"No other guide [...] a pleasure to read[...]"

". . . Excellently organized for the casual traveler who is looking for a mix of recreation and cultural insight."
Washington Post

★ ★ ★ ★ ★ (5-star rating) "Crisply written and remarkably personable. Cleverly organized so you can pluck out the minutest fact in a moment. Satisfyingly thorough."
Réalités

"The information they offer is up-to-date, crisply presented but far from exhaustive, the judgments knowledgeable but not opinionated."
New York Times

"The individual volumes are compact, the prose succinct, and the coverage up-to-date and knowledgeable . . . The format is portable and the index admirably detailed."
John Barkham Syndicate

". . . An abundance of excellent directions, diversions, and facts, including perspectives and getting-ready-to-go advice — succinct, detailed, and well organized in an easy-to-follow style."
Los Angeles Times

"They contain an amount of information that is truly staggering, besides being surprisingly current."
Detroit News

"These guides address themselves to the needs of the modern traveler demanding precise, qualitative information . . . Upbeat, slick, and well put together."
Dallas Morning News

". . . Attractive to look at, refreshingly easy to read, and generously packed with information." *Miami Herald*

"These guides are as good as any published, and much better than most." *Louisville* (Kentucky) *Times*

Stephen Birnbaum Travel Guides

Acapulco
Bahamas, and Turks & Caicos
Barcelona
Bermuda
Boston
Canada
Cancun, Cozumel & Isla Mujeres
Caribbean
Chicago
Disneyland
Eastern Europe
Europe
Europe for Business Travelers
Florence
France
Great Britain
Hawaii
Honolulu
Ireland
Italy
Ixtapa & Zihuatanejo
Las Vegas
London
Los Angeles
Mexico
Miami & Ft. Lauderdale
Montreal & Quebec City
New Orleans
New York
Paris
Portugal
Puerto Vallarta
Rome
San Francisco
South America
Spain
Toronto
United States
USA for Business Travelers
Vancouver
Venice
Walt Disney World
Washington, DC
Western Europe

CONTRIBUTING EDITORS

Hazel Lowe
Larry O'Conner

MAPS   Mark Stein Studios

SYMBOLS   Gloria McKeown

A Stephen Birnbaum Travel Guide

Birnbaum's
MONTREAL &
QUEBEC CITY
1993

Alexandra Mayes Birnbaum
EDITOR

Lois Spritzer
EXECUTIVE EDITOR

Laura L. Brengelman
Managing Editor

Mary Callahan
Jill Kadetsky
Susan McClung
Beth Schlau
Dana Margaret Schwartz
Associate Editors

Gene Gold
Assistant Editor

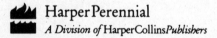
HarperPerennial
A Division of HarperCollins*Publishers*

To Stephen, who merely made all this possible.

BIRNBAUM'S MONTREAL & QUEBEC CITY 1993. Copyright © 1992 by HarperCollins Publishers. All rights reserved. Printed in the United States of America. No part of this book may be used or reproduced in any manner whatsoever without written permission except in the case of brief quotations embodied in critical articles and reviews. For information address HarperCollins*Publishers*, 10 East 53rd Street, New York, NY 10022.

FIRST EDITION

ISSN 0749-2561 (Stephen Birnbaum Travel Guides)
ISSN 1061-5415 (Montreal and Quebec City)
ISBN 0-06-278060-3 (pbk.)

93 94 95 96 97   CWI   10 9 8 7 6 5 4 3 2

Contents

GETTING READY TO GO

All the practical travel data you need to plan your vacation down to the final detail.

When and How to Go

Preparing

On the Road

Sources and Resources

USEFUL WORDS AND PHRASES

THE CITIES

A thorough, qualitative guide to Montreal and Quebec City. Each section offers a comprehensive report on the cities' most compelling attractions and amenities, designed to be used on the spot.

DIVERSIONS

A selective guide to more than a dozen active and/or cerebral vacation themes, including the best places to persue them.

For the Experience

For the Body

For the Mind

DIRECTIONS

Nine of the best walks in and around Montreal and Quebec City.

Montreal

Quebec City

A Word from the Editor

My husband Steve Birnbaum would fly hundreds — and one time an even thousand — of miles out of his way to order a plate of dry garlic spareribs at the late (and very lamented) *Ruby Foo's* restaurant in Montreal. And at the drop of a calorie, he would suggest a side trip to *Schwartz's* for a heaping helping of their French fries sprinkled with vinegar — the Canadian way. My introduction to this city, however, was when Steve took me there as a surprise birthday present. Until our arrival at New York's JFK Airport, my celebration destination was unknown.

I well remember my initial Montreal meeting: the first of what became many a romantic *calèche* ride around this charming city and, most particularly, a lighter-than-air chocolate soufflé that would have been the envy of any chef in Paris. It was Gallic heaven this side of the Atlantic. And not just because I come from a family of Anglophiles did I enjoy the city's enclaves that continue to cling to their very British heritage.

Next came Quebec City and a visit to the then current hot spot, which blared the then unknown Patti LaBelle's recording of "Voulez-Vous Coucher Avec Moi." A blizzard started at some point during the third chorus, and no, neither Steve nor I wanted to spend the night with Patti. We did, however, spend the next few days all but snowed in, occasionally making snowbound forays around Quebec's Old City, marveling at this beautiful French-speaking metropolis.

For visitors from the US, the foreign quality of Canada can take on quite a different cast from place to place. The dour demeanor of the Atlantic provinces is an extension (and occasionally an exaggeration) of the inscrutable mien that is regularly encountered in Maine. In contrast, the Canadian west — from the flat prairies of Saskatchewan and Manitoba to the islands of Vancouver Harbour — are almost unfailingly and heartily friendly; this is the segment of Canada where it is most difficult to realize that you have crossed a national border.

French Canada has come to be a somewhat different matter, and Montreal's advertisement of itself as "the second-largest French-speaking city in the world" has lately taken on new meaning. (We won't tell them that they've lately dropped to third place, behind Paris and Kinshasa.) As a vacation alternative to Paris, Montreal and Quebec City have substantial appeal both in their ambience and in the fact that the US dollar currently fares far better in Canada than in Europe. But the newly revitalized separatist spirit has shown its face in myriad ways, including the frequent reluctance of Montreal cabdrivers to speak English to US visitors. For the visitor, however, this slight inconvenience may prove welcome; it means that setting foot in a Montreal taxi now more closely approximates a foreign visitior's introduction to France.

My own evolution as a traveler (which happily continues) is mirrored by the evolution of our guidebook series. When we began our series of modern travel guides, we logically began with "area" books, attempting to publish guides that would include the widest possible number of attractive destinations. When the public seemed to accept our new way of delivering travel data, we added titles covering only a single country, and when these became popular Steve and I began our newest expansion phase, which centers on a group of books that deal with only a single city, or as is the case of the book you now hold, a pair of closely related cities. Now we can not only highlight our favorite urban destinations, but really describe how to get the very most out of a visit.

Such treatment of travel information only mirrors an increasingly pervasive trend among travelers — the frequent return to a treasured travel spot. Once upon a time, even the most dedicated travelers would visit distant parts of the world no more than once in a lifetime — usually as part of that fabled Grand Tour. But greater numbers of would-be sojourners are now availing themselves of the opportunity to visit a favored part of the world over and over again.

So where once it was routine to say you'd "seen" a particular city or country after a very superficial, once-over-lightly encounter, the more perceptive travelers of today recognize that it's entirely possible to have only skimmed the surface of a specific travel destination even after having visited that place more than a dozen times. Similarly, repeated visits to a single site permit true exploration of special interests, whether they be sporting, artistic, or intellectual.

For those of us who now have spent the last several years working out the special system under which we present information in this series, the luxury of being able to devote nearly as much space as we'd like to just a single or tandem cities is as close to paradise for guide writers and editors as any of us expects to come. But clearly this is not the first guide to the glories of Montreal or Quebec City — one suspects that guides of one sort or another have existed since the day when the fur traders made their way across the St. Lawrence to this uncharted land — so a traveler might logically ask why a new one is suddenly necessary.

Our answer is that the nature of travel to Montreal and Quebec City — and even of the travelers who now routinely make the trip — has changed dramatically of late. For the past 200 years or so, travel to even a town within our own country was considered an elaborate undertaking, one that required extensive advance planning. But with the advent of jet air travel in the late 1950s and of increased-capacity, wide-body aircraft during the late 1960s, travel to and around once distant destinations became extremely common. Attitudes as well as costs have changed significantly in the last couple of decades.

Obviously, any new guidebook to Montreal and Quebec City must keep pace with and answer the real needs of today's travelers. That's why we've tried to create a guide that's specifically organized, written, and edited for the more demanding modern traveler, one for whom qualitative information is infinitely more desirable than mere quantities of unappraised data. We think that this book, along with all the other guides in our series, represents a new generation of travel guides — one that is especially responsive to modern needs and interests.

But I should, I think, apologize for at least one indulgence in this text that is baldly chauvinistic, and that is our reference to citizens of the US as "Americans." Strictly speaking, Canadian citizens are just as much residents of the North American continent as US citizens, and we apoligize for any slight our Canadian readers may feel about our having appropriated this terminology. It was done strictly in an effort to simplify the narrative, rather than an attempt to appropriate a common continental distinction.

For years, dating back as far as Herr Baedeker, travel guides have tended to be encyclopedic, seemingly much more concerned with demonstrating expertise in geography and history than with a real analysis of the sorts of things that actually concern a typical modern tourist. But today, when it is hardly necessary to tell a traveler where Montreal or Quebec City are (in many cases, the traveler has been there nearly as often as the guidebook editors), it becomes the responsibility of those editors to provide new perspectives and to suggest new directions in order to make the guide genuinely valuable.

That's exactly what we've tried to do in this series. I think you'll notice a different, more contemporary tone to the text, as well as an organization and focus that are distinctive and more functional. And even a random reading of what follows will demonstrate a substantial departure from the standard guidebook orientation, for we've not only attempted to provide information of a more compelling sort, but we also have tried to present the data in a format that makes it particularly accessible.

Needless to say, it's difficult to decide just what to include in a guidebook of this size — and what to omit. Early on, we realized that giving up the encyclopedic approach precluded our listing every single route and restaurant, a realization that helped define our overall editorial focus. Similarly, when we discussed the possibility of presenting certain information in other than strict geographic order, we found that the new format enabled us to arrange data in a way that we feel best answers the questions travelers typically ask.

Large numbers of specific questions have provided the real editorial skeleton for this book. The volume of mail we regularly receive emphasizes that modern travelers want very precise information, so we've tried to organize our material in the most responsive way possible. Readers who want to know the best restaurants or the best places to shop for furs in Montreal or Quebec City will have no trouble extracting that data from this guide.

Travel guides are, understandably, reflections of personal taste, and putting one's name on a title page obviously puts one's preferences on the line. But I think I ought to amplify just what "personal" means. Like Steve, I don't believe in the sort of personal guidebook that's a palpable misrepresentation on its face. It is, for example, hardly possible for any single travel writer to visit thousands of restaurants (and nearly as many hotels) in any given year and provide accurate appraisals of each. And even if it were physically possible for one human being to survive such an itinerary, it would of necessity have to be done at a dead sprint, and the perceptions derived therefrom would probably be less valid than those of any other intelligent individual visiting the same establishments. It is, therefore, impossible (especially in a large, annually revised and updated guidebook *series* such as we offer) to have only one person provide all the data on the entire world.

I also happen to think that such individual orientation is of substantially less value to readers. Visiting a single hotel for just one night or eating one hasty meal in a random restaurant hardly equips anyone to provide appraisals that are of more than passing interest. No amount of doggedly alliterative or oppressively onomatopoeic text can camouflage a technique that is essentially specious. We have, therefore, chosen what I like to describe as the "thee and me" approach to restaurant and hotel evaluation and, to a somewhat more limited degree, to the sites and sights we have included in the other sections of our text. What this really reflects is a personal sampling tempered by intelligent counsel from informed local sources, and these additional friends-of-the-editor are almost always residents of the city and/or area about which they are consulted.

Despite the presence of several editors, writers, researchers, and local contributors, very precise editing and tailoring keep our text fiercely subjective. So what follows is the gospel according to Birnbaum, and it represents as much of our own taste and instincts as we can manage. It is probable, therefore, that if you like your cities stylish and prefer small hotels with personality to huge high-rise anonymities, we're likely to have a long and meaningful relationship. Readers with dissimilar tastes may be less enraptured.

I also should point out something about the person to whom this guidebook is directed. Above all, he or she is a "visitor." This means that such elements as restaurants have been specifically picked to provide the visitor with a representative, enlightening, stimulating, and above all pleasant experience. Since so many extraneous considerations can affect the reception and service accorded a regular restaurant patron, our choices can in no way be construed as an exhaustive guide to resident dining. We think we've listed all the best places, in various price ranges, but they were chosen with a visitor's enjoyment in mind.

Other evidence of how we've tried to tailor our text to reflect modern travel habits is most apparent in the section we call DIVERSIONS. Where once it was common for travelers to spend an urban visit in a determinedly passive state, the emphasis is far more active today. So we've organized every activity we could reasonably evaluate and arranged the material in a way that is especially accessible to activists of either athletic or cerebral bent. It is no longer necessary, therefore, to wade through a pound or two of superfluous prose just to find the very most elegant hostelry or the most dramatic ski slopes within a reasonable distance of these cities.

If there is a single thing that best characterizes the revolution in and evolution of current holiday habits, it is that most travelers now consider travel a right rather than a privilege. No longer is a family trip to the far corners of the world necessarily a once-in-a-lifetime thing; nor is the idea of visiting exotic, faraway places in the least worrisome. Travel today translates as the enthusiastic desire to sample all of the world's opportunities, to find that elusive quality of experience that is not only enriching but comfortable. For that reason, we've tried to make what follows not only helpful and enlightening, but the sort of welcome companion of which every traveler dreams.

Finally, I also should point out that every good travel guide is a living enterprise; that is, no part of this text is carved in stone. In our annual revisions, we refine, expand, and further hone all our material to serve your travel needs better. To this end, no contribution is of greater value to us than your personal reaction to what we have written, as well as information reflecting your own experiences while using the book. We earnestly and enthusiastically solicit your comments about this guide *and* your opinions and perceptions about places you have recently visited. In this way, we will be able to provide the most current information — including the actual experiences of recent travelers — and to make those experiences more readily available to others. Please write to us at 10 E. 53rd St., New York, NY 10022.

We sincerely hope to hear from you.

ALEXANDRA MAYES BIRNBAUM

How to Use This Guide

A great deal of care has gone into the special organization of this guidebook, and we believe it represents a real breakthrough in the presentation of travel material. Our aim is to create a new, more modern generation of travel books, and to make this guide the most useful and practical travel tool available today.

Our text is divided into five basic sections in order to present information in the best way on every possible aspect of a vacation to Montreal and Quebec City. This organization itself should alert you to the vast and varied opportunities available, as well as indicate all the specific data necessary to plan a successful visit. You won't find much of the conventional "swaying palms and shimmering sands" text here; we've chosen instead to deliver more useful and practical information. Prospective itineraries tend to speak for themselves, and with so many diverse travel opportunities, we feel our main job is to highlight what's where and to provide basic information — how, when, where, how much, and what's best — to assist you in making the most intelligent choices possible.

Here is a brief summary of the five basic sections of this book, and what you can expect to find in each. We believe that you will find both your travel planning and en route enjoyment enhanced by having this book at your side.

GETTING READY TO GO

This mini-encyclopedia of practical travel facts is a sort of know-it-all companion with all the precise information necessary to create a successful trip to Montreal and Quebec City. There are entries on more than 25 separate topics, including how to get where you're going, what preparations to make before leaving, what to expect, what your trip is likely to cost, and how to avoid prospective problems. The individual entries are specific, realistic, and, where appropriate, cost-oriented. Except where noted, all prices in this book are in US dollars.

We expect you to use this section most in the course of planning your trip, for its ideas and suggestions are intended to simplify this often confusing period. Entries are intentionally concise, in an effort to get to the meat of the matter with the least extraneous prose. These entries are augmented by extensive lists of specific sources from which to obtain even more specialized data, plus some suggestions for obtaining travel information on your own.

USEFUL WORDS AND PHRASES

Though most hotels and restaurants in Montreal and Quebec City have English-speaking staff, at smaller establishments a little knowledge of French will go a long way. This collection of often-used words and phrases will help you to make a hotel or dinner reservation, order a meal, mail a letter — and even buy toothpaste.

THE CITIES

Individual reports on Montreal and Quebec City have been prepared with the assistance of researchers, contributors, professional journalists, and other experts who live in the cities. Although useful at the planning stage, THE CITIES is really designed to be taken along and used on the spot. The reports offer a short-stay guide, including an essay introducing each city as a historic entity and as a contemporary place to visit. *At-a-Glance* material is actually a site-by-site survey of the most important, interesting, and sometimes most eclectic sights to see and things to do. *Sources and Resources* is a concise listing of pertinent tourist information meant to answer myriad potentially pressing questions as they arise — from simple things such as the address of the local tourism office, how to get around, which sightseeing tours to take, and when special events occur, to something more difficult, like where to find the best nightspot or hail a taxi, which are the chic places to shop and where to find the more irresistible bargains, and where the best museums and theaters are to be found. *Best in Town* lists our cost-and-quality choices of the best places to eat and sleep on a variety of budgets.

DIVERSIONS

This section is designed to help travelers find the best places in which to pursue a wide range of physical and cerebral activities, without having to wade through endless pages of unrelated text. This very selective guide lists the broadest possible range of activities, including all the best places to pursue them.

We start with a list of special places to stay and eat, and move to activities that require some perspiration — sports preferences and other rigorous pursuits — and go on to report on a number of more spiritual vacation opportunities. In every case, our suggestion of a particular location — and often our recommendation of a specific hotel — is intended to guide you to that special place where the quality of experience is likely to be highest. Whether you seek a historic hotel or museum or the best place to shop or ski, each category is the equivalent of a comprehensive checklist of the absolute best in Montreal and Quebec City.

DIRECTIONS

Here are nine walks that cover Montreal and Quebec City, along their main thoroughfares and side streets, past their most spectacular landmarks and magnificent parks. This is the only section of the book that is organized geographically; itineraries can be "connected" for longer sojourns, or used individually for short, intensive explorations.

Although each of this book's sections has a distinct format and a special function, they have all been designed to be used together to provide a complete inventory of travel information. To use this book to full advantage, take a few minutes to read the table of contents and random entries in each section to get a firsthand feel for how it all fits together.

Pick and choose needed information. Assume, for example, that you always wanted to visit Montreal and Quebec City and enjoy an authentic French crêpe on this side of the Atlantic or sample a slice of maple syrup pie, but never really knew how to organize it or where to go. Choose specific restaurants from the selections offered in "Eating Out" in THE CITIES, add some of those noted in each walking tour in DIRECTIONS, and cross-reference with those in the roundup of the best in the cities in the *Montreal and Quebec City's Best Restaurants* section in DIVERSIONS.

In other words, the sections of this book are building blocks designed to help you put together the best possible trip. Use them selectively as a tool, a source of ideas, a reference work for accurate facts, and a guidebook to the best buys, the most exciting sights, the most pleasant accommodations, the tastiest food — *the best travel experience* that you can possibly have.

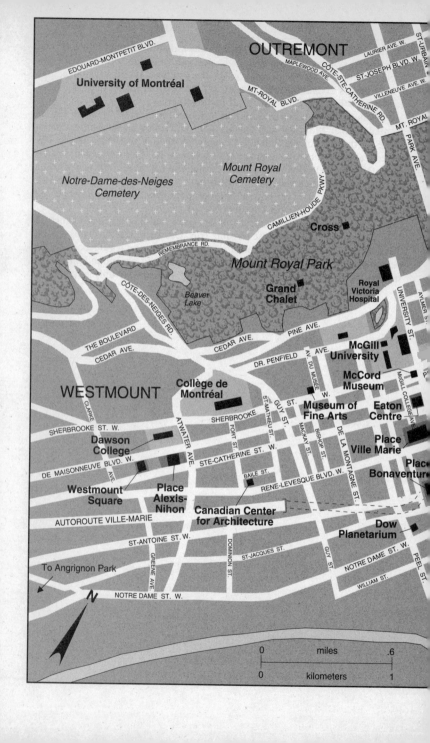

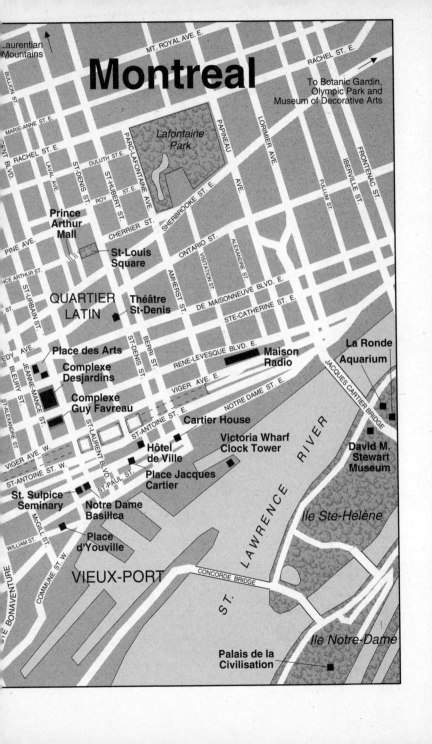

Montreal

Laurentian Mountains

To Botanic Gardin, Olympic Park and Museum of Decorative Arts

MT. ROYAL AVE. E.

RACHEL ST. E.

BULLION ST.

MARIE-ANNE ST. E.

RACHEL ST. E.

PARC-LAFONTAINE AVE.

Lafontaine Park

PAPINEAU AVE.

LORIMIER AVE.

FRONTENAC ST.

IBERVILLE ST.

FULLUM ST.

DULUTH ST E.

ST-DENIS ST.

LAVAL AVE.

ST-HUBERT ST.

ROY ST. E.

ROY

CHERRIER ST.

SHERBROOKE ST. E.

Prince Arthur Mall

PINE AVE.

CHERRIER ST.

CE ARTHUR ST.

NCE ARTHUR ST.

St-Louis Square

ONTARIO ST.

ALEXANDRE ST.

VISITATION ST.

ST-URBAIN ST.

ST.

QUARTIER LATIN

Théâtre St-Denis

AMHERST ST.

DE MAISONNEUVE BLVD. E.

STE-CATHERINE ST. E.

EDY AVE.

Place des Arts

ST-DENIS ST.

BERRI ST.

La Ronde

Aquarium

BLEURY ST.

JEANNE-MANCE ST.

Complexe Desjardins

RENE-LEVESQUE BLVD. E.

Maison Radio

JACQUES CARTIER BRIDGE

ST-ALEXANDRE ST.

Complexe Guy Favreau

VIGER AVE. E.

ST-LAURENT BLVD.

David M. Stewart Museum

VIGER AVE. W.

NOTRE DAME ST. E.

Cartier House

ST-ANTOINE ST. E.

Victoria Wharf Clock Tower

LAWRENCE RIVER

ST-ANTOINE ST. W.

Hôtel de Ville

ST-PAUL ST.

Place Jacques Cartier

St. Sulpice Seminary

Notre Dame Basilica

Ile Ste-Hélène

WILLIAM ST.

McGILL ST.

Place d'Youville

ST. LAWRENCE RIVER

E BONAVENTURE

COMMUNE ST. W.

VIEUX-PORT

CONCORDE BRIDGE

Ile Notre-Dame

Palais de la Civilisation

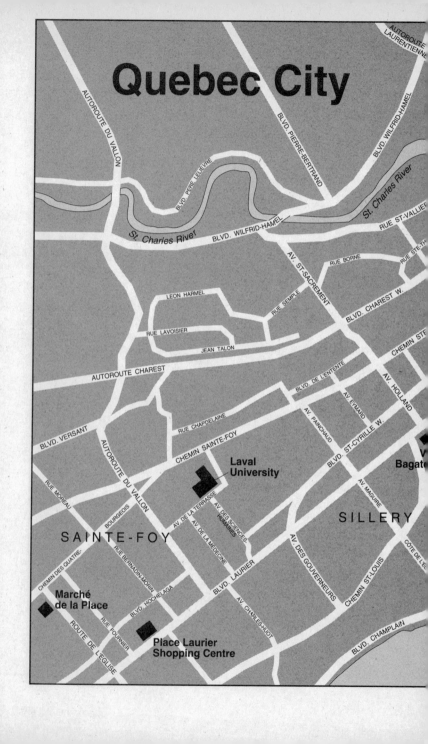

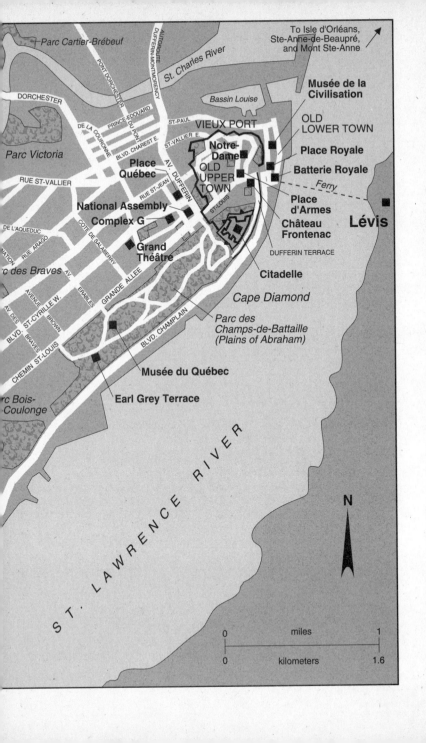

GETTING READY TO GO

When and How to Go

When to Go

There really isn't a "best" time to visit Montreal or Quebec City. Although the months of June through September traditionally have been the most popular vacation time, it is important to emphasize that more and more travelers who have the choice are enjoying the substantial advantages of off-season travel. Though some tourist attractions may close during the slower seasons, the majority remain open and tend to be less crowded. What's more, while winter sports such as skiing in the nearby Laurentians are in full swing, travel to and from Montreal and Quebec City during these seasons generally is less expensive.

For some, the most convincing argument in favor of off-season travel is the economic one. Getting there and staying there is more affordable during less popular travel periods, as airfares, hotel rooms, and car rental rates go down and less expensive package tours become available; the independent traveler can go farther on less, too.

A definite bonus to visiting during the off-season is that even the most basic services are performed more efficiently. In theory, off-season service is identical to that offered during high season, but the fact is that the absence of demanding crowds inevitably begets much more thoughtful and personal attention.

Even during the off-season, high-season rates also may prevail because of an important local event. Particularly in Montreal and Quebec City, special events and major trade shows or conferences held at the time of your visit also are sure to affect not only the availability of discounts on accommodations, but the basic availabilty of a place to stay.

In short, like many other popular places in Canada, the vacation appeal of Montreal and Quebec City has become multi-seasonal. But the noted exceptions notwithstanding, most travel destinations are decidedly less heavily trafficked and less expensive during the winter.

WEATHER: While there's no getting around Montreal's cold and snowy winters, its summers seem to make up for them, delivering pleasantly mild temperatures averaging 70F (21C). June and September evenings can be cooler, however. Spring temperatures average about 50F (10C) and in fall drop to 40F (5C). December through March ushers in frigid temperatures — the low averaging about 10F, the high about 25F (-12C) — and plenty of snow.

Quebec City is generally clear and sunny and has relatively low humidity because of its altitude — 350 feet above sea level. In the summer, the thermometer reading averages 78F (26C), and in the winter temperatures fall to 20F (-6C; though they can plummet to -10F/-23C in January and February). In addition to the cold weather, winter brings plenty of snow — 150 to 200 inches during the season.

Travelers can get current readings and extended forecasts through the *Weather Channel Connection,* the worldwide weather report center of the *Weather Channel,* a cable television station. By dialing 900-WEATHER and punching in either the first four letters of the city name or the area code for over 600 cities, an up-to-date recording will provide such information as current temperature, barometric pressure, relative humidity, and wind speed, as well as a general 2-day forecast. Boating and highway reports are also provided for some locations. Weather information for over 225 international destinations can be obtained by punching in the first 4 letters of the city name. To hear the weather report for Montreal, punch in MONT; for Quebec City, punch in 1 (for Q) then UEB. (To find out which cities or locations in a given country are covered, enter the first four letters of the *country* name.) Callers also can access information on the weather patterns for any time of the year in the area requested, as well as international travel information such as visa requirements, US State Department travel advisories, tipping, and voltage requirements. This 24-hour service can be accessed from any touch-tone phone in the US, and costs 95¢ per minute. The charge will show up on your phone bill. For additional information, contact the *Weather Channel Connection,* 2600 Cumberland Pkwy., Atlanta, GA 30339 (phone: 404-434-6800).

SPECIAL EVENTS: Every year during the period of *Lent,* Montreal hosts a 10-day snow carnival called *Fête des Neiges.* For music lovers, there's the popular annual *International Jazz Festival;* held in July, it draws jazz greats from around the world. Screen fans will enjoy Montreal's own *World Film Festival,* which features all the latest movies at the *Cinéma Parisien* along with the presence of some of Hollywood's luminaries.

In Quebec City, well over half a million people celebrate the *Carnaval de Québec,* a 10-day event that precedes *Lent.* International snow-sculpture contests, fireworks, a queen's coronation, and plenty of winter sports comprise this festive affair. During July, music fans will enjoy the *International Quebec Summer Festival,* which highlights top artists from the classical music, rock, and jazz world.

Traveling by Plane

Flying usually is the quickest and most efficient way to get to Montreal and Quebec City. When all costs are taken into account for traveling any substantial distance, plane travel usually is less expensive per mile than traveling by car. It also is the most economical way to go in terms of time. Although touring by car, bus, or train certainly is the most scenic way to travel, air travel is far faster and more direct — the less time spent in transit, the more time spent at your destination.

Despite recent attempts at price simplification by a number of major US carriers, the airlines offering flights to Canada continue to sell seats at a variety of prices under a vast spectrum of requirements and restrictions. Since you probably will spend more for your airfare than for any other single item in your travel budget, try to take advantage of the lowest available fare. You should know what kinds of flights are available, the rules and regulations pertaining to air travel, and all the special package options.

SCHEDULED FLIGHTS: Air service to Montreal and Quebec City is provided by two Canadian airlines and a number of US carriers. *Air Alliance* flies from Newark to Quebec City. *Air Canada* flies from Boston, Chicago, Newark, and New York to Montreal, where travelers can get a flight to Quebec City (connections can also be made in Toronto). *Canadian Airlines International* flies from Indianapolis, Dayton (OH), Columbus (OH), Pittsburgh, Harrisburg (PA), Allentown (PA), Los Angeles, and San Francisco to Toronto, where travelers can get a connection to Montreal or Quebec City. *American* provides service only from Chicago to Montreal. *Delta* has flights from

Atlanta, Boston, Hartford (CT), and New York to Montreal. *Northwest* flies from Detroit to Montreal, and from Boston to Quebec City. *USAir* has flights from Baltimore, Buffalo, Cleveland, Philadelphia, and Pittsburgh to Montreal.

Tickets – When traveling on one of the many regularly scheduled flights, a full-fare ticket provides maximum travel flexibility (although at considerable expense), because there are no advance booking requirements. A prospective passenger can buy a ticket for a flight right up to the minute of takeoff — if a seat is available. If your ticket is for a round trip, you can make the return reservation whenever you wish — months before you leave, or the day before you return. Assuming the foreign immigration requirements are met, you can stay at your destination for as long as you like. (Tickets generally are good for a year and can be renewed if not used.) On some airlines, you also may be able to cancel your flight at any time without penalty; on others, cancellation — even of a full-fare ticket — may be subject to a variety of restrictions. It pays to check with the individual carrier *before* booking your flight. In addition, while it is true that this category of ticket can be purchased at the last minute, it is advisable to reserve well in advance during popular vacation periods and around holiday times.

Fares – Airfares continue to change so rapidly that even the experts find it difficult to keep up with them. This ever-changing situation is due to a number of factors, including airline deregulation (in both the US and Canada), volatile labor relations, increasing fuel costs, and vastly increased competition.

Perhaps the most common misconception about fares on scheduled airlines is that the cost of the ticket determines how much service will be provided on the flight. This is true only to a certain extent. A far more realistic rule of thumb is that the less you pay for your ticket, the more restrictions and qualifications are likely to come into play before you board the plane (as well as after you get off). These qualifying aspects relate to the months (and the days of the week) during which you must travel, how far in advance you must purchase your ticket, the minimum and maximum amount of time you may or must remain away, your willingness to decide on a return date at the time of booking — and your ability to stick to that decision. It is not uncommon for passengers sitting side by side on the same wide-body jet to have paid fares varying by hundreds of dollars, and all too often the traveler paying more would have been equally willing (and able) to accept the terms of the far less expensive ticket.

In general, the great variety of US domestic fares, Canadian domestic fares, and fares between the two countries can be reduced to four basic categories, including first class, coach (also called economy or tourist class), and excursion or discount fares. A fourth category, called business class, has been added by many airlines in recent years. In addition, Advance Purchase Excursion (APEX) fares offer savings under certain conditions.

A **first class** ticket is your admission to the special section of the aircraft, with larger seats, more legroom, sleeperette seating on some wide-body aircraft, better (or, at least, more elaborately served) food, free drinks and headsets for movies and music channels, and, above all, personal attention. First class fares are about twice those of full-fare economy, although both first class passengers and those paying full economy fares are entitled to reserve seats and are sold tickets on an open reservation system. Sometimes, a first class ticket offers the additional advantage of allowing travelers to schedule any number of stops en route to or from their most distant destination — provided that certain set, but generous, restrictions regarding maximum mileage limits and flight schedules are respected.

Not too long ago, there were only two classes of air travel, first class and all the rest, usually called economy or tourist. Then **business class** came into being — one of the most successful recent airline innovations. At first, business class passengers were merely curtained off from the other economy passengers. Now a separate cabin or cabins — usually toward the front of the plane — is the norm. While standards of comfort and service are not as high as in first class, they represent a considerable improvement over conditions in the rear of the plane, with roomier seats, more leg and shoulder space between passengers, and fewer seats abreast. Free liquor and headsets, a choice of meal entrées, and a separate counter for speedier check-in are other induce-ments. As in first class, a business class passenger may travel on any scheduled flight he or she wishes, buy a one-way or round-trip ticket, and have the ticket remain valid for a year. There are no minimum or maximum stay requirements, no advance booking requirements, and sometimes (depending on the carrier), no cancellation penalties. If the particular airline allows first class passengers unlimited free stopovers, this privilege generally also is extended to those flying business class. Though airlines often have their own names for their business class service, such as Executive Class on *Air Canada* or Medallion Class on *Delta, Canadian Airlines International* simply refers to it as busi-ness class.

The terms of the **coach** or **economy** fare may vary slightly from airline to airline, and in fact from time to time airlines may be selling more than one type of economy fare. Coach or economy passengers sit more snugly, as many as 10 in a single row on a wide-body jet, behind the first class and business class sections. Normally, alcoholic drinks are not free, nor are the headsets. If there are two economy fares on the books, one (often called "regular economy") still may include a number of free stopovers. The other, less expensive fare (often called "special economy") may limit stopovers to one or two, with a charge (typically $25) for each one.

Like first class passengers, however, passengers paying the full coach fare are subject to none of the restrictions that usually are attached to less expensive excursion and discount fares. There are no advance booking requirements, no minimum stay require-ments, and often, no cancellation penalties — but beware, the rules regarding cancella-tion vary from carrier to carrier. Tickets are sold on an open reservation system: They can be bought for a flight right up to the minute of takeoff (if seats are available), and if the ticket is round trip, the return reservation can be made anytime you wish. Both first class and coach tickets generally are good for a year, after which they can be renewed if not used, and if you ultimately decide not to fly at all, your money may be refunded (again, policies vary). The cost of economy and business class tickets does not change much in the course of the year between the US and Canada, though on some routes they vary from a basic (low-season) price in effect most of the year to a peak (high-season) price — these seasonal demarcations vary according to the destination.

Excursion and other **discount** fares are the airlines' equivalent of a special sale and usually apply to round-trip bookings only. These fares generally differ according to the season and the number of travel days permitted. They are only a bit less flexible than full-fare economy tickets, and are, therefore, often useful for both business and holiday travelers. Most round-trip excursion tickets include strict minimum and maximum stay requirements and reservations can be changed only within the specified time limits. So don't count on extending a ticket beyond the prescribed time of return or staying less time than required. Again, different airlines may have different regulations concerning stopover privileges and sometimes excursion fares are less expensive midweek. The availability of these reduced-rate seats is most limited at busy times such as holidays. Discount or excursion fare ticket holders sit with the coach passengers and, for all intents and purposes, are indistinguishable from them. They receive all the same basic services, even though they may have paid anywhere between 30% and 55% less for the trip. Obviously, it's wise to make plans early enough to qualify for this less expensive transportation if possible.

These discount or excursion fares may masquerade under a variety of names, and they may vary from city to city (from the East Coast to the West Coast, especially), but they invariably have strings attached. A common requirement is that the ticket be purchased a certain number of days — usually between 7 and 21 days — in advance of departure, though it may be booked weeks or months in advance (it has to be "ticketed," or paid for, shortly after booking, however). The return reservation usually has to be made at the time of the original ticketing and often cannot be changed later than a certain number of days (again, usually 7 to 21 days) before the return flight. If events force a change in the return reservation after the date allowed, the passenger may have to pay the difference between the round-trip excursion rate and the round-trip coach rate, although some carriers permit such scheduling changes for a nominal fee. In addition, some airlines also may allow passengers to use their discounted fares by standing by for an empty seat, even if they don't otherwise have standby fares. Another common condition is a minimum and maximum stay requirement: for example 1 to 6 days or 6 to 14 days (but including at least a Saturday night). Last, cancellation penalties of up to 50% of the full price of the ticket have been assessed — if a refund is offered at all — so careful planning is imperative. Check the specific penalty in effect when you purchase your discount/excursion ticket.

On some airlines, the ticket bearing the lowest price of all the current discount fares is the ticket where no change at all in departure and/or return flights is permitted, and where the ticket price is totally nonrefundable. If you do buy such a nonrefundable ticket, you should be aware of a policy followed by *some* airlines that may make it easier to change your plans if necessary. For a fee — set by each airline and payable at the airport when checking in — you *may* be able to change the time or date of a return flight on a nonrefundable ticket. However, if the nonrefundable ticket price for the replacement flight is higher than that of the original (as often is the case when trading in a weekday for a weekend flight), you will have to pay the difference. Any such change must be made a certain number of days in advance — in some cases as little as 2 days — of either the original or the replacement flight, whichever is earlier; restrictions are set by the individual carrier. (Travelers holding a nonrefundable or other restricted ticket who must change their plans due to a family emergency should know that some carriers may make special allowances in such situations; for further information, see *Staying Healthy,* in this section.)

■**Note:** Due to recent changes in many US airlines' policies, nonrefundable tickets are now available that carry none of the above restrictions. Although passengers still may *not* be able to obtain a refund for the price paid, the time or date of a departing or return flight may be changed at any time (assuming seats are available) for a nominal service charge.

There also is a newer, often less expensive type of excursion fare, the **APEX**, or **Advance Purchase Excursion**, fare. As with traditional excursion fares, passengers paying an APEX fare sit with and receive the same basic services as any other coach or economy passengers, even though they may have paid up to 50% less for their seats. In return, they are subject to certain restrictions. In the case of flights to Canada, the ticket usually is good for a minimum of approximately 4 days away (spanning at least 1 weekend), and a maximum, currently, of 1 month to 1 year (depending on the airline and the destination); and as its name implies, it must be "ticketed," or paid for in its entirety, a certain period of time before departure — usually somewhere between 7 and 21 days.

The drawback to some APEX fares is that they penalize travelers who change their minds — and travel plans. Usually, the return reservation must be made at the time of the original ticketing, and if for some reason you change your schedule, you will have to pay a penalty of $100 or 10% of the ticket value, whichever is greater, as long as you travel within the validity period of your ticket. More flexible APEX fares recently have been introduced that allow travelers to make changes in the date or time of their flights for a nominal charge (as low as $25).

With either type of APEX fare, if you change your return to a date less than the minimum stay or more than the maximum stay, the difference between the round-trip APEX fare and the full round-trip coach rate will have to be paid. There also is a penalty of anywhere from $50 to $100 or more for canceling or changing a reservation *before* travel begins — check the specific penalty in effect when you purchase your ticket. No stopovers are allowed on an APEX ticket, but it is possible to create an open-jaw effect by buying an APEX on a split ticket basis; for example, flying to Toronto and returning from Quebec City. The total price would be half the price of an APEX to Toronto plus half the price of an APEX to Quebec City. Depending on the destination, APEX tickets to Canada may be sold at basic and peak rates (the peak season will vary) and may include surcharges for weekend flights.

Standby fares, at one time the rock-bottom price at which a traveler could fly to Canada, have become elusive. At the time of this writing, most major scheduled airlines did not regularly offer standby fares on direct flights to Canada. Because airline fares and their conditions constantly change, however, bargain hunters should not hesitate to ask if such a fare exists at the time they plan to travel.

While the definition of standby varies somewhat from airline to airline, it generally means that you make yourself available to buy a ticket for a flight (usually no sooner than the day of departure), then literally stand by on the chance that a seat will be empty. Once aboard, however, a standby passenger has the same meal service and frills (or lack of them) enjoyed by others in the economy class compartment.

Something else to check is the possibility of qualifying for a **GIT** (Group Inclusive Travel) fare, which requires that a specific dollar amount of ground arrangements be purchased, in advance, along with the ticket. The requirements vary as to number of travel days and stopovers permitted, and the minimum number of passengers required for a group. The actual fares also vary, but the cost will be spelled out in brochures distributed by the tour operators handling the ground arrangements. In the past, GIT fares were among the least expensive available from the established carriers, but the prevalence of discount fares has caused group fares to all but disappear from some air routes. Travelers reading brochures on group package tours to Canada will find that, in almost all cases, the applicable airfare given as a sample (to be added to the price of the land package to obtain the total tour price) is an APEX fare, the same discount fare available to the independent traveler.

The major airlines serving Canada from the US also may offer individual fare excursion rates similar to GIT fares, which are sold in conjunction with ground accommodation packages. Previously called ITX and sometimes referred to as individual tour-basing fares, these fares generally are offered as part of "air/hotel/car/transfer packages," and can reduce the cost of an economy fare by more than a third. The packages are booked for a specific amount of time, with return dates specified; rescheduling and cancellation restrictions and penalties vary from carrier to carrier. At the time of this writing, these fares were offered to popular destinations throughout Canada by *Air Canada, American, Canadian Airlines International, Delta,* and *USAir.* Note that their offerings may or may not represent substantial savings over standard economy fares, so check at the time you plan to travel. (For further information on package options, see *Package Tours,* in this section.)

Travelers looking for the least expensive possible airfares should, finally, scan the pages of their hometown newspapers (especially the Sunday travel section) for announcements of special promotional fares. Most airlines offer their most attractive special fares to encourage travel during slow seasons and to inaugurate and publicize new routes. Even if none of these factors applies, prospective passengers can be fairly sure that the number of discount seats per flight at the lowest price is strictly limited, or that the fare offering includes a set expiration date — which means it's absolutely necessary to move fast to enjoy the lowest possible price.

Among other special airline promotional deals for which you should be on the lookout are discount or upgrade coupons sometimes offered by the major carriers and found in mail-order merchandise catalogues. For instance, airlines sometimes issue coupons that typically cost around $25 each and are good for a percentage discount or an upgrade on an international airline ticket — including flights to Canada. The only requirement beyond the fee generally is that a coupon purchaser must buy at least one item from the catalogue. There usually are some minimum airfare restrictions before the coupon is redeemable, but in general these are worthwhile offers. Restrictions often include certain blackout days (when the coupon cannot be used at all), usually imposed during peak travel periods. These coupons are particularly valuable to business travelers who tend to buy full-fare tickets, and while the coupons are issued in the buyer's name, they can be used by others who are traveling on the same itinerary.

It's always wise to ask about discount or promotional fares and about any conditions that might restrict booking, payment, cancellation, and changes in plans. Check the prices from neighboring cities. A special rate may be offered in a nearby city but not in yours, and it may be enough of a bargain to warrant your leaving from that city. Ask if there is a difference in price for midweek versus weekend travel, or if there is a further discount for traveling early in the morning or late at night. Also be sure to investigate package deals, which are offered by virtually every airline. These may include a car rental, accommodations, and dining and/or sightseeing features, in addition to the basic airfare, and the combined cost of packaged elements usually is considerably less than the cost of the exact same elements when purchased separately.

If in the course of your research you come across a deal that seems too good to be true, keep in mind that logic may not be a component of deeply discounted airfares — there's not always any sane relationship between miles to be flown and the price to get there. More often than not, the level of competition on a given route dictates the degree of discount, and don't be dissuaded from accepting an offer that sounds irresistible just because it also sounds illogical. Better to buy that inexpensive fare while it's being offered and worry about the sense — or absence thereof — while you're flying to your desired destination.

When you're satisfied that you've found the lowest possible price for which you can conveniently qualify (you may have to call the airline more than once, because different airline reservations clerks have been known to quote different prices), make your booking. Then, to protect yourself against fare increases, purchase and pay for your ticket as soon as possible after you've received a confirmed reservation. Airlines generally will honor their tickets, even if the operative price at the time of your flight is higher than the price you paid; if fares go up between the time you *reserve* a flight and the time you *pay* for it, you likely will be out of luck. Finally, with excursion or discount fares, it is important to remember that when a reservations clerk says that you must purchase a ticket by a specific date, this is an absolute deadline. Miss the deadline and the airline may automatically cancel your reservation without telling you.

■ **Note:** Another wrinkle in the airfare scene is that if the fares go *down* after you purchase your ticket, you *may* be entitled to a refund of the difference. However, this is only possible in certain situations — availability and advance purchase restrictions pertaining to the lower rate are set by the airline. If you suspect that you may be able to qualify for such a refund, check with your travel agent or the airline.

Frequent Flyers – The leading carriers serving Montreal and Quebec City from the US — *Air Canada, American, Canadian Airlines International, Delta, Northwest,* and *USAir* — offer a bonus system to frequent travelers. After the first 10,000 miles, for example, a passenger might be eligible for a first class seat for the coach fare; after another 10,000 miles, he or she might receive a discount on his or her next ticket purchase. The value of the bonuses continues to increase as more miles are logged.

Bonus miles also may be earned by patronizing affiliated car rental companies or hotel chains, or by using one of the credit cards that now offer this reward. In deciding whether to accept such a credit card from one of the issuing organizations that tempt you with frequent flyer mileage bonuses on a specific airline, first determine whether the interest rate charged on the unpaid balance is the same as (or less than) possible alternate credit cards, and whether the annual "membership" fee also is equal or lower. If these charges are slightly higher than those of competing cards, weigh the difference against the potential value in airfare savings. Also ask about any bonus miles awarded just for signing up — 1,000 is common, 5,000 generally the maximum.

For the most up-to-date information on frequent flyer bonus options, you may want to send for the monthly newsletter *Frequent.* Issued by Frequent Publications, it provides current information about frequent flyer plans in general, as well as specific data about promotions, awards, and combination deals to help you keep track of the profusion — and confusion — of current and upcoming availabilities. For a year's subscription, send $33 to Frequent Publications, 4715-C Town Center Dr., Colorado Springs, CO 80916 (phone: 800-333-5937).

There also is a monthly magazine called *Frequent Flyer,* but unlike the newsletter mentioned above, its focus is primarily on newsy articles of interest to business travelers and other frequent flyers. Published by Official Airline Guides (PO Box 58543, Boulder, CO 80322-8543; phone: 800-323-3537), *Frequent Flyer* is available for $24 for a 1-year subscription.

Low-Fare Airlines – Increasingly, the stimulus for special fares is the appearance of airlines associated with bargain rates. On these airlines, all seats on any given flight generally sell for the same price, which tends to be somewhat below the lowest discount fare offered by the larger, more established airlines. It is important to note that tickets offered by these smaller companies frequently are not subject to the same restrictions as some of the discounted fares offered by the more established carriers. They may not require advance purchase or minimum and maximum stays, may involve no cancellation penalties, and may be available one way or round trip. A disadvantage to some low-fare airlines, however, is that when something goes wrong, such as delayed baggage or a flight cancellation due to equipment breakdown, their smaller fleets and fewer flights mean that passengers may have to wait longer for a solution than they would on one of the equipment-rich major carriers.

Taxes and Other Fees – Travelers who have shopped for the best possible flight at the lowest possible price should be warned that a number of extras will be added to that price and collected by the airline or travel agent who issues the ticket. For instance, the $6 International Air Transportation Tax is a departure tax paid by all passengers flying from the US to a foreign destination.

Still another fee is charged by some airlines to cover more stringent security procedures, prompted by recent terrorist incidents. The 10% federal US Transportation Tax applies to travel within the US or US territories. It does not apply to passengers flying between US cities or territories en route to a foreign destination, unless the trip includes a stopover of more than 12 hours at a US point. Someone flying from Los Angeles to New York and stopping in New York for more than 12 hours before boarding a flight to Canada, for instance, would pay the 10% tax on the domestic portion of the trip. When flying from Canada back to the US, a Canadian Departure Tax also is charged; this amounts to 5% of the ticket cost, plus CN$4, the total of which may not exceed CN$19. Note that these taxes *usually* (but not always) are included in advertised fares and in the prices quoted by airline reservation clerks.

Reservations – For those who don't have the time or patience to investigate personally all possible air departures and connections for a proposed trip, a travel agent can be of inestimable help. A good agent should have all the information on which flights go where and when, and which categories of tickets are available on each. Most have computerized reservation links with the major carriers, so that a seat can be reserved and confirmed in minutes. An increasing number of agents also possess fare-comparison computer programs, so they often are very reliable sources of detailed competitive price data. (For more information, see *How to Use a Travel Agent,* in this section.)

When making plane reservations through a travel agent, ask the agent to give the airline your home phone number, as well as your daytime business phone number. All too often the agent uses the agency number as the official contact for changes in flight plans. Especially during the winter, weather conditions hundreds or even thousands of miles away can wreak havoc with flight schedules. Aircraft are constantly in use, and a plane delayed in the Orient or on the West Coast can miss its scheduled flight from the East Coast the next morning. The airlines are fairly reliable about getting this sort of information to passengers if they can reach them; diligence does little good at 10 PM if the airline has only the agency's or an office number.

Reconfirmation is strongly recommended for all international flights (though it is not usually required on US domestic flights) and, in the case of flights to Canada, it is essential to confirm your round-trip reservations — especially the return leg — as well as any point-to-point flights within the country. Some (though increasingly fewer) reservations to and from international destinations are automatically canceled after a required reconfirmation period (typically 72 hours) has passed — even if you have a confirmed, fully paid ticket in hand. It always is wise to call ahead to make sure that the airline did not slip up in entering your original reservations, or in registering any changes you may have made since, and that it has your seat reservation and/or special meal request in the computer. If you look at the printed information on your ticket, you'll see the airline's reconfirmation policy stated explicitly. Don't be lulled into a false sense of security by the "OK" on your ticket next to the number and time of the flight. This only means that a reservation has been entered; a reconfirmation still may be necessary. If in doubt — call.

If you plan not to take a flight on which you hold a confirmed reservation, by all means inform the airline. Because the problem of "no-shows" is a constant expense for airlines, they are allowed to overbook flights, a practice that often contributes to the threat of denied boarding for a certain number of passengers (see "Getting Bumped," below).

Seating – For most types of tickets, airline seats usually are assigned on a first-come, first-served basis at check-in, although some airlines make it possible to reserve a seat at the time of ticket purchase. Always check in early for your flight, even with advance seat assignments. A good rule of thumb for international flights is to arrive at the airport *at least* 2 hours before the scheduled departure to give yourself plenty of time in case there are long lines.

Most airlines furnish seating charts, which make choosing a seat much easier, but there are a few basics to consider. You must decide whether you prefer a window, aisle, or middle seat. On flights where smoking is permitted, you also should indicate if you prefer the smoking or nonsmoking section.

The amount of legroom provided (as well as chest room, especially when the seat in front of you is in a reclining position) is determined by something called "pitch," a measure of the distance between the back of the seat in front of you and the front of the back of your seat. The amount of pitch is a matter of airline policy, not the type of plane you fly. First class and business class seats have the greatest pitch, a fact that figures prominently in airline advertising. In economy class or coach, the standard pitch ranges from 33 to as little as 31 inches — downright cramped.

The number of seats abreast, another factor determining comfort, depends on a combination of airline policy and airplane dimensions. First class and business class have the fewest seats per row. Economy generally has 9 seats per row on a DC-10 or an L-1011, making either one slightly more comfortable than a 747, on which there normally are 10 seats per row. Charter flights on DC-10s and L-1011s, however, often have 10 seats per row and can be noticeably more cramped than 747 charters, on which the seating normally remains at 10 per row.

Airline representatives claim that most aircraft are more stable toward the front and midsection, while seats farthest from the engines are quietest. Passengers who have long legs and are traveling on a wide-body aircraft might request a seat directly behind a door or emergency exit, since these seats often have greater than average pitch, or a seat in the first row of a given section, which offers extra legroom — although these seats are increasingly being reserved for passengers who are willing (and able) to perform certain tasks in the event of emergency evacuation. It often is impossible, however, to see the movie from these seats, which are directly behind the plane's exits. Be aware that seats in the first row of the economy section (called "bulkhead" seats) on a conventional aircraft (not a widebody) do *not* offer extra legroom, since the fixed partition will not permit passengers to slide their feet under it, and that watching a movie from these first-row seats can be difficult and uncomfortable. These bulkhead seats do, however, provide ample room to use a bassinet or safety seat and often are reserved for families traveling with children.

Despite all these rules of thumb, finding out which specific rows are near emergency exits or at the front of a wide-body cabin can be difficult because seating arrangements on two otherwise identical planes vary from airline to airline. There is, however, a quarterly publication called the *Airline Seating Guide* that publishes seating charts for most major US airlines and many foreign carriers as well. Your travel agent should have a copy, or you can buy the US edition for $39.95 per year and the international edition for $44.95. Order from Carlson Publishing Co., Box 888, Los Alamitos, CA 90720 (phone: 800-728-4877 or 213-493-4877).

Simply reserving an airline seat in advance, however, actually may guarantee very little. Most airlines require that passengers arrive at the departure gate at least 45 minutes (sometimes more) ahead of time to hold a seat reservation. *Air Canada,* for example, may cancel seat assignments and may not honor reservations of passengers who have not checked in some period of time — usually around 20 to 30 minutes, depending on the airport — before the scheduled departure time, and they *ask* travelers to check in at least 1 hour before all domestic flights and 2 hours before international flights. It pays to read the fine print on your ticket carefully and plan ahead.

A far better strategy is to visit an airline ticket office (or one of a select group of travel agents) to secure an actual boarding pass for your specific flight. Once this has been issued, airline computers show you as checked in, and you effectively own the seat you have selected (although some carriers may not honor boarding passes of passengers arriving at the gate less than 10 minutes before departure). This also is good — but not foolproof — insurance against getting bumped from an overbooked flight and is, therefore, an especially valuable tactic at peak travel times.

Smoking – One decision regarding choosing a seat has been taken out of the hands of many travelers who smoke. Effective February 25, 1990, the US government imposed a ban that prohibits smoking on all flights scheduled for 6 hours or less within the US and its territories. The new regulation applies to both domestic and international carriers serving these routes.

In the case of flights to Canada, by law these rules do not apply to nonstop flights from the US to destinations in Canada, or those with a *continuous* flight time of over 6 hours between stops in the US or its territories. As we went to press, however, all major carriers flying from the US to Canada included such flights in their "domestic" category in terms of nonsmoking rules, and no smoking was allowed on flights between the US and Canada with a continuous flight time of under 6 hours. (Note that there is no smoking on any *Air Canada* flight or any *Canadian Airlines International* flight.)

For a wallet-size guide, which notes in detail the rights of nonsmokers according to these regulations, send a self-addressed, stamped envelope to ASH (*Action on Smoking and Health*), Airline Card, 2013 H St. NW, Washington, DC 20006 (phone: 202-659-4310).

Meals – If you have specific dietary requirements, be sure to let the airline know well before departure time. The available meals include vegetarian, seafood, kosher, Muslim, Hindu, high-protein, low-calorie, low-cholesterol, low-fat, low-sodium, diabetic, bland, and children's menus (not all of these may be available on every carrier). There is no extra charge for this option. It usually is necessary to request special meals when you make your reservations — check-in time is too late. It's also wise to reconfirm that your request for a special meal has made its way into the airline's computer — the time to do this is 24 hours before departure. (Note that special meals generally are not available on intra-Canadian flights on small local carriers. If this poses a problem, try to eat before you board, or bring a snack with you.)

Baggage – Travelers from the US face two different kinds of rules. When you fly in on a US airline or on a major international carrier, US baggage regulations will be in effect. Though airline baggage allowances vary slightly, in general all passengers are allowed to carry on board, without charge, one piece of luggage that will fit easily under a seat of the plane or in an overhead bin and whose combined dimensions (length, width, and depth) do not exceed 45 inches. A reasonable amount of reading material, camera equipment, and a handbag also are allowed. In addition, all passengers are allowed to check two bags in the cargo hold: one usually not to exceed 62 inches when length, width, and depth are combined, the other not to exceed 55 inches in combined dimensions. Generally no single bag may weigh more than 70 pounds.

In general, baggage allowances follow these guidelines in Canada, but care should be exercised on regional and local airlines. If you are flying from the US to Canada and connecting to a domestic flight, you generally will be allowed the same amount of baggage as on the international flight. If you break your trip and then take a domestic flight, the local carrier's weight restrictions apply. Particularly if traveling to remote outposts, be aware that the smaller aircraft used by carriers serving these routes often have limited luggage capacity and also may have to carry mail and freight. When booking flights off the routes of major trunk carriers, always verify baggage allowances.

Charges for additional, oversize, or overweight bags usually are made at a flat rate; the actual dollar amount varies from carrier to carrier. If you plan to travel with any special equipment or sporting gear, be sure to check with the airline beforehand. Most have specific procedures for handling such baggage, and you may have to pay for transport regardless of how much other baggage you have checked. Golf clubs and skis may be checked through as luggage (most airlines are accustomed to handling them), but tennis rackets should be carried onto the plane. Some airlines require that bicycles be partially dismantled and packaged.

To reduce the chances of your luggage going astray, remove all airline tags from previous trips, label each bag inside and out — with your business address rather than your home address on the outside, to prevent thieves from knowing whose house might be unguarded. Lock everything and double-check the tag that the airline attaches to make sure that it is coded correctly for your destination: YUL for Dorval International Airport and YMX for Mirabel International Airport in Montreal; YQB for Saint-Foy Airport in Quebec City.

If your bags are not in the baggage claim area after your flight, or if they're damaged, report the problem to airline personnel immediately. Keep in mind that policies regarding the specific time limit within which you have to make your claim vary from carrier to carrier. Fill out a report form on your lost or damaged luggage and keep a copy of it and your original baggage claim check. If you must surrender the check to claim a damaged bag, get a receipt for it to prove that you did, indeed, check your baggage on the flight. If luggage is missing, be sure to give the airline your destination and/or a telephone number where you can be reached. Also take the name and number of the person in charge of recovering lost luggage.

Most airlines have emergency funds for passengers stranded away from home without their luggage, but if it turns out your bags are truly lost and not simply delayed, do not then and there sign any paper indicating you'll accept an offered settlement. Since the airline is responsible for the value of your bags within certain statuary limits ($1,250 per passenger for lost baggage on a US domestic flight; $9.07 per pound or $20 per kilo for checked baggage, and up to $400 per passenger for unchecked baggage on an international flight), you should take some time to assess the extent of your loss (see *Insurance,* in this section). It's a good idea to keep records indicating the value of the contents of your luggage. A wise alternative is to take a Polaroid picture of the most valuable of your packed items just after putting them in your suitcase.

Considering the increased incidence of damage to baggage, it's now more than ever a good idea to keep the sales slips that confirm how much you paid for your bags. These are invaluable in establishing the value of damaged luggage and eliminate any arguments. A better way to protect your precious gear from the luggage-eating conveyers is to try to carry it on board wherever possible.

Airline Clubs – Some US and foreign carriers often have clubs for travelers who pay for membership. These clubs are not solely for first class passengers, although a first class ticket *may* entitle a passenger to lounge privileges. Membership entitles the traveler to use the private lounges at airports along their route, to refreshments served in those lounges, and to check-cashing privileges at most of their counters. Extras include special telephone numbers for individual reservations, embossed luggage tags, and a membership card for identification. Airlines serving Canada that offer membership in such clubs include the following:

> *American:* The *Admiral's Club.* Single yearly membership $225 for the first year; $125 yearly thereafter; spouse an additional $70 per year.
>
> *Delta:* The *Crown Club.* Single yearly membership $150; spouse an additional $50 per year; 3-year and lifetime memberships also available.
>
> *Northwest:* The *World Club.* Single yearly membership $140 (plus a onetime $50 initiation fee); spouse an additional $50 per year; 3-year and lifetime memberships also available.
>
> *USAir:* The *USAir Club.* Single yearly membership $125; spouse an additional $25 per year; 3-year and lifetime memberships also available.

In addition, *very* frequent travelers who have flown over 60,000 miles on *Air Canada* and are members of the carrier's frequent flyer program — called *Aeroplan* (membership costs CN$20) — may use the carrier's *Maple Leaf Lounges* at major airports across Canada. Club members with an *Aeroplan Elite* card also may bring a guest.

Note that the companies above do not have club facilities in all airports. Other airlines also may offer a variety of special services in many airports.

Getting Bumped – A special air travel problem is the possibility that an airline will accept more reservations (and sell more tickets) than there are seats on a given flight. This is entirely legal and is done to make up for "no-shows," passengers who don't show up for a flight for which they have made reservations and bought tickets. If the airline has oversold the flight and everyone does show up, there simply aren't enough seats. When this happens, the airline is subject to stringent rules designed to protect travelers.

In such cases, the airline first seeks ticket holders willing to give up their seats voluntarily in return for a negotiable sum of money or some other inducement, such as an offer of upgraded seating on the next flight or a voucher for a free trip at some other time. If there are not enough volunteers, the airline may bump passengers against their wishes.

Anyone inconvenienced in this way, however, is entitled to an explanation of the criteria used to determine who does and does not get on the flight, as well as compensation if the resulting delay exceeds certain limits. If the airline can put the bumped passengers on an alternate flight that is *scheduled to arrive* at their original destination within 1 hour of their originally scheduled arrival time, no compensation is owed. If the delay is more than 1 hour but less than 2 hours on a domestic US flight, they must be paid denied-boarding compensation equivalent to the one-way fare to their destination (but not more than $200). If the delay is more than 2 hours beyond the original arrival time on a domestic flight or more than 4 hours on an international flight, the compensation must be doubled (not more than $400). The airline also may offer bumped travelers a voucher for a free flight instead of the denied-boarding compensation. The passenger may be given the choice of either the money or the voucher, the dollar value of which may be no less than the monetary compensation to which the passenger would be entitled. The voucher is not a substitute for the bumped passenger's original ticket; the airline continues to honor that as well.

Keep in mind that the above regulations and policies are only for flights leaving the US, and do *not* apply to charters or to inbound flights originating abroad, even on US carriers.

To protect yourself as best you can against getting bumped, arrive at the airport early, allowing plenty of time to check in and get to the gate. If the flight is oversold, ask immediately for the written statement explaining the airline's policy on denied-boarding compensation and its boarding priorities. If the airline refuses to give you this information, or if you feel it has not handled the situation properly, file a complaint with both the airline and the appropriate government agency.

Delays and Cancellations – The above compensation rules also do not apply if the flight is canceled or delayed, or if a smaller aircraft is substituted due to mechanical problems. Each airline has its own policy for assisting passengers whose flights are delayed or canceled or who must wait for another flight because their original one was overbooked. Most airline personnel will make new travel arrangements if necessary. If the delay is longer than 4 hours, the airline may pay for a phone call or telegram, a meal, and, in some cases, a hotel room and transportation to it.

■ **Caution:** If you are bumped or miss a flight, be sure to ask the airline to notify other airlines on which you have reservations or connecting flights. When your name is taken off the passenger list of your initial flight, the computer usually cancels all of your reservations automatically, unless *you* take steps to preserve them.

CHARTER FLIGHTS: By booking a block of seats on a specially arranged flight, charter tour operators offer travelers air transportation for a substantial reduction over the full coach or economy fare. These operators may offer air-only charters (selling transportation alone) or charter packages (the flight plus a combination of land arrangements such as accommodations, meals, tours, or car rentals). Charters are especially attractive to people living in smaller cities or out-of-the-way places, because they frequently take off from nearby airports, saving travelers the inconvenience and expense of getting to a major gateway.

From the consumer's standpoint, charters differ from scheduled airlines in two main respects: You generally need to book and pay in advance, and you can't change the itinerary or the departure and return dates once you've booked the flight. In practice, however, these restrictions don't always apply. Today, although most charter flights still require advance reservations, some permit last-minute bookings (when there are unsold seats available), and some even offer seats on a standby basis.

Some things to keep in mind about the charter game are:

1. It cannot be repeated often enough that if you are forced to cancel your trip, you can lose much (and possibly all) of your money unless you have cancellation insurance, which is a *must* (see *Insurance,* in this section). Frequently, if the cancellation occurs far enough in advance (often 6 weeks or more), you may forfeit only a $25 or $50 penalty. If you cancel only 2 or 3 weeks before the flight, there may be no refund at all unless you or the operator can provide a substitute passenger.
2. Charter flights may be canceled by the operator up to 10 days before departure for any reason, usually underbooking. Your money is returned in this event, but there may be too little time for you to make new arrangements.
3. Most charters have little of the flexibility of regularly scheduled flights regarding refunds and the changing of flight dates; if you book a return flight, you must be on it or lose your money.
4. Charter operators are permitted to assess a surcharge, if fuel or other costs warrant it, of up to 10% of the airfare up to 10 days before departure.
5. Because of the economics of charter flights, your plane almost always will be full, so you will be crowded, though not necessarily uncomfortable. (There is, however, a new movement among charter airlines to provide flight accommodations that are more comfort-oriented, so this situation may change in the near future.)

To avoid problems, *always* choose charter flights with care. When you consider a charter, ask your travel agent who runs it and carefully check the company. The Better Business Bureau in the company's home city can report on how many complaints, if any, have been lodged against it in the past. Protect yourself with trip cancellation and interruption insurance, which can help safeguard your investment if you, or a traveling companion, are unable to make the trip and must cancel too late to receive a full refund from the company providing your travel services. (This is advisable whether you're buying a charter flight alone or a tour package for which the airfare is provided by charter or scheduled flight.)

Booking – If you do fly on a charter, read the contract's fine print carefully and pay particular attention to the following:

Instructions concerning the payment of the deposit and its balance and to whom the check is to be made payable. Ordinarily, checks are made out to an escrow account, which means the charter company can't spend your money until your flight has safely returned. This provides some protection for you. To ensure the safe handling of your money, make out your check to the escrow account, the number of which must appear by law on the brochure, though all too often it is on the back in fine print. Write the details of the charter, including the destination and dates, on the face of the check; on the back, print "For Deposit Only." Your travel agent may prefer that you make out your check to the agency, saying that it will then pay the tour operator the fee minus commission. It is perfectly legal to write the check as we suggest, however, and if your agent objects too vociferously (he or she should trust the tour operator to send the proper commission), consider taking your business elsewhere. If you don't make your check out to the escrow account, you lose the protection of that escrow should the trip be canceled. Furthermore, recent bankruptcies in the travel industry have served to point out that even the protection of escrow may not be enough to safeguard a traveler's investment. More and more, insurance is becoming a necessity. The charter company should be bonded (usually by an insurance company), and if you want to file a claim against it, the claim should be sent to the bonding agent. The contract will set a time limit within which a claim must be filed.

Specific stipulations and penalties for cancellations. Most charters allow you to cancel up to 45 days in advance without major penalty, but some cancellation dates are 50 to 60 days before departure.

Stipulations regarding cancellation and major changes made by the charterer. US rules say that charter flights may not be canceled within 10 days of departure except when circumstances — such as natural disasters or political upheavals — make it physically impossible to fly. Charterers may make "major changes," however, such as in the date or place of departure or return, but you are entitled to cancel and receive a full refund if you don't wish to accept these changes. A price increase of more than 10% at any time up to 10 days before departure is considered a major change; no price increase at all is allowed during the last 10 days immediately before departure.

Canadian Airlines International offers charter flights through its subsidiary *Canadian Holidays* (191 The West Mall, Etobicoke, Ontario M9C 5K8, Canada; phone: 800-237-0314 from the US; call local offices in Canada), both within Canada and to foreign destinations. Bookings can be made through *Canadian Airlines International* or through a travel agent. *Travel Charter* (1120 E. Longlake Rd., Detroit, MI 48098; phone: 313-528-3570) also sometimes offers charters to Canada.

You also may want to subscribe to the travel newsletter *Jax Fax,* which regularly features a list of charter companies and packagers offering seats on charter flights and may be a source for other charter flights to and within Canada. For a year's subscription send a check or money order for $12 to *Jax Fax,* 397 Post Rd., Darien, CT 06820 (phone: 203-655-8746).

DISCOUNTS ON SCHEDULED FLIGHTS: Promotional fares often are called discount fares because they cost less than what used to be the standard airline fare — full-fare economy. Nevertheless, they cost the traveler the same whether they are bought through a travel agent or directly from the airline. Tickets that cost less if bought from some outlet other than the airline do exist, however. While it is likely that the vast majority of travelers flying to Canada in the near future will be doing so on a promotional fare or charter rather than on a "discount" air ticket of this sort, it still is a good idea for cost-conscious consumers to be aware of the latest developments in the budget airfare scene. Note that the following discussion makes clear-cut distinctions among the types of discounts available based on how they reach the consumer; in actual practice, the distinctions are not nearly so precise.

Net Fare Sources – The newest notion for reducing the costs of travel services comes from travel agents who offer individual travelers "net" fares. Defined simply, a net fare is the bare minimum amount at which an airline or tour operator will carry a prospective traveler. It doesn't include the amount that normally would be paid to the travel agent as a commission. Traditionally, such commissions amount to about 10% on domestic fares and from 10% to 20% on international fares — not counting significant additions to these commission levels that are paid retroactively when agents sell more than a specific volume of tickets or trips for a single supplier. At press time, at least one travel agency in the US was offering travelers the opportunity to purchase tickets and/or tours for a net price. Instead of earning its income from individual commissions, this agency assesses a fixed fee that may or may not provide a bargain for travelers; it requires a little arithmetic to determine whether to use the services of a net travel agent or those of one who accepts conventional commissions. One of the potential drawbacks of buying from agencies selling travel services at net fares is that some airlines refuse to do business with them, thus possibly limiting your flight options.

Travel Avenue is a fee-based agency that rebates its ordinary agency commission to the customer. For domestic flights, they will find the lowest retail fare, then rebate 7% to 10% (depending on the airline selected) of that price minus a $10 ticket-writing charge. The rebate percentage for international flights varies from 5% to 16% (again depending on the airline), and the ticket-writing fee is $25. The ticket-writing charge is imposed per ticket; if the ticket includes more than eight separate flights, an additional $10 or $25 fee is charged. Customers using free flight coupons pay the ticket-writing charge, plus an additional $5 coupon-processing fee.

Travel Avenue will rebate its commissions on all tickets, including heavily discounted fares and senior citizen passes. Available 7 days a week, reservations should be made far enough in advance to allow the tickets to be sent by first class mail, since extra charges accrue for special handling. It's possible to economize further by making your own airline reservation, then asking *Travel Avenue* only to write/issue your ticket. For travelers outside the Chicago area, business may be transacted by phone and purchases charged to a credit card. For information, contact *Travel Avenue* at 641 W. Lake St., Suite 201, Chicago, IL 60606-1012 (phone: 312-876-1116 in Illinois; 800-333-3335 elsewhere in the US).

Consolidators and Bucket Shops – Other vendors of travel services can afford to sell tickets to their customers at an even greater discount because the airline has sold the tickets to them at a substantial discount (usually accomplished by sharply increasing commissions to that vendor), a practice in which many airlines indulge, albeit discreetly, preferring that the general public not know they are undercutting their own "list" prices. Airlines anticipating a slow period on a particular route sometimes sell off a certain portion of their capacity at a very great discount to a wholesaler, or consolidator. The wholesaler sometimes is a charter operator who resells the seats to the public as though they were charter seats, which is why prospective travelers perusing the brochures of charter operators with large programs frequently see a number of flights designated as "scheduled service." As often as not, however, the consolidator, in turn, sells the seats to a travel agency specializing in discounting. Airlines also can sell seats directly to such an agency, which thus acts as its own consolidator. The airline offers the seats either at a net wholesale price, but without the volume-purchase requirement that would be difficult for a modest retail travel agency to fulfill, or at the standard price, but with a commission override large enough (as high as 50%) to allow both a profit and a price reduction to the public.

Travel agencies specializing in discounting sometimes are called "bucket shops," a term once fraught with connotations of unreliability in this country. But in today's highly competitive travel marketplace, more and more conventional travel agencies are selling consolidator-supplied tickets, and the old bucket shops' image is becoming respectable. Agencies that specialize in discounted tickets exist in most large cities, and usually can be found by studying the smaller ads in the travel sections of Sunday newspapers.

Before buying a discounted ticket, whether from a bucket shop or a conventional, full-service travel agency, keep the following considerations in mind: To be in a position to judge how much you'll be saving, first find out the "list" prices of tickets to your destination. Then do some comparison shopping among agencies. Also bear in mind that a ticket that may not differ much in price from one available directly from the airline may, however, allow the circumvention of such things as the advance-purchase requirement. If your plans are less than final, be sure to find out about any other restrictions, such as penalties for canceling a flight or changing a reservation. Most discount tickets are non-endorsable, meaning they can be used only on the airline that issued them, and they usually are marked "nonrefundable" to prevent their being cashed in for a list price refund.

A great many bucket shops are small businesses operating on a thin margin, so it's a good idea to check the local Better Business Bureau for any complaints registered against the one with which you're dealing — before parting with any money. If you still do not feel reassured, consider buying discounted tickets only through a conventional travel agency, which can be expected to have found its own reliable source of consolidator tickets — some of the largest consolidators, in fact, sell only to travel agencies.

A few bucket shops require payment in cash — we strongly advise *against* this — or by certified check or money order, but if credit cards are accepted, use that option. Note, however, if buying from a charter operator selling both scheduled and charter flights, that the scheduled seats are not protected by the regulations — including the use of escrow accounts — governing the charter seats. Well-established charter operators, nevertheless, may extend the same protection to their scheduled flights and, when this is the case, consumers should be sure that the payment option selected directs their money into the escrow account.

Following is a list of companies active in the North American market. Although, at press time, none offered discount fares to Canada, it might prove useful to call when planning your trip to see if Montreal or Quebec City is among the destinations served at the time.

Bargain Air (655 Deep Valley Dr., Suite 355, Rolling Hills, CA 90274; phone: 800-347-2345 or 213-377-2919).

Council Charter (205 E. 42nd St., New York, NY 10017; phone: 800-223-7402 or 212-661-0311).

TFI Tours International (34 W. 32nd St., 12th Floor, New York, NY 10001; phone: 212-736-1140).

Travac Tours and Charters (989 Ave. of the Americas, New York, NY 10018; phone: 800-TRAV-800 or 212-563-3303).

25 West Tours (2490 Coral Way, Miami, FL 33145; phone: 305-856-0810; 800-423-6954 in Florida; 800-252-5052 elsewhere in the US).

Unitravel (1177 N. Warson Rd., St. Louis, MO 63132; phone: 314-569-2501 in Missouri; 800-325-2222 elsewhere in the US).

■**Note:** Although rebating and discounting are becoming increasingly common, there is some legal ambiguity concerning them. Strictly speaking, it is legal to discount domestic tickets, but not international tickets. On the other hand, the law that prohibits discounting, the Federal Aviation Act of 1958, consistently is ignored these days, in part because consumers benefit from the practice and in part because many illegal arrangements are indistinguishable from legal ones. Since the line separating the two is so fine that even the authorities can't always tell the difference, it is unlikely that most consumers would be able to do so, and in fact it is not illegal to *buy* a discounted ticket. If the issue of legality bothers you, ask the agency whether any ticket you're about to buy would be permissible under the above-mentioned act.

Last-Minute Travel Clubs – Still another way to take advantage of bargain airfares is open to those who have a flexible schedule. A number of organizations, usually set up as last-minute travel clubs and functioning on a membership basis, routinely keep in touch with travel suppliers to help them dispose of unsold inventory at discounts of between 15% and 60%. A great deal of the inventory consists of complete package tours and cruises, but some clubs offer air-only charter seats and, occasionally, seats on scheduled flights.

Members pay an annual fee and receive a toll-free hotline telephone number to call for information on imminent trips. In some cases, they also receive periodic mailings with information on bargain travel opportunities for which there is more advance notice. Despite the suggestive names of the clubs providing these services, last-minute travel does not necessarily mean that you cannot make plans until literally the last minute. Trips can be announced as little as a few days or as much as 2 months before departure, but the average is from 1 to 4 weeks' notice.

Among the organizations regularly offering such discounted travel opportunities to Canada are the following:

Discount Travel International (Ives Building, 114 Forrest Ave., Suite 205, Narberth, PA 19072; phone: 800-334-9294 or 215-668-7184). Annual fee: $45 per household.

Encore/Short Notice (4501 Forbes Blvd., Lanham, MD 20706; phone: 301-459-8020; 800-638-0930 for customer service). Annual fee: $36 per family for its Short Notice program only; $48 per family to join the Encore program, which provides additional travel services.

Last Minute Travel (1249 Boylston St., Boston MA 02215; phone: 800-LAST-MIN or 617-267-9800). No fee.

Moment's Notice (425 Madison Ave., New York, NY 10017; phone: 212-486-0503). Annual fee: $45 per family.

Spur-of-the-Moment Tours and Cruises (10780 Jefferson Blvd., Culver City, CA 90230; phone: 310-839-2418 in Southern California; 800-343-1991 elsewhere in the US). No fee.

Traveler's Advantage (3033 S. Parker Rd., Suite 1000, Aurora, CO 80014; phone: 800-835-8747). Annual fee: $49 per family.

Vacations to Go (2411 Fountain View, Suite 201, Houston, TX 77057; phone: 800-338-4962). Annual fee: $19.95 per family.

Worldwide Discount Travel Club (1674 Meridian Ave., Miami Beach, FL 33139; phone: 305-534-2082). Annual fee: $40 per person; $50 per family.

■ **Note:** For additional information on last-minute travel discounts, a new "900" number telephone service called *Last Minute Travel Connection* (phone: 900-446-8292) provides recorded advertisements (including contact information) for discount offerings on airfares, package tours, cruises, and other travel opportunities. Since companies update their advertisements as often as every hour, listings are current. This 24-hour service is available to callers using touch-tone phones; the cost is $1 per minute (the charge will show up on your phone bill). For more information, contact *La Onda, Ltd.* (601 Skokie Blvd., Suite 224, Northbrook, IL 60062; phone: 708-498-9216).

Generic Air Travel – Organizations that apply the same flexible-schedule idea to air travel only and sell tickets at literally the last minute also exist. Their service sometimes is known as "generic" air travel, and it operates somewhat like an ordinary airline standby service except that the organizations running it offer seats on not one but several scheduled and charter airlines.

One pioneer of generic flights is *Airhitch* (2790 Broadway, Suite 100, New York, NY 10025; phone: 212-864-2000). Prospective travelers stipulate a range of at least five consecutive departure dates and their desired destination, along with alternate choices, and pay the fare in advance. They are then sent a voucher good for travel *on a space-available basis* on flights to their destination *region* (i.e., not necessarily the specific destination requested) during this time period. The week before this range of departure dates begins, travelers must contact *Airhitch* for specific information about flights that will probably be available and instructions on how to proceed for check-in.

(Return flights are arranged in the same manner as the outbound flights — a specified period of travel is decided upon, and a few days before this date range begins, prospective passengers contact *Airhitch* for details about flights that may be available.) If the client does not accept any of the suggested flights or cancels his or her travel plans after selecting a flight, the amount paid can be applied toward a future fare or the flight arrangements can be transferred to another individual (although, in both cases, an additional fee may be charged). No refunds are offered unless the prospective passenger does not ultimately get on any flight in the specified date range; in such a case, the full fare is refunded. (Note that *Airhitch*'s slightly more expensive "Target" program, which provides confirmed reservations on specific dates to specific destinations, offers passengers greater — but not guaranteed — certainty regarding flight arrangements.) At the time of this writing, *Airhitch* did not offer flights between the US and Canada, but do check at the time you plan to travel.

Bartered Travel Sources – Suppose a hotel buys advertising space in a newspaper. As payment, the hotel gives the publishing company the use of a number of hotel rooms in lieu of cash. This is barter, a common means of exchange among hotels, airlines, car rental companies, cruise lines, tour operators, restaurants, and other travel service companies. When a bartering company finds itself with empty airline seats (or excess hotel rooms, or cruise ship cabin space, and so on) and offers them to the public, considerable savings can be enjoyed.

Bartered travel clubs often offer discounts of up to 50% to members, who pay an annual fee (approximately $50 at press time) that entitles them to select from the flights, cruises, hotel rooms, or other travel services that the club obtained by barter. Members usually present a voucher, club credit card, or scrip (a dollar-denomination voucher negotiable only for the bartered product) to the hotel, which in turn subtracts the dollar amount from the bartering company's account.

Selling bartered travel is a perfectly legitimate means of retailing. One advantage to club members is that they don't have to wait until the last minute to obtain flight or room reservations.

Among the companies specializing in bartered travel, two that offer members travel services to and in Canada are *IGT (In Good Taste) Services* (1111 Lincoln Rd., 4th Floor, Miami Beach, FL 33139; phone: 800-444-8872 or 305-534-7900), with an annual fee of $48 per family, and *Travel Guild* (18210 Redmond Way, Redmond, WA 98052; phone: 206-861-1900), which charges $48 per family per year.

OTHER DISCOUNT TRAVEL SOURCES: An excellent source of information on economical travel opportunities is the *Consumer Reports Travel Letter,* published monthly by Consumers Union. It keeps abreast of the scene on a wide variety of fronts, including package tours, rental cars, insurance, and more, but it is especially helpful for its comprehensive coverage of airfares, offering guidance on all the options from scheduled flights on major or low-fare airlines to charters and discount sources. For a year's subscription, send $37 ($57 for 2 years) to *Consumer Reports Travel Letter* (PO Box 53629, Boulder, CO 80322-3629; phone: 800-234-1970). For information on other travel newsletters, see *Books, Magazines, and Newsletters,* in this section.

On Arrival

FROM THE AIRPORT TO THE CITY: Montreal's airports for both international and domestic flights are Dorval International Airport, which is located about 20 miles (32 km) from the city, and Mirabel International Airport, which is situated 34 miles (55 km) from the city. In Quebec City,

Saint-Foy Airport handles both international and domestic flights and is about 12 miles (20 km) outside the city.

Taxi – In Montreal, it takes about 25 minutes to get from Dorval Airport to the city; the fare is about CN$23. From Mirabel to the center of Montreal takes about 45 minutes; the fare costs CN$40. In Quebec City, the 35-minute ride from Saint-Foy Airport costs about CN$20.

Public Transportation – The most convenient way to get from Dorval Airport to downtown Montreal is to take the shuttle bus *Auto Car Connoisseur* (phone: 514-476-3010), which charges CN$8.50 for the 25-minute trip. From Mirabel Airport to downtown the *Aero-Plus* shuttle (phone: 514-476-1100) takes 1 hour, and costs CN$11.75. In Quebec City, *Maple Leaf Sightseeing Tours* (phone: 418-640-9226) operates a shuttle bus that goes to all the major hotels. It takes about 25 minutes, and costs CN$7.50.

CAR RENTAL: Unless planning to drive round-trip from home, most travelers who want to drive while on vacation simply rent a car.

Renting a car in Canada is not inexpensive, but it is possible to economize by determining your own needs and then shopping around among the car rental companies until you find the best deal. Ask about special rates or promotional deals, such as weekend or weekly rates, bonus coupons for airline tickets, or 24-hour rates that include gas and unlimited mileage.

Renting from the US – Travel agents can arrange foreign rentals for clients, but it is just as easy to call and rent a car yourself. Listed below are some of the major international rental companies that have representation in Montreal and Quebec City and have information and reservations numbers that can be dialed toll-free from the US:

Avis (phone: 800-331-1084 in the US; 800-387-7600 in Quebec; 800-268-2310 elsewhere in Canada). Has representatives at all airports as well as downtown Montreal and Quebec City.

Budget (phone: 800-527-0700 in the US; 800-268-8900 in Canada). Has representatives at the airports and downtown in both cities.

Hertz (phone: 800-654-3001 in the US; 800-263-0600 in Canada). Has representatives at the airports and downtown in both cities.

National Car Rental (phone: 800-CAR-RENT throughout the US and Canada). Has representatives at the airports and downtown in both cities.

Sears Rent-A-Car (phone: 800-527-0770 in the US; 800-268-8900 in Canada). Has representatives at the airports and downtown in both cities.

Thrifty Rent-A-Car (phone: 800-367-2277 throughout the US and Canada). Has representatives at the airports and downtown in both cities.

Tilden Rent-A-Car System: (phone: 800-CAR-RENT throughout the US and Canada). Largest Canadian firm, affiliated with *National* in the US.

It also is possible to rent a car before you go by contacting any number of smaller or less well known US companies that do not operate worldwide. These organizations may specialize in North American auto travel, including leasing and car purchase in addition to car rental, or may actually be tour operators with a well-established Canadian car rental program.

Requirements – Whether you decide to rent a car in advance from a large international rental company with Canadian branches or wait to rent from a local company, you should know that renting a car is rarely as simple as signing on the dotted line and roaring off into the night. To drive in Montreal or Quebec City, you need certain documents (see below), and will have to convince the renting agency that (1) you are personally creditworthy, and (2) you will bring the car back at the stated time. This will be easy if you have a major credit card; most rental companies accept credit cards in lieu of a cash deposit, as well as for payment of your final bill. If you prefer to pay in cash, leave your credit card imprint as a "deposit," then pay your bill in cash when you return the car.

If you are planning to rent a car once you're in Canada, *Avis, Budget, Hertz,* and other US rental companies usually *will* rent to travelers paying in cash and leaving either a credit card imprint or a substantial amount of cash as a deposit. This is not necessarily standard policy, however, as some of the other international chains and a number of local and regional Canadian companies will *not* rent to an individual who doesn't have a valid credit card. In this case, you will have to call around to find a company that accepts cash.

Also keep in mind that although the minimum age to drive a car in Canada is 16 years, the minimum age to rent a car is set by the rental company. (Restrictions vary from company to company, as well as at different locations.) Many firms have a minimum age requirement of 21 years, some raise that to between 23 and 25 years, and for some models of cars it rises to 30 years. The upper age limit at many companies is between 69 and 75; others have no upper limit or may make drivers above a certain age subject to special conditions.

Don't forget that all car rentals in the province of Quebec are subject to an 8% province tax, as well as the Canadian Goods and Services Tax (GST) of 7%. This tax rarely is included in the rental price that's advertised or quoted, but it always must be paid — whether you pay in advance in the US or pay it when you drop off the car.

Driving Documents – A valid driver's license from his or her own state of residence is required for a US citizen to drive in Canada. Proof of liability also is required and is a standard part of any car rental contract. Car rental companies also make provisions for breakdowns, emergency service, and assistance; ask for a number to call when you pick up the vehicle.

Rules of the Road – Driving in Canada is on the right side of the road, as in the US. Passing is on the left; the left turn signal must be flashing before and while passing, and the right indicator must be used when pulling back to the right.

According to law, those coming from the right at intersections have the right of way, as in the US, and pedestrians, provided they are in marked crosswalks, have priority over all vehicles.

In the city, speed limits usually are 50 kmh (about 30 mph). Outside the city, the speed limit is 100 kmh (about 60 mph) on freeways and 80 kmh (about 50 mph) on highways.

Gasoline – The major oil companies have stations in Canada: *Chevron, Exxon, Gulf, Shell, Sunoco,* and *Texaco.* Even more common are Canadian companies, like *Petro-Canada.* Gas is sold by the liter, which is slightly more than 1 quart; approximately 3.8 liters equal 1 US gallon. As in the US, regular, leaded, and diesel gas generally are available in several grades, and self-service (where you do the pumping) often is less expensive than full service. Similarly, gas paid for in cash often costs less that when you pay for it with a credit card.

Package Tours

If the mere thought of buying a package for your visit to Montreal or Quebec City conjures up visions of a trip marching in lockstep with a horde of frazzled fellow travelers, remember that packages have come a long way. For one thing, not all packages necessarily are escorted tours, and the one you buy does not have to include any organized touring at all — nor will it necessarily include traveling companions. If it does, however, you'll find that people of all sorts — many just like yourself — are taking advantage of packages today because they are economical and convenient, and save you an immense amount of planning time. Given the high cost of travel these days, packages have emerged as a particularly wise buy.

In essence, a package is just an amalgam of travel services that can be purchased in a single transaction. A Montreal or Quebec City package (tour or otherwise) may include any or all of the following: round-trip transportation, local transportation (and/or car rentals), accommodations, some or all meals, sightseeing, entertainment, transfers to and from the hotel, taxes, tips, escort service, and a variety of incidental features that might be offered as options at additional cost. In other words, a package can be any combination of travel elements, from a fully escorted tour offered at an all-inclusive price to a simple fly/drive booking that allows you to move about totally on your own. Its principal advantage is that it saves money: The cost of the combined arrangements invariably is well below the price of all of the same elements if bought separately, and, particularly if transportation is provided by discount flight, the whole package could cost less than just a round-trip economy airline ticket on a regularly scheduled flight. A package provides more than economy and convenience: It releases the traveler from having to make individual arrangements for each separate element of a trip.

Tour programs generally can be divided into two categories — "escorted" (or locally hosted) and "independent." An escorted tour means that a guide will accompany the group from the beginning of the tour through to the return flight; a locally hosted tour means that the group will be met upon arrival at each location by a different local host. On independent tours, there generally is a choice of hotels, meal plans, and sightseeing trips, as well as a variety of special excursions. The independent plan is for travelers who do not want a totally set itinerary, but who do prefer confirmed hotel reservations. Whether you choose an escorted or an independent tour, always bring along complete contact information for your tour operator in case a problem arises, although US tour operators often have local affiliates who can give additional assistance or make other arrangements on the spot.

To determine whether a package — or more specifically, *which* package — fits your travel plans, start by evaluating your interests and needs, deciding how much and what you want to spend, see, and do. Gather brochures on Montreal and Quebec City tours. Be sure that you take the time to read each brochure *carefully* to determine precisely what is included. Keep in mind that they are written to entice you into signing up for a package tour. Often the language is deceptive and devious. For example, a brochure may quote the lowest prices for a package tour based on facilities that are unavailable during the off-season, undesirable at any season, or just plain nonexistent. Information such as "breakfast included" (as it often is in packages to Canada) or "plus tax" (which can add up) should be taken into account. Note, too, that the prices quoted in brochures almost always are based on double occupancy: The rate listed is for each of two people sharing a double room, and if you travel alone, the supplement for single accommodations can raise the price considerably (see *Hints for Single Travelers,* in this section).

In this age of erratic airfares, the brochure most often will *not* include the price of an airline ticket in the price of the package, though sample fares from various gateway cities usually will be listed separately, as extras to be added to the price of the ground arrangements. Before figuring your actual costs, check the latest fares with the airlines, because the samples invariably are out of date by the time you read them. If the brochure gives more than one category of sample fares per gateway city —

such as an individual tour-basing fare, a group fare, an excursion, APEX, or other discount ticket — your travel agent or airline tour desk will be able to tell you which one applies to the package you choose, depending on when you travel, how far in advance you book, and other factors. (An individual tour-basing fare is a fare computed as part of a package that includes land arrangements, thereby entitling a carrier to reduce the air portion almost to the absolute minimum. Though it always represents a saving over full-fare coach or economy, lately the individual tour-basing fare has not been as inexpensive as the excursion and other discount fares that also are available to individuals. The group fare usually is the least expensive fare, and it is the tour operator, not you, who makes up the group.) When the brochure does include round-trip transportation in the package price, don't forget to add the cost of round-trip transportation from your home city to the departure city to come up with the total cost of the package.

Finally, read the general information regarding terms and conditions and the responsibility clause (usually in fine print at the end of the descriptive literature) to determine the precise elements for which the tour operator is — and is not — liable. Here the tour operator frequently expresses the right to change services or schedules as long as equivalent arrangements are offered. This clause also absolves the operator of responsibility for circumstances beyond human control, such as floods, avalanches, earthquakes, or injury to you or your property. While reading, ask the following questions:

1. Does the tour include airfare or other transportation, sightseeing, meals, transfers, taxes, baggage handling, tips, or any other services? Do you want all these services?
2. If the brochure indicates that "some meals" are included, does this mean a welcoming and farewell dinner, two breakfasts, or every evening meal?
3. What classes of hotels are offered? If you will be traveling alone, what is the single supplement?
4. Does the tour itinerary or price vary according to the season?
5. Are the prices guaranteed; that is, if costs increase between the time you book and the time you depart, can surcharges unilaterally be added?
6. Do you get a full refund if you cancel? If not, be sure to obtain cancellation insurance.
7. Can the operator cancel if too few people join? At what point?

One of the consumer's biggest problems is finding enough information to judge the reliability of a tour packager, since individual travelers seldom have direct contact with the firm putting the package together. Usually, a retail travel agent is interposed between customer and tour operator, and much depends on his or her candor and cooperation. So ask a number of questions about the tour you are considering. For example:

- Has the travel agent ever used a package provided by this tour operator?
- How long has the tour operator been in business? Check the Better Business Bureau in the area where the tour operator is based to see if any complaints have been filed against it.
- Is the tour operator a member of the *United States Tour Operators Association* (*USTOA;* 211 E. 51st St., Suite 12B, New York, NY 10022; phone: 212-944-5727)? *USTOA* will provide a list of its members on request; it also offers a useful brochure called *How to Select a Package Tour.*
- How many and which companies are involved in the package?
- If air travel is by charter flight, is there an escrow account in which deposits will be held; if so, what is the name of the bank?

This last question is very important. US law requires that tour operators deposit every charter passenger's deposit and subsequent payment in a proper escrow account (see "Charter Flights," above).

■ **A word of advice:** Purchasers of vacation packages who feel they're not getting their money's worth are more likely to get a refund if they complain in writing to the operator — and bail out of the whole package immediately. Alert the tour operator to the fact that you are dissatisfied, that you will be leaving for home as soon as transportation can be arranged, and that you expect a refund. They may have forms to fill out detailing your complaint; otherwise, state your case in a letter. Even if difficulty in arranging immediate transportation home detains you, your dated, written complaint should help in procuring a refund from the operator.

SAMPLE PACKAGES IN MONTREAL AND QUEBEC CITY: As discussed above, a typical package tour to Montreal or Quebec City might include round-trip transportation, accommodations, a sightseeing tour, and several meals. Although some packages just cover arrangements at a specific hotel, others offer more extensive arrangements and may be built around activities such as fishing, hunting, or skiing, or special interests such as history, archaeology, or nature exploration.

Following is a list of some of the major tour operators that offer packages to Montreal and/or Quebec City. Most tour operators offer several departure dates, depending on the length of the tour and areas visited. As indicated, some operators are wholesalers only, and will deal only with a travel agent.

Adventure Tours (9818 Liberty Rd., Randallstown, MD 21133; phone: 410-922-7000 in Baltimore; 800-638-9040 elsewhere in the US). Offers 2- to 4-night city packages to Montreal and Quebec City; extensions also available. This tour operator is a wholesaler, so use a travel agent.

American Express Travel Related Services (offices throughout the US; phone: 800-241-1700 for information and local branch offices). Offers city packages to Montreal and Quebec City, as well as an 11-day Eastern Highlights tour that includes stops in US and Canadian cities. The tour operator is a wholesaler, so use a travel agent.

Brenden Tours (15137 Califa St., Van Nuys, CA 91411-3021; phone: 818-785-9696 or 800-421-8446). Offers a 10-day French Canada and Ontario tour that includes stays in Montreal and Quebec City.

Cartan Tours (1304 Parkview Ave., Suite 210, Manhattan Beach, CA 90266; phone: 800-422-7826). Offers a variety of Canada packages that include stays in Montreal and Quebec City.

Collette Tours (162 Middle St., Pawtucket, RI 02860; phone: 800-752-2655 in Rhode Island, 800-832-4656 elsewhere in the US). Offers 7- to 11-day city packages that include stays in Montreal and Quebec City.

Maupintour (PO Box 807, Lawrence, KS 66044; phone: 800-255-4266). Offers 1- to 2-week escorted tours throughout Canada, including several packages that include Montreal and Quebec City. The operator is a wholesaler, so use a travel agent.

Tauck Tours (PO Box 5027, Westport, CT 06881-5027; phone: 800-451-4708 in Connecticut, 800-468-2825 elsewhere in the US). Offers several tours of Canada, including city packages to Montreal and Quebec City.

■ **Note:** Frequently, the best city packages are offered by the hotels, which are trying to attract guests during the weekends, when business travel drops off, and during other off-periods. These packages are sometimes advertised in local newspapers and in the Sunday travel sections of major metropolitan papers, such as *The New York Times,* which has a national edition available in most parts of the US. It's worthwhile asking about packages, especially family and special-occasion offerings, when you call to make a hotel reservation. Calling several hotels can garner you a variety of options from which to choose.

Preparing

How to Use a Travel Agent

 A reliable travel agent remains the best source of service and information for planning a trip, whether you have a specific itinerary and require an agent only to make reservations or you need extensive help in sorting through the maze of airfares, tour offerings, hotel packages, and the scores of other arrangements that may be involved in a trip to Canada.

Know what you want from a travel agent so that you can evaluate what you are getting. It is perfectly reasonable to expect your travel agent to be a thoroughly knowledgeable travel specialist, with information about your destination and, even more crucial, a command of current airfares, ground arrangements, and other wrinkles in the travel scene.

Most travel agents work through computer reservations systems (CRS). These are used to assess the availability and cost of flights, hotels, and car rental, and through them they can book reservations. Despite reports of "computer bias," in which a computer may favor one airline over another, the CRS should provide agents with the entire spectrum of flights available to a given destination, and the complete range of fares, in considerably less time than it takes to telephone the airlines individually — and at no extra cost to the client.

Make the most intelligent use of a travel agent's time and expertise; understand the economics of the industry. As a client, traditionally you pay nothing for the agent's services; with few exceptions, it's all free, from hotel bookings to advice on package tours. Any money the travel agent makes on the time spent arranging your itinerary — booking hotels, resorts, or flights, or suggesting activities — comes from commissions paid by the suppliers of these services — the airlines, hotels, and so on. These commissions generally run from 10% to 15% of the total cost of the service, although suppliers often reward agencies that sell their services in volume with an increased commission called an override.

A conventional travel agent sometimes may charge a fee for special services. These chargeable items may include long-distance telephone costs incurred in making a booking, for reserving a room in a place that does not pay a commission (such as a small, out-of-the-way hotel), or for special attention such as planning a highly personalized itinerary. A fee also may be assessed in instances of deeply discounted airfares.

Choose a travel agent with the same care with which you would choose a doctor or lawyer. You will be spending a good deal of money on the basis of the agent's judgment, so you have a right to expect that judgment to be mature, informed, and interested. At the moment, unfortunately, there aren't many standards within the travel agent industry to help you gauge competence, and the quality of individual agents varies enormously.

At present, only nine states have registration, licensing, or other form of travel agent–related legislation on their books. Rhode Island licenses travel agents; Florida, Hawaii, Iowa, and Ohio register them; and California, Illinois, Oregon, and Washington have laws governing the sale of transportation or related services. While state licensing of agents cannot absolutely guarantee competence, it can at least ensure that an agent has met some minimum requirements.

Perhaps the best way to find a travel agent is by word of mouth. If the agent (or agency) has done a good job for your friends over a period of time, it probably indicates a certain level of commitment and competence. Always ask for the name of the company *and* the name of the specific agent with whom your friends dealt, for it is that individual who will serve you, and quality can vary widely within a single agency.

Entry Requirements and Documents

ENTRY REQUIREMENTS: The only requirement for citizens and legal residents of the US crossing the US-Canada border in either direction is that they present one form of identification. For native US citizens, this can be a valid passport or a driver's license, original or certified birth certificate, baptismal certificate, voter registration card or draft card, or other identification that officially verifies their US citizenship. Proof of current residency also may be required. Naturalized US citizens should carry their naturalization certificate or some other evidence of citizenship. Permanent residents of the US who are not American citizens should have Alien Registration Receipt cards (US Form I-151 or Form I-551). Visitors under 18 years of age not accompanied by an adult should carry a letter from a parent or guardian giving them permission to travel to Canada.

Any visitor to Canada who is not a US citizen or a permanent resident of the US must have a valid passport from some other nation. In addition, a visa may be required of visitors other than British citizens. Foreign visitors to the US who cross into Canada and then return to the US should check with the US Immigration and Naturalization Service to make sure that they have all the papers they need for reentry into the US.

DUTY AND CUSTOMS: As a general rule, the requirements for bringing the majority of items *into Canada* is that they must be in quantities small enough not to imply commercial import.

Among the items that each person may take into Canada duty free are 50 cigars, 200 cigarettes, and 2.2 pounds (1 kilo) of manufactured tobacco, as well as 40 ounces (1.1 liters) of liquor or wine or 24 12-ounce cans or bottles of beer or ale. Personal effects and sports equipment appropriate for a pleasure trip also are allowed.

If you are bringing along a computer, camera, or other electronic equipment for your own use that you will be taking back to the US, you should register the item with the US Customs Service to avoid paying duty both entering and returning from Canada. (Also see *Customs and Returning to the US,* in this section.) For information on this procedure, as well as for a variety of pamphlets on US customs regulations, contact the local office of the US Customs Service or the central office, PO Box 7474, Washington, DC 20044 (phone: 202-566-8195).

■**One rule to follow:** When passing through customs, it is illegal not to declare dutiable items; penalties range from stiff fines and seizure of goods to prison terms. So don't try to sneak anything through — it just isn't worth it.

Insurance

 It is unfortunate that most decisions to buy travel insurance are impulsive and usually are made without any real consideration of the traveler's existing policies. Therefore, the first person with whom you should discuss travel insurance is your own insurance broker, not a travel agent or the clerk behind the airport insurance counter. You may discover that the insurance you already carry — homeowner's policies and/or accident, health, and life insurance — protects you adequately while you travel and that your real needs are in the more mundane areas of excess value insurance for baggage or trip cancellation insurance.

TYPES OF INSURANCE: To make insurance decisions intelligently, however, you first should understand the basic categories of travel insurance and what they cover. Then you can decide what you should have in the broader context of your personal insurance needs, and you can choose the most economical way of getting the desired protection: through riders on existing policies; with onetime, short-term policies; through a special program put together for the frequent traveler; through coverage that's part of a travel club's benefits; or with a combination policy sold by insurance companies through brokers, automobile clubs, tour operators, and travel agents.

There are seven basic categories of travel insurance:

1. Baggage and personal effects insurance
2. Personal accident and sickness insurance
3. Trip cancellation and interruption insurance
4. Default and/or bankruptcy insurance
5. Flight insurance (to cover injury or death)
6. Automobile insurance (for driving your own or a rented car)
7. Combination policies

Baggage and Personal Effects Insurance – Ask your insurance agent if baggage and personal effects are included in your current homeowner's policy, or if you will need a special floater to cover you for the duration of a trip. The object is to protect your bags and their contents in case of damage or theft any time during your travels, not just while you're in flight, where only limited protection is provided by the airline. Baggage liability varies from carrier to carrier, but generally speaking, on domestic flights, luggage usually is insured to $1,250 — that's per passenger, not per bag. For most international flights, including domestic portions of international flights, the airline's liability limit is approximately $9.07 per pound or $20 per kilo (which comes to about $360 per 40-pound suitcase) for checked baggage and up to $400 per passenger for unchecked baggage. Canadian airlines insure baggage for up to a maximum of $750 on domestic flights and $640 on flights originating in the US that cross the Canadian border only. These limits should be specified on your airline ticket, but to be awarded the specified amount, you'll have to provide an itemized list of lost property, and if you're including new and/or expensive items, be prepared for a request that you back up your claim with sales receipts or other proofs of purchase.

If you are carrying goods worth more than the maximum protection offered by the airline, consider excess value insurance. Additional coverage is available from airlines at an average, currently, of $1 to $2 per $100 worth of coverage, up to a maximum of $5,000. This insurance can be purchased at the airline counter when you check in, though you should arrive early enough to fill out the necessary forms and avoid holding up other passengers.

Major credit card companies provide coverage for lost or delayed baggage — and this coverage often also is over and above what the airline will pay. The basic coverage usually is automatic for all cardholders who use the credit card to purchase tickets, but to qualify for additional coverage, cardholders generally must enroll.

Additional baggage and personal effects insurance also is included in certain of the combination travel insurance policies discussed below.

■ **A note of warning:** Be sure to read the fine print of any excess value insurance policy; there often are specific exclusions, such as cash, tickets, furs, gold and silver objects, art, and antiques. Insurance companies ordinarily will pay only the depreciated value of the goods rather than their replacement value. The best way to protect your property is to take photos of your valuables, and keep a record of the serial numbers of such items as cameras, typewriters, laptop computers, radios, and so on. If an airline loses your luggage, you will be asked to fill out a Property Irregularity Report before you leave the airport. Also, report the loss to the police (since the insurance company will check with the police when processing your claim).

Personal Accident and Sickness Insurance – This covers you in case of illness during your trip or death in an accident. Most policies insure you for hospital and doctors' expenses, lost income, and so on. In most cases, it is a standard part of existing health insurance policies, though you should check with your insurance broker to be sure of the conditions for which your policy will pay. If your coverage is insufficient, take out a separate vacation accident policy or an entire vacation insurance policy that includes health and life coverage.

Two examples of such comprehensive health and life insurance coverage are the travel insurance packages offered by *Wallach & Co.*:

HealthCare Abroad: This program is available to individuals up to age 75. For $3 per day (minimum 10 days, maximum 90 days), policy holders receive $100,000 medical insurance and a $25,000 death benefit.

HealthCare Global: This insurance package, which can be purchased for periods of 10 to 180 days, is offered for two age groups: Men and women up to age 75 receive $25,000 medical insurance and a $50,000 death benefit; those from age 75 to 84 are eligible for $12,500 medical insurance and a $25,000 death benefit. For either policy, the cost for a 10-day period is $25, with decreasing rates up to 75 days, after which the rate is $1.50 per day.

Both of these basic programs also may be bought in combination with trip cancellation and baggage insurance at extra cost. For further information, write to *Wallach & Co.,* 107 W. Federal St., Box 480, Middleburg, VA 22117-0480 (phone: 703-687-3166 in Virginia; 800-237-6615 elsewhere in the US).

Trip Cancellation and Interruption Insurance – Most package tour passengers pay for their travel well before departure. The disappointment of having to miss a vacation because of illness or any other reason pales before the awful prospect that not all (and sometimes none) of the money paid in advance might be returned. So cancellation insurance for any package tour is a must.

Although cancellation penalties vary (they are listed in the fine print in every tour brochure, and before you purchase a package tour you should know exactly what they are), rarely will a passenger get more than 50% of this money back if forced to cancel within a few weeks of scheduled departure. Therefore, if you book a package tour, you should have trip cancellation insurance to guarantee full reimbursement or refund should you, a traveling companion, or a member of your immediate family get sick, forcing you to cancel your trip or *return home early.*

The key here is *not* to buy just enough insurance to guarantee full reimbursement for the cost of the package in case of cancellation. The proper amount of coverage should be sufficient to reimburse you for the cost of having to catch up with a tour after its departure or having to travel home at the full economy airfare if you have to forgo the return flight tied to the package. There usually is quite a discrepancy between an excursion or other special fare and the amount charged to travel the same distance on a regularly scheduled flight at full economy fare.

Trip cancellation insurance is available from travel agents and tour operators in two forms: as part of a short-term, all-purpose travel insurance package (sold by the travel agent); or as specific cancellation insurance designed by the tour operator for a specific charter tour. Generally, tour operators' policies are less expensive, but also less inclusive. Cancellation insurance also is available directly from insurance companies or their agents as part of a short-term, all-inclusive travel insurance policy.

Before you decide on a policy, read each one carefully. (Either type can be purchased from a travel agent when you book the charter or package tour.) Be sure to check the fine print for stipulations concerning "family members" and "pre-existing medical conditions," as well as allowances for living expenses if you must delay your return due to injury or illness.

Default and/or Bankruptcy Insurance – Although trip cancellation insurance usually protects you if *you* are unable to complete — or begin — your trip, a fairly recent innovation is coverage in the event of default and/or bankruptcy on the part of the tour operator, airline, or other travel supplier. In some travel insurance packages, this contingency is included in the trip cancellation portion of the coverage; in others, it is a separate feature. Either way, it is becoming increasingly important. Whereas sophisticated travelers have long known to beware of the possibility of default or bankruptcy when buying a tour package, in recent years more than a few respected airlines unexpectedly have revealed their shaky financial condition, sometimes leaving hordes of stranded ticket holders in their wake. While default/bankruptcy insurance will not ordinarily result in reimbursement in time to pay for new arrangements, it can ensure that you will get your money back, and even independent travelers buying no more than an airplane ticket may want to consider it.

Flight Insurance – Airlines have carefully established limits of liability for injury to or the death of passengers on international flights. For all international flights to, from, or with a stopover in the US, all carriers are liable for up to $75,000 per passenger. For all other international flights, the liability is based on where you purchase the ticket: If booked in advance in the US, the maximum liability is $75,000; if arrangements are made abroad, the liability is $10,000. But remember, these liabilities are not the same thing as insurance policies; every penny that an airline eventually pays in the case of death or injury may be subject to a legal battle.

But before you buy last-minute flight insurance from an airport vending machine, consider the purchase in light of your total existing insurance coverage. A careful review of your current policies may reveal that you already are amply covered for accidental death. Be aware that airport insurance, the kind typically bought at a counter or from a vending machine, is among the most expensive forms of life insurance coverage, and that even within a single airport, rates for approximately the same coverage vary widely.

If you buy your plane ticket with a major credit card, you generally receive automatic insurance coverage at no extra cost. Additional coverage usually can be obtained at extremely reasonable prices, but a cardholder must sign up for it in advance.

Automobile Insurance – All drivers in Canada are required by law to have automobile insurance for their car. The minimum coverage is determined by provincial law, but this minimum usually is too low for adequate protection. Your insurance agent can advise you on the proper amount of insurance necessary. There are several kinds of coverage you should have in Canada:

1. *Liability Insurance:* This provides protection if you are sued for injuring someone or his or her property. US motorists driving in Canada should obtain a Canadian Non-Resident Inter-Province Motor Vehicle Liability Insurance Card, which provides evidence of financial responsibility by a valid automobile liability insurance policy. This card is available only through insurance agents in the US. (There usually is no charge for this card.) All provinces in Canada require visiting motorists to produce evidence of financial responsibility should they be involved in an accident. Minimum liability requirements vary from CN$50,000 (in Quebec) to CN$200,000 (in other Canadian provinces). Information and advice regarding auto insurance may be obtained from the *Insurance Bureau of Canada,* 181 University Ave., Toronto, Ontario M5H 3M7, Canada (phone: 416-362-2031).
2. *Accident Insurance:* This protects against payments for death or bodily injury and includes loss of pay, medical expenses, and so on. These policies also include coverage against uninsured motorists. Note that the province of Quebec has no-fault insurance laws.
3. *Comprehensive and Collision Insurance:* This protects against loss of or damage to your car. There usually is a deductible amount indicated for this coverage; it either is paid by the policy holder toward the cost of repairs or deducted from the loss settlement.

When you rent a car, the rental company is required to provide you with collision protection. In your car rental contract, you'll see that for about $10 to $13 a day, you may buy optional collision damage waiver (CDW) protection.

If you do not accept the CDW coverage, you may be liable for as much as the full retail value of the rental car, and by paying for the CDW you are relieved of all responsibility for any damage to the car. Before agreeing to this coverage, however, check with your own broker about your own existing personal automobile insurance policy. It very well may cover your entire liability exposure without any additional cost, or you automatically may be covered by the credit card company to which you are charging the cost of your rental. To find out the amount of rental car insurance provided by major credit cards, contact the issuing institutions.

You also should know that an increasing number of the major international car rental companies automatically are including the cost of the CDW in their basic rates. Car rental prices have increased to include this coverage, although rental company ad campaigns may promote this as a new, improved rental package "benefit." The disadvantage of this inclusion is that you may not have the option to turn down the CDW — even if you already are adequately covered by your own insurance policy or through a credit card company.

Combination Policies – Short-term insurance policies, which may include a combination of any or all of the types of insurance discussed above, are available through retail insurance agencies, automobile clubs, and many travel agents. These combination policies are designed to cover you for the duration of a single trip.

Companies offering policies of this type include the following:

Access America International (PO Box 90310, Richmond, VA 23230; phone: 800-424-3391 or 804-215-3300).

Carefree Travel Insurance (Arm Coverage, 120 Mineola Blvd., Mineola, NY 11501; phone: 800-645-2424 or 516-294-0220).

NEAR Services (450 Prairie Ave., Suite 101, Calumet City, IL 60409; phone: 708-868-6700 in the Chicago area; 800-654-6700 elsewhere in the US and Canada).

Tele-Trip (3201 Farnam St., Omaha, NE 68131; phone: 402-345-2400 in Nebraska; 800-228-9792 elsewhere in the US).

Travel Assistance International (1133 15th St. NW, Suite 400, Washington, DC 20005; phone: 202-331-1609 in Washington, DC; 800-821-2828 elsewhere in the US).

Travel Guard International (1145 Clark St., Stevens Point, WI 54481; phone: 715-345-0505 in Wisconsin; 800-826-1300 elsewhere in the US).

Travel Insurance PAK c/o The Travelers Companies (Travelers Insurance Company, Travel Insurance Division 10NB, One Tower Sq., Hartford, CT 06183-5040; phone: 203-277-2319 in Connecticut; 800-243-3174 elsewhere in the US).

Hints for Handicapped Travelers

From 40 to 50 million people in the US alone have some sort of disability, and over half this number are physically handicapped. Like everyone else today, they — and the uncounted disabled millions around the world — are on the move. More than ever before, they are demanding facilities they can use comfortably, and they are being heard.

With the 1990 passage of the Americans with Disabilities Act, the physically handicapped increasingly will be finding better access to places and services throughout the US. The provisions of the act relating to public accommodations and transportation, which took effect in January 1992, mandate that means of access be provided except where the cost would be prohibitive, and creative alternatives are being encouraged. As the impact of the law spreads across the country, previous barriers to travel in the US should be somewhat ameliorated.

PLANNING: Make your travel arrangements well in advance and specify to all services involved the exact nature of your condition or restricted mobility. The best way to find out if your intended destination can accommodate a handicapped traveler is to write or call the local tourist authority or hotel and ask specific questions.

It is also advisable to call the hotel you are considering and ask specific questions. If you require a corridor of a certain width to maneuver a wheelchair or if you need handles on the bathroom walls for support, ask the hotel manager (many large hotels have rooms designed for the handicapped). A travel agent or the local chapter or national office of the organization that deals with your particular disability — for example, the *American Foundation for the Blind* or the *American Heart Association* — will supply the most up-to-date information on the subject.

The following organizations offer general information on access:

ACCENT on Living (PO Box 700, Bloomington, IL 61702; phone: 309-378-2961). This information service for persons with disabilities provides a free list of travel agencies specializing in arranging trips for the disabled; for a copy send a self-addressed, stamped envelope. It also offers a wide range of publications, including a quarterly magazine ($10 per year; $17.50 for 2 years, $25 for 3 years) for persons with disabilities.

Canadian Paraplegic Association (520 Sutherland Dr., Toronto, Ontario M4G 3V9, Canada; phone: 416-422-5644) is a good source of information on travel for the mobility-disabled. The association has a comprehensive library, offers accessibility information, and provides referral services.

Information Center for Individuals with Disabilities (27-43 Wormwood St., Ft. Point Pl., 1st Floor, Boston, MA 02210; phone: 800-462-5015 in Massachusetts; 617-727-5540/1 elsewhere in the US; both numbers provide voice and TDD — telecommunications device for the deaf). The center offers information and referral services on disability-related issues, publishes fact sheets on travel agents, tour operators, and other travel resources, and can help you research your trip.

Mobility International USA (MIUSA; PO Box 3551, Eugene, OR 97403; phone: 503-343-1284; both voice and TDD). This US branch of *Mobility International* (the main office is at 228 Borough High St., London SE1 1JX, England; phone: 011-44-71-403-5688), a nonprofit British organization with affiliates worldwide, offers members advice and assistance — including information on accommodations and other travel services, and publications applicable to the traveler's disability. *Mobility International* also offers a quarterly newsletter and a comprehensive sourcebook, *A World of Options for the 90s: A Guide to International Education Exchange, Community Service and Travel for Persons with Disabilities* ($14 for members; $16 for non-members). Membership includes the newsletter and is $20 a year; subscription to the newsletter alone is $10 annually.

National Rehabilitation Information Center (NRIC; 8455 Colesville Rd., Suite 935, Silver Spring, MD 20910; phone: 301-588-9284). A general information, resource, research, and referral service.

Paralyzed Veterans of America (PVA; PVA/ATTS Program, 801 18th St. NW, Washington, DC 20006; phone: 202-416-7708 in Washington, DC, 800-424-8200 elsewhere in the US). The members of this national service organization all are veterans who have suffered spinal-cord injuries, but it offers advocacy services and information to all persons with a disability. *PVA* also sponsors *Access to the Skies (ATTS)*, a program that coordinates the efforts of the national and international air travel industry in providing airport and airplane access for the disabled. Members receive several helpful publications, as well as regular notification of conferences on subjects of interest to the disabled traveler.

Royal Association for Disability and Rehabilitation (RADAR; 25 Mortimer St., London W1N 8AB, England; phone: 011-44-71-637-5400). Offers a number of publications for the handicapped, including *Holidays and Travel Abroad 1993/94 — A Guide for Disabled People,* a comprehensive guidebook focusing on international travel. This publication can be ordered by sending payment in British pounds to *RADAR.* As we went to press, it cost just over £3; call for current pricing before ordering.

Society for the Advancement of Travel for the Handicapped (SATH; 347 Fifth Ave., Suite 610, New York, NY 10016; phone: 212-447-7284). To keep abreast of developments in travel for the handicapped as they occur, you may want to join *SATH,* a nonprofit organization whose members include consumers as well as travel service professionals who have experience (or an interest) in travel for the handicapped. For an annual fee of $45 ($25 for students and travelers who are 65 and older) members receive a quarterly newsletter and have access to extensive information and referral services. *SATH* also offers two useful publications: *Travel Tips for the Handicapped* (a series of informative fact sheets) and *The United States Welcomes Handicapped Visitors* (a 48-page guide covering domestic transportation and accommodations, as well as useful hints for travelers with disabilities abroad); to order, send a self-addressed, #10 envelope and $1 per title for postage.

Travel Information Service (Moss Rehabilitation Hospital, 1200 W. Tabor Rd., Philadelphia, PA 19141-3099; phone: 215-456-9600 for voice; 215-456-9602 for

TDD). This service assists physically handicapped people in planning trips and supplies detailed information on accessibility for a nominal fee.

Blind travelers should contact the *American Foundation for the Blind* (15 W. 16th St., New York, NY 10011; phone: 212-620-2147 or 800-829-0500) and *The Seeing Eye* (PO Box 375, Morristown, NJ 07963-0375; phone: 201-539-4425); both provide useful information on resources for the visually impaired. *Note:* Seeing Eye dogs accompanied by their owners may enter Canada without certification or other restrictions.

The American Society for the Prevention of Cruelty to Animals (*ASPCA;* Education Dept., 424 E. 92 St., New York, NY 10128; phone: 212-876-7700) offers a useful booklet, *Traveling With Your Pet,* which lists inoculation and other requirements by country and territory. It is available for $5 (including postage and handling).

In addition, there are a number of publications — from travel guides to magazines — of interest to handicapped travelers. Among these are the following:

Access to the World, by Louise Weiss, offers sound tips for the disabled traveler. Published by Facts on File (460 Park Ave. S., New York, NY 10016; phone: 212-683-2244 in New York State; 800-322-8755 elsewhere in the US; 800-443-8323 in Canada), it costs $16.95. Check with your local bookstore; it also can be ordered by phone with a credit card.

The Diabetic Traveler (PO Box 8223 RW, Stamford, CT 06905; phone: 203-327-5832) is a useful quarterly newsletter for travelers with diabetes. Each issue highlights a single destination or type of travel and includes information on general resources and hints for diabetics. A 1-year subscription costs $18.95. When subscribing, ask for the free fact sheet including an index of special articles; back issues are available for $4 each.

Guide to Traveling with Arthritis, a free brochure available by writing to the Upjohn Company (PO Box 307-B, Coventry, CT 06238), provides lots of good, commonsense tips on planning your trip and how to be as comfortable as possible when traveling by car, bus, train, cruise ship, or plane.

Handicapped Travel Newsletter is regarded as one of the best sources of information for the disabled traveler. It is edited by wheelchair-bound Vietnam veteran Michael Quigley, who has traveled to 93 countries around the world. Issued every 2 months (plus special issues), a subscription is $10 per year. Write to *Handicapped Travel Newsletter,* PO Box 269, Athens, TX 75751 (phone: 903-677-1260).

Handi-Travel: A Resource Book for Disabled and Elderly Travellers, by Cinnie Noble, is a comprehensive travel guide full of practical tips for those with disabilities affecting mobility, hearing, or sight. To order this book, send $12.95, plus shipping and handling, to the *Canadian Rehabilitation Council for the Disabled,* 45 Sheppard Ave. E., Suite 801, Toronto, Ontario M2N 5W9, Canada (phone: 416-250-7490; both voice and TDD).

The Itinerary (PO Box 2012, Bayonne, NJ 07002-2012; phone: 201-858-3400). This quarterly travel magazine for people with disabilities includes information on accessibility, listings of tours, news of adaptive devices, travel aids, and special services, as well as numerous general travel hints. A subscription costs $10 a year.

The Physically Disabled Traveler's Guide, by Rod W. Durgin and Norene Lindsay, rates accessibility of a number of travel services and includes a list of organizations specializing in travel for the disabled. It is available for $9.95, plus $2 shipping and handling, from Resource Directories, 3361 Executive Pkwy., Suite 302, Toledo, OH 43606 (phone: 419-536-5353 in the Toledo area; 800-274-8515 elsewhere in the US).

Ticket to Safe Travel offers useful information for travelers with diabetes. A reprint of this article is available free from local chapters of the *American Diabetes Association.* For the nearest branch, contact the central office at 149 Madison Ave., 7th Floor, New York, NY 10016 (phone: 212-725-4925 in New York State; 800-232-3472 elsewhere in the US).

Travel for the Patient with Chronic Obstructive Pulmonary Disease, a publication of the George Washington University Medical Center, provides some sound practical suggestions for those with emphysema, chronic bronchitis, asthma, or other lung ailments. To order, send $2 to Dr. Harold Silver, 1601 18th St. NW, Washington, DC 20009 (phone: 202-667-0134).

Traveling Like Everybody Else: A Practical Guide for Disabled Travelers, by Jacqueline Freedman and Susan Gersten, offers the disabled tips on traveling by car, cruise ship, and plane, as well as lists of accessible accommodations, tour operators specializing in tours for disabled travelers, and other resources. It is available for $11.95, plus postage and handling, from Modan Publishing, PO Box 1202, Bellmore, NY 11710 (phone: 516-679-1380).

Travel Tips for Hearing-Impaired People, a free pamphlet for deaf and hearing-impaired travelers, is available from the *American Academy of Otolaryngology* (One Prince St., Alexandria, VA 22314; phone: 703-836-4444). For a copy, send a self-addressed, stamped, business-size envelope to the academy.

Travel Tips for People with Arthritis, a 31-page booklet published by the *Arthritis Foundation,* provides helpful information regarding travel by car, bus, train, cruise ship or plane, planning your trip, medical considerations, and ways to conserve your energy while traveling, and includes listings of helpful resources, such as associations and travel agencies that operate tours for disabled travelers. For a copy, contact your local *Arthritis Foundation* chapter, or send $1 to the national office, 1314 Spring St. NW, Atlanta, GA 30309 (phone: 404-872-7100 or 800-283-7800).

A few more basic resources to look for are *Travel for the Disabled,* by Helen Hecker ($19.95) and, by the same author, *Directory of Travel Agencies for the Disabled* ($19.95). *Wheelchair Vagabond,* by John G. Nelson, is another useful guide for travelers confined to a wheelchair (hardcover, $14.95; paperback, $9.95). All three titles are published by Twin Peaks Press, PO Box 129, Vancouver, WA 98666 (phone: 800-637-CALM or 206-694-2462). For $2, the publisher also will send you a catalogue of 26 books on travel for the disabled.

PLANE: The US Department of Transportation (DOT) has ruled that US airlines must accept all passengers with disabilities. As a matter of course, US airlines were pretty good about accommodating handicapped passengers even before the ruling, although each airline has somewhat different procedures. Canadian airlines also are good about accommodating the disabled traveler, but, again, policies may vary somewhat from carrier to carrier. Ask for specifics when you book your flight.

Disabled passengers always should make reservations well in advance, and should provide the airline with all relevant details of their conditions. These details include information on mobility and equipment that you will need the airline to supply — such as a wheelchair for boarding or portable oxygen for in-flight use. Be sure that the person to whom you speak fully understands the degree of your disability — the more details provided, the more effective help the airline can give you.

On the day before the flight, call back to make sure that all arrangements have been prepared, and arrive early on the day of the flight so that you can board before the rest of the passengers. It's a good idea to bring a medical certificate with you, stating your specific disability or the need to carry particular medicine.

Because most airports have jetways (corridors connecting the terminal with the door of the plane), a disabled passenger usually can be taken as far as the plane, and sometimes right onto it, in a wheelchair. If not, a narrow boarding chair may be used to take you to your seat. Your own wheelchair, which will be folded and put in the baggage compartment, should be tagged as escort luggage to assure that it's available at planeside upon landing rather than in the baggage claim area. Travel is not quite as simple if your wheelchair is battery-operated: Unless it has non-spillable batteries, it might not be accepted on board, and you will have to check with the airline ahead of time to find out how the batteries and the chair should be packaged for the flight. Usually people in wheelchairs are asked to wait until other passengers have disembarked. If you are making a tight connection, be sure to tell the attendant.

Passengers who use oxygen may not use their personal supply in the cabin, though it may be carried on the plane as cargo when properly packed and labeled (the tank must be emptied). If you will need oxygen during the flight, the airline will supply it to you (there is a charge) provided you have given advance notice — 24 hours to a few days, depending on the carrier.

Useful information on every stage of air travel, from planning to arrival, is provided in the booklet *Incapacitated Passengers Air Travel Guide.* To receive a free copy, write to the *International Air Transport Association* (Publications Sales Department, 2000 Peel St., Montreal, Quebec H3A 2R4, Canada; phone: 514-844-6311). Another helpful publication is *Air Transportation of Handicapped Persons,* which explains the general guidelines that govern air carrier policies. For a copy of this free booklet, write to the US Department of Transportation (Distribution Unit, Publications Section, M-443-2, Washington, DC 20590) and ask for "Free Advisory Circular #AC-120-32." *Access Travel: A Guide to the Accessibility of Airport Terminals,* a free publication of the *Airport Operators Council International,* provides information on more than 500 airports worldwide — including major airports in Canada — and offers ratings of 70 features, such as wheelchair accessibility to bathrooms, corridor width, and parking spaces. For a copy, contact the Consumer Information Center, Dept. 563W, Pueblo, CO 81009 (phone: 719-948-3334).

Among the major carriers serving Canada, the following airlines have TDD toll-free lines for the hearing-impaired:

Air Canada: 800-361-8071 only in Canada.
American: 800-582-1573 in Ohio; 800-543-1586 elsewhere in the US.
Canadian Airlines International: 800-465-3611 only in Canada.
Delta: 800-831-4488 throughout the US.
Northwest 800-328-2298 throughout the US.
USAir: 800-245-2966 throughout the US.

GROUND TRANSPORTATION: Perhaps the simplest solution to getting around is to travel with an able-bodied companion who can drive. If you are accustomed to driving your own hand-controlled car and want to rent one, you may be in luck. Some rental car companies will fit cars with hand controls. *Avis* (phone: 800-331-1084) can convert a car to hand controls with as little as 24 hours' notice, though it's a good idea to make arrangements more than one day in advance. *Hertz* (phone: 800-654-3001) can also convert a car to hand controls. Neither company charges extra for hand controls, but will fit them only on mid- or full-size cars. Both companies can provide hand-controlled cars in Montreal, but neither has them available in Quebec City. Other car rental companies provide hand-control cars at some locations; however, as there usually are only a limited number available, call well in advance.

The *American Automobile Association (AAA)* publishes a useful book, *The Handicapped Driver's Mobility Guide.* Contact the central office of your local *AAA* club for availability and pricing, which may vary at different branch offices.

TOURS: Programs designed for the physically impaired are run by specialists who have researched hotels, restaurants, and sites to be sure they present no insurmountable obstacles. The following travel agencies and tour operators specialize in making group and individual arrangements for travelers with physical or other disabilities.

Access: The Foundation for Accessibility by the Disabled (PO Box 356, Malverne, NY 11565; phone: 516-887-5798). A travelers' referral service that acts as an intermediary with tour operators and agents worldwide, and provides information on accessibility at various locations. A membership program, *Access* charges a onetime $35 registration fee.

Accessible Journeys (35 W. Sellers Ave., Ridley Park, PA 19078; phone: 215-747-0171). Arranges for medical professionals to be traveling companions — registered or licensed practical nurses, therapists, or doctors (all are experienced travelers). Several prospective companions' profiles and photos are sent to the client for perusal and, if one is acceptable, the "match" is made. The client usually pays all travel expenses for the companion, plus a set fee to compensate for wages the companion would be making at his or her usual job.

Accessible Tours/Directions Unlimited (720 N. Bedford Rd., Bedford Hills, NY 10507; phone: 914-241-1700 in New York State; 800-533-5343 elsewhere in the continental US). Arranges group or individual tours for disabled persons traveling in the company of able-bodied friends or family members. Accepts the unaccompanied traveler if completely self-sufficient.

Evergreen Travel Service (4114-198th St. SW, Suite 13, Lynnwood, WA 98036-6742; phone: 206-776-1184 or 800-435-2288 throughout the US and Canada). It offers worldwide tours for people who are disabled (Wings on Wheels Tours), sight-impaired/blind (White Cane Tours), hearing-impaired/deaf (Flying Fingers Tours), or mentally disabled (Happiness Tours). It also offers program for people who are not disabled but who want a slower pace (Lazybones Tours), and arranges special programs for people who need dialysis.

Flying Wheels Travel (143 W. Bridge St., Box 382, Owatonna, MN 55060; phone: 507-451-5005 or 800-535-6790 throughout the US and Canada). Handles both tours and individual arrangements.

Sprout (893 Amsterdam Ave., New York, NY 10025; phone: 212-222-9575). Arranges travel programs for mildly and moderately disabled teens and adults.

USTS Travel Horizons (11 E. 44th St., New York, NY 10017; phone: 212-687-5121 in New York State or 800-487-8787 elsewhere in the US). Travel agent and registered nurse Mary Ann Hamm designs trips for individual travelers requiring all types of kidney dialysis and handles arrangements for the dialysis.

Whole Person Tours (PO Box 1084, Bayonne, NJ 07002-1084; phone: 201-858-3400). Owner Bob Zywicki travels the world with his wheelchair and offers a lineup of escorted tours (many conducted by him) for the disabled. Call for current itinerary at the time you plan to travel. *Whole Person Tours* also publishes *The Itinerary,* a quarterly newsletter for disabled travelers (see the publication source list above).

Travelers who would benefit from being accompanied by a nurse or physical therapist also can hire a companion through *Traveling Nurses' Network,* a service provided by Twin Peaks Press (PO Box 129, Vancouver, WA 98666; phone: 800-637-CALM or 206-694-2462). For a $10 fee, clients receive the names of three nurses, whom they can then contact directly; for a $125 fee, the agency will make all the hiring arrangements for the client. Travel arrangements also may be made in some cases — the fee for this further service is determined on an individual basis.

A similar service is offered by *MedEscort International* (ABE International Airport, PO Box 8766, Allentown, PA 18105; phone: 800-255-7182 in the continental US;

elsewhere, call 215-791-3111). Clients can arrange to be accompanied by a nurse, paramedic, respiratory therapist, or physician through *MedEscort*. The fees are based on the disabled traveler's needs. This service also can assist in making travel arrangements.

Hints for Single Travelers

Just about the last trip in human history on which the participants were neatly paired was the voyage of Noah's Ark. Ever since, passenger lists and tour groups have reflected the same kind of asymmetry that occurs in real life, as countless individuals set forth to see the world unaccompanied (or unencumbered, depending on your outlook) by spouse, lover, companion, or relative. Unfortunately, traveling alone can turn a traveler into a second class citizen.

The truth is that the travel industry is not very fair to people who vacation by themselves. People traveling alone almost invariably end up paying more than individuals traveling in pairs. Most travel bargains, including package tours, accommodations, resort packages, and cruises, are based on *double occupancy* rates. This means that the per-person price is offered on the basis of two people traveling together and sharing a double room (which means they each will spend a good deal more on meals and extras). The single traveler will have to pay a surcharge, called a single supplement, for exactly the same package. In extreme cases, this can add as much as 35% — and sometimes more — to the basic per-person rate.

Don't despair, however. In Montreal and Quebec City, there are scores of smaller hotels and other hostelries where, in addition to a cozier atmosphere, prices still are quite reasonable for the single traveler.

The obvious, most effective alternative is to find a traveling companion. Even special "singles' tours" that promise no supplements usually are based on people sharing double rooms. Perhaps the most recent innovation along these lines is the creation of organizations that "introduce" the single traveler to other single travelers. Some charge fees, while others are free, but the basic service offered is the same: to match an unattached person with a compatible travel mate. Among such organizations are the following:

Odyssey Network (118 Cedar St., Wellesley, MA 02181; phone: 617-237-2400). Originally founded to match single women travelers, this company now includes men in its enrollment. *Odyssey* offers a quarterly newsletter for members who are seeking a travel companion, and occasionally organizes small group tours. Membership (which includes newsletter subscription) is $50.

Partners-in-Travel (PO Box 491145, Los Angeles, CA 90049; phone: 213-476-4869). Members receive a list of singles seeking traveling companions; prospective companions make contact through the agency. The membership fee is $40 per year and includes a chatty newsletter (6 issues per year).

Travel Companion Exchange (PO Box 833, Amityville, NY 11701; phone: 516-454-0880). This group publishes a newsletter for singles and a directory of individuals looking for travel companions. On joining, members fill out a lengthy questionnaire and write a small listing (much like an ad in a personal column). Based on these listings, members can request copies of profiles and contact prospective traveling companions. It is wise to join well in advance of your planned vacation so that there's enough time to determine compatibility and plan a joint trip. Membership fees, including the newsletter, are $30 for 6 months or $60 a year for a single-sex listing.

Travel in Two's (239 N. Broadway, Suite 3, N. Tarrytown, NY 10591; phone: 914-631-8409). For city programs, this company matches up solo travelers and then customizes programs for them. The firm also puts out a quarterly *Singles Vacation Newsletter,* which costs $5 per issue or $15 per year.

In addition, a number of tour packagers cater to single travelers. These companies offer packages designed for individuals interested in vacationing with a group of single travelers or in being matched with a traveling companion. Among the better established of these agencies are the following:

Cosmos: This tour operator offers a number of package tours with a guaranteed-share plan whereby singles who wish to share rooms (and avoid paying the single supplement) are matched by the tour escort with individuals of the same sex and charged the basic double-occupancy tour price. Contact the firm at one of its three North American branches: 95-25 Queens Blvd., Rego Park, NY 11374 (phone: 800-221-0090 or 718-268-7000); 5301 S. Federal Circle, Littleton, CO 80123 (phone 800-221-0090); 1061 Eglinton Ave. W., Toronto, Ontario M6C 2C9, Canada (phone: 416-787-1281). As we went to press, *Cosmos* was not offering any tours that included Montreal or Quebec City, but it's worth checking when planning your trip.

Grand Circle Travel (347 Congress St., Boston, MA 02210; phone: 617-350-7500 or 800-221-2610). Arranges extended vacations, escorted tours and cruises for the over-50 traveler. Membership, which is automatic when you book a trip through *Grand Circle,* includes travel discounts and other extras, such as a Pen Pals service for singles seeking travel companions.

Marion Smith Singles (611 Prescott Pl., North Woodmere, NY 11581; phone: 516-791-4852, 516-791-4865, or 212-944-2112). Specializes in tours for singles ages 20 to 50, who can choose to share accommodations to avoid paying single-supplement charges.

Saga International Holidays (120 Boylston St., Boston MA 02116; phone: 617-451-6808 or 800-343-0273). A subsidiary of a British company specializing in older travelers, many of them single, *Saga* offers a broad selection of packages for people age 60 and over or those 50 to 59 traveling with someone 60 or older. Although anyone can book a *Saga* trip, a $15 club membership includes a subscription to their newsletter, as well as other publications and travel services — such as a matching service for single travelers.

Singles in Motion (545 W. 236th St., Suite 1D, Riverdale, NY 10463; phone: 718-884-4464). Offers a number of packages for single travelers, including tours, cruises, and excursions focusing on outdoor activities such as hiking and biking.

Umbrella Singles (PO Box 157, Woodbourne, NY 12788; phone: 914-434-6871; 800-537-2797 in the continental US). Specializes in weekend and holiday trips for singles, including bus tours to Montreal, Quebec City, and Niagara Falls in Ontario.

A good book for single travelers is *Traveling On Your Own,* by Eleanor Berman, which offers tips on traveling solo and includes information on trips for singles. Available in bookstores, it also can be ordered by sending $12.95, plus postage and handling, to Random House, Order Dept., 400 Hahn Rd., Westminster, MD 21157 (phone: 800-733-3000).

Single travelers also may want to subscribe to *Going Solo,* a newsletter that offers helpful information on going on your own. Issued eight times a year, a subscription costs $29. Contact Doerfer Communications, PO Box 1035, Cambridge, MA 02239 (phone: 617-876-2764).

Hints for Older Travelers

Special discounts and more free time are just two factors that have given Americans over age 65 a chance to see the world at affordable prices. Senior citizens make up an ever-growing segment of the travel population, and the trend among them is to travel more frequently and for longer periods of time.

PLANNING: When planning a vacation, prepare your itinerary with one eye on your own physical condition and the other on your interests. One important factor to keep in mind is not to overdo anything and to be aware of the effects that the weather may have on your capabilities.

Older travelers may find the following publications of interest:

Going Abroad: 101 Tips for the Mature Traveler offers tips on preparing for your trip, commonsense precautions en route, and some basic travel terminology. This concise free booklet is available from *Grand Circle Travel,* 347 Congress St., Boston, MA 02210 (phone: 800-221-2610 or 617-350-7500).

The International Health Guide for Senior Citizen Travelers, by Dr. W. Robert Lange, covers such topics as trip preparations, food and water precautions, adjusting to weather and climate conditions, finding a doctor, motion sickness, jet lag, and so on. Also includes a list of resource organizations that provide medical assistance for travelers. It is available for $4.95 plus $1 in postage, from Pilot Books, 103 Cooper St., Babylon, NY 11702 (phone: 516-422-2225).

Mature Traveler is a monthly newsletter that provides information on travel discounts, places of interest, useful tips, and other topics of interest for travelers 49 and up. To subscribe, send $24.95 to GEM Publishing Group, PO Box 50820, Reno, NV 89513 (phone: 702-786-7419).

Senior Citizen's Guide To Budget Travel In The US And Canada, by Paige Palmer, provides specific information on economical travel options for senior citizens. To order, send $4.95, plus postage and handling, to Pilot Books (address above).

Take a Camel to Lunch and Other Adventures for Mature Travelers, by Nancy O'Connell, offers offbeat and unusual adventures for travelers over 50. Available at bookstores or directly from Bristol Publishing Enterprises for $8.95 (plus shipping and handling), PO Box 1737, San Leandro, CA 94577 (phone: 800-346-4889 or 510-895-4461).

Travel Tips for Older Americans is a useful booklet that provides good, basic advice. This US State Department publication (stock number: 044-000-02270-2) can be ordered by sending a check or money order for $1 to the Superintendent of Documents (US Government Printing Office, Washington, DC 20420) or by calling 202-783-3238 and charging the order to a credit card.

Unbelievably Good Deals & Great Adventures That You Absolutely Can't Get Unless You're Over 50, by Joan Rattner Heilman, offers travel tips for older travelers, including discounts on accommodations and transportation, as well as a list of organizations for seniors. It is available for $7.95 (plus shipping and handling) from Contemporary Books, 180 N. Michigan Ave., Chicago, IL 60601 (phone: 312-782-9181).

HEALTH: Health facilities generally are maintained by individual Canadian provinces, but Blue Cross usually is honored throughout Canada. Pre-trip medical and dental checkups are strongly recommended. In addition, be sure to take along any prescription medication you need, enough to last *without a new prescription* for the duration of your trip; pack all medications with a note from your doctor for the benefit of airport authorities. If you have specific medical problems, bring prescriptions and a "medical file" composed of the following:

1. A summary of your medical history and current diagnosis.
2. A list of drugs to which you are allergic.
3. Your most recent electrocardiogram, if you have heart problems.
4. Your doctor's name, address, and telephone number.

DISCOUNTS AND PACKAGES: Since guidelines change from place to place, it is a good idea to inquire in advance about discounts on accommodations, transportation, tickets to theater and concert performances and movies, entrance fees to museums, national monuments, and other attractions. Senior citizens with identification are eligible for a large variety of discounts across Canada. Some discounts are only available to Canadians, but many others are available to anyone over 65. For instance, depending on the local management, discounts of 10% to 25% often are available at a variety of hotel chains, including *Holiday Inn, Howard Johnson,* and *Sheraton.* In addition, both *Air Canada* and *Canadian Airlines International* offer discounts on fares to senior citizens 62 and over (and often one traveling companion per senior). For more information on current prices and applicable restrictions, contact the individual carriers.

Some discounts, however, are extended only to bona fide members of certain senior citizens organizations. Because the same organizations frequently offer package tours to both domestic and international destinations, the benefits of membership are twofold: Those who join can take advantage of discounts as individual travelers and also reap the savings that group travel affords. In addition, because the age requirements for some of these organizations are quite low (or nonexistent), the benefits can begin to accrue early.

In order to take advantage of these discounts, you should carry proof of your age (or eligibility). For Canadians, a special card issued by the province; for older visitors from the US and other countries, a driver's license, passport, birth certificate, membership card in a recognized senior citizens organization, or a Medicare card should be sufficient. Among the organizations dedicated to helping older travelers see the world are the following:

American Association of Retired Persons (AARP; 601 E St. NW, Washington, DC 20049; phone: 202-434-2277). The largest and best-known of these organizations. Membership is open to anyone 50 or over, whether retired or not; dues are $8 a year, $20 for 3 years, or $45 for 10 years, and include spouse. The *AARP* Travel Experience Wordwide program, available through *American Express Travel Related Services,* offers members travel programs designed exclusively for older travelers. Members can book these services by calling *American Express* at 800-927-0111 for land and air travel.

Mature Outlook (Customer Service Center, 6001 N. Clark St., Chicago, IL 60660; phone: 800-336-6330). Through its *Travel Alert,* tours, cruises, and other vacation packages are available to members at special savings. Hotel and car rental discounts and travel accident insurance also are available. Membership is open to anyone 50 years of age or older, costs $9.95 a year, and includes a bimonthly newsletter and magazine, as well as information on package tours.

National Council of Senior Citizens (1331 F St. NW, Washington, DC 20004; phone: 202-347-8800). Here, too, the emphasis is on keeping costs low. This nonprofit organization offers members a different roster of package tours each year, as well as individual arrangements. Although most members are over 50, membership is open to anyone (regardless of age) for an annual fee of $12 per person or couple, or $30 for 3 years. Lifetime membership costs $150. For information, contact its affiliated travel agency *Vantage Travel Service* (phone: 800-322-6677).

Certain travel agencies and tour operators offer special trips geared to older travelers. Among them are the following:

Evergreen Travel Service (4114 198th St. SW, Suite 13, Lynnwood, WA 98036-6742; phone: 206-776-1184 or 800-435-2288 throughout the US and Canada). This specialist in trips for persons with disabilities recently introduced Lazy-bones Tours, a program offering leisurely trips for older travelers. Most programs are first class or deluxe, and include an escort.

Gadabout Tours (700 E. Tahquitz, Palm Springs, CA 92262; phone: 619-325-5556 or 800-521-7309 in California; 800-952-5068 elsewhere in the US). Offers escorted tours and cruises throughout Canada.

Grand Circle Travel (347 Congress St., Boston, MA 02210; phone: 800-221-2610 or 617-350-7500). Caters exclusively to the over-50 traveler and packages a large variety of escorted tours, cruises, and extended vacations. Membership, which is automatic when you book a trip through *Grand Circle,* includes discount certificates on future trips and other travel services, such as a matching service for single travelers and a helpful free booklet, *Going Abroad: 101 Tips for Mature Travelers* (see the source list above).

OmniTours (104 Wilmot Rd., Deerfield, IL 60015; phone: 800-962-0060 or 708-374-0088). Offers combination air and rail group tours designed for travelers 50 years and older. Their itineraries include a 9-day rail tour that visits Montreal, Ottawa, Quebec City, and Toronto.

Saga International Holidays (120 Boylston St., Boston MA 02116; phone: 617-451-6808 or 800-343-0273). A subsidiary of a British company catering to older travelers, *Saga* offers a broad selection of packages for people age 60 and over or those 50 to 59 traveling with someone 60 or older. Although anyone can book a *Saga* trip, a $15 club membership includes a subscription to their newsletter, as well as other publications and travel services.

Many travel agencies, particularly the larger ones, are delighted to make presentations to help a group of senior citizens select destinations. A local chamber of commerce should be able to provide the names of such agencies. Once a time and place are determined, an organization member or travel agent can obtain group quotations for transportation, accommodations, meal plans, and sightseeing. Larger groups usually get the best breaks.

Another choice open to older travelers is a trip that includes an educational element. *Elderhostel,* a nonprofit organization, offers educational programs at schools worldwide. Most Canadian programs run for 1 week, and include double occupancy accommodations in hotels or student residence halls and all meals. Elderhostelers must be at least 60 years old (younger if a spouse or companion qualifies), in good health, and not in need of special diets. For a free catalogue describing the program and current offerings, contact *Elderhostel* (75 Federal St., Boston, MA 02110; phone: 617-426-7788) or *Elderhostel Canada* (308 Wellington St., Kingston, Ontario K7K 7A7, Canada; phone: 613-530-2222). Those interested in the program also can borrow slides at no charge or purchase an informational videotape for $5.

Hints for Traveling with Children

 What better way to encounter the world's variety than in the company of the young, wide-eyed members of your family? Their presence does not have to be a burden or an excessive expense. The current generation of discounts for children and family package deals can make a trip together quite reasonable.

A family trip to Montreal or Quebec City will be an investment in your children's future, making geography and history come alive to them, and leaving a sure memory that will be among the fondest you will share with them someday. Their insights will be refreshing to you; their impulses may take you to unexpected places with unexpected dividends.

PLANNING: Here are several hints for making a trip with children easy and fun.

1. Children, like everyone else, will derive more pleasure from a trip if they know something about their destination before they arrive. Begin their education about a month before you leave. Using maps, travel magazines, and books, give children a clear idea of where you are going and how far away it is.

2. Children should help to plan the itinerary, and where you go and what you do should reflect some of their ideas. If they already know something about the sites they'll visit, they will have the excitement of recognition when they arrive.

3. When traveling in Montreal and Quebec City, it is helpful to learn the language with your children — a few basics like *"bonjour"* ("hello"), *"au revoir"* ("good-bye"), and *"merci bien"* ("thanks a lot").

4. Familiarize your children with Canadian dollars. Give them an allowance for the trip and be sure they understand just how far it will or won't go.

5. Give children specific responsibilities: The job of carrying their own flight bags and looking after their personal things, along with some other light chores, will give them a stake in the journey.

6. Give each child a travel diary or scrapbook to take along.

One useful resource to which you may want to refer is the *Berlitz Jr. French Phrasebook* instructional series for children. The series combines an illustrated storybook with a lively 60-minute audiocassette. Each book features a character, Teddy, who goes to school and learns to count and spell and speak French phrases. The book/cassette package is available for $19.95, plus shipping and handling, from Macmillan Publishing Company, Front and Brown Sts., Riverside, NJ 08075 (phone: 800-257-5755).

Children's books about Canada provide an excellent introduction to the country and culture and can be found at many general bookstores and in libraries.

And for parents, *Travel With Your Children* (*TWYCH;* 45 W. 18th St., 7th Floor, New York, NY 10011; phone: 212-206-0688) publishes a newsletter, *Family Travel Times,* that focuses on families with young travelers and offers helpful hints. An annual subscription (10 issues) is $35 and includes a copy of the "Airline Guide" issue (updated every other year), which focuses on the subject of flying with children. This special issue is also available separately for $10.

Another newsletter devoted to family travel is *Getaways.* This quarterly publication provides reviews of family-oriented literature, activities, and useful travel tips. To subscribe, send $25 to *Getaways,* Att. Ms. Brooke Kane, PO Box 8282, McLean, VA 22107 (phone: 703-534-8747).

Also of interest to parents traveling with their children is *How to Take Great Trips With Your Kids,* by psychologist Sanford Portnoy and his wife, Joan Flynn Portnoy. The book includes helpful tips from fellow family travelers, tips on economical accommodations and touring by car, recreational vehicle, and train, as well as over 50 games to play with your children en route. It is available for $8.95, plus shipping and handling, from Harvard Common Press, 535 Albany St., Boston, MA 02118 (phone: 617-423-5803).

Another book on family travel, *Travel with Children* by Maureen Wheeler, offers a wide range of practical tips on traveling with children, and includes accounts of the author's family travel experiences. It is available for $10.95, plus shipping and handling, from Lonely Planet Publications, 155 Filbert St., Oakland, CA 94607 (phone: 510-893-8555).

Adventure Travel North America, by Pat Dickerman (Adventure Guides, 36 E. 57th St., New York, NY 10022; phone: 800-252-7899 or 212-355-6334; $18, plus shipping and handling), is a good source of companies featuring family travel adventures. Also see *Great Vacations with Your Kids,* by Dorothy Jordan (Dutton; $12.95), *What to Do with the Kids This Year: One Hundred Family Vacation Places with Time Off for You!,* by Jane Wilford and Janet Tice (Globe Pequot Press; $8.95), and *Super Family Vacations,* by Martha Shirk (HarperCollins; $14).

Finally, parents arranging a trip with their children may want to contact *Let's Take the Kids* (1268 Devon Ave., Los Angeles, CA 90024; phone: 800-726-4349 or 213-274-7088), an information service specializing in family travel. Although they do not arrange or book trips, this organization provides parents with information and advice on questions they may have about accommodations, itineraries, transportation, and other aspects of a planned vacation. They also offer a parent travel network, whereby parents who have been to a particular destination can evaluate it for others.

PLANE: Begin early to investigate all available discounts and charter flights, as well as any package deals and special rates offered by the major airlines. Booking is sometimes required up to 2 months in advance. You may well find that charter companies offer no reductions for children, or not enough to offset the risk of last-minute delays or other inconveniences to which charters are subject. The major scheduled airlines, on the other hand, almost invariably provide hefty discounts for children.

When you make your reservations, tell the airline that you are traveling with a child. Children ages 2 through 11 generally travel at about a 20% to 30% discount off regular full-fare adult ticket prices on international flights. This children's fare, however, usually is much higher than the excursion fare, which is applicable to any traveler regardless of age. An infant under 2 years of age usually can travel free if it sits on an adult's lap. A second infant without a second adult would pay the fare applicable to children ages 2 through 11.

Although some airlines will, on request, supply bassinets for infants, most carriers encourage parents to bring their own safety seat on board, which then is strapped into the airline seat with a regular seat belt. This is much safer — and certainly more comfortable — than holding the child in your lap. If you do not purchase a seat for your baby, you have the option of bringing the infant restraint along on the off-chance that there might be an empty seat next to yours — in which case some airlines will let you use that seat at no charge for your baby and infant seat. However, if there is no empty seat available, the infant seat no doubt will have to be checked as baggage (and you may have to pay an additional charge), since it generally does not fit under the seat or in the overhead racks. The safest bet is to pay for a seat.

Be forewarned: Some safety seats designed primarily for use in cars do not fit into plane seats properly. Although nearly all seats manufactured since 1985 carry labels indicating whether they meet federal standards for use aboard planes, actual seat sizes may vary from carrier to carrier. At the time of this writing, the FAA was in the process of reviewing and revising the federal regulations regarding infant travel and safety devices — it was still to be determined if children should be *required* to sit in safety seats and whether the airlines will have to provide them.

If using one of these infant restraints, you should try to get bulkhead seats, which will provide extra room to care for your child during the flight. You also should request a bulkhead seat when using a bassinet — again, this is not as safe as strapping the child in. On some planes bassinets hook into a bulkhead wall; on others they are placed on the floor in front of you. (Note that bulkhead seats often are reserved for families traveling with children.) As a general rule, babies should be held during takeoff and landing.

Request seats on the aisle if you have a toddler or if you think you will need to use the bathroom frequently. Carry onto the plane all you will need to care for and occupy your children during the flight — formula, diapers, a sweater, books, favorite stuffed animals, and so on. Dress your baby simply, with a minimum of buttons and snaps, because the only place you may have to change a diaper is at your seat or in a small lavatory.

On some airlines, you also can ask for a hot dog, hamburger, or even a fruit plate instead of the airline's regular lunch or dinner if you give at least 24 hours' notice. Some, but not all, airlines have baby food aboard and the flight attendant can warm a bottle for you. While you should bring along toys from home, also ask about children's diversions. Some carriers have terrific free packages of games, coloring books, and puzzles.

When the plane takes off and lands, make sure your baby is nursing or has a bottle, pacifier, or thumb in its mouth. This sucking will make the child swallow and help to clear stopped ears. A piece of hard candy will do the same for an older child.

Parents traveling by plane with toddlers, children, or young teenagers may want to consult *When Kids Fly,* a free booklet published by Massport (Public Affairs Department, 10 Park Plaza, Boston, MA 02116-3971; phone: 617-973-5600), which includes helpful information on airfares for children, infant seats, what to do in the event of overbooked or cancelled flights, and so on.

■ **Note:** Newborn babies, whose lungs may not be able to adjust to the altitude, should not be taken aboard an airplane. And some airlines may refuse to allow a pregnant woman in her 8th or 9th month to fly. Check with the airline ahead of time, and carry a letter from your doctor stating that you are fit to travel — and indicating the estimated date of birth.

Things to Remember

1. If you are visiting many sites, pace the days with children in mind. Break the trip into half-day segments, with running around or "doing" time built in.
2. Don't forget that a child's attention span is far shorter than an adult's. Children don't have to see every sight or all of any sight to learn something from their trip; watching, playing with, and talking to other children can be equally enlightening.
3. Let your children lead the way sometimes; their perspective is different from yours, and they may lead you to things you would never have noticed on your own.
4. Remember the places that children love to visit: aquariums, zoos, amusement parks, nature trails, and so on. Among the activities that may pique their interest are bicycling, boat trips, visiting planetariums and children's museums, and viewing natural habitat exhibits. Children's favorites in Montreal include the *Theatre Biscuit,* which has puppet shows, and *La Ronde Amusement Park.* In Quebec City, they will enjoy the city zoo and aquarium, as well as *Village des Sports,* which offers a variety of sports activities for children and their parents.

On the Road

Credit and Currency

 It may seem hard to believe, but one of the greatest (and least understood) costs of travel is money itself. Your one single objective in relation to the care and retention of your travel funds is to make them stretch as far as possible. When you do spend money, it should be on things that expand and enhance your travel experience, with no buying power lost due to carelessness or lack of knowledge. This requires more than merely ferreting out the best airfare or the most charming budget hotel. It means being canny about the management of money itself. Herewith, a primer on making money go as far as possible when traveling.

CURRENCY: Travelers from the US should have little difficulty with matters of exchange in Canada. Both countries have money systems based on 100 cents to the dollar, although the US dollar and the Canadian dollar are not equal in value. The value of Canadian currency in relation to the US dollar fluctuates daily, affected by a wide variety of phenomena.

Although US dollars usually are accepted in Canada, you certainly will lose a percentage of your dollar's buying power if you do not take the time to convert it into the local legal tender. By paying for goods and services in local currency, you save money by not negotiating invariably unfavorable exchange rates for every small purchase, and avoid difficulty where US currency is not readily — or happily — accepted. *Throughout this book, unless specifically stated otherwise, prices are given in US dollars.*

There is no limit to the amount of US currency that can be brought into Canada. To avoid problems anywhere along the line, it's advisable to fill out any customs forms provided when leaving the US on which you can declare all money you are taking with you — cash, traveler's checks, and so on. US law requires that anyone taking more than $10,000 into or out of the US must report this fact on customs form No. 4790, which is available at all international airports or from any office of US Customs. If taking over $10,000 out of the US, you must report this *before* leaving the US; if returning with such an amount, you should include this information on your customs declaration. Although travelers usually are not questioned by customs officials about currency when entering or leaving, the sensible course is to observe all regulations just to be on the safe side.

In Montreal and Quebec City, as in the rest of Canada, you will find the official rate of exchange posted in banks, airports, money exchange houses, hotels, and some shops. As a general rule, expect to get more local currency for your US dollar at banks than at any other commercial establishment. Exchange rates do change from day to day, and most banks offer the same (or very similar) exchange rates. (In a pinch, the convenience of cashing money in your hotel — sometimes on a 24-hour basis — *may* make up for the difference in the exchange rate.) Don't try to bargain in banks or hotels — no one will alter the rates for you.

Money exchange houses are financial institutions that charge a fee for the service of exchanging dollars for local currency. When considering alternatives, be aware that although the rate varies among these establishments, the rates of exchange offered are bound to be less favorable than the terms offered at nearby banks — again, don't be surprised if you get fewer Canadian dollars for your US dollar than the rate published in the papers.

That said, however, the following rules of thumb are worth remembering.

Rule number one: Never (repeat: *never*) exchange more than $10 for foreign currency at hotels, restaurants, or retail shops. If you do, you are sure to lose a significant amount of your US dollar's buying power. If you do come across a storefront exchange counter offering what appears to be an incredible bargain, there's too much counterfeit specie in circulation to take the chance.

Rule number two: Estimate your needs carefully; if you overbuy, you lose twice — buying and selling back. Every time you exchange money, someone is making a profit, and rest assured it isn't you. Use up foreign notes before leaving, saving just enough for last-minute incidentals, and tips.

Rule number three: Learn the local currency quickly and keep abreast of daily fluctuations in the exchange rate. These are listed in the *International Herald Tribune* daily for the preceding day, as well as in every major newspaper in Canada. Rates change to some degree every day. For rough calculations, it is quick and safe to use round figures, but for purchases and actual currency exchanges, carry a small pocket calculator to help you compute the exact rate. Inexpensive calculators specifically designed to convert currency amounts for travelers are widely available.

When changing money, don't be afraid to ask how much commission you're being charged, and the exact amount of the prevailing exchange rate. In fact, in any exchange of money for goods or services, you should work out the rate before making any payment.

TRAVELER'S CHECKS: It's wise to carry traveler's checks instead of (or in addition to) cash, since it's possible to replace them if they are stolen or lost. Issued in various denominations and available in both US and Canadian dollars, with adequate proof of identification (credit cards, driver's license, passport), traveler's checks are as good as cash in most hotels, restaurants, stores, and banks.

You will be able to cash traveler's checks fairly easily throughout Canada. However, even in metropolitan areas, don't assume that restaurants, small shops, and other establishments are going to be able to change checks of large denominations.

Although traveler's checks are available in some foreign currencies, such as Canadian dollars, the exchange rates offered by the issuing companies in the US generally are far less favorable than those available from banks both in the US and abroad. Therefore, it usually is better to carry the bulk of your travel funds abroad in US dollar–denomination traveler's checks.

Every type of traveler's check is legal tender in banks around the world, and each company guarantees full replacement if checks are lost or stolen. After that the similarity ends. Some charge a fee for purchase, others are free; you can buy traveler's checks at almost any bank, and some are available by mail. Most important, each traveler's check issuer differs slightly in its refund policy — the amount refunded immediately, the accessibility of refund locations, the availability of a 24-hour refund service, and the time it will take for you to receive replacement checks. For instance, *American Express* guarantees replacement of lost or stolen traveler's checks in under 3 hours at any *American Express* office — other companies may not be as prompt. (Travelers should keep in mind that *American Express*'s 3-hour policy is based on a traveler's being able to provide the serial numbers of the lost checks. Without these numbers, refunds can take much longer.)

We cannot overemphasize the importance of knowing how to replace lost or stolen checks. All of the traveler's check companies have agents around the world, both in their own name and at associated agencies (usually, but not necessarily, banks), where refunds can be obtained during business hours. Most of them also have 24-hour toll-free telephone lines, and some even will provide emergency funds to tide you over on a Sunday.

Be sure to make a photocopy of the refund instructions that will be given to you by the issuing institution at the time of purchase. To avoid complications should you need to redeem lost checks (and to speed up the replacement process), keep the purchase receipt and an accurate list, by serial number, of the checks that have been spent or cashed. You may want to incorporate this information in an "emergency packet," also including the numbers of the credit cards you are carrying, and any other bits of information you shouldn't be without. Always keep these records separate from the checks and the original records themselves (you may want to give them to a traveling companion to hold).

Several of the major traveler's check companies charge 1% for the acquisition of their checks; others don't. To receive fee-free traveler's checks you may have to meet certain qualifications — for instance, *Thomas Cook* checks issued in US currency are free if you make your travel arrangements through its travel agency; *American Express* traveler's checks are available without charge to members of the *American Automobile Association (AAA)*. Holders of some credit cards (such as the *American Express Platinum* card) also may be entitled to free traveler's checks. The issuing institution (e.g., the particular bank at which you purchase them) may itself charge a fee. If you purchase traveler's checks at a bank in which you or your company maintains significant accounts (especially commercial accounts of some size), the bank may absorb the 1% fee as a courtesy.

American Express, Bank of America, Citicorp, MasterCard, Thomas Cook, and *Visa* all offer traveler's checks. Here is a list of the major companies issuing traveler's checks and the numbers to call in the event that loss or theft makes replacement necessary:

- *American Express:* To report lost or stolen checks in the US and Canada, call 800-221-7282.
- *Bank of America:* To report lost or stolen checks in the US, call 800-227-3460. In Canada, call 415-624-5400, collect, 24 hours.
- *Citicorp:* To report lost or stolen checks in the US, call 800-645-6556. In Canada, call 813-623-1709, collect.
- *MasterCard:* Note that *Thomas Cook Travel* (below) is now handling all *MasterCard* traveler's checks, inquiries, and refunds.
- *Thomas Cook MasterCard:* To report lost or stolen checks in the US, call 800-223-7373; in Canada, call 609-987-7300, collect.
- *Visa:* To report lost or stolen checks throughout the US and Canada, call 800-227-6811.

CREDIT CARDS: Some establishments you may encounter during the course of your travels may not honor any credit cards and some may not honor all cards, so there is a practical reason to carry more than one. Most US credit cards, including the principal bank cards, are honored in Canada. The following is a list of credit cards that enjoy wide domestic and international acceptance:

- *American Express:* Cardholders can cash personal checks for traveler's checks and cash at *American Express* or its representatives' offices in the US and Canada up to the following limits (within any 21-day period): $1,000 for *Green* and *Optima* cardholders; $5,000 for *Gold* cardholders; and $10,000 for *Platinum* cardholders. Check cashing also is available to cardholders who are guests at participating hotels in the US and Canada (up to $250) and, for holders of airline tickets, at participating airlines (up to $50). Free travel accident, baggage, and car rental insurance is provided if the ticket or rental is charged to the card; additional insurance also is available for additional cost. For further information or to report a lost or stolen *American Express* card, call 800-528-4800 throughout the continental US and Canada.

Carte Blanche: Free travel accident, baggage, and car rental insurance if ticket or rental is charged to card; additional insurance also is available at additional cost. For medical, legal, and travel assistance worldwide, call 800-356-3448 throughout the US and Canada. For further information or to report a lost or stolen *Carte Blanche* card, call 800-525-9135 throughout the US and Canada.

Diners Club: Emergency personal check cashing for cardholders staying at participating hotels and motels in the US (up to $250 per stay). Free travel accident, baggage, and car rental insurance if ticket or rental is charged to card; additional insurance also is available for an additional fee. For medical, legal, and travel assistance worldwide, call 800-356-3448 throughout the US and Canada. For further information or to report a lost or stolen *Diners Club* card, call 800-525-9135 throughout the US and Canada.

Discover Card: Offered by a subsidiary of *Sears, Roebuck & Co.,* it provides cardholders with cash advances at numerous automatic teller machines and *Sears* stores throughout the US. For further information and to report a lost or stolen *Discover* card, call 800-DISCOVER throughout the US; in Canada, call 302-323-7834, collect.

MasterCard: Cash advances are available at participating banks worldwide. Check with your issuing bank for information. *MasterCard* also offers a 24-hour emergency lost card service; call 800-826-2181 throughout the US and Canada; in Canada you can also call 314-275-6690, collect.

Visa: Cash advances are available at participating banks worldwide. Check with your issuing bank for information. *Visa* also offers a 24-hour emergency lost card service; call 800-336-8472 throughout the US. Once in Canada, call 415-570-3200, collect.

SENDING MONEY ABROAD: If you have used up your traveler's checks, cashed as many emergency personal checks as your credit card allows, drawn on your cash advance line to the fullest extent, and still need money, have it sent to you via one of the following services:

American Express (phone: 800-926-9400 for an operator). Offers a service called "MoneyGram," completing money transfers generally within 15 minutes. The sender can go to any *American Express Travel Office* or MoneyGram agent location in the US and transfer money by presenting cash or credit card — *Discover, MasterCard, Visa* or *American Express Optima* card (no other *American Express* or other credit cards are accepted). *American Express Optima* cardholders also can arrange for this transfer over the phone. To collect at the other end, the receiver must show identification (passport, driver's license, or other picture ID) or answer a test question at an *American Express Travel Office* (there are over 3,000) or at a branch of an affiliated bank in Canada. For further information on this service, call 800-543-4080.

Western Union Telegraph Company (phone: 800-325-4176 throughout the US). A friend or relative can go, cash in hand, to any *Western Union* office in the US, where, for a charge of $50 or less (it varies with the amount of the transaction), the funds will be transferred to one of *Western Union*'s branch offices. When the money arrives, you will not be notified — you must go to the *Western Union* branch office to inquire. Transfers generally take only about 15 minutes. The funds will be turned over in Canadian currency, based on the rate of exchange in effect on the day of receipt. For a higher fee, the US party to this transaction may call *Western Union* with a *MasterCard* or *Visa* number to send up to $2,000.

If you are literally down to your last cent, and you have no other way to obtain cash, the nearest US consulate (see *Legal Aid and Consular Services,* in this section) will let you call home to set these matters in motion.

CASH MACHINES: Automatic teller machines (ATMs) are increasingly common worldwide. If your bank participates in one of the international ATM networks (most do), the bank will issue you a "cash card" along with a personal identification code or number (also called a PIC or PIN). You can use this card at any ATM in the same electronic network to check your account balances, transfer monies between checking and savings accounts, and — most important for a traveler — withdraw cash instantly. Network ATMs generally are located in banks, commercial and transportation centers, and near major tourist attractions.

Some financial institutions offer exclusive automatic teller machines for their own customers only at bank branches. At the time of this writing, ATMs which *are* connected generally belong to one of the following two international networks:

   CIRRUS: Has over 75,000 ATMs worldwide, including 133 in Montreal and 6 in Quebec City. *MasterCard* and *Visa* cardholders also may use their cards to draw cash against their credit lines. For more information on the *CIRRUS* network and the location of the nearest ATM call 800-4-CIRRUS; for all other information contact your financial institution.

   PLUS: Has over 60,000 automatic teller machines worldwide, including 300 in Montreal and 2 in Quebec City. *MasterCard* and *Visa* cardholders also may use their cards to draw cash against their credit lines. For a free directory listing the locations of these machines and further information on the *PLUS* network, call 800-THE-PLUS.

Information about these networks is available at member bank branches, where you can obtain free booklets listing the locations worldwide. Note that a recent change in banking regulations permits financial institutions to subscribe to *both* the *CIRRUS* and *PLUS* systems, allowing users of either network to withdraw funds from ATMs at participating banks.

Time Zones, Business Hours, and Public Holidays

 TIME ZONES: Canada is divided into six time zones, but because the two most northeasterly zones — Newfoundland standard time and Atlantic standard time — are only a half hour apart, there is no more than a 5½-hour difference between its east and west coasts. Traveling west from Atlantic standard time, the zones get earlier by hour intervals.

Greenwich Mean Time — the time in Greenwich, England, at longitude 0°0' — is the base from which all other time zones are measured. Areas in zones west of Greenwich have earlier times and are called Greenwich Minus; those to the east have later times and are called Greenwich Plus. For example, New York City — which falls into the Greenwich Minus 5 time zone — is 5 hours earlier than Greenwich, England.

Montreal and Quebec City are in the eastern standard time zone, which means that the time is 5 hours earlier than it is in Greenwich, England.

Daylight savings time in Canada, as in the US, begins on the first Sunday in April and continues until the last Sunday in October.

Canadian timetables use a 24-hour clock to denote arrival and departure times, which means that hours are expressed sequentially from 1 AM. By this method, 9 AM is recorded as 0900, noon as 1200, 1 PM as 1300, 6 PM as 1800, midnight as 2400, and so on. For example, the departure of a train at 7 AM will be announced as "0700"; one leaving at 7 PM will be announced as "1900."

BUSINESS HOURS: In Montreal and Quebec City, as throughout Canada, business hours are fairly standard and similar to those in the US: 9 AM to 5 PM, Mondays through Fridays. While an hour lunch break is customary, employees often take it in shifts so that service is not interrupted, especially at banks and other public service operations.

Banks traditionally are open from 10 AM to 3 PM, Mondays through Thursdays, and until 6 PM on Fridays, but, as in the US, the trend is toward longer hours. Banks generally are closed on Saturdays and Sundays, although in major cities some banks offer services on Saturday mornings.

Retail stores usually are open from 9 or 9:30 AM to 5 or 5:30 PM. They often are open until 9 PM on Thursday or Friday nights. Most major stores are open on Saturdays.

PUBLIC HOLIDAYS: In Montreal and Quebec City the public holidays (and their dates this year) are as follows:

New Year's Day (January 1)
Good Friday (April 9)
Easter Monday (April 12)
Victoria Day (May 24)
Fête Nationale (June 24)
Canada Day (July 1)
Labour Day (September 6)
Thanksgiving (October 11)
Remembrance Day (November 11)
Christmas Day (December 25)
Boxing Day (December 26)

Mail, Telephone, and Electricity

 MAIL: The post offices in Montreal (1025 St-Jacques St., W.) and Quebec City (300 St-Paul St.) are open from 9 AM to 5:30 PM, Mondays through Fridays. Other offices may have Saturday hours. Stamps also are available at most hotel desks. Vending machines for stamps are outside post offices and in shopping centers.

Letters between Canada and the US have been known to arrive in as short a time as 5 days, but it is a good idea to allow at least 10 days for delivery in either direction. If your correspondence is important, you may want to send it via a special courier service: *Federal Express* (1175 University St., Montreal; phone: 514-345-0130; or 222 2nd Ave., Hangar 5, Quebec City; phone: 800-463-3339 throughout Canada); *DHL*

(632 Albert De Niverville, Dorval, Montreal; phone: 514-636-8703; or 900 Pierre Bertrand, Suite 240, Ville Vanier, Quebec City; phone: 418-683-9536). The cost is considerably higher than sending something via the postal service — but the assurance of its timely arrival may be worth it.

There are several places that will receive and hold mail for travelers in Montreal and Quebec City. Mail sent to you at a hotel and clearly marked "Guest Mail, Hold for Arrival" is one safe approach. Canadian post offices, including the main city offices, also will extend this service to you if the mail is sent to you in care of General Delivery. To inquire about this service, in Montreal call the post office at 514-283-2556; in Quebec City, call 418-648-3340. Also, don't forget to bring identification (driver's license, credit cards, birth certificate, or passport) with you when you go to collect it. Mail must be collected in person.

If you are an *American Express* customer (a cardholder, a carrier of *American Express* traveler's checks, or traveling on an *American Express Travel Related Services* tour) you can have mail sent to its office in Montreal or Quebec City. Letters are held free of charge — registered mail and packages are not accepted. You must be able to show an *American Express* card, traveler's checks, or a voucher proving you are on one of the company's tours to qualify. Those who aren't clients cannot use the service. Mail should be addressed to you, care of *American Express,* and should be marked "Client Mail Service."

While the US Embassy and consulates in Canada will not under ordinary circumstances accept mail for tourists, they *may* hold mail for US citizens in an emergency situation or if the papers sent are particularly important. It is best to inform them either by separate letter or cable, or by phone (particularly if you are in the country already), that you will be using their address for this purpose.

 TELEPHONE: The procedure for calling any number in Canada is the same as when calling within the US: dial the area code + the local number. The reverse procedure — dialing a number in the US from Canada — is the same.

The area code for Montreal is 514; for Quebec City it is 418.

Public telephones are available just about everywhere if you are in a city or town — including transportation terminals, hotel lobbies, restaurants, drugstores, libraries, post offices, and other municipal buildings. They also may be found at rest stops along major highways, at major tourist centers, and in resort areas. Roadside booths can be found just about anywhere. The average price of a local call is CN 25¢. *Note:* US coins can be used in pay phones.

Although you can use a telephone-company credit card number on any phone, pay phones that take major credit cards (*American Express, MasterCard, Visa,* and so on) are increasingly common, particularly in transportation and tourism centers. Also now available is the "affinity card," a combined telephone calling card/bank credit card that can be used for domestic and international calls. Cards of this type include the following:

> *AT&T/Universal* (phone: 800-662-7759).
> *Executive Telecard International* (phone: 800-950-3800).
> *Sprint Visa* (phone: 800-877-4646).

Similarly, *MCI VisaPhone* (phone: 800-866-0099) can add phone card privileges to the services available through your existing *Visa* card. This service allows you to use your *Visa* account number, plus an additional code, to charge calls on any touch-tone phone in the US and Canada.

The nationwide number for information is the same as in the US, 555-1212. If you need a number in another area code, dial the area code + 555-1212. (If you don't know the area code, simply dial 0 for an operator who can tell you.) In some metropolitan areas, you also have the option of dialing 411 for local information.

Long-distance rates are charged according to when the call is placed: weekday daytime; weekday evenings; and nights, weekends, and holidays. Least expensive are the calls you dial yourself from a private phone at night, and on weekends and major holidays. It generally is more expensive to call from a pay phone than it is to call from a private phone, and you must pay for a minimum 3-minute call. If the operator assists you, calls are more expensive. This includes credit card, bill-to-a-third-number, collect, and time-and-charge calls, as well as person-to-person calls, which are the most expensive. Rates are fully explained in the front of the white pages of every telephone directory.

Hotel Surcharges – Avoiding operator-assisted calls can cut costs considerably and bring rates into a somewhat more reasonable range — except for calls made through hotel switchboards. One of the most unpleasant surprises travelers encounter in many foreign countries is the amount they find tacked on to their hotel bill for telephone calls, because foreign hotels routinely add on astronomical surcharges. Before calling from your hotel room, inquire about any surcharges the hotel may impose. These can be excessive, but are avoidable by calling collect, using a telephone credit card (see above), or calling from a public pay phone. (Note that when calling from your hotel room, even if the call is made collect or charged to a credit card number, some establishments still may add on a nominal line usage charge — so ask before you call.)

Emergency Number – As in the US, dial 911 in Montreal in the event of an emergency. Operators at this number will get you the help you need from the police, fire department, or ambulance service. In Quebec City, dial "0" for the operator, who will connect you directly with the service you need.

■**Note:** An excellent resource for planning your trip is *AT&T's Toll-Free 800 Directory,* which lists thousands of companies with 800 numbers, both alphabetically (white pages) and by category (yellow pages), including a wide range of travel services — from travel agents to transportation and accommodations. Issued in a consumer edition for $9.95 and a business edition for $14.95, both are available from *AT&T Phone Centers* or by calling 800-426-8686. Another useful directory for use before you leave and on the road is the *Toll-Free Travel & Vacation Information Directory* ($4.95 postpaid from Pilot Books, 103 Cooper St., Babylon, NY 11702; phone: 516-422-2225).

ELECTRICITY: Canada has the same electrical current system as that in the US: 110 volts, 60 cycles, alternating current (AC). US appliances running on standard current can be used throughout Canada without adapters or convertors.

Staying Healthy

The surest way to return home in good health is to be prepared for medical problems that might occur while on vacation. Below we've outlined some things about which you need to think before you go.

BEFORE YOU GO: Older travelers or anyone suffering from a chronic medical condition, such as diabetes, high blood pressure, cardiopulmonary disease, asthma, or ear, eye, or sinus trouble, should consult a physician before leaving home.

Those with conditions requiring special consideration when traveling should think about seeing, in addition to their regular physician, a specialist in travel medicine. For a referral in a particular community, contact the nearest medical school or ask a local doctor to recommend such a specialist. Dr. Leonard Marcus, a member of the *American Committee on Clinical Tropical Medicine and Travelers' Health,* provides a directory of more than 100 travel doctors around the world. For a copy, send a 9- by 12-inch self-addressed, stamped envelope to Dr. Marcus at 148 Highland Ave., Newton, MA 02165 (phone: 617-527-4003).

Also be sure to check with your insurance company ahead of time about the applicability of your hospitalization and major medical policies away from home; many policies do not apply. Older travelers should know that Medicare does not make payments outside the US and its territories. If your medical policy does not protect you while you're traveling, there are comprehensive combination policies specifically designed to fill the gap. (For a discussion of medical insurance and a list of inclusive combination policies, see *Insurance,* in this section).

First Aid – Put together a compact, personal medical kit including Band-Aids, first-aid cream, antiseptic, nose drops, insect repellent, aspirin, an extra pair of prescription glasses or contact lenses (and a copy of your prescription for glasses or contact lenses), sunglasses, over-the-counter remedies for diarrhea, indigestion, and motion sickness, a thermometer, and a supply of those prescription medicines you take regularly.

In a corner of your kit, keep a list of all the drugs you have brought and their purpose, as well as duplicate copies of your doctor's prescriptions (or a note from your doctor). As brand names may vary in different countries, it's a good idea to ask your doctor for the generic name of any drugs you use so that you can ask for their equivalent should you need a refill. It also is a good idea to ask your doctor to prepare a medical identification card that includes such information as your blood type, your social security number, any allergies or chronic health problems you have, and your medical insurance information. Considering the essential contents of your medical kit, keep it with you, rather than in your checked luggage.

MINIMIZING THE RISKS: Travelers to Canada do not face the same health risks as might be encountered in visiting some other destinations in this hemisphere (such as Mexico and South America). Certainly travel always entails *some* possibility of injury or illness, but neither is inevitable and, with some basic precautions, your trip should proceed untroubled by ill health.

Sunburn – Even in Canada the burning power of the sun can quickly cause severe sunburn or sunstroke. To protect yourself against these ills, wear sunglasses, take along a broad-brimmed hat and cover-up, and, most important, use a sunscreen lotion.

Food and Water – Tap water in Canada generally is quite pure, so feel free to drink it. However, in rural areas, the local water supply may not be thoroughly purified, and local residents either have developed immunities to the natural bacteria or boil the water for drinking. You also should avoid swimming in or drinking water from freshwater streams, rivers, or pools, as they may be contaminated with leptospira, which cause a bacterial disease called leptospirosis (the symptoms resemble influenza). Milk is pasteurized throughout Canada, and dairy products are safe to eat, as are fruit, vegetables, meat, poultry, and fish.

MEDICAL AID ABROAD: Nothing ruins a vacation or business trip more effectively than sudden injury or illness. Fortunately, should you need medical attention, competent health professionals perfectly equipped to handled any medical problem can be found throughout the country. All hospitals are prepared for emergency cases, and many hospitals also have walk-in clinics to serve people who do not really need emergency service, but who have no place to go for immediate medical attention. Medical institutes in Canada, especially in the larger cities, generally provide the same basic specialties and services that are available in the US.

Emergency Treatment – You will find, in the event of an emergency, that most tourist facilities — transportation companies and hotels — are equipped to handle the situation quickly and efficiently. If a bona fide emergency occurs, the fastest way to get attention may be to take a taxi to the emergency room of the nearest hospital. In Montreal go to *Montreal General Hospital* (1650 Cedar Ave.; phone: 514-937-6011); in Quebec City, go to *Jeffrey Hale Hospital* (1250 St-Foy Rd.; phone: 418-683-4471). They are major hospitals with advanced equipment and technology to deal with acute medical situations, and most or all of the staff speak English. An alternative is to dial the free national "emergency" number — 911 in Canada — used to summon the police, fire department, or an ambulance.

Non-Emergency Care – If a doctor is needed for something less than an emergency, there are several ways to find one. If you are staying in a hotel or at a resort, ask for help in reaching a doctor or other emergency services, or for the house physician, who may visit you in your room or ask you to visit an office.

It also usually is possible to obtain a referral through a US consulate (see addresses and phone numbers below) or directly through a hospital, especially if it is an emergency.

Pharmacies and Prescription Drugs – If you have a minor medical problem, a pharmacist might offer some help. In Montreal, one 24-hour drugstore is the *Dubois Pharmacy* (51 22 Côte-Des-Neiges, Montreal; phone: 514-738-8464). At the time of this writing, there were no 24-hour pharmacies available in Quebec City.

Bring along a copy of any prescription you may have from your doctor in case you should need a refill. In the case of minor complaints, Canadian pharmacists *may* fill a foreign prescription; however, do not count on this. In most cases, you will need a local doctor to rewrite the prescription. Even in an emergency, a traveler will more than likely be given only enough of a drug to last until a local prescription can be obtained.

ADDITIONAL RESOURCES: Emergency assistance also is available from the various medical programs designed for travelers who have chronic ailments or whose illness requires them to return home:

International Association for Medical Assistance to Travelers (*IAMAT;* 417 Center St., Lewiston, NY 14092; phone: 716-754-4883). Entitles members to the services of participating doctors around the world, as well as clinics and hospitals in various locations. Participating physicians agree to adhere to a basic charge of around $50 to see a patient referred by *IAMAT.* To join, simply write to *IAMAT;* in about 3 weeks you will receive a membership card, the booklet of members, and an inoculation chart. A nonprofit organization, *IAMAT* appreciates donations; with a donation of $25 or more, you will receive a set of worldwide climate charts detailing weather and sanitary conditions. (Delivery can take up to 5 weeks, so plan ahead.)

International Health Care Service (New York Hospital–Cornell Medical Center, 525 E. 68th St., Box 210, New York, NY 10021; phone: 212-746-1601). This service provides a variety of travel-related health services, including a complete range of immunizations at moderate per-shot rates. A pre-travel counseling and immunization package costs $255 for the first family member and $195 for each additional member; a post-travel consultation is $175 to $275, plus lab work. Consultations are by appointment only, from 4 to 8 PM Mondays through Thursdays, although 24-hour coverage is available for urgent travel-related problems. In addition, sending $4.50 (with a self-addressed envelope) to the address above will procure the service's publication, *International Health Care Travelers Guide,* a compendium of facts and advice on health care and diseases around the world.

International SOS Assistance (PO Box 11568, Philadelphia, PA 19116; phone: 800-523-8930 or 215-244-1500). Subscribers are provided with telephone access — 24 hours a day, 365 days a year — to a worldwide, monitored, multilingual network of medical centers. A phone call brings assistance ranging from a telephone consultation to transportation home by ambulance or aircraft, or, in some cases, transportation of a family member to wherever you are hospitalized. Individual rates are $35 for 2 weeks of coverage ($3.50 for each additional day), $70 for 1 month, or $240 for 1 year; couple and family rates also are available.

Medic Alert Foundation (2323 N. Colorado, Turlock, CA 95380; phone: 800-ID-ALERT or 209-668-3333). If you have a health condition that may not be readily perceptible to the casual observer — one that might result in a tragic error in an emergency situation — this organization offers identification emblems specifying such conditions. The foundation also maintains a computerized central file from which your complete medical history is available 24 hours a day by phone (the telephone number is clearly inscribed on the emblem). The onetime membership fee (between $35 and $50) is based on the type of metal from which the emblem is made — the choices range from stainless steel to 10K gold-filled.

TravMed (PO Box 10623, Baltimore, MD 21204; phone: 800-732-5309 or 301-296-5225). For $3 per day, subscribers receive comprehensive medical assistance while abroad. Major medical expenses are covered up to $100,000, and special transportation home or of a family member to wherever you are hospitalized is provided at no additional cost.

Helpful Publications – Practically every phase of health care — before, during, and after a trip — is covered in *The New Traveler's Health Guide,* by Drs. Patrick J. Doyle and James E. Banta. It is available for $4.95, plus postage and handling, from Acropolis Books Ltd., 13950 Park Center Rd., Herndon, VA 22071 (phone: 800-451-7771 or 703-709-0006).

The *Traveling Healthy Newsletter,* which is published six times a year, also is brimming with health-related travel tips. For a year's subscription, which costs $24, contact Dr. Karl Neumann (108-48 70th Rd., Forest Hills, NY 11375; phone: 718-268-7290). A sample issue is available for $4. Dr. Neumann also is the editor of the useful free booklet *Traveling Healthy,* which is available by writing to the *Travel Healthy Program* (Clark O'Neill Inc., 1 Broad Ave., Fairview, NJ 07022; phone: 201-947-3400).

For more information regarding preventive health care for travelers, contact the *International Association for Medical Assistance to Travelers* (*IAMAT;* 417 Center St., Lewiston, NY 14092; phone: 716-754-4883). The Centers for Disease Control also publishes an interesting booklet, *Health Information for International Travel.* To order send a check or money order for $5 to the Superintendent of Documents (US Government Printing Office, Washington, DC 20402), or charge it to your credit card by calling 202-783-3238. For information on vaccination requirements, disease outbreaks, and other health information pertaining to traveling abroad, you also can call the Centers for Disease Control's 24-hour International Health Requirements and Recommendations Information Hotline: 404-332-4559.

■ **Note:** Those who are unable to take a reserved flight due to personal illness or who must fly home unexpectedly due to a family emergency should be aware that airlines may offer a discounted airfare (or arrange a partial refund) if the traveler can demonstrate that his or her situation is indeed a legitimate emergency. Your inability to fly or the illness or death of an immediate family member usually must be substantiated by a doctor's note or the name, relationship, and funeral home from which the deceased will be buried. In such cases, airlines often will waive certain advance purchase restrictions or you may receive a refund check or voucher for future travel at a later date. Be aware, however, that this bereavement fare may not necessarily be the least expensive fare available and, if possible, it is best to have a travel agent check all possible flights through a computer reservations system (CRS).

Legal Aid and Consular Services

There are crucial places to keep in mind when outside the US, namely, the US Embassy (100 Wellington St., Ottawa, Ontario K1P 5T1, Canada; phone: 613-238-4470) and the US consulates (1155 Saint Alexandre St., Montreal, Quebec H2Z 1Z2, Canada; phone: 514-398-9695; and 2 Terrasse-Dufferin, Quebec City, Quebec G1R 4N5, Canada; phone: 418-692-2095).

If you are injured or become seriously ill, or if you encounter legal difficulties, the consulate is the first place to turn, although its powers and capabilities are limited. It will direct you to medical assistance and notify your relatives if you are ill; it can advise you of your rights and provide a list of English-speaking lawyers if you are arrested, but it cannot interfere with the local legal process.

For questions about US citizens arrested abroad, how to get money to them, and other useful information, call the *Citizen's Emergency Center* of the Office of Special Consular Services in Washington, DC, at 202-647-5225. (For further information about this invaluable hotline, see below.)

A consulate exists to aid citizens in serious matters, such as illness, destitution, and the above legal difficulties. It is not there to aid in trivial situations, such as canceled reservations or lost baggage, no matter how important these matters may seem to the victimized tourist. If you should get sick, the US consul can provide names of English-speaking doctors and dentists, as well as the names of local hospitals and clinics; the consul also will contact family members in the US and help arrange special ambulance service for a flight home. In a situation involving "legitimate and proven poverty" of an US citizen stranded abroad without funds, the consul will contact sources of money (such as family or friends in the US), apply for aid to agencies in foreign countries, and in a last resort — which is *rarely* — arrange for repatriation at government expense, although this is a loan that must be repaid. And in case of natural disasters or civil unrest, consulates around the world handle the evacuation of US citizens if it becomes necessary.

As mentioned above, the US State Department operates a *Citizens' Emergency Center,* which offers a number of services to US citizens traveling abroad and their families at home. In addition to giving callers up-to-date information on trouble spots, the center will contact authorities abroad in an attempt to locate a traveler or deliver an urgent message. In case of illness, death, arrest, destitution, or repatriation of a US citizen on foreign soil, it will relay information to relatives at home if the consulate is unable to do so. Travel advisory information is available 24 hours a day to people with touch-tone phones (phone: 202-647-5225). Callers with rotary phones can get information at this number from 8:15 AM to 10 PM (eastern standard time) on weekdays; 9 AM to 3 PM on Saturdays. In the event of an emergency, this number also may be called during these hours. For emergency calls only, at all other times, call 202-634-3600 and ask for the duty officer.

Drinking and Drugs

 DRINKING: The legal drinking age is 18 in Montreal and Quebec City. The province of Quebec has the most liberal drinking laws in the country. Beer and wine are sold at retail grocery stores; hard liquor is available at government liquor stores.

Licensed restaurants, hotels, lounges, and bars are found throughout Montreal and Quebec City, though some may sell only wine or beer. The hours during which bars and restaurants may serve liquor vary, though traditionally bar closing time is between midnight and 3 AM. Liquor stores are required to close on Sundays and holidays, but some alcoholic beverages may be purchased on Sundays, usually only with meals, at authorized dining rooms, restaurants, and private clubs.

Visitors to Canada may bring in 40 ounces (about 1 gallon) of liquor or wine, or 288 ounces of beer or ale (twenty-four 12-ounce cans, eighteen 16-ounce cans) as personal baggage, duty-free. Anything in excess of this amount is subject to duties and taxes and requires a provincial permit. If excess liquor is declared, it will be held by Canada Customs at the point of entry for 30 days. A receipt will be issued, and the owner can claim it upon return. People leaving Canada from a point other than their point of entry can make arrangements to have their property returned at the point of departure.

DRUGS: Illegal narcotics are as prevalent in Canada as in the US, but the moderate legal penalties and vague social acceptance that marijuana has gained in the US has no equivalent in Canada. Due to the international war on drugs, enforcement of drug laws is becoming increasingly strict throughout the world. Local Canadian narcotics officers and customs officials are renowned for their absence of understanding and lack of a sense of humor — especially where foreigners are involved.

Opiates and barbiturates, and other increasingly popular drugs — "white powder" substances like heroin and cocaine, and "crack" (the cocaine derivative) — continue to be of major concern to narcotics officials. It is important to bear in mind that the type or quantities of drugs involved is of minor importance. According to a spokesperson for the Royal Canadian Mounted Police, stiff penalties have been imposed on drug offenders convicted of possessing mere *traces* of illegal drugs. Persons arrested are subject to the laws of the country they are visiting, and there isn't much the US consulate can do for drug offenders beyond providing a list of lawyers. The best advice we can offer is this: Don't carry, use, buy, or sell illegal drugs.

Those who carry medicines that contain a controlled drug should be sure to have a current doctor's prescription with them. Ironically, travelers can get into almost as much trouble coming through US Customs with over-the-counter drugs picked up abroad that contain substances that are controlled in the US. Cold medicines, pain relievers, and the like often have codeine or codeine derivatives that are illegal, except by prescription, in the US. Throw them out before leaving for home.

■ **Be forewarned:** US narcotics agents warn travelers of the increasingly common ploy of drug dealers asking travelers to transport a "gift" or other package back to the US. Don't be fooled into thinking that the protection of US law applies abroad — accused of illegal drug trafficking, you will be considered guilty until you prove your innocence. In other words, do not, under any circumstances, agree to take anything across the border for a stranger.

Tipping

While tipping is at the discretion of the person receiving the service, CN 50¢ is the rock-bottom tip for anything, and CN$1 is the current customary minimum for small services. *(Please note that the gratuities suggested below are given in Canadian dollars.)*

In restaurants, tip between 10% and 20% of the bill's total before tax is added. For average service in an average restaurant, a 15% tip to the waiter is reasonable, although one should never hesitate to penalize poor service or reward excellent and efficient attention by leaving less or more.

Although it's not necessary to tip the maître d' of most restaurants — unless he or she has been especially helpful in arranging a special party or providing a table (slipping him something in a crowded restaurant *may,* however, get you seated sooner or procure a preferred table) — when tipping is appropriate, the least amount should be CN$5. In the finest restaurants, where a multiplicity of servers are present, plan to tip 5% to the captain. The sommelier (wine waiter) is entitled to a gratuity of approximately 10% of the price of the bottle of wine.

In allocating gratuities at a restaurant, pay particular attention to what has become the standard credit card charge form, which now includes separate places for gratuities for waiters and/or captains. If these separate boxes are not on the charge slip, simply ask the waiter or captain how these separate tips should be indicated. In some establishments, tips indicated on credit card receipts may not be given to the help, so you may want to leave tips in cash.

In a large hotel, where it's difficult to determine just who out of a horde of attendants actually performed particular services, it is perfectly proper for guests to ask to have an extra 10% to 15% added to their bill. For those who prefer to distribute tips themselves, a chambermaid generally is tipped at the rate of around CN$1 a day. Tip the concierge and hall porter for specific services only, with the amount of such gratuities dependent on the level of service provided. For any special service you receive in a hotel, a tip is expected — CN$1 being the minimum for a small service.

Bellhops, doormen, and porters at hotels and transportation centers generally are tipped at the rate of CN$1 per piece of luggage, along with a small additional amount if a doorman helps with a cab or car. Taxi drivers should get about 15% of the total fare. And if you arrive without Canadian currency, tip in US dollars.

Miscellaneous tips: Sightseeing tour guides should be tipped. If you are traveling in a group, decide together what you want to give the guide and present it from the group at the end of the tour ($1 per person is a reasonable tip). If you have been individually escorted, the amount paid should depend on the degree of your satisfaction, but it should not be less than 10% of the tour price. Museum and monument guides usually are tipped, and it is a nice touch to tip a caretaker who unlocks a small church or turns on the light in a chapel. In barbershops and beauty parlors, tip also are expected, but the percentages vary according to the type of establishment — 10% in the most expensive salons; 15% to 20% in less expensive establishments. (As a general rule, the person who washes your hair should get a small additional tip.) Washroom attendants should get a small tip — they usually set out a little plate with a coin already on it indicating the suggested denomination.

Tipping always is a matter of personal preference. In the situations covered above, as well as in any others that arise where you feel a tip is expected or due, feel free to express your pleasure or displeasure. Again, never hesitate to reward excellent and efficient attention and to penalize poor service. Give an extra gratuity and a word of thanks when someone has gone out of his or her way for you. Either way, the more personal the act of tipping, the more appropriate it seems. And if you didn't like the service — or the attitude — don't tip.

Duty-Free Shopping and Goods and Services Tax

DUTY-FREE SHOPS: If common sense says that it always is less expensive to buy goods in an airport duty-free shop than to buy them at home or in the streets of a foreign city, travelers should be aware of some basic facts. Duty-free, first of all, does not mean that the goods travelers buy will be free of duty when they return to the US. Rather, it means that the shop has paid no import tax in acquiring goods of foreign make, because the goods are not to be used in the country where the shop is located. This is why duty-free goods are available only in the restricted, passengers-only area of international airports or are delivered to departing passengers on the plane. In a duty-free store, travelers save money only on goods of foreign make because they are the only items on which an import tax would be charged in any other store. There usually is no saving on locally made items, but in provinces such as Quebec that impose provincial sales and good and services taxes (see below) that are refundable to foreigners, the prices in airport duty-free shops also subtract this tax, sparing travelers the often cumbersome procedures they otherwise have to follow to obtain a PST or GST refund.

Beyond this, there is little reason to delay buying locally made merchandise and/or souvenirs until reaching the airport. In fact, because airport duty-free shops usually pay high rents, the locally made goods they sell may well be more expensive than they would be in downtown stores. The real bargains are foreign goods, but — let the buyer beware — not all foreign goods are automatically less expensive in an airport duty-free shop. You can get a good deal on even small amounts of perfume, costing less than the usually required minimum purchase, tax-free. Other fairly standard bargains include spirits, smoking materials, cameras, clothing, watches, chocolates, and other food and luxury items — but first be sure to know what these items cost elsewhere. Terrific savings do exist (they are the reason for such shops, after all), but so do overpriced items that an unwary shopper might find equally tempting. In addition, if you wait to do your shopping at airport duty-free shops, you will be taking the chance that the desired item is out of stock or unavailable.

Duty-free shops are located at all three major airports in Quebec: Dorval International Airport and Mirabel International Airport in Montreal, and Saint-Foy Airport in Quebec City.

GOODS AND SERVICES TAX: Commonly abbreviated as GST, this 7% tax is levied by Canada on a wide range of purchases and payments for services, including package tours, car rentals, accommodations, and meals.

The tax is intended for residents (and already is included in the price tag), but visitors are also required to pay it unless they have purchases shipped by the store directly to an address abroad. If visitors pay the tax and take purchases with them, however, they generally are entitled to a refund.

The amount of the tax rebate claimed must be for a minimum of CN$7 — which means your expenditures in Canada for accommodations and other applicable purchases (there's no GST refund for food) must be at least CN$100 (CN$107, including the tax). Visitors are entitled to make up to four rebate claims per year, or purchases can be accumulated on any number of visits and one claim made for the calendar year. Visitors can mail the rebate forms after returning home (again, forms are available where goods are purchased), or at instant-rebate centers at points of departure from Canada such as duty-free shops and border crossings. (Any rebate claim for tax on a day's expenditure of CN$500 or more must be processed by mail.) Note that rebates through the mail are issued in US dollars; instant rebates are in Canadian dollars. If you have any questions about the tax while you're in Canada, call the information hotline that has been set up by Revenue Canada: 800-267-6620. For the hearing impaired, call 800-465-5770 (in Canada only).

In addition, most provinces impose a Provincial Sales Tax (PST) on most items, including food and lodging. These taxes vary from province to province; in Quebec it is 8% and a tax refund is provided to foreign visitors. If you spend at least CN$500 in Quebec, you will be eligible for a refund of the PST on your expenditures. Forms to use when applying for the refund are available at retail shops or by contacting Revenue Quebec, PO Box 3000, Station Desjardins, Montreal, Quebec H5B 1A4, Canada (phone: 514-873-4692).

■ **Buyer Beware:** You may come across shops *not* at airports that call themselves duty-free shops. These require shoppers to show a foreign passport but are subject to the same rules as other stores, including paying import duty on foreign items. What "tax-free" means in the case of these establishments is something of an advertising strategy: They are announcing loud and clear that they do, indeed, offer the PST/GST refund service — sometimes on the spot (minus a fee for higher overhead). Prices may be no better at these stores, and could be even higher due to this service.

Customs and Returning to the US

 When you return to the United States, you must declare to the US Customs official at the point of entry everything you have bought or acquired while in Canada. To speed up the process, keep all your receipts handy and try to pack your purchases together in an accessible part of your suitcase.

DUTY-FREE ARTICLES: In general, the duty-free allowance for US visitors returning from abroad is $400. This duty-free limit covers purchases that accompany you and are for personal use. This limit includes items used or worn while in Canada, souvenirs for friends, and gifts received during the trip. A flat 10% duty based on the "fair retail value in country of acquisition" is assessed on the next $1,000 worth of merchandise brought in for personal use or gifts. Amounts above these two levels are dutiable at a variety of rates. The average rate for typical tourist purchases is about 12%, but you can find out rates on specific items by consulting *Tariff Schedules of the United States* in a library or at any US Customs Service office.

Families traveling together may make a joint declaration to customs, which permits one member to exceed his or her duty-free exemption to the extent that another falls short. Families also may pool purchases dutiable under the flat rate. A family of three, for example, would be eligible for up to a total of $3,000 at the 10% flat duty rate (after each member had used up his or her $400 duty-free exemption) rather than three separate $1,000 allowances. This grouping of purchases is extremely useful when considering the duty on a duty-tariff item, such as jewelry or a fur coat. (Keep in mind, however, that the $25 exemption may not be grouped with family members.)

Personal exemptions can be used once every 30 days; in order to be eligible, an individual must have been out of the country for more than 48 continuous hours. If any portion of the exemption has been used once within any 30-day period or if your trip is less than 48 hours long, the duty-free allowance is cut to $25.

There are certain articles, however, that are duty-free only up to certain limits. The $25 limit includes the following: 10 cigars (not Cuban), 50 cigarettes, and 4 ounces of perfume. Individuals eligible for the full $400 duty-free limit are allowed 1 carton of cigarettes (200), 100 cigars, and 1 liter of alcoholic beverages if the traveler is over 21. Under federal law, alcohol above this allowance is liable for both duty and an Internal Revenue tax. Note, however, that states are allowed to impose additional restrictions and penalties of their own, including (in Arizona and Utah, for example) confiscation of any quantities of liquor over the statutory limit. Antiques, if they are 100 or more years old and you have proof from the seller of that fact, are duty-free, as are paintings and drawings if done entirely by hand.

To avoid paying duty twice, register the serial number of computers, watches, and electronic equipment with the nearest US Customs bureau before departure; receipts of insurance policies also should be carried for other foreign-made items.

Gold, gold medals, bullion, and up to $10,000 in currency or negotiable instruments may be brought into the US without being declared. Sums over $10,000 must be declared in writing.

The allotment for individual "unsolicited" gifts mailed from abroad (no more than one per day per recipient) is $50 retail value per gift. These gifts do not have to be declared and are not included in your duty-free exemption (see below). Although you should include a receipt for the purchases with each package, the examiner is empowered to impose a duty based on his or her assessment of the value of the goods. The duty owed is collected by the US Postal Service when the package is delivered. More information on mailing packages home from abroad is contained in the US Customs Service pamphlet *Buyer Beware, International Mail Imports* (see below for where to write for this and other useful brochures).

CLEARING CUSTOMS: This is a simple procedure. If your purchases total no more than the $400 duty-free limit, you need only make an oral declaration to the customs inspector. If entering with more than $400 worth of goods, you must submit a written declaration.

It is illegal not to declare dutiable items; not to do so, in fact, constitutes smuggling, and the penalty can be anything from stiff fines and seizure of the goods to prison sentences. There is a basic rule to buying goods abroad, and it should never be broken: *If you can't afford the duty on something, don't buy it.* Your list or verbal declaration should include all items purchased in Canada, as well as gifts received there, purchases made at the behest of others, the value of repairs, and anything brought in for resale in the US.

Do not include in the list items that do not accompany you, i.e., purchases that you have mailed or had shipped home. These are dutiable in any case, even if for your own use and even if the items that accompany your return from the same trip do not exhaust your duty-free exemption. It is a good idea, if you have accumulated too much while abroad, to mail home any personal effects (made and bought in the US) that you no longer need rather than your foreign purchases. These personal effects pass through US Customs as "American goods returned" and are not subject to duty.

FORBIDDEN IMPORTS: US residents are prohibited from bringing certain goods into the US from Canada, including any Cuban-made goods and items from North Korea, Vietnam, or Cambodia.

Narcotics, plants (unless specifically exempt and free of soil), and many types of food are not allowed into the US. Drugs are totally illegal, with the exception of medication prescribed by a physician. It's a good idea not to travel with too large a quantity of any given prescription drug (however, in the event that a pharmacy is not open when you need it, bring along several extra doses) and to have the prescription on hand in case any question arises either abroad or when re-entering the US.

Tourists have long been forbidden to bring into the US foreign-made, US-trade-marked articles purchased abroad (if the trademark is recorded with US Customs) without written permission. It's now permissible to enter with one such item in your possession as long as it's for personal use.

Tourists who want to bring Canadian plants into the US should know that house-plants usually are permitted; however, those transporting outdoor plants and fruit trees must have a plant certificate from an office of Agriculture Canada. For more information, contact Plant Protection Division, Export Division, Food Production and Inspection Branch, Agriculture Canada, Ottawa, Ontario K1A 0C6, Canada (phone: 613-995-7900).

The US Customs Service implements the rigorous Department of Agriculture regulations concerning the importation of vegetable matter, seeds, bulbs, and the like. Living vegetable matter may not be imported without a permit, and everything must be inspected, permit or not. Approved items (which do not require a permit) include dried bamboo and woven items made of straw; beads made of most seeds (but not jequirity beans — the poisonous scarlet and black seed of the rosary pea) and some viable seeds; cones of pine and other trees; roasted coffee beans; most flower bulbs; flowers (without roots); dried or canned fruits, jellies, or jams; polished rice, dried beans and teas; herb plants (not with witchweed); nuts (but not acorns, chestnuts, or any nuts with outer husks); dried lichens, mushrooms (including truffles), shamrocks, and seaweed; and most dried spices.

Other processed foods and baked goods usually are okay. Regulations on meat products generally depend on the country of origin and manner of processing. As a rule, commercially canned meat, hermetically sealed and cooked in the can so that it can be stored without refrigeration, is permitted, but not all canned meat fulfills this requirement.

The US Customs Service also enforces federal laws that prohibit the entry of articles made from the furs or hides of animals on the endangered species list. Beware of shoes, bags, and belts made of crocodile and certain kinds of lizard, and anything made of tortoiseshell; this also applies to preserved crocodiles, lizards, and turtles sometimes sold in gift shops. Most coral — particularly black coral — also is restricted (although small quanitites of coral incorporated into jewelry or other craft items usually are permitted). And if you're shopping for big-ticket items, beware of fur coats made from the skins of spotted cats. They are sold abroad, but they will be confiscated upon your return to the US, and there will be no refund. For information about other animals on the endangered species list, contact the Department of the Interior, US Fish and Wildlife Service (Publications Unit, 4401 N. Fairfax Dr., Room 130, Arlington, VA 22203; phone: 703-358-1711), and ask for the free publication *Facts About Federal Wildlife Laws.*

Also note that some foreign governments prohibit the export of items made from certain species of wildlife, and the US honors any such restrictions. Before you go shopping in any foreign country, check with the US Department of Agriculture (G110 Federal Bldg., Hyattsville, MD 20782; phone: 301-436-8010) and find out what items are prohibited from the country you will be visiting.

The US Customs Service publishes a series of free pamphlets with customs information. It includes *Know Before You Go,* a basic discussion of customs requirements pertaining to all travelers; *Buyer Beware, International Mail Imports; Travelers' Tips on Bringing Food, Plant, and Animal Products into the United States; Importing a Car; GSP and the Traveler; Pocket Hints; Currency Reporting; Pets, Wildlife, US Customs; Customs Hints for Visitors (Nonresidents);* and *Trademark Information for Travelers.*

For the entire series or individual pamphlets, write to the US Customs Service (PO Box 7474, Washington, DC 20044) or contact any of the seven regional offices — in Boston, Chicago, Houston, Long Beach (California), Miami, New Orleans, and New York.

Note that the US Customs Service has a tape-recorded message whereby callers using touch-tone phones can obtain free pamphlets on various travel-related topics; the number is 202-566-8195. These pamphlets provide great briefing material, but if you still have questions when you're in Canada, contact the nearest US consulate or the US Embassy.

Religion on the Road

 The surest source of information on religious services in an unfamiliar country is the desk clerk of the hotel or guesthouse in which you are staying; the local tourist information office, a US consul, or a church of another religious affiliation also may be able to provide this information. For a full range of options, joint religious councils often print circulars with the addresses and times of services of houses of worship in the area. These often are printed as part of general tourist guides provided by the local tourist and convention center, or as part of a "what's going on" guide to the city. Many newspapers also print a listing of religious services in their area in weekend editions. You also can check the yellow pages of the phone book under "Churches" and call for more information.

You may want to use your vacation to broaden your religious experience by joining an unfamiliar faith in its service. This can be a moving experience, especially if the service is held in a church, synagogue, or temple that is historically significant or architecturally notable. You almost always will find yourself made welcome and comfortable.

■ **Note:** For those interested in a spiritual stay while in Canada, *Catholic America: Self-Renewal Centers and Retreats,* by Patricia Christian-Meyer, lists approximately 20 self-renewal centers throughout Canada. To order, send $13.95 to John Muir Publications, PO Box 613, Sante Fe, NM 87504 (phone: 800-888-7504 or 505-982-4078).

Sources and Resources

Tourist Information Offices

 The Canadian tourist offices and consulates in the US generally are the best sources of local travel information, and most of their many, varied publications are free for the asking. For the best results, request general information on specific provinces or cities, as well as publications relating to your particular areas of interest: accommodations, special events, sports, guided tours, and facilities for specific sports. There is no need to send a self-addressed, stamped envelope with your request, unless specified. For information on Montreal and Quebec City, contact Tourisme Québec (PO Box 20000, Quebec City, Quebec G1K 7X2, Canada), or call INFOTOURIST (800-363-7777 or 514-873-2015).

Canadian Embassy and Consulates in the US

The Canadian government maintains an embassy and several consulates in the US. These are empowered to sign official documents and to notarize copies of US documents, which may be necessary for those papers to be considered legal abroad. Below is a list of the Canadian Embassy and consulates in the US.

Atlanta: Canadian Consulate (1 CNN Center, Suite 400, South Tower, Atlanta, GA 30303; phone: 404-577-6810).

Dallas: Canadian Consulate (750 N. St. Paul, Suite 1700, Dallas, TX 75201; phone: 214-922-9806).

Los Angeles: Canadian Consulate (300 S. Grand Ave., Los Angeles, CA 90071; phone: 213-687-7432).

New York City: Canadian Consulate (1251 Ave. of the Americas, New York, NY 10020; phone: 212-768-2442).

San Francisco: Canadian Consulate (50 Fremont St., Suite 2100, San Francisco, CA 94105; phone: 415-495-6021).

Washington, DC: Canadian Embassy (501 Pennsylvania Ave. NW, Washington, DC 20001; phone: 202-682-1740).

Theater and Special Event Tickets

 As you read this book, you will learn about events that may spark your interest — everything from music festivals and special theater seasons to sporting championships — along with telephone numbers and addresses to which to write for descriptive brochures, reservations, or tickets. The Canadian government tourist offices can supply information on these and other special events and festivals that take place in Montreal and Quebec City, though they cannot in all cases provide the actual program or detailed information on ticket prices.

Since many of these occasions often are fully booked well in advance, think about having your reservation in hand before you go. In some cases, tickets may be reserved over the phone and charged to a credit card, or you can send an international money order or foreign draft. If you do write, remember that any request from the US should be accompanied by an International Reply Coupon to ensure a response (send two of them for an airmail response). These international coupons, money orders, and drafts are available at US post offices.

Books, Magazines, and Newsletters

 BOOKS: Throughout GETTING READY TO GO, numerous books and brochures have been recommended as good sources of further information on a variety of topics. In many cases, these are publications of the various tourism authorities and are available in any of their offices both here and abroad.

Suggested Reading – The list below comprises books we have come across and think worthwhile; it is by no means complete, but meant merely to start you on your way. Unless indicated, all the books listed here are in print, but you also may want to do some additional research at your local library. These titles include some informative guides to special interests, solid historical accounts, and books that call attention to things you might not notice otherwise.

General Travel

The Adventure Guide to Canada, by Pam Hobbs (Hunter Publishing; $15.95).

The Best Bicycle Tours of Eastern Canada: Twelve Breathtaking Tours Through Quebec, Ontario, Newfoundland, Nova Scotia, New Brunswick, & Prince Edward Island, by Jerry Dennis (Henry Holt; $14.95).

The Best of Montreal and Quebec City: A Guide to the Places, Peoples, and Pleasures of French Canada, by Martin Kevan (Random House; $14).

Birnbaum's Canada 1993, edited by Alexandra Mayes Birnbaum (HarperCollins; $17).

Budget Traveler's Guide to Great Off-Beat Vacations in the US and Canada, by Paige Palmer (Pilot Books; $4.95).

Canada: A Travel Survival Kit, by Mark Lightbody and Tom Smallman (Lonely Planet; $19.95).

Canadian Bed and Breakfast Guide, by Gerda Pantel (Chicago Review Press; $12.95).

The Canadian Canoeing Companion: An Illustrated Guide to Paddling Canada's Wilderness, by Alex Narvey (Thunder Enlightening Press; $16.95).

Country Inns, Lodges, and Historic Hotels, Canada, by Anthony Hitchcock (Burt Franklin Press; $10.95).

Montreal Night and Day, by Daniel Desjardins (Ulysses Books & Maps; $11.95).

O Canada: Travels in an Unknown Country, by Jan Morris (HarperCollins Publishers; $20).

History and Culture

Canadian Folklore, by Edith Fowke (Oxford University Press; $9.95).

Contours of Canadian Thought, by A. B. McKillop (University of Toronto Press; $13.95).

France and England in North America, by Francis Parkman (Library of America; 2 volumes, $32.50 per volume).

The Independence Movement in Quebec: 1945-1980, by William Coleman (University of Toronto Press; $16.95).

Oh Canada! Oh Quebec!: Requiem for a Divided Country, by Mordecai Richler (Random House; $23).

The Penguin History of Canada, by Kenneth McNaught (Penguin Books; $8.95).

A Reader's Guide to Canadian History, edited by D. A. Muise (University of Toronto Press; 2 volumes, $14.95 per volume).

Sweet Promises: A Reader in Indian-White Relations in Canada, edited by J. R. Miller (University of Toronto Press; $24.95).

Literature

The Apprenticeship of Duddy Kravitz, by Mordecai Richler (Penguin; $9.95).

Anne Hébert: Selected Poems (Bookslinger; $10).

Black Robe, by Brian Moore (Fawcett Books; $4.99).

The Enthusiasms of Robertson Davies, by Robertson Davies; edited by Judith Skelton Grant (Penguin; $9.95).

Friend of My Youth, by Alice Munro (Penguin; $8.95).

Home Sweet Home: My Canadian Album, by Mordecai Richler (Random House; $16.95).

Intimate Strangers: New Stories from Quebec, edited by Matt Cohen and Wayne Grady (Penguin; $6.95).

The Oxford Book of Canadian Ghost Stories, edited by Alberto Manguel (Oxford University Press; $15.95).

The Oxford Book of Canadian Short Stories in English, edited by Margaret Atwood (Oxford University Press; $27.95).

The Oxford Book of French-Canadian Short Stories, edited by Richard Teleky (Oxford University Press; $14.95).

The Oxford Illustrated Literary Guide to Canada, by Albert and Theresa Moritz (Oxford University Press; $39.95).

Surfacing, by Margaret Atwood (Fawcett Books; $4.95).

In addition, *Culturgrams* is a handy series of pamphlets that provides a good sampling of information on the people, cultures, sights, and bargains to be found in over 90 countries around the world. Each four-page, newsletter-size leaflet covers one country, and Canada is included in the series. The topics included range from customs and courtesies to lifestyles and demographics. These fact-filled pamphlets are published by the David M. Kennedy Center for International Studies at Brigham Young University; for an order form contact the group c/o Publication Services (280 HRCB, Provo, UT 84602; phone: 801-378-6528). When ordering from 1 to 5 *Culturgrams,* the price is $1 each; 6 to 49 pamphlets, 50¢ each; for 50 or more, the per-copy price is even lower.

MAGAZINES: As sampling the regional fare is likely to be one of the highlights of any visit, you will find reading about local edibles worthwhile either before you go or after you return. *Gourmet,* a magazine specializing in food, frequently carries mouthwatering articles on food and restaurants in Canada, although its scope is much broader. It is available at newsstands for $2.50 an issue, or as a subscription for $18 a year from *Gourmet* (PO Box 53789, Boulder, CO 80322; phone: 800-365-2454).

There are numerous additional magazines for every special interest available; check at your library information desk for a directory of such publications, or look over the selection offered at a well-stocked newsstand.

NEWSLETTERS: Throughout GETTING READY TO GO we have mentioned specific newsletters which our readers may be interested in consulting for further information. One of the very best sources of detailed travel information is *Consumer Reports Travel Letter.* Published monthly by Consumers Union (PO Box 53629, Boulder, CO 80322-3629; phone: 800-234-1970), it offers comprehensive coverage of the travel scene on a wide variety of fronts. A year's subscription costs $37; 2 years, $57.

In addition, the following travel newsletters provide useful up-to-date information on travel services and bargains:

> *Entree* (PO Box 5148, Santa Barbara, CA 93150; phone: 805-969-5848). This newsletter caters to a sophisticated, discriminating traveler with the means to explore the places mentioned. Subscribers have access to a 24-hour hotline providing information on restaurants and accommodations around the world. Monthly; a year's subscription costs $59.
>
> *The Hideaway Report* (Harper Assocs., PO Box 50, Sun Valley, ID 83353; phone: 208-622-3193). This monthly source highlights retreats — including Canadian idylls — for sophisticated travelers. A year's subscription costs $90.
>
> *Romantic Hideaways* (217 E. 86th St., Suite 258, New York, NY 10028; phone: 212-969-8682). This newsletter leans toward those special places made for those traveling in twos. A year's subscription for this monthly publication costs $65.
>
> *Travel Smart* (Communications House, 40 Beechdale Rd., Dobbs Ferry, NY 10522; phone: 914-693-8300 in New York; 800-327-3633 elsewhere in the US). This monthly covers a wide variety of trips and travel discounts. A year's subscription costs $44.

■ **Computer Services:** Anyone who owns a personal computer and a modem can subscribe to a database service providing everything from airline schedules and fares to restaurant listings. Two such services of particular use to travelers are *CompuServe* (5000 Arlington Center Blvd., Columbus, OH 43220; phone: 800-848-8199 or 614-457-8600; $39.95 to join, plus a $2 monthly fee and usage fees of $6 to $22 per hour) and *Prodigy Services* (445 Hamilton Ave., White Plains, NY 10601; phone: 800-822-6922, 800-PRODIGY, or 914-993-8000; $12.95 per month's subscription, plus variable usage fees). Before using any computer bulletin-board services, be sure to take precautions to prevent downloading of a computer "virus." First install one of the programs designed to screen out such nuisances.

Weights and Measures

When traveling in Canada, you'll find that just about every quantity, whether it is distance, length, weight, or capacity, will be expressed in unfamiliar terms. In fact, this is true for travel almost everywhere in the world, since the US is one of the last countries to make its way to the metric system. Your trip to Montreal or Quebec City may serve to familiarize you with what may one day be the weights and measures at your grocery store.

There are some specific things to keep in mind during your trip. Fruits and vegetables at a market generally are recorded in kilos (kilograms), as are your luggage at the airport and your body weight. (This latter is particularly pleasing to people of significant size, who, instead of weighing 220 pounds, hit the scales at a mere 100 kilos.) A kilo equals 2.2 pounds and 1 pound is .45 of a kilo. Body temperature usually is measured in degrees centigrade or Celsius rather than on the Fahrenheit scale, so that a normal body temperature is 37C, not 98.6F, and freezing is 0 degrees C versus 32F.

Gasoline is sold by the liter (approximately 3.8 to a 1 gallon). Tire pressure gauges and other equipment measure in kilograms per square centimeter rather than pounds per square inch. Highway signs are written in kilometers rather than miles (1 mile equals 1.6 km; 1 km equals .62 mile). And speed limits are in kilometers per hour, so think twice before hitting the gas when you see a speed limit of 100. That means 62 miles per hour.

The tables and conversion factors listed below should give you all the information you will need to understand any transaction, road sign, or map you encounter during your travels.

CONVERSION TABLES METRIC TO US MEASUREMENTS		
Multiply:	**by:**	**to convert to:**
LENGTH		
millimeters	.04	inches
meters	3.3	feet
meters	1.1	yards
kilometers	.6	miles
CAPACITY		
liters	2.11	pints (liquid)
liters	1.06	quarts (liquid)
liters	.26	gallons (liquid)
WEIGHT		
grams	.04	ounces (avoir.)
kilograms	2.2	pounds (avoir.)
US TO METRIC MEASUREMENTS		
LENGTH		
inches	25.0	millimeters
feet	.3	meters
yards	.9	meters
miles	1.6	kilometers
CAPACITY		
pints	.47	liters
quarts	.95	liters
gallons	3.8	liters
WEIGHT		
ounces	28.0	grams
pounds	.45	kilograms
TEMPERATURE $°F = (°C \times 9/5) + 32$ $°C = (°F - 32) \times 5/9$		

APPROXIMATE EQUIVALENTS		
Metric Unit	Abbreviation	US Equivalent
LENGTH		
meter	m	39.37 inches
kilometer	km	.62 mile
millimeter	mm	.04 inch
CAPACITY		
liter	l	1.057 quarts
WEIGHT		
gram	g	.035 ounce
kilogram	kg	2.2 pounds
metric ton	MT	1.1 tons
ENERGY		
kilowatt	kw	1.34 horsepower

Cameras and Equipment

 Vacations are everybody's favorite time for taking pictures and home movies. After all, most of us want to remember the places we visit — and show them off to others. Here are a few suggestions to help you get the best results from your travel photography or videography. For more information see *A Shutterbug's View* in DIVERSIONS.

BEFORE THE TRIP

If you're taking your camera or camcorder out after a long period in mothballs, or have just bought a new one, check it thoroughly before you leave to prevent unexpected breakdowns or disappointing pictures.

1. Still cameras should be cleaned carefully and thoroughly, inside and out. If using a camcorder, run a head cleaner through it. You also may want to have your camcorder professionally serviced (opening the casing yourself will violate the manufacturer's warranty). Always use filters to protect your lens while traveling.
2. Check the batteries for your camera's light meter and flash, and take along extras just in case yours wear out during the trip. For camcorders, bring along extra Nickel-Cadmium (Ni-Cad) batteries; if you use rechargeable batteries, a recharger will cut down on the extras.
3. Using all the settings and features, shoot at least one test roll of film or one videocassette, using the type you plan to take along with you.

EQUIPMENT TO TAKE ALONG

Keep your gear light and compact. Items that are too heavy or bulky to be carried comfortably on a full-day excursion will likely remain in your hotel room.

1. Invest in a broad camera or camcorder strap if you now have a thin one. It will make carrying the camera much more comfortable.
2. A sturdy canvas, vinyl, or leather camera or camcorder bag, preferably with padded pockets (not an airline bag), will keep your equipment organized and easy to find. If you will be doing much shooting around the water, a waterproof case is best.
3. For cleaning, bring along a camel's hair brush that retracts into a rubber squeeze bulb. Also take plenty of lens tissue, soft cloths, and plastic bags to protect equipment from dust and moisture.

FILM AND TAPES: If you are concerned about airport security X-rays damaging rolls of undeveloped still film (X-rays do not affect processed film) or tapes, store them in one of the lead-lined bags sold in camera shops. This possibility is not as much of a threat as it used to be, however. In both the US and Canada, incidents of X-ray damage to unprocessed film (exposed or unexposed) are few because low-dosage X-ray equipment is used virtually everywhere. If you're traveling without a protective bag, you may want to ask to have your photo equipment inspected by hand. One type of film that should never be subjected to X-rays is the very high speed ASA 1000 film; there are lead-lined bags made especially for it — and, in the event that you are refused a hand inspection, this is the only way to save your film. The walk-through metal detector devices at airports do not affect film, though the film cartridges may set them off.

You should have no problem finding film or tapes in Montreal and Quebec City. When buying film, tapes, or photo accessories the best rule of thumb is to stick to name brands with which you are familiar. The availability of film processing labs and equipment repair shops will vary.

USEFUL WORDS
AND PHRASES

Useful Words and Phrases

 Frequent travelers to France who've begun to pick up the language there are bound to be surprised by their first encounters with French-speaking Canadians. Don't be stunned if when settled into a taxi at the airport you're left speechless, not able to understand a word of the fast-talking cabbie. But rest easy. Parisians themselves at first cannot make head nor tail of their mother tongue spoken in parts of Canada. Yet once beyond those initial uncomfortable moments, you'll begin to pick up the differences in inflection, pronunciation, and vocabulary and find that your high school French is understood by Quebeckers, even though at times you may still be at sea.

What travelers tend not to think about is that the French language of Canadians, like the Spanish of Mexicans, has developed in isolation from the tongue of their forebears. Indeed, for centuries the French Canadian language and culture have gone it alone, so many words and phrases used in the province of Quebec are not used in France and vice versa. What the French of Canada do *not* share with their European counterparts, however, is a reputation for being either snobbish or brusque to tourists. *Au contraire.* French Canadians are almost unfailingly cordial and helpful, especially when you attempt to speak even a few words of their language. So don't be afraid of misplaced accents or misconjugated verbs — in most cases you will be understood and appreciated, and even pointed in the right direction. Those familiar with everyday phrases and a common French vocabulary on the other side of the Atlantic, however, will notice in the list below many differences between the two, not the least of which is a sense of informality (and colloquialism) — alien to Parisian purists.

In Montreal and parts of Quebec City, services in stores, restaurants, hotels, and almost all centers of tourism are a bilingual courtesy. Montreal, in particular, prides itself in being an international city and it's common for hotels to publish their service directories in three or four languages; most staff reception desks and conference facilities have multilingual personnel. A lot has been made about French-only signs in Quebec, but most travelers don't need an English sign to tell them a department store is a department store. Motorists, however, would do well to pick up a French phrase book — or at least learn the French words for the days of the week (*lundi, mardi, mercredi, jeudi, vendredi, samedi, dimanche*) to understand signs for street parking. Hope for the best when coping with the coin meters in Montreal's parking lots. The directions are complicated enough to confuse drivers in any language.

French words are stressed on the vowel preceding the last consonant in the word except that a final accented *e* (*è*) is stressed. Final consonants are pronounced only if they precede words beginning with vowels. Vowels preceding nasals (*m, n*) are nasalized (i.e., pronounced with emission of air through the nose) and the *m* or *n* is not pronounced.

French consonants are pronounced almost as in English with these exceptions:

ch is pronounced like *sh* in *push*
c before *e, i,* or *y* is pronounced *s;* otherwise as *k*

ç is pronounced as *s* before *a, o,* and *u*
s is pronounced as *z* between vowels
gn is pronounced like *ny* in canyon
g before *e,i,* or *y* is pronounced like *si* in vision; otherwise like *g* in *go*
j is pronounced like *si* in vision
ll following *i* is pronounced like *y* in year
qu is pronounced as *k* (not *kw*)
h is silent

French vowels are different from those in English, but usually can be pronounced intelligibly following these rules:

Final unaccented *e* is silent; it signals that a preceding consonant is pronounced.
é is pronounced like the *a* in *late*
è is pronounced as in *met*
i is pronounced as in *machine*
o is pronounced like *ou* in *ought*
u is pronounced like *e* in *beet* but with the lips rounded
an and *en* are pronounced like the *a* in *father* but nasalized
in is pronounced with the vowel of *met* but nasalized
ai is pronounced like *e* in *met*
au is pronounced like *o* in *cold*
oi and *oy* are pronounced *wa*
ou is pronounced as in *youth*
eu is pronounced like the *e* of *men* but with the lips rounded
Final *er* is pronounced like the *ay* of *delay*

Greetings and Everyday Expressions

Hello, goodbye, cheers, good luck!	*Salut!*
Good morning! (Hello!)	*Bonjour!*
Good afternoon, good evening!	*Bonsoir!*
How are you?	*Ça va?*
Not bad.	*Pas pire.*
No better than that?	*Pas plus que ça?*
I feel bad, eh?	*Je suis mauvais, la?*
Pleased to meet you!	*Enchanté!*
Good-bye!	*Au revoir!*
See you soon!	*A bientôt!*
Good night!	*Bonne nuit!*
Yes!	*Oui!*
No!	*Non!*
Please!	*S'il vous plaît!*
Thank you!	*Merci!*
You're welcome!	*De rien!*
Excuse me!	*Excusez-moi!* or *Pardonnez-moi!*
It doesn't matter.	*Ca m'est égal.*
I don't speak French.	*Je ne parle pas français.*
Do you speak English?	*Parlez-vous anglais?*
Please repeat.	*Répétez, s'il vous plaît.*
I don't understand.	*Je ne comprends pas.*
Do you understand?	*Vous comprenez?*

My name is . . .	*Je m'appelle . . .*
What is your name?	*Comment vous appelez-vous?*
You're very nice.	*Tu es bien gentil.*
Where is the men's/ladies' room?	*Où est le petit coin?*
French resident of Quebec	*Québécois/e*
old pioneer stock	*la vieille souche*
100% French lineage (also, pure wool)	*pure laine*
miss	*mademoiselle*
madame	*madame*
mister/sir	*monsieur*
open	*ouvert*
closed	*fermé*
entrance	*entrée*
exit	*sortie*
push	*poussez*
pull	*tirez*
today	*aujourd'hui*
tomorrow	*demain*
yesterday	*hier*
Help!	*Au secours!*
ambulance	*l'ambulance*
Get a doctor!	*Appelez le médecin!*

Checking In

I have (don't have) a reservation.	*J'ai une (Je n'ai pas de) réservation.*
I would like . . .	*Je voudrais . . .*
a single room	*une chambre pour une personne*
a double room	*une chambre pour deux*
a quiet room	*une chambre tranquille*
with bath	*avec salle de bain*
with shower	*avec douche*
with air conditioning	*une chambre climatisée*
with balcony	*avec balcon*
overnight only	*pour une nuit seulement*
a few days	*quelques jours*
a week (at least)	*une semaine (au moins)*
with full board	*avec pension complète*
with half board	*avec demi-pension*
Does that price include breakfast?	*Est-ce que le petit dejeuner est inclus?*
Are taxes included?	*Est-ce que les taxes sont compris?*
Do you accept traveler's checks?	*Acceptez-vous les chèques de voyage?*
Do you accept credit cards?	*Acceptez-vous les cartes de crédit?*

Eating Out

bottle	*une bouteille*
cup	*une tasse*
fork	*une fourchette*
knife	*un couteau*
spoon	*une cuillère*
napkin	*une serviette*
plate	*une assiette*
menu	*le carte*
wine list	*le carte des vins*
ashtray	*un cendrier*
(extra) chair	*une chaise (en sus)*
table	*une table*
coffee	*café*
black coffee	*café noir*
coffee with milk	*café au lait*
cream	*crème*
fruit juice	*jus de fruit*
lemonade	*citron pressé*
milk	*lait*
mineral water	
(non-carbonated)	*l'eau minérale*
(carbonated)	*l'eau gazeuse*
orangeade	*orange pressé*
tea	*thé*
water	*eau*
beer	*bière*
port	*vin de porto*
sherry	*vin de Xérès*
red wine	*vin rouge*
white wine	*vin blanc*
rosé	*rosé*
sweet	*doux*
(very) dry	*(très) sec*
cold	*froid*
hot	*chaud*
bacon	*bacon*
bread	*pain*
butter	*beurre*
eggs	*oeufs*
soft boiled	*à la coque*
hard boiled	*oeuf dur*
fried	*sur le plat*
scrambled	*brouillé*
poached	*poché*
omelette	*omelette*
ham	*jambon*

honey	*miel*
sugar	*sucre*
jam	*confiture*
juice	*jus*
orange	*jus d'orange*
tomato	*jus de tomate*
pepper	*poivre*
salt	*sel*
Waiter!	*Monsieur!* (Never *Garçon!* in Quebec.)
Waitress!	*Madame!* or *Mademoiselle!*
May I check my coat?	*Est-ce que je peux vous laisser mon manteau?*
I'll have . . .	*Je vais prendre . . .*
a snack	*une bouchée*
a glass of	*un verre de*
a bottle of	*une bouteille de*
a half bottle of	*une demie-bouteille*
a liter of	*un litre de*
a carafe of	*une carafe de*
The check, please.	*L'addition, s'il vous plaît.*
Can you change a $20?	*Avez-vous du change pour vingt piasses?*
Is the service charge included?	*Le service, est-il compris?*
I think there is a mistake in the bill.	*Je crois qu'il y a une erreur dans l'addition.*

Shopping

bakery	*boulangerie*
barber	*barbier*
bookstore	*librairie*
butcher store	*boucherie*
camera shop	*magasin de photographie*
clothing store	*magasin de vêtements*
convenience store	*dèpanneur*
delicatessen	*charcuterie*
department store	*grand magasin*
drugstore (for medicine)	*pharmacie*
grocery	*épicerie*
jewelry store	*bijouterie*
newsstand	*kiosque à journaux*
outfitting company for outdoor sports	*pouvoirie*
notions shop	*mercerie*
pastry shop	*pâtisserie*
perfume (and cosmetics) store	*parfumerie*
pharmacy/drugstore	*pharmacie*
shoestore	*magasin de chaussures*
supermarket	*supermarché*
tobacconist	*bureau de tabac*

cheap	*bon marché*
expensive	*cher*
large	*grand*
larger	*plus grand*
too large	*trop grand*
small	*petit*
smaller	*plus petit*
too small	*trop petit*
long	*long*
short	*court*
old	*vieux*
new	*nouveau*
used	*d'occasion*
handmade	*fabriqué à la main*

Is it machine washable?	*Est-ce que c'est lavable à la machine?*
How much does this cost?	*Quel est le prix?/Combien?*

What is it made of?	*De quoi est-il fait?*
camel's hair	*poil de chameau*
cotton	*coton*
corduroy	*velours côtelé*
filigree	*filigrane*
lace	*dentelle*
leather	*cuir*
linen	*lin*
silk	*soie*
suede	*daim*
synthetic	*synthétique*
wool	*laine*
wood	*bois*
brass	*cuivre jaune*
copper	*cuivre*
gold (plated)	*or (plaqué)*
silver (plated)	*argent (plaqué)*

May I have a sales tax rebate form?	*Puis-je avoir la forme pour la détaxe?*
May I pay with this credit card?	*Puis-je payer avec cette carte de crédit?*
May I pay with a traveler's check?	*Puis-je payer avec chèques de voyage?*

Getting around

north	*le nord*
south	*le sud*
east	*l'est*
west	*l'ouest*

right	*droite*
left	*gauche*
Go straight ahead	*tout droit*
far	*loin*
near	*proche*
map	*carte*
airport	*l'aéroport*
automobile	*le char*
bus	*autobus*
bus stop	*l'arrêt de bus*
gas station	*station service*
subway	*le métro*
trams	*le petits chars*
gasoline	*le gaz*
regular (leaded)	*ordinaire*
super (leaded)	*super*
unleaded	*sans plomb*
diesel	*diesel*
Fill it up, please.	*De plein, s'il vous plaît.*
tires	*les pneus*
oil	*l'huile*
train station	*la gare*
gate	*porte*
track	*voie*
one-way ticket	*aller simple*
round-trip ticket	*un billet aller et retour*
sleeping car	*le char dortois*
in first class	*en première*
in second class	*en deuxième*
no smoking	*défense de fumer*
Does this subway/bus go to . . . ?	*Est-ce que ce métro/bus va à . . . ?*
What time does it leave?	*A quelle heure part-il?*
Danger	*Danger*
Caution	*Attention*
Detour	*Détour*
Dead End	*Cul-de-sac*
Do Not Enter	*Défense de stationner*
No Parking	*Défense de garer*
No Passing	*Défense de doubler*
No U-turn	*Défense de faire demi-tour*
One way	*Sens interdit*
Pay toll	*Péage*
Pedestrian Zone	*Zone piétonnière*
Reduce Speed	*Ralentissez*

square (plaza)	*carré (place)*
Steep Incline	*Côte à forte inclination*
Stop	*Arrêt*
Use Headlights	*Allumez les phares*
Yield	*Cédez*
Where is the . . . ?	*Où se trouve . . . ?*
How many kilometers are we from . . . ?	*Combien de kilomètres sommes-nous de . . . ?*

Personal Items and Services

aspirin	*aspirine*
Band-Aids	*pansements*
bath	*bain*
bathroom	*salle de bain*
beauty shop	*salon de coiffeur*
condom	*préservatif*
dentist	*dentiste*
disposable diapers	*couches*
dry cleaner	*nettoyage à sec or teinturerie*
hairdresser	*coiffeur pour dames*
laundromat	*laundrette or blanchisserie automatique*
post office	*bureau de poste*
postage stamps (air mail)	*timbres (par avion)*
razor	*rasoir*
sanitary napkins	*serviettes hygiéniques*
shampoo	*shampooing*
shaving cream	*mousse à raser*
shower	*douche*
soap	*savon*
tampons	*tampons*
tissues	*mouchoirs (en papier)*
toilet	*le petit coin*
toilet paper	*papier hygiénique*
toothbrush	*brosse à dents*
toothpaste	*pâte dentrifice*

Days of the Week

Monday	*lundi*
Tuesday	*mardi*
Wednesday	*mercredi*
Thursday	*jeudi*
Friday	*vendredi*
Saturday	*samedi*
Sunday	*dimanche*

Months

January	*janvier*
February	*février*
March	*mars*
April	*avril*
May	*mai*
June	*juin*

July	*juillet*
August	*août*
September	*septembre*
October	*octobre*
November	*novembre*
December	*décembre*

Numbers

zero	*zéro*
one	*un*
two	*deux*
three	*trois*
four	*quatre*
five	*cinq*
six	*six*
seven	*sept*
eight	*huit*
nine	*neuf*
ten	*dix*
eleven	*onze*
twelve	*douze*
thirteen	*treize*
fourteen	*quatorze*
fifteen	*quinze*
sixteen	*seize*
seventeen	*dix-sept*
eighteen	*dix-huit*
nineteen	*dix-neuf*
twenty	*vingt*
twenty-one	*vingt-et-un*
thirty	*trente*
forty	*quarante*
fifty	*cinquante*
sixty	*soixante*
seventy	*soixante-dix*
eighty	*quatre-vingts*
ninety	*quatre-vingt-dix*
one hundred	*cent*
1993	*mille neuf cent quatre-vingt treize*

Colors

black	*noir*
blue	*bleu*
brown	*brun*
gray	*gris*
green	*vert*
orange	*orange*
pink	*rose*
purple	*violet*
red	*rouge*
yellow	*jaune*
white	*blanc*

Writing Reservations Letters

Restaurant/Hotel Name
Street Address
Quebec City or Montreal, Quebec
Postal Code, Canada

Dear Sir:

I would like to reserve a table for (number of) persons for lunch/dinner on (day and month), 199?, at (hour) o'clock.

or

I would like to reserve a room for (number of) people for (number of) nights.

Would you be so kind as to confirm the reservation as soon as possible?

I am very much looking forward to meeting you. (The French usually include a pleasantry such as this.)

With my thanks,
(Signature, followed by your typed name and address)

Monsieur:

Je voudrais réserver une table pour (number) personnes pour le déjeuner/dîner du (day and month) 199?, à (time using the 24-hour clock) heures.

or

Je voudrais réserver une chambre à (number) personne(s) pour (number) nuits.

Auriez-vous la bonté de bien vouloir me confirmer cette réservation dès que possible?

J'attends avec impatience la chance de faire votre connaissance.

Avec tous remerciements,

THE CITIES

THE CITIES

MONTREAL

Since 1535 — when Jacques Cartier first laid eyes on the St. Lawrence River village of Hochelaga, climbed with its Indian residents to the top of its 764-foot mountain, took a look at the 50-mile view, and exclaimed, "What a royal mount!" — the place has emerged as Canada's second-largest city, and is the third-largest French-speaking city (after Paris and Kinshasa, Zaire) in the world.

Yet some of the most dramatic changes on the face of Montreal have been etched in the past 30 years, with the construction of luxury hotels; the addition of a vast underground network of shops and services linked by a clean, efficient Métro system; an accretion of fashionable boutiques and excellent restaurants; and careful restorations in the historic quarter. Montreal's new look was sparked by a complete midtown face-lift during the 1960s, a renovation that gained momentum during *EXPO '67,* a world's fair that drew over 50 million people to Montreal and brought the city international attention. The increase in tourism continued throughout the early 1970s, and reached a peak in 1976, when Montreal hosted the *Summer Olympic Games.*

A second building boom in the 1980s transformed the downtown area with the completion of 12 major construction projects worth $1 million or more. They include the conversions of the former *Mount Royal* and *Windsor* hotels, both on Peel Street, into chic shopping, condo, and office complexes, along with the construction of several showy office towers.

The transformation has been so complete that some residents now claim they can't remember what Montreal looked like before. They exaggerate for effect. One of the first priorities when construction began was the preservation of Vieux Montréal (Old Montreal). No one considered destroying the historic city a reasonable way of effecting change, and as a result preservation and progress proceeded apace. The protection of special buildings extends to modern Montreal as well: The city's *Olympic Stadium* has become a spectacular sports facility open to the public, and the *EXPO '67* grounds on Ile Notre Dame (also part of the world's fair acreage) are now the site of the *Palais de la Civilisation,* the former French pavilion, which features one major cultural event each summer.

Compelling and cosmopolitan, Montreal sits on an anvil-shape island 32 miles long and 10 miles wide in the middle of the St. Lawrence River, some 170 miles (274 km) northeast of Lake Ontario. The river borders the city on the south and east and provides the crucial navigable link between the inland Great Lakes and the Atlantic Ocean. (The other great French city on the St. Lawrence, Quebec City, is 153 miles/245 km north of Montreal.) A narrow branch of the St. Lawrence, known as Rivière des Prairies, borders the city on the west and the north. From the top of Mount Royal residents can see all the surrounding river country. Except for Mount Royal, the island is flat.

The most appealing fact about Montreal, especially for Americans, is its Frenchness. Without jet lag and with a minimum of cost and bother, Americans have easy access to what is essentially a European city, providing the very best of the traditional French experience. Two-thirds of Montreal's more than 3 million inhabitants are of French origin. It only takes about two steps into the city to discover that you are truly in a foreign country. Montreal — like all of the surrounding province of Quebec — is proudly French, and it is the French Canadian patois that is heard all around. Nearly everyone is bilingual, but there is no question of the primary tongue.

What makes a visit to Montreal such a different experience from a visit to Quebec City is its size and sophistication: Montreal is simply more cosmopolitan. This is due in part to the city's more diverse population, which includes more than 100 ethnic groups. Sixteen percent of the non-French population is Anglo-Saxon; the remainder have roots in Central Europe, Greece, Italy, Hungary, or China. Montrèal has the country's largest Jewish population and a Chinese community of more than 50,000. Groups of Italians (the third-largest ethnic group), Hungarians, Greeks, Germans, and West Indians also have brought their traditions to Montreal.

The character of Montreal has not been radically changed by the influx of immigrants of varied cultures, however, as it has, for example, in Toronto. When large numbers of European settlers moved into Toronto, they managed to break the English-only monopoly on politics, money, and culture that had held the city in thrall since its founding, and transformed the nature of life there. Not so in Montreal. There is no mistaking that its population is predominantly and profoundly French. However, perhaps because Montreal was never the headquarters of the Catholic church (as was Quebec City), or because it passed some part of this century as a "sin city," it seems more ebullient and easygoing than Quebec City. The reasons for this subtle flavor of life — everywhere palpable but rarely tangible — must lie in its history.

When explorer-entrepreneur Samuel de Champlain reached Montreal's shores in 1603, he foresaw the great value of this natural transportation crossroad as an inland port and returned in 1611 to erect a trading post near the foot of the Lachine Rapids. (The ravages of warring tribes had left no trace of the Indian village of Hochelaga, first seen by Cartier.) The spot was christened Place Royale and is still a nucleus of commercial activity.

Champlain was followed by a succession of missionaries determined to convert the Indians to Christianity. In 1642 the permanent community of Ville Marie was founded at Place Royale (in what is now known as Vieux Montréal) by a small group led by the French career soldier Paul de Chomedey, Sieur de Maisonneuve. Shortly after their arrival, the colonists narrowly escaped being swept away in a disastrous flood. As a token of gratitude to God for their survival, they climbed Mount Royal's eastern slope and planted a wooden cross at the top. Today, the illuminated 100-foot steel cross that stands in its stead — and on a different site — can be seen for miles on clear nights.

While the flood did not obliterate Ville Marie, the Indians very nearly did. During the next 60 years, the rapidly growing colony of traders, explorers, and missionaries was besieged by numerous attacks; an open state of war existed with the Iroquois until an Indian treaty was signed in 1701.

In the 18th century, Montreal (the name Ville Marie was dropped during this period) prospered through its burgeoning fur trade, though not without difficulties. The Indians were quieted, but trouble with the English and Americans took its toll on the French settlement. In 1759, when Quebec City fell to the British as a result of the battle on the Plains of Abraham, the capital of New France moved briefly to Montreal. A year later Montreal, too, fell to the British.

During the American Revolution, the Americans eyed Montreal and Quebec City as potential extensions of the original 13 colonies. In November 1775, General Richard Montgomery marched on Montreal and occupied it without firing a shot. The American occupation lasted only 7 months, however, until June 1776, when Montgomery failed to capture Quebec City and Montreal returned to British rule.

Montreal's expansion under the British gained momentum during the early 19th century, when fur trading, shipbuilding, and railroading reached a crescendo. In 1832 Montreal was incorporated as a city, and by 1843 it was the capital of the province of Canada (an 1841 union of Upper and Lower Canada, encompassing today's provinces of Ontario and Quebec).

The city's expansion during the early 1900s began a period when Montreal justifiably bore the reputation of being a "wicked city"; prostitution, illegal gambling, and other vices flourished, mostly under the well-paid protection of the authorities.

By the end of the 1940s, the central section of Montreal was a dreary core of slums and run-down buildings (since completely vanished). A war on corruption, mounted during the 1950s by city official Jean Drapeau, wiped out the modern blot on the face of Montreal.

Called to act as public prosecutor in the city's police inquiry in 1950, Drapeau earned a reputation as an uncompromising foe of vice; this reputation got him elected Mayor of Montreal for the first time in 1954. Drapeau's administration initiated a time of change in both the face and feeling of Montreal as he presided over *EXPO '67* and the *Summer Olympic Games* of 1976, and remained a dominant force in city life and politics until his retirement a decade later.

The first renovation in Montreal was *Place Ville Marie,* an underground complex of shops, restaurants, and services in the heart of downtown, built to hide the ugly pityards of the *Canadian National Railway. Place Ville Marie* was only the first of six underground complexes in Montreal, each of which provides weatherproof access to hotels, office buildings, banks, stores, and two railway stations in different parts of the city, and is linked by the city's modern, quiet Métro system.

It was no sooner than the Métro began operation in 1966 that more than 50 million visitors flooded the city for *EXPO '67,* the 1967 world exposition.

The success of *EXPO* contributed to an explosion of daring construction undertaken by the city. During the 1960s and 1970s Montreal put up a stunning cultural and performing arts center, *Place des Arts* (home of the *Montreal Symphony Orchestra*); became one of the two Canadian cities with a major league baseball team, the Montreal *Expos* (Toronto has the *Blue Jays*); and hosted the *1976 Summer Olympics*.

At the same time that the city was acquiring its new look, municipal and provincial ordinances wisely assured the preservation of Vieux Montréal, designating the 95-acre waterfront sector a historical site.

The city spreads out in all directions from the peaks on Mount Royal, and probably the best way to appreciate the mountain and its surrounding Mount Royal Park is to hire one of the omnipresent *calèches*. These horse-drawn carriages seem to be stationed at every important tourist area around the city, and they can't be beaten as a means of sightseeing locomotion. Gone are the days when the *calèches* routinely changed the wheels of their carriages for sleigh runners, but during special occasions in winter you can still ride in a one-horse open sleigh through the snow and ice of Mount Royal Park; it's a magical experience.

In the course of meandering through Mount Royal Park, it's possible to assimilate a little local sociology along with an appreciation of the scenic beauty and arboreal pleasures. It is certainly no secret that a certain tension has always existed between the descendants of the original French founders and the progeny of the British conquerors. They live a fairly cordial coexistence, although former antipathies are still evident in Montreal's neighborhood patterns. To the west is Westmount, the "bedroom" for Montreal's prosperous English community. On the other side of the mountain is Outremont, the turf of the wealthy French inhabitants. Each community is equally affluent, but entirely separate, and it is easy to distinguish the lines of demarcation. As you ride along, just note the names of the passing apartment buildings. When the names cease being such Anglophilic gems as "The Trafalgar" and begin to take on the markedly Gallic cast of "Le Trianon," you'll know that you have "crossed the channel."

While England and France are enhancing their connections with the channel tunnel and the European Economic Community, Montreal and the province of Quebec seem to get farther and farther away from unity with English-speaking Canada. The province of Quebec's separatist movement found new momentum after Manitoba and Newfoundland refused to ratify the Meech Lake Accord, which (among other things) formally acknowledged the distinctiveness of French Canada. Since the failure of the accord in 1990, opinion polls in the province have shown support for independence running between 50% and 70%, based on continued economic ties with the rest of Canada.

But whichever course the province follows, it's safe to say that the city of Montreal always will offer a wide spectrum of sites and sounds. It would probably take about a week's conscientious effort to see just the most important sights, so visitors have to be a bit selective their first time around. But no one ever visits Montreal just once, so console yourself with the inevitability of there being a next time.

MONTREAL AT-A-GLANCE

SEEING THE CITY: Montreal has several vantage points from which to capture the sweep of the city, its mountain — 764-foot Mount Royal — the St. Lawrence River, and, on a clear day, beyond to the mountains of New York and Vermont. Two lookout points on Mount Royal itself offer spectacular views. To reach the Mount Royal Chalet Lookout, follow the path up from the Mount Royal Park parking lot or walk up Peel Street from downtown. Those traveling by car have access to an impressive view of the north and east at the lookout on the eastern slope of Camillien Houde Parkway, the only road over the mountain on which automobiles are permitted. From the *Olympic Stadium*'s 620-foot-high tower the view extends more than 50 miles on a clear day. A cable car with bay windows takes visitors to the top in 2 minutes. Closed from mid-January to mid-February. Admission charge.

The Westmount Lookout, also accessible by car, has an excellent view of the southwestern section of the city and surroundings. Arrows on the lookout's ledge indicate 22 points of interest, extending to the Green Mountains of Vermont and New York's Adirondacks. Ile Ste-Hélène and Ile Notre Dame offer magnificent views of downtown with a mountain backdrop.

The old clock tower on Victoria Wharf, refurbished and now an interpretative center tracing the Old Port's past, yields a vista of the harbor from its top story. From St. Joseph's Oratory (3800 Queen Mary Rd.) there is an excellent view of the northern part of the city.

Still other panoramas of Montreal can be seen while having lunch, cocktails, or dinner at the *Château Champlain*'s *L'Escapade* (1050 Gauchetière St. W.; phone: 878-1688); at *Le Grand* hotel's *Tour de Ville* (777 University St.; phone: 879-1370); or at the *Point de Vue* restaurant in the *Sheraton Centre* hotel (1201 René-Lévesque Blvd. W.; phone: 878-2000).

SPECIAL PLACES: The best way to get a feel for Montreal is by walking through its streets and parks. Because of its layout, Montreal is easy to cope with on foot. Though not exactly true in direction, Montreal's street plan is laid out on a north-south, east-west axis. Each block covers approximately 100 numbers. The east-west numbering starts at St. Lawrence Boulevard, so the street number 900 West, for example, is 9 blocks west of St. Lawrence. The north-south numbers start at the river and run north, following the same formula. Most interesting to the visitor is the area wedged between the river on the south and east and Mount Royal on the north and west.

Anyone who wearies quickly or would like to visit places farther afield should head for the nearest Métro station and hop aboard a soundless, rubber-tired train. The city's four subway lines put visitors within proximity of the most important attractions.

UNDERGROUND MONTREAL

Also called *la ville souterraine,* this below-street-level network of commercial-business-residential complexes is for many as vital a part of Montreal as the city above ground. Conceived by architect I. M. Pei and developer William Zeckendorf during the 1950s, *Place Ville Marie,* Montreal's first subterranean complex, opened in 1962. Montrealers took to it immediately, moving underground to shop, socialize, and seek refuge from inclement weather and city traffic. Its successful reception prompted a gradual expansion into other sections of the city, and today the network extends some 16 pedestrian miles. All the centers, known as *"places,"* are linked by the Métro system. Plans exist for further subterranean development in the first decade of the 21st century.

Because there is such a wide variety of attractions and services underground, it's possible to spend days in Montreal without ever going outside. Many Montrealers do just that — especially when winter dumps 100 inches of snow on the city. The complex networks offer access to the city's main sports facilities, exhibits, and performing arts centers, about 1,700 shops, 200 restaurants, 8 major hotels, the 2 main rail and bus terminals, numerous banks and apartment buildings, 34 cinemas and theaters, some 13,000 indoor parking spaces, and even a municipal library branch at the McGill Métro station. Reasonably priced tours of Underground Montreal are conducted by *Guidatour* (phone: 844-4021), *Visites de Montréal* (phone: 933-6674), *Gray Line* (phone: 934-1222), and *Hertz Tourist Guide* (phone: 937-6690).

Place Ville Marie – The city's first underground complex has had a face-lift since its debut and now houses over 85 boutiques and stores as well as *Les Cours de la Place,* an elegant marble and brass fast-food market with everything from Baskin-Robbins ice cream to Oriental snacks. Interconnecting promenades link *Place Ville Marie* with *Place Bonaventure* and *Place du Canada,* forming an underground core of some 200 shops, 20 restaurants and bars, and entrances to three major hotels — the *Queen Elizabeth,* Hilton's *Bonaventure International* hotel, and *Château Champlain.* Enter *Place Ville Marie* through the *Queen Elizabeth* (900 René-Lévesque Blvd.), or on Cathcart St. at the foot of McGill College Ave.

Place Bonaventure – Linked to *Place Ville Marie* by walkways leading through Central Station, this 6-acre arcade houses about 100 shops that carry fashions, handicrafts, and furniture from around the world. Above the shopping concourse are a merchandise market, an exhibition hall, and the *Bonaventure International* hotel. Enter *Place Bonaventure* through the *Bonaventure International* hotel (at the corner of Gauchetière and Mansfield Sts.), or through *Château Champlain* (1050 Gauchetière St. W.).

Place Montreal Trust – One of the newer additions to the Underground City network, this 5-level atrium houses 145 shops, including 120 specialty stores, in a sunny, California-style setting of cool pastels, waterfalls, reflecting pools, and greenery. Sunlight filters through a rooftop skylight into the second basement level. The *Place* has underground links with its neighbors above and below Ste-Catherine Street. Following the Métro corridors, shoppers can walk from here to *Eaton Centre, Les Promenades de la Cathédrale,* and *La Baie.* Enter via McGill Métro station or 1600 McGill College.

Eaton Centre (Le Centre Eaton de Montréal) – The largest shopping center in downtown Montreal opened in 1990 with 5 tiers of boutique-lined galleries under its glass roof. Linked to *Eaton's* department store, the center maintains 250 stores and also houses restaurants and fast-food outlets. A cinema complex of five theaters is on the top floor. Part of the Underground City, it opens into McGill Métro station. Street level entrance, 705 Ste-Catherine St. W.

Les Promenades de la Cathédrale – Two levels of underground shopping are hidden away beneath Christ Church Cathedral, with more than 100 shops linked to *La Baie, Eaton Centre,* and the Métro. Enter via McGill Métro station or 652 Ste-Catherine St. W.

2020 University – With 30 retail outlets, this University Street complex is part of the underground commerical core linked to the Ste-Catherine Street group through McGill Métro station.

Les Cours Montréal – Four levels of elegant commercial space have been incorporated into this complex within the remodeled *Sheraton Mount Royal* hotel. *Les Cours* houses 60 boutiques, 3 restaurants, a fast-food court, and a cinema. Enter via Peel Métro station; street-level entrances at 1455 Peel St. and 1550 Metcalf St.

Place Dupuis – One of a cluster of small, interconnected shopping centers opening into Berri-UQAM Métro station, the *Place* adjoins *Les Galeries Dupuis*. Together they have 40 retail and service outlets and both have access to *Les Atriums,* a shopping mall with 2 levels of 30 boutiques. Enter *Place Dupuis* through the Métro or 845 Ste-Catherine St. E.; *Les Atriums* via the Métro or 870 de Maisonneuve Blvd. E.

Bell-Banque Nationale Towers – Joined to the pedestrian passageway between *Place Victoria* and the Beaver Hall Hill building, these two office towers have increased the Underground City's shopping and dining potential with a 2-tiered mall of boutiques, and a large restaurant complex on the lower level. It is also connected to the *Place Victoria* Métro station.

Place Victoria – Facing Victoria Square, this massive office tower is the tallest building in Montreal (47 stories) and home to the Montreal Stock Exchange and yet another underground shopping mall. Stock Exchange tours are given by reservation only. Admission charge (phone: 871-2424). The complex is connected to *Le Grand* hotel and the *Place Victoria* Métro station.

Place Alexis Nihon – A short subway ride away from the central core, this plaza offers more weatherproofed shopping. Some 80,000 people pass through the complex each day en route to the office building, apartment tower, 3-floor shopping mall, and covered parking levels. 1500 Atwater; take the Métro to Atwater.

Westmount Square – French high-fashion designers are represented in this poshest of Montreal's underground plazas, just a stroll away from *Place Alexis Nihon.* Situated directly beneath three gleaming office towers designed by Mies van der Rohe are a deli, restaurants, cinemas, and china and jewelry shops. But the main attractions are the salons of *Guy Laroche* and *Cacharel.* Take the Métro to Atwater.

Place des Arts – The heart of Montreal's cultural life is its lavish performing arts center, which contains a stunning and acoustically superb concert hall and theater accommodating over 5,000 people. Home of the *Montreal Symphony Orchestra, Les Grands Ballets Canadiens,* and the *Montreal Opera,* it is also the setting for chamber music concerts, ballet recitals, and plays. On Sunday mornings, the lobby of the center hosts *"Sons et Brioche,"* informal concerts served up with a continental breakfast. (Tickets — very reasonably priced ones, at that — are available at *Place des Arts* half an hour prior to performance.) 175 Ste-Catherine St. W.; take the Métro to *Place des Arts* (phone: 842-2112 for program and ticket information).

Complexe Desjardins – This impressive complex contains meeting halls, offices, and an enclosed shopping center with some 100 boutiques and specialty stores and 20 restaurants. Sculptures, fountains, plants, and a regular series of entertainment events and special exhibits make it a popular gathering place. It's linked by an underground walkway to *Place des Arts.*

Complexe Guy Favreau – Yet another complex, this one houses offices, apartments, and boutiques, as well as the *National Film Board*'s movie theater, and connects to the *Complexe Desjardins* and the city's old convention center. The convention center mall also melds with the Chinatown pedestrian plaza, lined with Oriental shops and restaurants.

OLD MONTREAL

Both private enterprise and government funds are contributing to the restoration of important buildings in Vieux Montréal, the city's historic waterfront section. The area can be toured by car or horse-drawn *calèche,* but the best way to get a feel for it is by strolling through the narrow streets, armed with a detailed guidebook to the area. Get a free copy of *A Walking Tour of Vieux Montréal* from INFOTOURISTE, in the Dominion Square Building (Dorchester Sq. at Peel St.; phone: 871-1595), or its satellite center (on the corner of Pl. Jacques-Cartier and Notre Dame St. in Old Montreal). Highlights include the following:

Notre Dame Basilica – Opened in 1829, this building was designed in neo-Gothic style by New York architect James O'Donnell, whose grave lies in the church basement. In addition to its monumental altar and exquisite woodcarvings and paintings, the church houses an organ with 5,772 pipes and a small museum in the sacristy, open on weekends only from 9 AM to 5 PM for a small admission fee. Adjacent to the main church is the restored Sacred Heart Chapel (Sacré-Coeur). The stained glass windows depict the early history of Montreal. Before leaving, step into the Place d'Armes and glance up at the twin spires to get a true perspective of the church's scale. Open daily. Place d'Armes (phone: 849-1070).

Saint Sulpice Seminary – Sightseers aren't welcome inside the oldest building in Montreal (1685) because it's still a private home for Sulpician priests, but they can admire its weathered gray-stone façade through the wrought-iron gateway to the front courtyard. Photographers and students of historic architecture admire the symmetrical windows and dormers and the campanile over the main entrance, which, according to local historians, is the oldest outdoor clock in North America (1710). 130 Notre Dame St. W.

Place Jacques-Cartier – This cobblestone square, the largest in Old Montreal, was once the main marketplace. Now it's the hub of Old Montreal activity and is lined with attractive restaurants and restored houses. Dominating the square is a statue of Horatio Nelson atop a 35-foot column (erected in 1809). In warm weather, there is a flower market at the base of the column, offering blossoms of every conceivable size and hue; in autumn, apples and pumpkins are sold. Alfresco cafés line both sides of the square, perfect for relaxing and drinking in the flavor of the early 19th century. Between St-Paul and Notre Dame.

Vieux Port – Developed as a government project a decade ago, the Old Port is now a summertime entertainment center. The port itself has undergone extensive renovation of late with the addition of parkland, flowers, and fountains along the length of the federally owned dock area. Now strollers may rest on a bench and take in the waterfront as it was some 100 years ago. Bikers can rent wheels at the port to explore its waterfront trails, and the park area has been extended to include a new marina for pleasure craft at Basin Bonsecours. Encouraged by this government move to bring back the once-neglected harbor, nearby companies and property owners have refurbished their buildings with charming courtyards and outdoor cafés. The *Vieux Port Festival* kicks off the season on *St-Jean-Baptiste Day* (June 24), and events continue until *Labour Day*. Daily activities include puppet shows, clowns, movies, dancing, and theater (all free); at night, the large outdoor stage facing the harbor might host the *Montreal Symphony Orchestra* or various rock groups. There also are summer exhibitions in the Vieux Port at the *Expotec* (phone: 496-4629) and *Image du Futur* (phone: 849-1612). The *IMAX Cinema* has a giant 7-story-high screen (phone: 496-IMAX). An immense flea market with piles of secondhand bargains is here, too. The former Louis-Jolliet passenger ship terminal hosts exhibitions every summer. A favorite summer stop is the garden restaurant at *Gibby's* in the Youville courtyard (near the waterfront, at the foot of Pl. d'Youville; phone: 282-1837).

Château Ramezay – The manor, built in 1705, originally served as the residence of French governors in Montreal. It later housed the offices of the West India Company and, still later, was the residence of English governors. During the American occupation between 1775 and 1776, the Continental Army, under Generals Richard Montgomery and Benedict Arnold, established its headquarters here. Today the château is a fine historical museum, with exhibits reflecting its own past as well as that of Montreal. Closed Mondays except from June through August. Admission charge. 280 Notre Dame St. E. (phone: 861-3708).

Notre Dame de Bonsecours Chapel – One of the city's oldest churches, it is also called the Sailors' Chapel because of the large number of sailors who worship here. Built originally in 1657, it was destroyed by fire and twice rebuilt and modified. The present chapel dates from 1771, the façade from 1895. Inside, note the votive lamps in the shape of model ships, placed there by mariners as tokens of their faith. A series of dolls and miniatures in a small museum upstairs depicts the life of Ste-Marguerite Bourgeoys, foundress of the Congregation of Notre Dame order of nuns and Canada's first saint. (Marguerite Borgeoys was French-born; Marguerite d'Youville, canonized in 1990, was the first Canadian-born saint.) More energetic visitors may hike to the spire's summit for an uplifting view of the harbor and historic quarter. Church open daily; museum closed Mondays. Admission charge for the museum. 400 St. Paul St. E. (phone: 845-9991).

Place d'Youville – One of the first civic centers built in Montreal, Place d'Youville is now surrounded by monuments and historic sites. An interesting landmark is Fire Station 1, which has been restored and now houses the *Montreal History Centre,* which was completely revamped in 1990 and today presents various exhibits on the cultural mosaic of the city. It has a synchronized audiovisual presentation that leads visitors through 11 display rooms and 400 years of history. Permanent exhibits include an old streetcar, a "talking" telephone booth, and a simulated shoe factory. Periodic expositions feature Montreal's past. Closed Mondays, holidays, and from mid-September to mid-May. Admission charge. South of St-Paul St. W. For information, call 872-3207.

ELSEWHERE IN THE CITY

Angrignon Park – A 262-acre recreational oasis summer and winter, this park is at its busiest from mid-December to late March, when it becomes the city's winter wonderland, a place for all kinds of free outdoor fun, from cross-country skiing, snowshoeing, and skating on the decorated rink to thrilling slides down the icy toboggan run. 3400 Trinitaires Blvd. Get off at Angrinon Métro station.

Olympic Park – Having hosted the *1976 Summer Olympic Games,* Montreal is now using these spectacular facilities for all types of sports events and exhibits. The Montreal *Expos* play at the all-weather stadium, with its tower and retractable roof. A restaurant and observation deck offer panoramic views of the city. Meets, classes, and public swimming periods are held regularly in the 50-meter pool and 50-foot diving pool. The guided tour that offers a behind-the-scenes look at the facilities is 45 minutes well spent. The tour explains some of the facility's impressive, technologically advanced features — the ripple and bubble machines, for example, enable diving coaches to instantly create air bubbles on the surface of the pool to protect a diver from the impact of a bad dive. Tours in English are conducted daily, except holidays. Admission charge. 4545 Pierre-de-Coubertin Ave.; take the Métro to Viau (phone: 252-8687 or 252-4737).

Biodome of Montreal – Part of the Olympic Park, this new environmental museum of four ecosystems is flourishing in the former *Velodrome,* where cyclists competed in the *1976 Olympic Games.* The building houses reconstructions of a quartet of natural environments — found in South, Central, and North America — in a combined zoo, aquarium, and botanical garden complex. Environments include tropical and Laurentian forests and St. Lawrence marine and polar ecosystems. Bilingual tours are conducted daily. Admission charge. 4545 Pierre-de-Coubertin Ave. (phone: 252-8687 or 252-4737).

Botanical Garden – Across from the Olympic Park, this noted horticultural showplace was founded by naturalist Brother Marie Victorin. Actually a complex of some 30 specialized gardens and 10 greenhouses, there are more than 26,000 different species and varieties of plants on display, grouped according to use (economical, medicinal, ornamental) and habitat. The garden, said to have North America's most complete collection of bonsai trees and the country's largest and grandest exhibition greenhouse, is in the midst of expansion. The highly acclaimed Japanese gardens opened during the summer of 1988, and the Insectarium, a giant bug house with thousands of live insects on display, was completed in 1990. With the recent addition of the traditional Chinese Garden, Montreal's botanical garden has become the second-largest in the world (after London's Kew Gardens). The visitors' reception center presents video, art, and photographic displays on the world of botany. A mini-train tour is conducted by bilingual guides. Open daily. Admission charge for greenhouses. 4101 Sherbrooke St. E. (phone: 872-1400).

Mount Royal – Because it dominates the city scene, visitors can't avoid seeing Mount Royal from one angle or another (the mountain has two peaks: Mount Royal and Westmount). But lovely Mount Royal Park, planned by the renowned landscape architect Frederick Law Olmsted, of New York City's Central Park fame, is worth a closer look. Not only is it a fine vantage point from which to view the St. Lawrence River, Montreal, and the mountains beyond, it is also a good spot from which to observe Montrealers at their leisure. Local residents use the 500-acre park year-round, but it's especially busy in winter, when there's skiing, skating, and horse-drawn sleigh rides (they're for hire in the park). In summer, Beaver Lake is the site of twice-weekly folk dancing, and the audience is invited to participate. The Université de Montréal, the second-largest French-speaking university in the world, is located on the north side of Mount Royal; and St. Joseph's Oratory, described below, is on Westmount's north slope. The park is bounded by Avenue du Parc on the east and, continuing counterclockwise, Avenue du Mont-Royal, Camillien Houde Parkway, Chemin Remembrance, Côte des Neiges, and Avenue des Pins.

St. Joseph's Oratory – For more than 2 million people each year, a visit to this shrine is reason enough for a trip to Montreal. Even those who don't make a pilgrimage up the 99 steps to the basilica will notice the oratory's monumental dome as a distinctive landmark on the city's skyline. The church was founded in 1904 by Brother André of the Congregation de Ste-Croix for the glorification of St. Joseph, the patron saint of Canada. Brother André, said to have had great healing power, is entombed here. Organ recitals are given on Wednesdays during the summer at 8 PM (admission charge), and the children's choir *Les Petits Chanteurs du Mont-Royal* performs Sundays at 11 AM. Crèches from around the world are featured every *Christmas*. The building is open daily from 6:30 AM to 9:30 PM; the museum is open daily from 10 AM to 5 PM. 3800 Queen Mary Rd. (phone: 733-8211).

St-Denis Street – This area, known as Montreal's Latin Quarter, is the site of the Université du Québec à Montréal campus. It features a pleasant square with an agora, fountains, and an art gallery. The façade of historic St-Jacques Cathedral has been integrated into the institution's main building. St-Denis Street and its theater (*Théâtre St-Denis*) were the original hosts to the city's annual *Jazz Festival* in early July, and they still provide the sites for many events in this now much-expanded 10-day musicfest (see *Special Events*). The street is also popular for its restaurants and attracts an academic crowd to its bookshops, art galleries, and coffeehouses. St-Denis, above Sherbrooke Street, has gained a reputation as a fashion hub due to the many up-and-coming Quebec designers who have showrooms and boutiques here.

Westmount – This mountainside "city within a city" was traditionally the enclave of Montreal's wealthy English-speaking population. Today, the residents of this high-rent district must still be wealthy to maintain themselves in Westmount fashion, but the "English only" requisite has eased somewhat as the city's cultures have blended. This is the section of town for house staring, or more appropriately, mansion staring. West Mount, the palatial stone house that gave the area its name and was owned by *Beaver Steamship Line*'s William Murray, has been torn down, but there are a number of other impressive examples of 19th- and early-20th-century homes (and a few even earlier landmarks) to fill the gap. The sturdy of limb can take the Métro to Atwater station, which is linked to elegant Westmount Square, and start a walking tour of the area from there. But because of Westmount's hills, the less hearty may prefer to see it by car. The most interesting sights fall between Ste-Catherine and Edgehill Streets, from Greene Avenue to Victoria Avenue.

Outremont – The traditional French-speaking counterpart to English-speaking Westmount is the "ville" of Outremont, hidden on the northeast slope of Mount Royal. Incorporated in 1875, the village was principally made up of large tracts of farmland owned and cultivated by elite residents. While the farms have long since been divided into smaller building lots, some of the original old farmhouses still exist. Outremont's terrain is easily as rugged as Westmount's, so it is best explored by car. The section's main thoroughfare, Côte Ste-Catherine, and the parallel Maplewood Avenue display the best of Outremont's marvelous mansions, and Laurier Avenue is lined with smart boutiques and cafés. Try *Café Laurier* (394 Laurier W.; phone: 273-2484) for a relaxing coffee break. Bounded north and south by Glendale Avenue and Mont Royal Boulevard, east and west by Hutchinson and Canterbury Avenues.

Museum of Fine Arts – Galleries in this neo-classical building house an impressive permanent collection of European, Canadian, and Eastern art as well as frequent special exhibits. Canada's oldest fine arts museum (1860), it has staged a string of highly regarded international exhibitions, including Picasso, Miró, the Vatican Collection, Leonardo da Vinci, and Chagall. Across the street and linked to the older building by an underground passage is Israeli-born architect Moshe Safdie's striking new addition, opened in 1991. Safdie, a graduate of McGill University, is best known for designing the *National Gallery of Canada* in Ottawa and *La Musée de la Civilisation* in Quebec City. The new complex triples the museum's display space, which has been used for both traveling shows and to display works of art that have spent years in storage vaults. Free guided tours of permanent and temporary exhibitions. Closed Mondays. Admission charge. 1379 Sherbrooke St. W. (phone: 285-1600).

McCord Museum of Canadian History – Reopened last spring after a major expansion project as part of Montreal's 350th anniversary celebrations, the museum has one of the largest Amerindian and Inuit collections in Canada. History buffs will delight in the Notman Photographic Archives of more than 700,000 glass negatives and plates, recording an intimate history of Montreal, its people, buildings, and street scenes between 1856 and the early years of the 20th century. Open Tuesdays, Wednesdays, and Fridays, 10 AM to 6 PM; Thursday, 10 AM to 9 PM; Saturdays and Sundays, 10 AM to 5 PM. Closed Mondays and holidays. Admission charge. 690 Sherbrooke St. W. (phone: 398-7100).

McGill University – Chartered in 1821, this prestigious school was built with funds from the estate of Scottish immigrant James McGill, who amassed a fortune as a fur trader and served in Lower Canada's Parliament. The campus is close to the site of the 16th-century Indian town of Hochelaga, discovered by Cartier in 1535. A stroll around the campus and down fashionable Sherbrooke Street reveals a number of interesting architectural façades, including some fine old mansions that now belong to the university. Guided tours of the university grounds can be arranged by calling 398-6555. During the summer, McGill provides inexpensive accommodations in its dormitories, with cafeteria service and sports facilities available to guests. Call 398-6367 for information.

University of Montreal (Université de Montréal) – Opened in 1876 as a branch of Quebec City's Laval University, the "U of M" has developed into the largest French-language university outside of Paris, with 58,000 students and 220 undergraduate programs. The Mount Royal campus opened in 1943 and now accommodates 13 faculties, more than 60 research units, and affiliated schools of engineering and commerce, as well as a huge sports complex. 2900 Edouard-Montpetit Blvd. (phone: 343-6111).

Mackay to de la Montagne – A concentration of restaurants, pubs, discos, trendy fashion boutiques, and art galleries ensconced in brownstone and gray-stone Victorian houses is centered in this 9-square-block downtown area that visitors are bound to discover sooner or later. Whether for browsing, shopping, or bar-hopping, this is where the action is, and in good weather much of it is out on the street. *Thursdays* (1449 Crescent St.; phone: 288-5656) is a nice place to eat or have a drink. Mackay, Bishop, Crescent, and de la Montagne (Mountain in English) Sts. between Sherbrooke St. and René-Lévesque Blvd.

Prince Arthur Pedestrian Mall – Once a quiet residential street, part of McGill's low-cost student ghetto from the 1950s to the early 1970s, today the stretch of Prince Arthur from St. Laurent Boulevard to St. Louis Square has been transformed into an attractive mall. Enhanced by a fountain, overflowing tubs of flowers, and street lamps, it is currently home to an array of moderately priced restaurants that run the gamut of ethnicities from Greek and Italian to Vietnamese, Polish, and Quebecoise. People watchers will find summer a great time to take advantage of one of the many outdoor cafés that line this lovely street. Most of the restaurants are BOW (bring own wine). Summer is also the season for outdoor performances by local musicians, magicians, and acrobats.

Dow Planetarium – Outer space is highlighted in this giant theater of the stars, the first of Canada's planetariums, a gift to the city from Dow Brewery Ltd. in the mid-1960s. Its special programs change at various times of the year and are narrated in French and English on alternate hours (call for times). Closed Mondays during the day, and on some holidays. Admission charge. 1000 St-Jacques W. (phone: 872-4656).

Maison Radio–Canada – One of the world's largest and most modern radio and television centers, the Canadian Broadcasting Company (CBC) headquarters of French and English broadcasting sprawls over 25 acres in downtown Montreal. The 23-story hexagonal building that houses the studios also has galleries and an extensive collection of paintings, sculptures, and graphics done mostly by artists of Quebec and the Atlantic Provinces. Visitors are allowed at only a limited number of shows. Call ahead for more information. 1400 René-Lévesque Blvd. (phone: 597-7787).

St. Lawrence Seaway – Montreal is the starting point of this modern engineering miracle, which makes it possible for ocean-bound ships to travel all the way through the Great Lakes. Often missed by the average visitor, the observatory at the St. Lambert Lock offers a close look at the intricate locking procedures. Ships from the ocean must be raised and lowered some 15 feet as they pass through the lock. The observation tower also commands a fine view of Montreal's skyline across the St. Lawrence River. A scenic bicycle path runs along the lock. Open May to mid-October; weekends only September and October. No admission charge. Take the Victoria Bridge from downtown across to St. Lambert Lock on Route 132 on the south shore of the river (phone: 672-4110).

■**EXTRA SPECIAL:** The largest of Montreal's St. Lawrence River satellite islands is Ile Ste-Hélène, which Samuel de Champlain named after his wife, Hélène Boulé. It was once the site of a military installation and, more recently, part of the extensive grounds of *EXPO '67*, which also included its neighboring island, Ile Notre Dame. (When the fair was over, these facilities were renamed Man and His World, after *EXPO*'s main theme.) There's plenty to do on these two islands, which are linked to the city proper by two bridges — Pont de la Concorde and Pont Jacques-Cartier — as well as by the Métro system. Get off at the Ile Ste-Hélène stop on the Métro.

Ile Notre Dame – Its annual *Floralies* flower show has been so successful that the island has become a popular year-round park. Pedal-boat rentals are an ideal way to explore the island's canals in summer. This is also the site of Montreal's first downtown beach. In winter, the frozen canals become huge ice skating rinks. Snowshoeing, cross-country skiing, and horse-drawn sleigh rides can also be enjoyed. Other sites here include the *Olympic* rowing basin, which is transformed into a skating rink during winter; the *Canadian Grand Prix* racetrack, *Gilles Villeneuve Circuit;* and the *Palais de la Civilisation* exhibition center. Exhibition center open May to October. Admission charge for exhibition center only (phone: 872-4560).

Ile Ste-Hélène – *La Ronde,* a rollicking amusement park, covers 135 acres of this island. In addition to rides, *La Ronde* has spirited restaurants and pubs that Montrealers frequent on warm summer evenings (especially from the end of May to mid-June when it's the launching pad for a 10-day *Fireworks Festival*), and an Aquapark with waterslides, and swimming and wading pools. Open mid-June to *Labour Day.* Admission charge (phone: 872-6222).

The *David M. Stewart Museum* (formerly the *Military and Marine Museum*) in Ile Ste-Hélène's Old Fort (built in the early 1820s by order of the Duke of Wellington) houses historic uniforms, military equipment, and model ships. It features special historical displays June to November (weather permitting), and also hosts several temporary exhibitions during the year. In the summer, two colorfully uniformed resident companies of colonial troops — La Compagnie Franche de la Marine (French) and Fraser's Highlanders (Scottish) — perform authentic 18th-century drills and marches. Open daily, except Tuesdays, year-round. Admission charge (phone: 861-6701).

The *Festin du Gouverneur* restaurant in the Old Fort invites diners to enjoy an 18th-century banquet served by costumed performers who sing, dance, and draw patrons into the act. Reservations required (phone: 879-1141). The island is also the site of *Hélène de Champlain* restaurant in an attractive mock Normandy–style building overlooking the river and the rose gardens that remain from *EXPO '67* (phone: 395-2424).

Every winter, in late January, Iles Ste-Hélène and Notre Dame and Old Montreal play host to *La Fête des Neiges,* a 10-day pre-*Lenten* snow carnival that includes costume balls on ice, skating races, sledding, and other outdoor activities, all aided and abetted by plentiful refreshments. Imaginative snow sculptures are part of the fun. The frosty art has become so popular that it has made its way across the St. Lawrence and can be seen in Vieux Montréal as well (phone: 872-0210).

■**Note:** The Laurentian Mountains — called Les Laurentides by French Canadians — extend from 20 to 80 miles (32 to 128 km) north of Montreal and contain some of the best ski and all-season resorts in eastern North America (see *Skiing* in DIVERSIONS).

SOURCES AND RESOURCES

TOURIST INFORMATION: INFOTOURISTE (1001 Dorchester Sq.; phone: 873-2015; 800-363-7777 from the US) has visitors' information, maps, brochures, and a city guidebook for the handicapped. These also are available at the tourist bureau kiosks at the international tourist reception center in the Dorchester Square Building off Peel Street, in Place Jacques-Cartier, and in the Dorval and Mirabel airports.

Local Coverage – There is one daily English-language newspaper, the *Montreal Gazette,* available at newsstands every morning. The free weekly English newspaper *Mirror,* available in restaurants, cafés, and bars, gives a complete listing of entertainment and cultural activities. The monthly *Scope* magazine, available at newsstands, also has entertainment and restaurant listings.

Food – INFOTOURISTE publishes an annual restaurant guide. Restaurant reviews appear regularly in the newspapers and *Scope* magazine.

 TELEPHONE: The area code for Montreal is 514.

 CURRENCY: All prices are quoted here in US dollars unless otherwise indicated.

Sales Tax – Quebec has a provincial sales tax of 7% to 9%, depending on what is being purchased. In addition, a 7% federal tax, called the Goods and Services Tax (GST), is levied on most purchases. In many cases, visitors can receive refunds of both the provincial and federal taxes. For details on Quebec tax rebates, call 800-567-4692. For GST rebate information see *Calculating Costs* in GETTING READY TO GO.

GETTING AROUND: Car Rental – Montreal is served by *Avis* (1225 Metcalfe St.; phone: 866-7906); *Budget* (1460 Guy St.; phone: 937-9121); *Hertz* (1076 de la Montagne St.; phone: 393-1717); *Thrifty* (1600 Berri St.; phone: 845-5954); *Tilden* (1200 Stanley St.; phone: 878-2771), and *Via Route* (1255 Mackay St.; phone: 871-1166). See also "Car Rental" in *On Arrival,* GETTING READY TO GO.

Métro and Bus – *STCUM,* the city transit system, is an efficient network linking various areas of the city with four different underground lines and 150 bus lines. (The same tickets are used on the Métro and the buses.) Métro trains are clean and quiet, whizzing underground on rubber-tired wheels. The price of the Métro ride (about $1.50 per ride; about $6 for six tickets) also admits visitors to a veritable underground art gallery of murals, sculptures, stained glass windows, enameled steel frescoes, and ceramics built into exhibits in the 65 stations of the system. *STCUM* issues a helpful, complimentary map of the routes, available at hotel desks and all Métro station ticket booths. For 24-hour information about service, call 288-6287.

Harbor Cruises – A scenic and restful way to see the entire island is from the St. Lawrence; *Montreal Harbor Cruises* has several tours departing from Victoria Pier at the foot of Berri Street daily from May 1 through October 15. Ticket prices vary with the cruise (phone: 842-3871). In addition, *Amphibustour* (phone: 386-1298) travels on both the streets and waters of the port; a ferryboat runs from Jacques Cartier Pier to Cité du Havre island park daily, from noon to 10 PM.

Horse-Drawn Carriage – A romantic way to see the town is by *calèche;* these are stationed at Dorchester Square, Place Jacques-Cartier, and atop Mount Royal. One company that operates both carriages and one-horse sleighs (in winter) is *Boisvert* (phone: for information, 653-0751).

Taxi – Cabs may be hailed on the street; taxi stands are located on the corners of main intersections near the railway stations and hotels. The drop fee is about CN$2.50.

Tours – Some taxicab drivers are licensed tour guides. Tours can be arranged by calling *Taxi LaSalle* (phone: 277-7552); the rate is $25 an hour, four people maximum. Sightseeing tours leaving from INFOTOURISTE at Dorchester Square are provided by *Autocar Connoisseur Gray Line* (Rue du Sq. Dorchester; phone: 934-1222). Other private companies offering a variety of tours include *Guidatour* (phone: 844-4021), *Hertz Tourist Guides* (phone: 937-6690), *Step-on-Guides* (phone: 935-5131), and *Visites de Montréal* (phone: 933-6674). *Voyages Astral* (phone: 866-1001), located at IN-FOTOURISTE, offers group tours. For more information on private guided tours call INFOTOURISTE (phone: 873-2015 or 800-363-7777). *A Walking Tour of Vieux Montréal,* available free from the tourism bureau, is a must for those who choose to go it alone. Also see *Walk 2: Vieux Montréal* in DIRECTIONS.

LOCAL SERVICES: For additional information about local services not listed here, call the Greater Montreal Convention and Tourism Bureau (phone: 873-2051).

   Audiovisual Equipment – *Corpav* (460 St-Paul St. E.; phone: 842-1440); *Inter-Cité Video* (8270 Mayrand St.; phone: 342-4545).

   Baby-sitting – *Baby Sitting Service,* 367 Henri Bourassa Blvd. E. (phone: 381-5616).

   Business Services – *Travelex Business Center,* 1253 McGill College Ave. (phone: 871-8616) rents furnished offices by the hour, day, or week, and provides bilingual secretarial and telephone answering services, photocopying, telex, fax, and word processing.

   Computer Rental – *Centre Micro Informatique CIAP* (1690 Gilford St.; phone: 522-2427); *Ordiloc* (5780 Decelles St.; phone: 737-4002); *Vernon Rental & Leasing* (3500 de Maisonneuve Blvd. W.; phone: 843-8888).

   Dry Cleaner/Tailor – *Milton Dry Cleaning & Tailoring* (1447 Drummond St.; phone: 843-6132; and 1001 University St.; phone: 875-7928); *Nettoyeur 60 Minutes* (Central Station, 935 Rue de la Gauchetière W.; phone: 861-8003).

   Limousine – *Contact Limousine* (phone: 875-8746); *Phoenix Limousine* (phone: 875-8715).

   Mechanic – *Nelson Garage* (1100 Décarie Blvd.; phone: 481-0155); *Darmo Auto Inc.* (21 Somerville Ave.; phone: 486-0785).

   Medical Emergency – *Montreal Children's Hospital* (2300 Tupper St.; phone: 934-4499); *Montreal General Hospital* (1650 Cedar Ave.; phone: 934-8090); *Royal Victoria Hospital* (687 Pine Ave. W.; phone: 843-1610). For dental emergency call the *Dental Center* (1414 Drummond St.; phone: 281-1023).

   Messenger Services – *Express Service Courier* (1481 Amherst St.; phone: 345-0130); *Purolator Courier Ltd.* (6395 Côte de Liesse; phone: 342-6040).

   Pharmacy – *Jean Coutu* has 27 locations in central Montreal (among them 865 Ste-Catherine St. E.; phone: 842-9622; for late-night service try 1836 Ste-Catherine St. W.; phone: 933-4221).

   Photocopies – *Copiemont* (1447 Drummond St.; phone: 288-7592); *Recan Reproductions* (2024 Peel St.; phone: 849-3279).

   Post Office – Downtown Station A (1025 St-Jacques St. W.; phone: 283-2567); Station B (1250 University St.; phone: 283-2576).

   Professional Photographer – *The Professionals* (490 Guy St.; phone: 933-5728); *René Delbuguet Photo Media* (1209 Guy St.; phone: 932-1630).

   Secretary/Stenographer – *A & A Secretarial Services* (117 Ste-Catherine St. W.; phone: 288-3795); *Travelex Business Center* (1253 McGill College Ave.; phone: 871-8616).

   Teleconference Facilities – *Bonaventure International* (1 Pl. Bonaventure: phone: 878-2332); *Le Centre Sheraton* (1201 René-Lévesque Blvd. W.; phone 878-2000); *Château Champlain* (1050 Rue de la Gauchetière; phone: 878-9000); *Four Seasons* (1050

Sherbrooke St. W.; phone: 284-1100); *Queen Elizabeth* (900 René-Lévesque Blvd. W.; phone: 861-3511); *Ramada Renaissance Du Parc* (2625 Av. du Parc; phone: 288-6666); *Ritz-Carlton* (1228 Sherbrooke St. W.; phone 842-4212).

Telex – *Telepublic,* many locations throughout the city, including 1015 Côte du Beaver Hall (phone: 861-2841).

Translator – *Berlitz Translation & Interpretation Service,* 2020 University St. (phone: 288-3111).

Typewriter Rental – *Admaco Business Machines,* 5343 Décarie Blvd. (phone: 341-3020).

SPECIAL EVENTS: Last year Montreal celebrated the 350th anniversary of its founding. But even during non-anniversary years, the city hosts several big annual affairs. *Place Bonaventure*'s exhibition hall is the site of numerous shows throughout the year, ranging from Canada's largest antiques show to boat and camping exhibits. For information, call 397-2205. During the period prior to *Lent,* Old Montreal and Iles Ste-Hélène and Notre Dame host a 10-day snow carnival, *Fête des Neiges* (see "Extra Special," *Montreal At-a-Glance*).

Now in its 7th year, the *Tour de l'Ile de Montréal,* with over 40,000 cyclists competing, is fast becoming one of the most popular bicycle races in North America. Held in early June, the route encircles the island of Montreal via Sherbrooke Street (phone: 847-8687). The *Grand Prix du Canada* is a Formula One racing car event held in mid-June at the 4.41-km *Gilles Villeneuve* track on Ile Notre Dame. For information, call 392-0000.

The 10-day *International Jazz Festival* draws jazz greats — and more than 1 million of their fans — every year in early July. The major concerts are held at *Place des Arts,* with many more intimate events happening along Ste-Catherine Street and in the *Théâtre St-Denis* and the *Spectrum* (call 288-5363 for information). Also in early July, the *Just for Laughs Festival* is a 10-day comedy event attracting stand-up comics from all over the world who test their wits against each other in French and English. It is held at the *Comedy Nest* (1234 Bishop St.), the *Théâtre St-Denis* (St-Denis St.), and *Place des Arts.* For tickets and information, call 845-3155.

The *Palais de la Civilisation* on Ile Notre Dame presents an outstanding exhibit every summer. Past exhibits include "China: Treasures and Splendors," "Gold of the Thracian Horsemen," and *"Cités Ciné."* For more information, call 872-4560. During the last week in August, the *World Film Festival* brings the latest movies and their stars to Montreal's *Cinéma Parisien* (phone: 866-3856), *Place des Arts* (phone: 848-3883), and *Complexe Desjardins* (phone: 288-3141). Another film event, nearly 20 years old, the *Montreal Festival of New Cinema and Video* presents avant-garde filmworks in late September (call 843-4725 for dates and places). *Labour Day* in Canada is celebrated the same day as in the US (the first Monday in September; this year on September 6), and Canada's *Thanksgiving Day* is the second Monday of October (October 11 this year).

MUSEUMS: In addition to those mentioned in *Special Places,* above, and *For the Mind,* in DIVERSIONS, other notable Montreal museums include the following:

Bank of Montreal Museum – Early currency and bank memorabilia. Open from 10 AM to 4 PM, Mondays through Fridays; closed weekends and holidays. No admission charge. 129 St-Jacques St. at Place d'Armes (phone: 877-6892).

Canadian Center for Architecture – An architectural masterpiece in itself, this museum is a study center devoted to architecture. It contains 47,000 prints and drawings, plus 45,000 photographs, 35,000 books, and important architectural archives, including works by Leonardo da Vinci and Michelangelo. Open Wednesdays and

Fridays, 11 AM to 6 PM; Thursdays, 10 AM to 8 PM; Saturdays and Sundays, 11 AM to 5 PM; closed Mondays and Tuesdays. Admission charge. 1920 Baile St. (phone: 939-7026).

Fur Trade Museum – A historic home displays memorabilia from the area's rich fur-trading past. Open daily May 15 through Oct. 20; closed December 8 through February 20; open Wednesdays through Sundays the rest of the year. No admission charge. 1255 St. Joseph Blvd. at 12th Ave., Lachine (phone: 637-7433).

Marc-Aurèle Fortin Museum – Works and memorabilia of the Canadian artist. Open daily except Mondays, 11 AM to 5 PM. Admission charge. 118 St-Pierre St. (phone: 845-6108).

Marguerite d'Youville Centre – Motherhouse of the Grey Nuns (the Sisters of Charity of Montreal), a religious order founded by Marguerite d'Youville, who in 1990 was canonized, becoming the first Canadian-born saint. Guided tours are given of the chapel and crypt where the founder is buried. Open Wednesdays through Sundays from 1:30 to 4:30 PM. No admission charge. 1185 St. Matthew St. (phone: 937-9501).

Montreal History Center – Audiovisual tour through 11 display rooms describing Montreal's history. From mid-June to mid-September, open daily from 10 AM to 6 PM; from mid-September to mid-May, open Tuesdays through Sundays, 11 AM to 4:30 PM. Closed Mondays and holidays. Admission charge. Pl. d'Youville at St. Pierre St. (phone: 872-3207).

Montreal Museum of Decorative Arts – International design from 1940 to the present, including glass and textile exhibits. The museum is also called *Château Dufresne.* Open Wednesdays through Sundays only, 11 AM to 5 PM. Admission charge. Métro stop: Piè IX. Corner of Piè IX and Sherbrooke Sts. (phone: 259-2575).

Museum of Contemporary Art – Canadian and international works. Open 10 AM to 6 PM, except Mondays. No admission charge. The museum is still settling into its new location at *Place des Arts* (phone: 873-2878).

Redpath Museum – An impressive anthropological collection, including Egyptian mummies and rare fossils. From September through May, open Mondays through Fridays, 9 AM to 5 PM; June through September, Mondays through Thursdays, 9 AM to 5 PM. No admission charge. Métro stop: Peel or McGill. 859 Sherbrooke St. W. (phone: 398-4086).

Saidye Bronfman Centre – Contemporary works by national and international artists. Closed Saturdays. No admission charge. 5170 Côte Ste-Catherine (phone: 739-2301).

Saint Laurent Museum of Art – This arts and crafts center is housed in the old chapel that once served the Collège St-Laurent. Open daily, except Saturdays and Mondays, noon to 5 PM. No admission charge. Métro stop: Du College. 615 Ste-Croix Blvd., St-Laurent (phone: 747-7367).

Sir George-Etienne Cartier House – This national historic park was the Montreal home of one of Canada's founding fathers. Some of the rooms have been restored to their former Victorian glory and others are reserved for various exhibitions. Mid-May to *Labour Day,* open daily, 9 AM to 5 PM; *Labour Day* to mid-May, open Wednesdays through Sundays, 10 AM to 5 PM. No admission charge. Métro stop: Champs-de-Mars. 458 Notre Dame St. E. (phone: 283-2282).

 SHOPPING: Since the duty-free allowance for US citizens returning from Canada after a 2-day or longer stay has been raised to CN$400 (about US$340), and the US dollar is at a premium north of the border, there are excellent bargains to be found on a shopping spree in Montreal. Canadian import tariffs are different from those in the US, so in some cases this may mean even better buys. It also usually means a wider selection of imported products.

The underground shopping areas (see *Special Places*) provide a great enough variety of shops — 1,700 total, including branches of many Paris fashion houses — to satisfy most shopping needs. But Montreal's department stores have fine selections of clothing, china, crystal, and furniture. Three of the best-known in Canada are on Ste-Catherine Street West, between de la Montagne and Union Streets in the heart of downtown: *Eaton, Ogilvy,* and *The Bay.* In general, shopping hours are from 9 or 9:30 AM to 6 PM on weekdays, except on Thursdays and Fridays, when many stores stay open until 9 PM, and on Saturdays, until 5 PM. For more information also see *Best Shopping* in DIVERSIONS.

DEPARTMENT STORES

The Bay (La Baie) – Founded in 1845 as *Henry Morgan and Company,* it was purchased by the Hudson's Bay Company in 1969. It is strong on new trends, French boutique styles, and campus fashions. The store, however, no longer sells furs. The variety of dining spots includes a buffet cafeteria, a licensed dining room, and *Le Soupière,* which serves soup and sandwiches. 585 Ste-Catherine St. W., at Phillips Sq. (phone: 281-4631).

Eaton – This Montreal branch of the Canadian department store chain was founded by Timothy Eaton and dates back to 1925. Its merchandise runs the gamut from appliances to works of art, and a personalized shopping service will do all the work for reluctant shoppers. The Art Deco restaurant on the 9th floor is modeled after the dining room of the *Ile de France,* the favorite vessel of Lady Eaton. 677 Ste-Catherine St. W. (phone: 284-8484).

Holt Renfrew – For true chic in furs. The firm traces its heritage to the 1837 furriers Henderson, Holt, and Renfrew. It is still known for its exceptional fur fashions as well as haute couture lines, its *Gucci* boutique, and stylish men's clothing (see *Best Shopping* in DIVERSIONS). 1300 Sherbrooke St. W. (phone: 842-5111).

Ogilvy – This once tartan-trimmed testament to days gone by has been transformed into a glossy new complex of chic boutiques and elegant counters. However, the columns and grand main-floor chandeliers have been retained, and traditional goods can still be found. The store's Scottish heritage continues to manifest itself every day at noon when shoppers hear the skirl of the bagpipes played by a kilted piper. Every *Christmas* since 1947, Montrealers have looked forward to *Ogilvy*'s main window display of animated Steiff toys, a spectacle that ushers in the holiday season. 1307 Ste-Catherine St. W. (phone: 842-7711).

ANTIQUES

Antiques Retro-Ville – On Notre Dame Street West's "attic row," a 10-block stretch of antiques and secondhand shops, this store deals mainly in nostalgia — old signs, toys, magazines, sports collectibles, and the like. 2652 Notre Dame St. W. (phone: 989-1307).

Blue Pillow Antiques – A tiny shop in the *Queen Elizabeth* hotel's underground shopping mall, it might offer such treasures as a Royal Crown Derby tea set or a platinum- and diamond-encrusted brooch. Its specialty is estate jewelry. *Queen Elizabeth,* 900 René-Lévesque Blvd. (phone: 871-0225).

Coach House Antiques – The Westmount branch is the place to look for a sterling silver tea service or mahogany-framed hunting prints. Both outlets feature fine antiques, art, and estate jewelry. 135 Greene Ave., Westmount (phone: 486-8418); 5372 Queen Mary Rd., Snowdon (phone: 486-8418).

Daniel J. Malynowsky Antiques – Sterling silver and fine bone china stand out in this place, along with marble-topped Victorian tables, *étagères* and the cracked leather seats of high-backed chairs. 1642 Notre Dame St. W. (phone: 937-3727).

Deuxièmement – A grab-bag of secondhand furniture, household items, china, and toys. 1880 Notre Dame St. W. (phone: 933-8560).

Petit Musée – Probably one of the most intriguing and expensive of Montreal's antiques shops, it is really more of a fine-arts gallery with its eclectic collection of fine furniture, china, and objets d'art from Europe, the Middle East, and the Orient. 1494 Sherbrooke St. W. (phone: 937-6161).

ART

Dominion Gallery – Easily recognizable by Rodin's *Bourgeois de Calais* and Henry Moore's *Upright Motif* on the plaza in front of its limestone townhouse, it is a leader in the Canadian art world, displaying and selling paintings and sculptures by international and Canadian artists. 1438 Sherbrooke St. W. (phone: 845-7471).

Galerie d'Art, Musée des Beaux Arts – A part of the new addition to the *Museum of Fine Arts,* this attractive gallery also rents museum art for display. 1446 Sherbrooke St. W. (phone: 285-1611).

Galerie Claude Lafitte – A showcase for the best of Canadian art, including the work of Jean-Paul Riopelle as well as international masters such as Chagall and Ernst. 1480 Sherbrooke St. W. (phone: 939-9898).

Galerie Jean-Pierre Valentin – Canadian and European paintings in a downtown gallery. 1434 Sherbrooke St. W. (phone: 849-3637).

Galerie Lippel – One of the few sources of pre-Columbian carving and artwork in Montreal. 1324 Sherbrooke St. W. (phone: 842-6369).

Galerie Tansu – An art and antiques gallery specializing in Japanese and Chinese antiques, bronzes, embroidered silks, lacquer works, kimonos, obis, and ancient dolls. Open 7 days a week. 1460 Sherbrooke St. W. (phone: 845-8604).

Galerie Walter Klinkhoff – This family-owned gallery is among the most respected in the city. The Klinkhoffs show primarily Canadian artists, although they have international works as well. 1200 Sherbrooke St. W. (phone: 288-7306).

Images Boréales – Formerly the *Eskimo Art Gallery,* it displays a varied collection of soapstone, jade, and other carvings, in addition to prints created by artists from the Canadian north. 1434 Sherbrooke St. W. (phone: 844-4080).

BOOKS

Bibliomania Booke Shoppe – A haven for browsers, its shelves are well stocked with titles, old and new, in French and English. Some rare collectors' items as well. 4872 Park Ave. (phone: 278-6401).

Coles – There are outlets of this bookstore all over the city, selling a variety of French and English publications. The flagship store on Ste-Catherine St. W. has been expanded. 1171 Ste-Catherine St. W. (phone: 849-8825).

Double Hook – Housed in a quaint Victorian house in Westmount, this bookshop specializes in Canadian authors and its cozy atmosphere welcomes browsers. 1235 Greene Ave., Westmount (phone: 932-5093).

Paragraph – A bookstore-cum–coffee shop, it attracts serious bibliophiles and students from nearby English-speaking McGill University. The store often features lectures and readings by well-known Canadian authors. 2065 Mansfield St. (phone: 845-5811).

Russell – Though shabby and located in a run-down part of town, its shelves are well dressed with out of print and secondhand books. A must stop for collectors. 275 St. Antoine St. W. (phone: 866-0564).

W.H. Smith – Best sellers, paperbacks, magazines, and international newspapers are its stock in trade. Two branches: *Place Ville Marie* (phone: 861-1736), and Central Station (phone: 861-5567).

Ulysses – All kinds of travel publications on Canada, Montreal, and the world, plus globes, travel cases, and a jumble of guides to take travelers around the world. Three locations: 1307 Ste-Catherine St. (phone: 842-7711, ext. 362); 560 President Kennedy Ave. (phone: 289-0993); and 4176 St-Denis St. (phone: 843-9447).

SWEETS

Laura Secord – Canada's answer to Fanny Farmer maintains branches all over the city, selling chocolates, goodie baskets, and ice cream. Some central outlets include 1045 Ste-Catherine St. W. (phone: 843-5708); *Place Bonaventure* (phone: 861-0339); and *Place Ville-Marie* (phone: 861-7867).

Lenôtre Paris – For chocolate and pastries with European flair, the Montreal branches of this French *pâtisserie* are worth the trip. 1050 Laurier Ave. W. (phone: 270-2702) and 1277 Greene Ave., Westmount (phone: 939-6000).

Pâtisserie La Brioche Lyonnaise – This distinctly Quebecois pastry shop is also a restaurant where you can sip coffee, savor a cream-filled cake or two, and overhear the "Franglais" of fellow patrons. An outdoor terrace is open spring and summer. 1593 St-Denis St. (phone: 842-7017).

CHILDREN'S WEAR

Gamineries – A neat little boutique on the street level of a 19th-century townhouse specializes in expensive but unusual European- and US-made fashions for chic children up to 12 years. 1458 Sherbrooke St. W. (phone: 843-4614).

Jacadi – Sweaters and pleated skirts, knitted suits, and smart *chapeaux* from France are in the affordable range in this *Eaton Centre* boutique for fashion-conscious kids. 705 Ste-Catherine St. W. (phone: 282-1933).

Oink-Oink – It's a rewarding trip off the beaten track to catch the children's fashions in this Westmount "two-stop shop" where neighborhood moms shop. There's also a nice selection of toys. For little ones: 1361 Greene Ave. (phone: 939-2634); for teens: 1359 Greene Ave. (phone: 937-7829).

Olly de Hollande – All the brightest colors in the rainbow go into the designer wear featured in this boutique for the young. Styles are sporty, cheerful, and definitely distinctive. 2165 Crescent St. (phone: 844-1220).

FASHION

Agatha – Stylish young Quebecoise career women swear by this boutique in the trendy Laurier Avenue area. 1054 Laurier Ave. (phone: 272-9313).

Alfred Sung – A white marble salon in *Place Montreal Trust* features haute couture for women and children by one of Canada's best known designers. 1500 McGill College Ave. (phone: 843-3539).

Aquascutum – Three branches of the British fashion house feature the best of raincoats, blazers, and other classic clothing. All garments carry the seal "By Appointment to H.M. Queen Elizabeth, The Queen Mother." *Ogilvy,* 1307 Ste-Catherine St. W., 2nd floor for women (phone: 843-7836); main floor for men (phone: 843-8428); 1 *Place Ville-Marie* for men and women (phone: 843-7010); and *Les Cours Mont-Royal,* 1455 Peel St., for women (phone: 843-7319).

Brisson & Brisson – Catering to the well-dressed Montreal male since 1934, it offers elegant European-style tweeds, suits, vests, and designer silk ties. 1472 Sherbrooke St. W. (phone: 937-7456).

Chakok – Youthful styles incorporating riots of color distinguish the designs in this French import boutique. 1 Westmount Sq. (phone: 931-6055).

Clubissimo – Tailored ensembles by Sonja Rykiel drape the mannequins in one of the Sherbrooke shopping strip's niftier salons. 1320 Sherbrooke St. W. (phone: 844-5555).

Jaeger – The *Ogilvy* branch of one of Britain's finest top-of-the-line fashion houses carries fine English woolens, tweeds, classic suits, coats, and dresses. 1307 Ste-Catherine St. W. (phone: 845-5834).

Laura Ashley – Romantic prints, little girl frocks — for big girls — and flowing skirts inspired by the late London designer, nestled appropriately, in an old Victorian row house. There are also flowery bed linens, fabric, and matching wallpaper. 2110 Crescent St. (phone: 284-9225).

Marks & Spencer – The Montreal outpost of Britain's venerable fashion and food chain carries a wide selection of men's, women's, and children's clothing that's both affordable and serviceable. *Place Montreal Trust,* 1500 McGill College Ave. (phone: 499-8558).

Parachute – One of Canada's best known fashion success stories for avant-garde, casual designs. 3526 St. Lawrence Blvd. (phone: 845-7865); also *Les Cours Mont-Royal,* 1455 Peel St. (phone: 843-5437).

Polo Ralph Lauren – A townhouse has been transformed into a showcase for New England fashions by the internationally popular designer. 1316 Sherbrooke St. W. (phone: 288-3988).

Rodier Paris – Knits and ensembles from the exclusive French house. Two branches: 1014 Ste-Catherine St. W. (phone: 875-6899) and *Place Desjardins* (phone: 844-5010).

L'Uomo Boutique – Store windows created with uncompromising flair display trend-setting men's wear. 1452 Peel St. (phone: 844-1008).

FUR

Alexandor's – One of the finer salons dealing in Canadian-made furs, this showroom isn't large but it's filled with luxury fashions. 2015 Rue de la Montagne. (phone: 288-1119).

Birger Christensen – The Danish fur fashion house has its Quebec store and storage vaults at *Holt Renfrew* (once founded by furriers Henderson, Holt and Renfrew). The former *Holt*'s salon presented Queen Elizabeth II with a Labrador mink coat as a wedding gift in 1947. 1300 Sherbrooke St. W. (phone: 842-5111).

Desjardins Fourrures – The large, 2-story house of furs has served generations of customers at its east end location. 325 René-Lévesque Blvd. E. (phone: 288-4151).

Grizzly Fourrure – Bargain-priced new and secondhand furs. 3692 St-Denis St. (phone: 288-9959).

McComber – Canadian-made fur coats for women, plus a small selection of fur coats for men. 440 de Maisonneuve Blvd. W. (phone: 845-1167).

Oslo Fourrures – Basically a manufacturing house, it opens its showroom to the retail market, as well. 4316 St. Lawrence Blvd. (phone: 499-1777).

Shuchat – Known for its high-fashion designs in furs. 402 de Maisonneuve Blvd. W. (phone: 849-2113).

FURNITURE

Décors et Confort de France – Elegant French furniture and decorative fixtures are featured here, all of them expensive. 1434 Sherbrooke St. W. (phone: 281-9281).

Dixversions Mobilier – Splashy modern furniture and household items, ranging from the fun and comic to the new and useful, fill the three showrooms of this popular Montreal chain. 4361 St-Denis St. (phone: 284-9374); *Maison Alcan,* 1188 Sherbrooke St. W. (phone: 284-1013); and 6874 Jean-Talon Ave. E. (phone: 899-0140).

Roche-Bobois – For those who prefer the latest in leather sectionals, chrome-frame furniture, and glass-topped tables on arty pedestals. 1425 René-Lévesque Blvd. W. (phone: 871-9070).

GLASS ART AND HANDICRAFTS

Canadian Guild of Crafts, Quebec – Devoted to authentic Inuit carvings, prints, and other crafts, the collection is open to viewing, while the boutique is regarded as the best place in Montreal to learn about the artists of Canada's far north. Each piece is signed by the artist. Knowledgeable, helpful staff. 2055 Peel St. (phone: 849-6091).

Centre de Céramique Bonsecours – Original ceramics and sculpture by Quebec artists are displayed and sold here. Closed Saturdays. 444 Rue St-Gabriel, Vieux Montréal (phone: 866-6581).

Galerie Le Chariot – In the heart of the historic *quartier,* this place stocks a wide selection of signed Inuit carvings from Cape Dorset and other parts of the Canadian north. 446 Pl. Jacques-Cartier (phone: 875-4994).

Galerie Elena Lee-Verre d'Art – The one-of-a-kind pieces on display in this gallery/boutique are true works of art, rendered in huge plates, vases and other "objets" the artist infuses with glowing color. 1518 Sherbrooke St. W. (phone: 932-3896).

Le Rouet Métiers d'Art – A trio of crafts boutiques features tasteful, reasonably priced Quebec-made ceramics, weaving, copper and enamel jewelry, wooden toys, and carvings. 136 Rue St-Paul, Vieux Montréal (phone: 861-8401); 1 *Place Ville-Marie* (phone: 866-4774); and 700 Ste-Catherine St. W. (phone: 861-8401).

JEWELRY

Birks – Montreal's most prestigious jewelry store with branches all over North America, it's been the source of sterling silver, china, and crystal for generations of Canadians. Crystal chandeliers and marble pillars set the tone in the downtown store. 1240 Phillips Sq. (phone: 397-2511); *Place Montreal Trust,* 1500 McGill College Ave. (phone: 397-2503).

Cartier – Probably the city's most exclusive jewelry store, this treasure chest of a boutique carries a small selection of *Les Must de Cartier* (absolute necessities) from the famous Paris *joaillier.* 1498 Sherbrooke St. W. (phone: 939-0000).

Kaufmann – A long-established midtown company where watches by Rolex and Piaget share display cases with diamond rings and things. 2195 Crescent St. (phone: 848-0595).

Mappins – A loyal local clientele shops here for classic, reasonably priced jewelry, charms, gold and silver chains, and watches. 1000 Ste-Catherine St. W. (phone: 866-7431).

Oz Bijoux – Young fashionables on a budget patronize this costume jewelry boutique known for its original designs in chunky silver and copper. 3900 St-Denis St. (phone: 845-9568).

LINEN

Linen Chest – The largest branch of this Canadian enterprise stocks a bountiful supply of bed and bath linen, china, crystal, gift items, and home accessories. Les Promenades de la Cathédrale, 625 Ste-Catherine St. W. (phone: 282-9525).

Porthault – Connoisseurs of fine linen (especially beautiful print designs) and fond grandparents shop here for hand-embroidered imports and exclusive infants' wear. The boudoir boutique is the only outlet in Canada for the famous *Floris of London* toiletries. 2137 Crescent St. (phone: 286-9320).

Pratesi – Gift shoppers and brides buy their imported and high-fashion bed, bath and table linen here. The store also carries an enchanting selection of imported toiletries. 1448 Sherbrooke St. W. (phone: 285-8909).

SHOES

Bally – The affordable, yet stylish men's and women's shoes and boots sold at *Bally* of Canada (not Switzerland) are available at branches throughout the city, several of which are listed here. 1500 McGill College Ave. (phone: 499-9766); 1125 Ste-Catherine St. W. (phone: 288-5040); *Place Bonaventure* (phone: 866-5410).

Brown's – A popular salon for high-fashion women's shoes, boots, and bags. 1 *Place Ville-Marie* (phone: 861-8925).

Pegabo – For the latest in youthful footwear for women, particularly boots, this boutique chain is a good bet. A main store is at 4065 St-Denis St. (phone: 848-0272).

Roots – Canada's own health-shoe company is a big hit in a walkers' city like Montreal where fashion-conscious men and women like to combine style with comfort. 716 Ste-Catherine St. W. (phone: 875-4374).

TOBACCO

Davidoff – This up-market tobacconist stocks imported products of the weed in all its forms (including Cuban cigars — it's legal to sell them here), pipes, lighters, and other accessories. 1452 Sherbrooke St. W. (phone: 289-9118).

SPORTS: Baseball – The National League *Expos* baseball team plays at the spectacular *Olympic Stadium* (see *Special Places*) with a capacity of 53,858. For information, call 253-3434. Olympic Park is situated in the east end of the city, in the block bounded by Sherbrooke, Viau, and Pierre de Coubertin; take the Métro to Viau.

Biking – The Vieux Port rents bicycles to visitors who want to explore its waterfront trails. In addition, the island of Montreal has 20 bike paths, 12 of them city-run (phone: 872-6211). For information on commercial rentals, call *Vélo-Québec* (phone: 252-VELO). Rentals also are available from *Cycle Peel* (6665 St-Jacques St.; phone: 486-1148) and *La Cordée* (2159 Ste-Catherine E. St.; phone: 524-1515).

Golf – The 9-hole *Golf Municipal de Montréal* is located at Sherbrooke and Viau Sts. (phone: 872-1143, for information). Reciprocal agreements with private clubs in the US make two of the best clubs anywhere — the *Royal Montreal Golf Club* and the *Beaconsfield Golf Club* — available to golfers with letters of introduction from their home pros. The *Royal Montreal* (25 Southridge Rd., Ile Bizard; phone: 626-3977), where members first drove the green in 1873, is one of the most exclusive tournament class clubs in the country, and only 6 months younger than the *Royal Quebec Golf Club,* the oldest club in North America (see "Golf" in *Quebec City*). The *Beaconsfield* (49 Golf Ave., Pointe Claire; phone: 695-2661) is an 18-hole, tournament class gem that has hosted three LPGA events in the past decade. Both are located west of downtown Montreal. In addition, golfers can find more than 30 courses on the island of Montreal and in the surrounding area.

Hockey – From October through April, the ice is hotly contested at the *Forum* by *Les Canadiens* and their NHL challengers (Métro stop: Atwater; 2313 Ste-Catherine St. W.; phone: 932-6131). Concordia University boasts one of the leading collegiate hockey teams in the country. The *Stingers* play in the university's *Loyola Arena* (phone: 848-3850).

Horse Racing – Harness racing takes place nightly, except Tuesdays and Thursdays, at *Blue Bonnets Race Track.* Races begin at 7:30 PM, except on Sundays, when post time is 1:30 PM. 7440 Décarie Blvd. (phone: 739-2741).

Jet-boat Tours – Organized expeditions over the Lachine Rapids, in large hydrofoil-like crafts, leave from Victoria Pier at the foot of Berri St. in Vieux Montréal. From May to late September they depart daily every other hour from 10 AM to 6 PM (phone: 284-9607).

Jogging – Mount Royal Park and Angrignon Park both have paved trails for taking a pleasant run. There is another good trail from Old Montreal to St. Louis Lake.

Swimming – The stunning Olympic-size pool at Olympic Park is open to the public year-round (phone: 252-4622); the city of Montreal also runs over 50 indoor and outdoor pools, including the large public pools at Ile Ste-Hélène (phone: 872-6211).

Two of the best indoor pools are the *Cegep du Vieux Montréal* (255 Ontario St. E.; phone: 872-2644) and the *Centre Claude-Robillard* (1000 Emile-Journault; phone: 872-6900). Montreal's only downtown beach is on Ile Notre Dame (Métro stop: Ile Ste-Hélène).

Tennis – The *Player's Limited International Championships* are held each summer at the *Jarry Tennis Stadium,* alternating between men's and women's events (men's tournaments are held in odd-numbered years; women's tournaments in even-numbered years; Jarry Park; phone: 273-1515). The city of Montreal operates more than 200 municipal courts that are open to the public, either at no charge or for a nominal fee. For information and court reservations, call 872-6763.

Winter Sports – There's ice skating, snowshoeing, cross-country skiing, and tobogganing in parks all over town once winter sets in. All told, the city has close to 200 skating rinks; 11 cross-country ski areas, each with several trails; 11 large snowshoeing areas; 7 alpine slopes; and 9 toboggan runs among its facilities. From January to March, snowshoeing and cross-country skiing are popular on Ile Notre Dame, as is skating along its 1.2-mile-long basin. Close to 1,000 Parks Department employees keep it all in condition. For information, call the municipal recreation department at 872-6211.

 THEATER: French-language productions are presented at more than a dozen theaters around town, including such well-known stages as *Théâtre de Quat' Sous, Théâtre du Nouveau Monde,* and *Théâtre du Rideau Vert. Centaur Theatre* schedules a regular season of mainly English-language drama and musicals, as well as workshop productions in the smaller of its two theaters. Works by Canadian writers are featured on both stages, which occupy a historic building that once housed the Montreal Stock Exchange. Local newspapers and in-hotel magazine guides list current attractions. *Centaur Theatre,* 453 St-François-Xavier (phone: 288-3161).

 CINEMA: Visitors to Montreal can see the latest film releases from Hollywood in English and from France, Algiers, and other French-language ports of call in French. Most movies are screened in multi-theater complexes like the five-theater entertainment hub on the top floor of the *Eaton Centre* (705 Ste-Catherine St. W.; phone: 282-1933), where films are shown in both languages. Other centrally located cinema complexes include *Cineplex Odéon* (1616 Ste-Catherine St. W.; 932-2121); *Cinema Place Bonaventure* (901 Rue de la Gauchetière W.; phone: 861-7437); *Palace 6* (698 Ste-Catherine St. W.; phone: 866-6991); and *Egyptien* (1455 Peel St.; phone: 843-3112).

The National Film Board, Canada's main government-supported film organization, presents a regular program of made-in-Canada film fare, some of which have won international acclaim, at *Cinématèque Québécoise* (225 de Maisonneuve Blvd. E.; phone: 842-9763). Devoted chiefly to Quebec cinema, the theater presents two different films a day, not all of which originate with the NFB. Screenings are scheduled Tuesdays through Saturdays at 6:35 and 8:35 PM; Sundays at 3, 6:35, and 8:35 PM. Closed Mondays.

 MUSIC: Since music transcends all language barriers, visitors can enjoy all that Montreal has to offer, from grand symphony at the *Place des Arts* to French folk music at *boîtes à chanson,* Quebec-style cafés. Again, the guides mentioned above should have up-to-date schedules. The *Montreal Symphony Orchestra* performs at *Salle Wilfrid Pelletier* at the *Place des Arts* (175 Ste-Catherine

St. W.; phone: 842-2112), as do *Les Grand Ballets Canadiens, L'Opéra de Montréal,* and other guest companies and soloists. Programs of chamber music are given at the *Place des Arts' Théâtre Maisonneuve* and *Théâtre Port-Royale* (phone: 842-2112). *Pollack Concert Hall* also regularly schedules varied musical programs (555 Sherbrooke St. W.; phone: 398-4547). Throughout the year rock stars perform at the *Forum* (phone: 932-6131) and *Olympic Stadium* (phone: 253-3434). Special productions, such as a summer *Mozart Festival,* and *Christmastime* performances of Handel's *Messiah,* are presented at Notre Dame Basilica (Place d'Armes; call the *Montreal Symphony* office, 842-3402) and at other Montreal churches.

 NIGHTCLUBS AND NIGHTLIFE: Nightlife for the younger set centers around Crescent, de la Montagne, and St-Denis Streets. The supper club crowd can choose from among the many hotel and restaurant dining-entertainment spots. The *Château Champlain*'s *Le Caf'Conc'* supper club is reminiscent of Paris's *Moulin Rouge;* you can go for dinner and the show or for drinks only at showtime. The hotel's *L'Escapade* restaurant on the 36th floor offers a good view along with music (1050 Rue de la Gauchetière; phone: 878-9000). *Le Stage Dinner Theatre,* at *La Diligence* restaurant, serves up a menu of supper and drama (7385 Décarie Blvd.; phone: 731-7771). *Solmar* (111 St. Paul St. E.; phone: 861-4562) has fado music and Portuguese cuisine. *Vieux Munich* (1170 St-Denis St.; phone: 288-8011) features a Bavarian orchestra and dancing every night after 6 PM, while the *Sabayon* (666 Sherbrooke St. W.; phone: 288-0373) features a dance band as well as Greek music and food. *Csarda* restaurant (3479 St. Lawrence Blvd.; phone: 843-7519) features dinner theater productions Saturday and Sunday nights.

Dance bands play at the the *Méridien*'s *Le Café Fleuri* restaurant (4 *Complexe Desjardins;* phone: 285-1450); and *Le Grand* hotel's revolving *Tour de Ville* restaurant (777 University St.; phone: 879-1370). The *Ritz-Carlton*'s *Café de Paris* (1228 Sherbrooke St. W; phone: 842-4212) features piano music.

Disco and bar-hopping abound around Crescent, de la Montagne, St-Denis, St. Lawrence, Bishop, and Mackay Streets and a number of side streets between René-Lévesque Boulevard and Sherbrooke. Currently popular are *Club Soda* (5240 Park Ave.; phone: 270-7848), dean of Montreal's rock rooms; *Grand Prix Bar* (1228 Sherbrooke St. W.; phone 843-4212), *Ritz-Carlton*'s rendezvous for mature singles with fat expense accounts; *Lola's Paradise Café* (3604 St. Lawrence Blvd.; phone: 282-9944), a trendy destination for late-late diners where a disc jockey plays jazz until 6 AM; at *Talullah Darling,* the upstairs bar stays open until 3 AM; *LUX* (5220 St. Lawrence Blvd.; phone: 271-9272), stays open round-the-clock to accommodate piano bar patrons and the dawn patrol. More nightlife can be found at *Thursday's* (1449 Crescent St.; phone 288-5656), the city's original singles bar; *Biddles,* for great jazz and ribs (2060 Aylmer St.; phone: 842-8656); *Le Business* disco (3510 St. Lawrence Blvd., above Sherbrooke; phone: 844-3988); *Cheers* (1260 Mackay St.; phone: 932-3138); *L'Esprit* (1234 de la Montagne St.; phone: 397-1711); *Metropolis,* a turn-of-the-century theater with six bars and dancing on 3 floors (59 Ste-Catherine St. E.; phone: 288-5559); *Salsathèque,* for Latin music and dancing (1220 Peel St.; phone: 875-0016); *Sir Winston Churchill Pub* (1459 Crescent St.; phone: 288-0616); and *Winnie's* (1455 Crescent St.; phone: 288-0623).

Vieux Montréal is fast becoming a hot nightspot area. Favorites include *Le Bijou* (300 Le Moyne St.; phone: 288-5508); *La Cage aux Sports,* a hangout popular with sports personalities (395 Le Moyne; phone: 288-1115); *Chez Brandy* (25 St. Paul St. E.; phone: 871-9178); *L'Air du Temps* (191 St. Paul St. W.; phone: 842-2003); and *Zhivago* for caviar, vodka, and dancing (419 St-Pierre St.; phone: 284-0333).

BEST IN TOWN

CHECKING IN: With more than 16,000 hotel rooms in the Montreal area, there is no difficulty finding suitable accommodations. Hotels in all categories dot Montreal's downtown center, close to shopping, restaurants, and the city's other attractions. Even some of the luxury hotels offer weekend packages that are real bargains, including the small extras that make a stay more pleasant. Double room rates will run about $120 or more in the expensive category and about $60 to about $85 in the moderate category. A number of firms handle bed and breakfast lodgings; they include *B & B Chez Antonio* (101 Northview Ave.; phone: 486-6910); *Bed & Breakfast de Chez Nous* (3717 Ste-Famille St.; phone: 845-7711); *Bed & Breakfast Downtown Network* (3458 Laval Ave.; phone: 289-9749); *Bed & Breakfast Montreal* (PO Box 575, Snowdon Station, H3X 3T8; phone: 738-9410); *Bed & Breakfast Mount Royal* (3458 Laval Ave.; phone: 289-9749); *Relais Montréal Hospitalité* (3977 Laval Ave.; phone: 287-9635); and *Welcome Bed & Breakfast* (3950 Laval Ave.; phone: 844-5897).

The downtown *YMCA* (1451 Stanley St.; phone: 849-8393) and *YWCA* (1355 René-Lévesque Blvd. W.; phone: 866-9941), as well as the youth hostel (3541 Aylmer; phone: 843-3317) offer inexpensive accommodations. In the summer, McGill University (phone: 398-6367; see *Montreal At-a-Glance*), Université de Montréal (phone: 343-6531), MacDonald College in Ste-Anne de Bellevue (phone: 398-7716), and the Collège Français (on Fairmont St. W.; phone: 495-2581) also have inexpensive rooms to let. In addition, *KOA* runs a campground on South Shore at St-Philippe (phone: 659-8626). All telephone numbers are in the 514 area code unless otherwise indicated.

Bonaventure International – In a unique 2-story penthouse location — 17 stories above the *Place Bonaventure* — is Hilton International's 394-room establishment. Standing in the rooftop lobby, looking at the open-air gardens and heated outdoor pool, it is hard to believe that you are right above one of Montreal's busiest office and commercial complexes. The outside rooms have a lovely view of a good portion of the center of the city (often including the St. Lawrence Seaway). The inside rooms (preferred by many) look out on a contemplative, Japanese-style central garden that contains a brook, a multitude of trees and bushes, and a couple of waterfalls, and the year-round open-air pool, all on the roof. *Le Castillion* restaurant is an elegant luncheon or dinner setting. 1 *Place Bonaventure* (phone: 878-2332; 800-268-9275 in Canada or 800-445-8667 in the US; fax: 878-3881). Expensive.

Le Centre Sheraton – This 824-room hostelry has posh suites on the top 5 floors, dubbed appropriately *Le Sommet de la Tour* (the Top of the Tower). Its *Point de Vue* restaurant is quickly gaining a reputation for fine nouvelle cuisine. 1201 René-Lévesque Blvd. W. (phone: 878-2000 or 800-325-3535; fax: 878-4659). Expensive.

Château Champlain – The huge, arched picture windows covering the 36-story façade of this Canadian Pacific property make it a distinctive landmark on Montreal's skyline (it's known to locals as the cheese grater). Its 617 rooms and suites are spacious and elegantly furnished, and there also is a health club and a swimming pool. 1050 Rue de la Gauchetière W. (phone: 878-9000; 800-828-7447 in Canada or 800-528-0444 in the US; fax: 878-6761). Expensive.

La Citadelle – An old *Quality Inn* high-rise has been completely refurbished to create this European-style hotel with 182 comfortable rooms, a health spa, and pool. *C'est La Vie,* the lobby bar, attracts a lively crowd for its happy hour. 410 Sherbrooke St. W. (phone: 844-8851; 800-363-0363; fax: 844-0912). Expensive.

Delta – Here is a luxury high-rise with 453 rooms (most with balconies), a health club, pools, and an innovative "Creativity Center" designed to keep young travelers occupied while their parents are sightseeing. Convenient downtown location. On the corner of Sherbrooke and City Councillors Sts. (phone: 286-1986; 800-268-1133 in Canada or 800-877-1133 in the US; fax: 284-4342). Expensive.

Four Seasons (Quatre Saisons) – This superb member of the Canadian-owned group has 300 rooms, including deluxe suites and 2 extraordinary split-level penthouses. European touches include the efficient services of a 24-hour concierge and a free nightly shoeshine. Among the facilities are a heated outdoor pool, a sauna, a whirlpool bath, and an exercise room. The *Pierre de Coubertin* restaurant is now a private dining and meeting room, though the Szechuan-style *Zen* restaurant (see *Eating Out*), and a downstairs café, *Le Restaurant,* are open to the public. 1050 Sherbrooke St. W. (phone: 284-1110; 800-268-6282 in Canada or 800-332-3442 in the US; fax: 845-3025). Expensive.

Holiday Inn Crowne Plaza – The largest and most convenient of the several *Holiday Inns* in the area, this 489-room link in the chain also has an indoor pool. 420 Sherbrooke St. W. (phone: 842-6111 or 800-HOLIDAY; fax: 842-9381). Expensive.

Inter-Continental Montreal – Opened in 1991 in the heart of the city's downtown financial district, this Montreal member of the international hotel chain combines a new 25-story tower of 359 rooms and suites with a restored historic property. Connected by an interior bridge, both buildings are linked to the *World Trade Centre* complex. The main restaurant, *Les Continents,* is part of the guestroom tower and *Les Voûtes,* a steak and seafood restaurant, is down in the vaults of the refurbished Nordheimer Building. At one time the building was home to the Nordheimer Piano Company and the *Nordheimer Music Hall,* where such diverse performers as Sarah Bernhardt and Tom Thumb once appeared. The 10th-floor health club, with a 50-foot lap pool, opens onto a rooftop garden. 360 St-Antoine St. W. (phone: 987-9900 or 800-327-0200; fax: 987-9904). Expensive.

Maritime – Centrally located, this place has 214 rooms, an indoor pool, and sauna. About a 10-minute walk from the *Forum,* the hotel offers special hockey packages that include accommodations, meals, and tickets to see the *Canadiens.* 1155 Guy St. (phone: 932-1411 or 800-363-6255; fax: 932-0446). Expensive.

Le Méridien Montréal – This 601-room property is the focal point of the enclosed commercial-business complex at *Complexe Desjardins,* adjacent to *Place des Arts,* Montreal's performing arts center. The atmosphere is French at this local member of the Air France hotel chain. There also are indoor and outdoor pools. 4 *Complexe Desjardins,* enter at 4 Jeanne Mance St. (phone: 285-1450; 800-361-8234 in Canada or 800-543-4300 in the US; fax: 285-1243). Expensive.

De la Montagne – A 132-room hostelry is within a stone's throw of the chic boutiques and restaurants in the Crescent Street–de la Montagne Street area. Its rooftop pool and terrace are popular for summer rendezvous, and its dining room, *Le Lutetia,* is highly regarded. 1430 Rue de la Montagne (phone: 288-5656 or 800-361-6262; fax: 288-9658). Expensive.

Queen Elizabeth (Reine Elizabeth) – A king-size, 1,046-room property, it is the city's largest hotel. With direct access to underground *Place Ville Marie*'s shops and services and *Canadian National's* Central Station, it is one of the most conveniently located, too. In addition to the restaurants in the hotel, including the well-known *Beaver Club* (see *Eating Out*), the building features an elegant shopping arcade in the lower lobby, separate from the shops of *Place Ville Marie.* 900

René-Lévesque Blvd. W. (phone: 861-3511; 800-268-9411 in Canada or 800-828-7447 in the US; fax: 954-2256). Expensive.

Ramada Inn Centreville – Of the three in the Montreal area, this 205-room member of the chain is the most convenient to downtown. An outdoor pool and complimentary parking are among its attractions. 1005 Guy St. (phone: 938-4611 or 800-268-8998; fax: 938-8718). Expensive.

Ritz-Carlton – In the manner of the grand hotels of Europe, this 240-room property on a tree-lined street caters to a loyal international clientele by providing personalized service (two staff members to each guest) and impeccable decor. This is one of the rare instances in which M. César Ritz himself was on hand for the inauguration more than 80 years ago. The hotel is now managed by the Kempinski Group, a German chain, but service has remained distinguished. During the summer, lunch, tea, and dinner are served alfresco at the garden restaurant, which overlooks the manicured lawn and flower-fringed duck pond in the hotel's center court. 1228 Sherbrooke St. W. (phone: 842-4212; 800-363-0366 in Canada or 800-223-6800 in the US; fax: 842-3386). Expensive.

Shangrila – This high-rise has a pleasant sidewalk café, *Café Park Express,* 167 well-appointed rooms, and an agreeable ambience. 3407 Peel St. (phone: 288-4141 or 800-361-7791; fax: 288-3021). Expensive.

Vogue – An ultra-chic, deluxe version of an *hôtel particulièr,* it has 126 rooms and suites, furnished in the late Empire style. The *pièce de résistance* is the penthouse floor with its 11 dramatically furnished black-on-black suites. The *Société Café* restaurant and adjoining bar echo the classical/modernist design. 142 Rue de la Montagne (phone: 285-5555; 800-363-0363 in Canada or 800-243-1166 in the US; fax: 849-8903). Expensive.

Le Grand – An ambitious establishment with 737 rooms, it has a 40-foot-high atrium lobby with glass-enclosed elevators, an indoor pool, a sauna, and a massage room. *Chez Antoine,* an Art Deco oasis in the corridor linking the hotel to *Place Victoria,* serves an innovative menu featuring seafood and meat grilled over charcoal flavored with mesquite, applewood, sassafras, and hickory. *Le Tour de Ville* is the city's only revolving rooftop restaurant. 777 University St. (phone: 879-1370 or 800-361-8155; fax: 879-1761). Expensive to moderate.

Manoir LeMoyne – Just a few blocks from the *Montreal Forum,* it has 286 rooms, most of which are actually apartments with fully equipped kitchens, dining alcoves, and spacious balconies. *Le Fréderic* is its fairly good restaurant and piano bar. There's an indoor pool and sauna, too. 2100 de Maisonneuve Blvd. (phone: 931-8861 or 800-361-7191; fax: 931-7726). Expensive to moderate.

Ramada Renaissance Du Parc – The hub of another major office-apartment-shopping complex at the base of Mount Royal, this 463-room hostelry, a member of the well-known chain, has an attractive lobby lounge and piano bar, indoor and outdoor pools, a sauna, and indoor tennis. *Puzzles* restaurant is a popular spot. 3625 Av. du Parc (phone: 288-6666; 800-268-8998 in Canada or 800-2-RAMADA in the US; fax: 288-2469). Expensive to moderate.

Château Versailles – A small, European-style hotel with 70 deluxe rooms, fast becoming a favorite with repeat visitors. It only serves breakfast, but its advantage is being in an area abounding in good, moderately priced restaurants. 1659 Sherbrooke St. W. (phone: 933-3611 or 800-361-7199 in Canada; 800-361-3664 in the US; fax: 933-7102). Moderate.

De l'Institut – Located near the University of Québec à Montréal, this 42-room establishment is part of the province's School of Tourism and is managed by teachers and students. Meals served here are generally quite good. 3535 St-Denis (phone: 282-5120; fax: 873-9893). Moderate.

Lord Berri – This 154-room hostelry is close to the Berri Métro station and Voyageur bus terminal in the city's east end. The *Café-Bistro* restaurant offers a reasonably priced menu. 1199 Berri St., near René-Lévesque Blvd. E. (phone: 845-9236 or 800-363-0363 in Canada and New England; fax: 849-9855). Moderate.

Sinomonde Garden – *Holiday Inn's* latest property in the financial district has added an exotic new dimension to Montreal's small Chinese quarter with its illuminated rooftop pagodas and reflection pool and cascade in the dining area. Conveniently located across the street from the *Palais des Congrès* (convention center), it has 235 well-appointed rooms, 6 suites, and an executive floor. There's also a mini-mall (40 shops) and a fitness center with an indoor pool and exercise room. 99 Viger Ave. W. (phone: 878-9888 or 800-HOLIDAY; fax: 878-6341). Moderate.

Tour Versailles – This 107-room hotel was opened in 1988 by the owners of *Château Versailles* in a converted high-rise apartment building across the street from their smaller property. Rooms have Shaker-style furniture and the bathrooms are decorated with Italian marble. The more deluxe rooms have a Jacuzzi, microwave oven, and refrigerator. There's a bistro-style restaurant. 1659 Sherbrooke St. W. (phone: 933-3611; 800-361-7199 in Canada or 800-361-3664 in the US; fax: 933-7102). Moderate.

EATING OUT: For the Gallic gourmand, that unique gastronomic malcontent for whom foreign means nothing but French, Montreal provides a cornucopia of delights comparable to anything available on the far side of the Atlantic. Here is the opportunity to have your crêpe and eat it too. Indeed, even homegrown French Canadian cuisine takes a back seat to the French variety. Except for *Les Filles du Roy* (see below), it pays to head to the countryside for such native fare as *ragoût de pattes* (pig's feet in a garlic mixture) or *ragoût de boulettes* (meatball stew made with lean ground pork) — although many metropolitan dining spots do offer oka cheese, the strong-smelling soft cheese made by Trappist monks for more than a century in the village of the same name. Many of the city's ethnic restaurants, as well as its seafood- and steakhouses, are excellent. Montrealers seem to live to eat and they have high dining standards; the ambience of a restaurant is as important a consideration as its food. Our choices reflect this native concern. Expect to pay $90 or more for a dinner for two in the very expensive range; $70 to $90 in the expensive category; $35 to $65 in a moderate restaurant; and under $30 in an inexpensive one. Prices do not include drinks, wine, or tips. By law, all menus must be posted outside the establishment. All telephone numbers are in the 514 area code unless otherwise indicated.

Café de Paris – The most exclusive of city establishments, this salon serves high society with long-practiced panache and grace. Quebec dishes are the specialties, including Gaspé salmon, venison and game birds, and "Gourmet Impérial," a selection of caviar, is a $150 appetizer. The decor is sumptuous: silk-paneled walls, velvet banquettes, and a wall of French doors. Open daily. Reservations advised. Major credit cards accepted. 1228 Sherbrooke St. W. (phone: 842-4212). Very expensive.

Beaver Club – As the name implies, this was once a private club, exclusively for those hearty souls who had journeyed to the Northwest Territories in search of furs. Now the public is welcome (at very high prices), though trophies and pelts from the early fur trading days still decorate the dining room. Nouvelle cuisine selections have been added to the already extensive menu. The bouillabaisse — made with a whole Canadian lobster, halibut, scallops, and fish stock thickened with butter — served with fresh greens is delicious. For dessert, don't pass up the delightful fresh fruit sherbets. Open daily. Reservations advised. Major credit cards accepted. In the *Queen Elizabeth Hotel,* 900 René-Lévesque Blvd. (phone: 861-3511). Expensive.

Les Chênets – A small, intimate French place, decorated with copper pots. Try the oysters from France (called Portuguese), mussels marinière, fresh Pacific salmon, pheasant with mushrooms — or anything else, it's all very good. The wine list is also good and includes 60 kinds of cognac. Pricey, but one of the finest meals in town. Open daily. Reservations advised. Major credit cards accepted. 2075 Bishop St. (phone: 844-1842). Expensive.

Chez Delmo – Well-prepared seafood draws Montrealers to this restaurant in the financial district of Old Montreal. There is dining room service, and at lunchtime seafood is also served up at the Victorian-style mahogany bar. Closed Sundays and some holidays. Reservations advised. Major credit cards accepted. 211 Notre Dame St. W. (phone: 849-4061). Expensive.

Chez Desjardins – A Montreal favorite since 1892, it features a menu inspired by the sea. Yet this is no nets-hanging-from-the-ceiling, buoys-bobbing-in-your-face kind of place. The nautical decor is tastefully appointed in this most elegant of settings. Open daily. Reservations advised. Major credit cards accepted. 1175 Mackay St. (phone: 866-9741). Expensive.

Chez la Mère Michel – In this fine old stone house converted to an attractive, dark-beamed, candlelit dining spot, French cuisine achieves authentic excellence. The lobster soufflé is a special treat, and don't miss a chance for a drink in the snug downstairs bar. Closed Sundays. Reservations necessary. Major credit cards accepted. 1209 Guy St. (phone: 934-0473). Expensive.

Daberto – Probably Montreal's most sophisticated Italian restaurant offers up true culinary artistry of its own. Be sure to try shrimps à la Berci; also fine are any of a multitude of pasta dishes. Closed Sundays except for groups with prior arrangements. Reservations advised. Major credit cards accepted. 1172 Rue de la Montagne (phone: 866-2191). Expensive.

Gibby's – If you are after good steak and atmosphere, try this spot in Old Montreal's restored, early-18th-century Youville Stables. While filling yourself on the large portions, you can take your time and enjoy the attractive stone-walled, beamed interior. Though most diners order a beef dish, there are other entrées as well, all accompanied by fresh, hot bread and a generous salad. Open daily. Reservations necessary. Major credit cards accepted. 298 Pl. d'Youville (phone: 282-1837). Expensive.

Les Halles – A special dining place in a converted, 2-story townhouse that has been divided into several intimate dining areas. You may be greeted at the door by an oversized cherub who will insist on planting the traditional French kiss of greeting on both your cheeks before letting you out of the foyer. That goes for both ladies and gentlemen. He will then lead you into one of several small dining alcoves and present a menu that is both classic and creative. Try the specialties such as *pamplemousse Marie Louise* (baked grapefruit stuffed with seafood) or the fine tournedos. Closed Sundays and holidays. Reservations necessary. Major credit cards accepted. 1450 Crescent St. (phone: 844-2328). Expensive.

La Marée – Housed in a carefully restored Old Montreal house and owned by the same gentleman who operates *Le Saint Amable,* this establishment specializes in *fruits de mer* (seafood). *Turbot au champagne,* imported French whitefish prepared in champagne, is one of the fine dishes. Open daily, but generally closed Sundays during the winter. Reservations necessary. Major credit cards accepted. 404 Pl. Jacques-Cartier (phone: 861-8126). Expensive.

Les Mignardises – Currently *the* place to dine, this elegant little establishment owes its reputation to owner-chef Jean-Pierre Monnet, former executive chef of *Les Halles* (see above). The host's distinctive touch enhances the extensive haute cuisine, featuring such house specialties as quails sautéed in armagnac, saddle of rabbit with rhubarb compote, and guinea fowl in orange sauce. Closed Sundays. Reservations necessary. Major credit cards accepted. 3035-07 St-Denis St. (phone: 842-1151). Expensive.

Prego – The first restaurant to bring word of nouvelle cuisine to the upper reaches of St. Lawrence Boulevard, it adapts classic Italian dishes to the *cuisine légère* method of the French school. Dishes are light and fresh and diners can watch their meals being prepared in the open kitchen. Best choices include unusual pasta combinations and veal entrées, one of which combines veal with fresh fruit in a creamy liqueur-laced sauce. Open daily. Reservations advised. Major credit cards accepted. 5142 St. Lawrence Blvd. (phone: 271-3234). Expensive.

Le Saint Amable – Located in a lovely old stone house overlooking Place Jacques-Cartier in the heart of Old Montreal, this French dining place owned by Pierre Garcin has long held a high rank for its cuisine, service, and atmosphere. *Tournedos Opéra* — filet mignon in a pastry crust — is a specialty. Open daily except *Christmas*. Reservations necessary. Major credit cards accepted. 188 St-Amable St. (phone: 866-3471). Expensive.

Les Trois Arches – A highly rated restaurant in suburban Pierrefonds, about 15 minutes from downtown Montreal. Located in a century-old gray-stone mansion, formerly the home of Canadian Army Brigadier General Meighen, its specialty is fine French dishes. Of particular note are the *canard aux olives* (duck with olives), sorrel salmon, and sweetbreads with truffles. Closed Sundays. Lunch served weekdays only. Reservations advised. Major credit cards accepted. 11,131 Meighen St. (yes, that's the right street address) in Pierrefonds (phone: 683-8200). Expensive.

Vent Vert – An award-winning menu boasts such specialties as quail pâté layered in *mille feuilles* (puff pastry), freshly poached scallops, and watercress mousse in wine sauce. Dine on the glassed-in terrace at the front, the small, romantic main dining room, or the back room, designed to accommodate larger groups. Open daily. Reservations advised. Major credit cards accepted. 2105 Rue de la Montagne (phone: 842-2482). Expensive.

Zen – The only North American branch of the London-based house of *Zen,* this is the city's best source of haute cuisine, Szechuan-style. "Aromatic Crispy Duck" is a long-standing favorite among the chef's specialities, which also include lobster, prepared six different ways, sesame shrimp, and whole abalone. Open daily. Reservations advised. Major credit cards accepted. *Four Seasons Hotel,* 1050 Sherbrooke St. W. (phone: 284-1110). Expensive.

Auberge le Vieux Saint-Gabriel – Long favored for its good French Canadian food and old-time ambience, this restaurant rambles through an Old Montreal building that dates from fur-trading days, complete with a tunnel leading to a room (now a cozy bar) once used to hide furs from raiding Indians. For a taste of Old Quebec, this is the place. Open daily. Reservations advised. Major credit cards accepted. 426 St-Gabriel St. (phone: 878-3562). Expensive to moderate.

Bagel-Etc. – Perfect for the insomniac, this jazzy all-night rendezvous prepares everything from caviar dishes to beef stew. Terrific hamburger menu, too. Sunday brunch features the widest variety of egg dishes in town. Open daily. Brunch reservations advised. Major credit cards accepted. 4320 St. Lawrence Blvd. (phone: 845-9462). Expensive to moderate.

Bonaparte – An attractive little dining room in the heart of Vieux Montréal, this place specializes in French cuisine and seafood. Ask for one of the balcony tables, overlooking the street. Open nightly for dinner, weekdays for lunch. Reservations advised for lunch. Major credit cards accepted. 433 St-François Xavier St. (phone: 844-4368). Expensive to moderate.

Claude Postel – One of Montreal's finest French restaurants (formerly *Le Petit Havre*) is located in Old Montreal in the old *Richelieu* hotel. Specialties include venison with raspberry sauce; salmon in a sherry, shallot, and cream sauce; smoked seafood; and homemade pastries. Open daily. Reservations advised. Major credit cards accepted. 443 St. Vincent (phone: 875-5067). Expensive to moderate.

Le Fadeau – Seventeenth-century ambience and excellent food and service are offered at this classic French restaurant in an Old Montreal house. Selections from an excellent wine cellar complement the cuisine. Closed Sundays. Reservations necessary. Major credit cards accepted. 423 St-Claude St. (phone: 878-3959). Expensive to moderate.

LUX – This futuristic-style bistro in the up-and-coming neighborhood around Boulevard St-Laurent is open 24 hours a day and serves French-influenced American food. Built in a converted textile mill, it has a spacious circular main room with a steel floor and a glass-enclosed second level, reached by two spiral staircases. Open daily. Reservations necessary for parties of 6 or more. Major credit cards accepted. 5220 Blvd. St-Laurent (phone: 271-9272). Expensive to moderate.

Le Mas des Oliviers – If you're gearing up for a night in Montreal's best disco area (Stanley, Mountain, and Bishop Streets), start off the way Montrealers do — by having dinner here. Try the lamb dishes — they're Chef Jacques Muller's specialty. Open daily. Reservations necessary. Major credit cards accepted. 1216 Bishop St. (phone: 861-6733). Expensive to moderate.

Le Pavillon de l'Atlantique – This seafood establishment, with its classic nautical decor, dominates the atrium of the Alcan Building. Service, even on busy Sunday evenings, is friendly and efficient. Among the best dishes are the grilled scampi, lobster thermidor, and Arctic char. *Moby Dick's* is the lively bar section, a popular lunchtime destination, where lunch and dinner menus are stripped-down versions of *Le Pavillon's* seafood specials. Open daily. Reservations advised. Major credit cards accepted. 1188 Sherbrooke St. W. (phone: 285-1636). *Moby Dick's,* closed Sundays. Reservations advised for lunch. Entrance at 2121 Drummond St. (phone: 285-1637) Expensive to moderate.

Les Serres de Marguerite – A greenhouse dining room that is always humming, particularly in the summer when cooling ceiling fans spin lazily overhead. Full-course dinners, generous salads, and quiche are the fare. Closed Sundays. Reservations advised. Major credit cards accepted. 417 St-Pierre St. (phone: 288-9788). Expensive to moderate.

Arigato – The sushi and sashimi combinations at this Japanese restaurant draw a loyal lunchtime crowd. Open daily. Reservations advised. Major credit cards accepted. 75 Rue de la Gauchetière W., on the Chinatown Mall (phone: 395-2470). Moderate.

Le Caveau – French food is served in this cozy little house in the heart of midtown. Checkered tablecloths and candlelight add to the intimate atmosphere. The less expensive of the two menus offers good value and has almost the same selection as the regular menu. The tournedos, house wine, and crème caramel are all of high quality. Open daily. Reservations advised. Major credit cards accepted. 2063 Victoria St. (phone: 844-1624). Moderate.

Les Copines de Chine – This Chinese restaurant has an attractive setting in the tropical, plant-filled atrium of *Place Dupuis*. Its appetizing Szechuan dishes are served by an attentive staff. Open daily. Reservations advised. Major credit cards accepted. 870 de Maisonneuve Blvd. E. (phone: 842-8325). Moderate.

Le Latini – A different pasta dish is featured every day, and the veal specialties are tasty and tender. In summer, guests may dine alfresco on the terrace. Closed Sundays. Reservations necessary. Major credit cards accepted. 1130 Jeanne Mance St., near *Complexe Desjardins* (phone: 861-3166). Moderate.

Le Paris – Yet another fine French eatery with an atmosphere that is truly Parisian. Closed Sundays and holidays. Reservations necessary. Major credit cards accepted. 1812 Ste-Catherine W. St. (phone: 937-4898). Moderate.

Le Père St-Vincent – Nestled in the oldest house in Old Montreal (1658), this eatery specializes in French dishes served beside a cozy hearth (there are three working fireplaces). The decor is rough-hewn, early Montreal, but the walls display an impressive collection of contemporary Quebec art. Open daily. Reservations advised. Major credit cards accepted. 429 St-Vincent St. (phone: 397-9610). Moderate.

La Tulipe Noire – This Parisian-style café and pastry shop in the Alcan building is one of the few midtown restaurants where you can get a moderately priced bite after the theater. A full dinner menu until 11:30 PM. A busy spot for breakfast, lunch, and Sunday brunch, it overlooks a garden court and its own summer café terrace. Open daily. No reservations. Major credit cards accepted. 2100 Stanley St. (phone: 285-1225). Moderate.

Les Filles du Roy – A popular tourist haunt offering hearty French Canadian fare in a 17th-century Quebec setting. The waitresses wear costumes fashioned after the period's "daughters of the king" who came to New France to marry eligible settlers. Order the spicy *tourtière* (meat pie), the *soupe aux pois* (pea soup), or the *ragoût de boulettes* (meatball stew). Sunday brunch is a special treat. Open daily. Reservations advised. Major credit cards accepted. 415 Bonsecours St. (phone: 849-3535). Moderate to inexpensive.

Bonsai – A Vietnamese restaurant, though it's named for the artistic miniature Japanese trees, it serves light meals accented with tasty soup and spring rolls. Ask for a table in the back dining room, which overlooks the Old Port. Closed Sundays. Reservations advised. Major credit cards accepted. 138 St. Paul St. E. (phone: 861-6640). Inexpensive.

Briskets – This Montreal deli chain offers some of the best smoked meat (a sort of mating of corned beef and pastrami) in this or any other town. At the Beaver Hall Hill branch, owner Jack Indri will be happy to give you a crash course in the slow art of smoking the beef — it's an interesting way to pass the time while waiting for your meal. Closed Sundays. No reservations. Major credit cards accepted. Three downtown locations: 1073 Beaver Hall Hill (phone: 878-3641); 2055 Bishop St. (phone: 843-3650); 4006 Ste-Catherine St. W. (phone: 932-3071). Inexpensive.

Chez Vito – In the Côte-des-Neiges area, near the University of Montreal, this popular place has fine Italian fare and a good disco upstairs. Open daily. No reservations. Major credit cards accepted. 5408-12 Côte-des-Neiges (phone: 735-3623). Inexpensive.

Jardin Lung Fung – Located in Chinatown, this place has an extensive Cantonese and Szechuan menu. House specialties include shrimp toast as an appetizer; "Great Vegetable Mix," a combination of Chinese stir-fried vegetables; and chicken stuffed with chopped meat in oyster sauce. It also serves the best egg rolls in town. Open daily. Reservations unnecessary. Major credit cards accepted. 1071 St-Urbain (phone: 879-0622). Inexpensive.

Magic Pan – For the best crêpes in town do as the students and professors of McGill do and head for this breezy little spot in the historic *Place Montreal Trust*. Dessert crêpes filled with pralines are a house favorite, and chocoholics will not be disappointed with the rich chocolate crêpes. Fillings include chicken, seafood, and cheese, too. Salads, sandwiches, and other light fare are served in this simple place with contemporary touches. Open daily. Reservations unnecessary. Major credit cards accepted. 1500 McGill College Rd. (phone: 849-4265). Inexpensive.

La Maison Greque – Very reasonable no-frills place featuring moussaka and *brochette au poisson*. Diners must bring their own wine, but it's worth a stop at the liquor store when a meal for two costs about $13. Open daily. Reservations advised. Major credit cards accepted. 450 Duluth St. E. (phone: 842-0969). Inexpensive.

Montreal Hebrew Delicatessen and Steak House – Known locally as *Schwartz's*, this deli is famous for its smoked meat and grilled steaks, and draws a cross section of Montrealers. You'll share a crowded table with other diners, and the French fries may be the best on this continent. Be sure to sprinkle them with vinegar like a true Montrealer. No liquor license, but plenty of Dr. Brown's cream soda. Closed *Yom Kippur*. No reservations. No credit cards accepted. 3895 St. Lawrence Blvd. (phone: 842-4813). Inexpensive.

Rôtisserie Laurier – Chicken, roasted Quebec-style, and served with a side of barbecue sauce. Open daily. No reservations. Major credit cards accepted. 381 Laurier W. (phone: 273-3671). Inexpensive.

Stash's Café Bazaar – Just beside Notre Dame Church in Old Montreal, this establishment specializes in Polish food. The decor is simple and the atmosphere friendly. Open daily. No reservations. Major credit cards accepted. 461 St-Sulpice St. (phone: 861-2915). Inexpensive.

Sucrerie de la Montagne – Anyone with a sweet tooth should make the trip to this sugaring-off spot 20 miles (32 km) southwest of the city. The maple sugar feast includes *tourtière* (meat pie) and baked beans, finished off with the traditional maple syrup pie, more commonly served in Quebec City. A full meal runs about $6.50 per person. Open 11 AM to 8 PM all year. Reservations necessary for groups. 300 Rang St-Georges, off Rte. 40 (phone: 451-5204 or 451-0831). Inexpensive.

Swensen's – An outlet of the San Francisco–based chain of old-fashioned ice cream parlors serves some of the richest, creamiest ice cream found from the American West to the Canadian East. There are 27 flavors to choose from, including sticky chewy chocolate, black raspberry cheesecake, butterscotch marble, Swiss orange chocolate chip — each one better than the last. Open daily. At the corner of Ste-Catherine St. W. and Mansfield Ave. (phone: 874-0695). Inexpensive.

QUEBEC CITY

The key battle that determined the fate of French Canada lasted only about 20 minutes. It occurred on the morning of September 13, 1759, on the Plains of Abraham in Quebec City, the capital of New France. The city had been under siege by the British General James Wolfe since July, but had stood firm against the attacks. On the evening of September 12, however, Wolfe led a group of soldiers up the steep hill from Anse au Foulon (formerly called Wolfe's Cove) and assembled the force on the Plains of Abraham. That is where the astonished and horrified French found them the following morning when the Marquis de Montcalm, commander of the city's defenses, rushed his troops into battle. In the ensuing struggle, both Wolfe and Montcalm were killed (Wolfe died on the battlefield, Montcalm shortly after in the city) and the French were decisively defeated. The British had won. But according to legend, as smoke obscured the battlefield and the dream of New France died with its last defenders, a voice was heard across the Plains, crying: "*Je me souviens*" — "I remember."

Those words have become the motto of Quebec Province, and nowhere do they resound with more conviction than in Quebec City, itself the most vivid and tangible remnant of New France in Canada. Rising on the massive cliff of Cape Diamond some 350 feet above the St. Lawrence River, Quebec City is the foundation of French culture and the rock upon which Canadian federalism often has come close to foundering. Though the English won control of Canada, Quebec City retained its French language, culture, and heritage. And through subsequent invasions by the British and Americans in the course of its history and the contemporary French-English controversy concerning the independence of Quebec, the city survives as a stronghold of French culture on an English-speaking continent.

In no other city in Canada can you see so clearly the places where the two worlds of the French and English collide. The Wolfe-Montcalm Monument in Lower Town, for example, commemorates both the victors and the vanquished. At the *Musée du Fort,* the guide explaining the diorama of the fateful battle in 1759 refers to the British as "the enemy." Few places have devoted so much space — 250 acres of parkland at the Plains of Abraham — to their defeat. Even in the sports world, French and English clashes of Canadian culture reveal themselves: Quebec City nationalists charged that top hockey prospect Eric Lindros was anti-French when he turned down an offer to play for the hometown *Nordiques.*

Quebec City was the first French settlement in North America, and despite 2 centuries of English rule, it is still fiercely French today. Of the metropolitan population of 600,000, 95% is of French stock, primarily from Normandy and Brittany on the northwest coast of France. Yet immigration to Quebec of people from French-speaking countries has not kept pace with immigration of English-speaking people to the rest of Canada, so these Quebecois tend to have a deeply rooted heritage that in most cases has little to do with France. True Quebecois are those who have never left the province — some actually trace their ancestry back to the 17th century. They are a family-oriented, traditional people, and their city reflects this attitude toward life.

Most everyone here speaks French; newspapers, plays, and conversations generally are in French, though many people can and do speak English, particularly those who work in businesses catering to tourists.

Many of the buildings in the old section of the city are restored 17th- and 18th-century stone houses, similar to those in the villages of provincial France. The cuisine is French or hearty Quebecois — thick pea soups, meat pies, and rich maple syrup pies for dessert. Street signs, store names, and customs attest to the city's French character. Even the walls that surround the Old City of Quebec (Quebec City is the only walled city on the continent) seem to protect its insular culture, and they demarcate historic Quebec from the newer parts of the city, where modern hotels, shopping malls, and office buildings acknowledge the 20th century.

The French-inspired architecture and the dramatic natural setting of Quebec City combine to make it one of the most beautiful cities in North America. Sometimes called the Gibraltar of America, Quebec City is carved into the 350-foot cliff of Cape Diamond.

At the foot of the cliff is the St. Lawrence River, caught midway on its long journey from Lake Ontario to the Atlantic Ocean at the Gulf of St. Lawrence. As huge as the St. Lawrence is — and it is miles wide at points both above and below Quebec City — Cape Diamond almost seems to tame it. As it lunges eastward toward its confluence with a small tributary, the St. Charles, the river narrows to a mere three-quarters of a mile.

To the southeast stands another promontory that forms the foundation of the town of Lévis. Some 25 miles (40 km) to the northeast, the hills culminate in the high peak of Mont Ste-Anne, one of the finest ski areas in Canada. Quebec City is a city on a hill, with a spectacular panoramic view. To the northeast is the Gaspé Peninsula, with its poor but picturesque villages; to the south, Montreal, a mere 153 miles (246 km) away; straight up to the north are the fabulous Laurentian slopes, which the Quebecois call the Laurentides.

The history of Quebec City seems to be stratified, starting at the land along the shore and progressing up the hill as the young settlement developed. Its history flows from the river, where the Indians inhabited the land for thousands of years, using it as their main source of transportation. And although explorer Jacques Cartier, the Breton sailor, gave Cape Diamond its name in 1535, Samuel de Champlain came to stay. Attracted by the strategically located site, Champlain founded the city in 1608 and established his first "habitation" here, a trading post comprised of a store, a few houses, and surrounding fortifications. The site of this development, now known as Place Royale, is located along the river. Place Royale became the center of a fur-trading colony — a meeting place for the merchants who governed the community as well as a commercial center and residential area where wealthy

Quebec merchants built their homes. As more colonists and missionaries arrived, the settlement began to expand up the hillside. In 1647, the Château St-Louis was built as a governor's residence at the top of the cliff (today the spectacular *Château Frontenac* hotel occupies this site).

The Canadian headquarters of the Roman Catholic church also was established in Old Upper Town soon after Bishop François de Montmorency Laval settled in Quebec City in 1659. The church played a major part in the development and character of the province. For more than 3 centuries, it acted as a cultural force in the city, initially conservative, but becoming more liberal in recent years.

Quarrels between the church and the trading company motivated King Louis XIV to send over a royal *intendant* — a royal overseer of sorts — to administer the province in 1663. Jean Talon, the first intendant, and Comte Louis de Buade de Frontenac, the governor, dealt with this conflict and also settled problems with various Indian tribes that had been attacking the young settlement. Together they fostered an atmosphere of peace and security during which the town developed as the center of New France.

This period was cut short by a much more significant struggle for power — between the two major colonizing forces, France and England. In 1690, Frontenac subdued an attack on the city led by Sir William Phipps, the British Governor of Massachusetts. Three years later, walls were constructed to fortify the city's defenses. In 1759, during the Seven Years' War, Quebec City fell to the British following the Battle of the Plains of Abraham. The settlement, known as the Act of Quebec (1774) guaranteed French Canadians "as much as British laws would allow" in terms of cultural and religious rights. But the battle had a profound effect on the Quebecois psyche. Many members of the aristocratic class returned to France. Those who stayed taught their children what had been lost on the Plains of Abraham: *"Je me souviens."*

But the British weren't the only ones with an interest in Quebec. In 1775, the Quebecois resisted an invasion by American troops led by General Richard Montgomery and Colonel Benedict Arnold. This siege lasted a little more than a month, ending with the arrival of the British fleet and the retreat of the exhausted American troops. Concerned over further attacks, the English completed the wall surrounding the city.

Throughout the 19th century, Quebec City remained an important political center and was named the province's capital in 1867. Peace also brought economic change. Timber and shipbuilding became the two major industries, and the city maintained its position as a significant commercial center until the mid-19th century, when Montreal and Toronto surpassed it.

But Quebec City remains the most important historical center of Canada. The Old City walls, which the United Nations declared a historic site in 1985, have been restored, and they surround the most historic section of the city, Old Quebec. The Quebec government declared the area around Place Royale a special zone in the 1960s, and more than 90% of the 17th- and 18th-century houses and buildings have been restored. Museums, cultural centers, and restaurants now occupy these restored houses. The Old Upper Town is a well-preserved area of narrow cobblestone streets lined with historic buildings. For a real taste of Old Quebec, go to one of its oldest buildings, now *Aux Anciens Canadiens* restaurant, for a hearty Quebecois meal topped off with maple syrup pie served with heavy cream (see *Eating Out*).

Beyond the city walls, farther up the hill, lies 20th-century Quebec. Here is a concentration of all the amenities found in any other modern provincial capital — a convention center; an underground shopping gallery, *Place Québec,* connected to the *Quebec Hilton International;* several other luxurious high-rise hotels; and the stately buildings of the National Assembly, as the legislature is called. Beyond spreads the suburb of Ste-Foy, rapidly developed in the past 3 decades to accommodate a growing population. Many Quebecois work in Ste-Foy at the suburb's two major shopping malls or at Laval University, a major employer and, with 40,000 students, also a big draw to the city. The largest employer of all is the provincial government, with more than 53,000 civil servants.

Around Parliament Hill stands further evidence that Quebec City's present is inextricably bound with its past. Sculptures of historically prominent Canadians are carved into niches in the National Assembly. These figures and the nearby Plains of Abraham and Citadelle — the star-shaped fortress that won the city the sobriquet "Gibraltar of America" — record Quebec City's struggle to become what it is today.

In many ways the struggle still continues, though its form has changed. The weapons are words rather than cannons, but the French-English controversy in Canada still simmers. During the late 1950s and early 1960s, what historians refer to as the Quiet Revolution swept Quebec. A liberal government headed by Premier Jean Lesage introduced major education and social reforms that are often associated with the growth of Quebec nationalism.

At the same time a growing feeling of exclusion from the mainstream of Canadian political-economic life gave rise to a new political party: the Parti Québecois. Headed by René Lévesque, it was determined to lead the province to political independence from English-speaking Canada, while still maintaining an economic link. The PQ was elected to provincial power in 1976 and re-elected in 1981, though a provincial referendum on independence in 1980 was rejected. In the 1985 and 1989 provincial elections, the PQ was defeated by the less separatism-oriented Liberal Party.

Canada has once again come to a critical point in its history. It's often said if you scratch the surface you will find some level of nationalism in every Quebecois; that has seldom been as true as it is now. Indeed, separatists note that today they have more than emotions going for them. The last decade has seen the emergence of a new era, one that finds Quebeckers themselves economically confident and turning to the world at large for fresh opportunities. It is fair to say that the province's current generation, well represented by a pragmatic government, aspires to economic stability rather than political turmoil. (Even the once fiercely separatist Parti Québecois wants to continue using the Canadian dollar and Canadian passports and to maintain trade relations with the rest of Canada.) Indeed, despite warnings from some critics that sovereignty would cripple the province economically, one poll of Quebec business leaders showed 72% believed that the economy of an independent Quebec would actually improve over time.

Quebec's current constitutional crisis began with its refusal to sign the Constitution, and in 1987 Prime Minister Mulroney proposed the Meech Lake Accord to give all the provinces more power. Under the accord, Quebec would have been recognized as a "distinct society" and, along with the other provinces, would have been given a veto power over future constitutional changes. When Manitoba and Newfoundland refused to ratify the agreement, the accord, which required unanimous approval, failed — giving rise to a new movement toward Quebec's secession from Canada. Since the accord's failure in 1990, opinion polls have shown support for independence in Quebec running between 50% and 70%. (According to newspaper accounts, the people of Quebec City are particularly supportive of independence, due to their primarily French Canadian heritage and to the fact that becoming the new nation's capital would likely mean new jobs and added prosperity for the city.)

But whatever the outcome of the independence movement, Quebec City will certainly remain — as it has through almost four centuries and six invasions — authentically French. The strength of its collective memory (*"Je me souviens"*) continues to hold fast.

QUEBEC CITY AT-A-GLANCE

SEEING THE CITY: *L'Astral,* the *Loews Le Concorde* hotel's revolving rooftop restaurant-bar, is situated on the highest point of Cape Diamond, and has a great panorama of Quebec City and surrounding areas, day or night. On a clear day, you can see as far as Ile d'Orléans, in summer a verdant island of fruit farms and country homes, and, some 25 miles away, a chain of mountains dominated by Mont Ste-Anne, the region's best ski resort. *L'Astral* is open from 11:45 AM to 3 PM and 6 to 11 PM except on Sundays, when it opens at 10 AM for brunch. The restaurant's bar is open daily from 11 AM to midnight (1225 Pl. Montcalm; phone: 647-2222). Also check out the view from the city's highest observation point, the 31st floor of Edifice Marie-Guyart (Complexe G) at 1037 St-Amable just off the Grande Allée. While enjoying the free view you can tour exhibitions of works by some of Quebec's best artists in the sky-high *Galerie Anima G* (phone: 644-9841). For more information, see *Walk 4: "New" Quebec* in DIRECTIONS/QUEBEC CITY.

There are many fine views of the river, but two of the best are from Dufferin Terrace, a boardwalk flanking the *Château Frontenac* hotel, and Earl Grey Terrace, an observatory adjoining the Plains of Abraham, between Wolfe and Montcalm Streets, in Parc des Champs de Bataille.

SPECIAL PLACES: The best way to see Quebec City is by strolling down its streets and alleys. Visitors definitely should ride the funicular, the outdoor elevator that links the Lower and Upper towns. But Quebec City is more a feast for feet, a people-size place where the scale of sites is that of an easy day's perambulation. The rewards for lazy, languid strolls are quaint cobbled streets, historic houses, and the sort of secure claustrophobia conferred by a city that you can almost drape around your shoulders. But first it's important to get a good map. The streets are laid out in a haphazard fashion, particularly in the older sections. Old Lower Town revolves around Place Royale at river level. To the north and west, there's a new cluster of cafés, pubs, art galleries, boutiques, and antiques stores in what used to be the city's financial district. (The stock exchange and the old banks closed after Quebec's importance as a trading center waned.) Just a few more blocks north is the spruced-up port area, with old warehouses reincarnated as fashionable boutiques. Place d'Armes, at the top of the funicular next to the *Château Frontenac,* stands at the center of Old Upper Town. Parliament Hill, farther up, is the site of government buildings abutting sleek high-rise hotels. Beyond them all are the suburbs. The Plains of Abraham have been made into a lovely park (Parc des Champs de Battaille), with miles of walking and jogging paths, picnic tables, bird-feeding stations, gardens, and great river views.

OLD LOWER TOWN

Place Royale – This small, cobblestone square is known as Canada's "cradle of French civilization." It was here that Champlain built his first *habitation* in 1608, which included buildings for lodging, a store, a stockade, and gardens. During the French regime, the square was used as a marketplace, and successful merchants built their homes here. In the center of the square is a bronze bust of Louis XIV. The area has been declared a special historic zone by the Quebec government, and its restoration is almost complete. Despite the destruction of some of the houses, the *place* and the streets leading off it are lined with the greatest concentration of 17th- and 18th-century buildings in North America. Most of the buildings clustered around the Church of Notre-Dame-des-Victoires are architectural gems that began life as the houses of wealthy merchants. As the centuries slipped by, the area went downhill and the townsfolk simply forgot its history. Then, in 1960, a fire bared some strange brick walls. "They don't build walls like that anymore," noted assorted passersby — until some of them realized that these were genuine historic treasures. The main floors of a number of these homes are open to the public as museums, cultural centers, art galleries, and restaurants, while the upper floors are home to modern-day Quebeckers, many of whom own businesses in the area. Off Notre-Dame at the foot of Cape Diamond near the river.

Place de Paris – In 1984, France paid tribute to this city and province by inaugurating the Place au Québec in Paris. To reciprocate, a monument was erected on the exact spot where the French first set foot on Quebec soil — at the corner of today's Rue de la Place and Rue de l'Union — and dubbed it Place de Paris.

Maisons Bruneau, Drapeau, and Rageot – The multimedia production, "Place Royale: Business Centre of New France," which describes the business activities of the area during colonial times, is presented here daily. No admission charge. 3A Pl. Royale, beside La Maison des Vins (see below).

La Batterie Royale – Built in 1691, this artillery emplacement, one of the oldest in Quebec City, has been entirely restored. On the corner of Rues Sous le Fort and St-Pierre.

Entrepôt Thibodeau – This house is now the Place Royale tourist reception center. Stop here first to pick up the "Place Royale" brochure, which describes points of interest in the area. Guided tours (in English) are available. Open daily from 10 AM to 6 PM May 15 until the end of September. No admission charge. Pl. Marché Finlay (phone: 643-6631 from June 1 through September; phone: 643-2158 at other times).

Maison Fornel – With foundations dating back to 1658 and vaulted cellars constructed in 1735, this restored house is now an exhibition center; its reconstruction in 1964 initiated the Place Royale restoration project. The exhibition "Place Royale: 400 Years of History" provides a good perspective on the area's past and ongoing restoration; a brochure (in English) is available. Open daily from mid-May through September 10 AM to 6 PM. No admission charge. 25 Rue St-Pierre, just south of Ruelle de la Place (phone: 643-6631).

Notre-Dame-des-Victoires – Our Lady of Victories was built in 1688 and renamed to commemorate the triumph of the French over the English during the attacks of 1690 and 1711. The small stone structure was rebuilt in 1759, after the bombardment, in accordance with the original design. The exterior is quite modest, yet inside look for the exquisite woodwork, including a main altar minutely carved in the shape of an old fort, paintings from the school of Rubens, and old battle flags. Mass is said every Saturday at 7 PM and Sunday (call for hours). Open daily May 15 to October 15. Off-season, closed Mondays. No admission charge. Pl. Royale (phone: 692-1650).

Maison des Vins – This restored home now houses an excellent wine store with an extensive selection of imported wines. The establishment is worth a visit for a look at its exposed brick walls, vaulted candlelit wine cellars, and its array of bottles ranging from a Mouton Rothschild 1879 (valued between about $13,000 and $21,000) to the local specialty, caribou, a potent mixture of wine and alcohol (a favorite of some Quebeckers for helping them get through the long, cold winters). Open Tuesdays through Saturdays. Reservations are essential for guided tours. No admission charge. 1 Pl. Royale (phone: 643-1214).

Maison Chevalier – These three buildings, constructed in the 17th and 18th centuries for several merchants, including Jean-Baptiste Chevalier, have been linked to form an interesting ethnographic museum. Exhibits vary, but include old toys, costumes, furniture, and folk art. Open daily from June 22 to September 3. No admission charge. Corner of Cul-de-Sac and Notre-Dame (phone: 643-9689).

Maison Jolliet – This restored house was the home of explorer Louis Jolliet, who, accompanied by Jacques Marquette, discovered the Mississippi River in 1672. His house now contains the entrance to the *funiculaire,* which for 75¢ saves you the trouble of having to climb back up to Upper Town. In operation daily from 7:30 AM to 11 PM. Opposite Sous le Fort at the foot of Escalier du Petit Champlain (phone: 692-1132).

Vieux Port de Québec (Old Port) – The old port area of Quebec has a new look. The $100-million development, including a 6,000-seat open-air amphitheater, a tent theater that seats 1,000, and a café theater, is connected by enclosed aerial walkways. At the confluence of the St. Lawrence and St. Charles rivers lies a lock-controlled marina big enough to accommodate several hundred pleasure craft; ocean-going merchant vessels and cruise ships moor along the wharf; the area also houses restaurants, pubs, and cafés. Easily accessible by strollers and cyclists from the waterfront promenade. 160 Rue Dalhousie (phone: 648-4370).

Port of Quebec in the 19th Century Interpretation Center – Four exhibition floors in a refurbished cement factory trace the salty history of Old Quebec when it was the center of Canada's lumber and shipbuilding trade in the days when 40% of the population was English-speaking. Run by Parks Canada, it displays a ship's prow, rum kegs, and a working capstan set up for visitors to try their hand. The top floor affords views of the city skyline and marina. Open daily during spring and summer; open with reservations only December through February, except during *Carnaval* when it is open daily. No admission charge. 100 Rue St-André (phone: 648-3330).

Musée de la Civilisation – Located between Place Royale and the Old Port near the St. Lawrence River, this building, designed by architect Moshe Safdie, won an award for the way in which its modern architecture is integrated into the historic neighborhood of the Old Port. Along with galleries, a stone house built in 1732 is enclosed in this large museum. Open daily June 24 to *Labour Day;* Tuesdays through Sundays the rest of the year. No admission charge for children under 16. 85 Rue Dalhousie, near Pl. Royale (phone: 643-2158).

OLD UPPER TOWN

Place d'Armes – A small square that served as a meeting place and parade ground during the French regime. In the center of the square stands a Gothic fountain surmounted by the granite and bronze Monument of Faith, constructed in 1916 in memory of the Récollets (Franciscan) missionaries who arrived in 1615. Today the square is a good orientation point in Old Upper Town, the section of Old Quebec built above the cliff, where military, religious, and residential buildings from the 17th, 18th, and 19th centuries have been restored. One of the loveliest, La Maison Vallée (which dates from 1732), has become the home of the Tussaud-like wax museum (*Musée de Cire;* 22 Rue Ste-Anne; phone: 692-2289). For traditional French Canadian fare and decor, check out *Aux Anciens Canadiens* (see *Eating Out*), in a house built in 1677 and named after the classic Canadian volume whose author, Philippe Aubert de Gaspé, once lived on the premises.

Château Frontenac – This grand hotel owned by C.P. Hotels, Ltd., in all its classic French glory, is Quebec City's most recognizable landmark. Everything about this structure, built in 1893, announces its grandeur, from its broad, slanting copper roof, its turrets and towers, and its imposing red brick walls to its magnificent setting high above the St. Lawrence River. The site on which it is built has undergone numerous transitions. First a fort built by Champlain in 1620, it became a fortress in 1636, and eventually became known as Château St-Louis, a regal residence of the Governors of New France. Two centuries later, in 1834, it was razed by fire. History buffs will find an interesting display tracing the château's past in the main lobby. Stroll around the lobby, the inner courtyard, or enjoy the majestic river view from the circular cocktail lounge. The Dufferin Terrace, built in 1834, with its spectacular view of Old Lower Town and the Ile d'Orléans, is a favorite spot for relaxing on summer nights. At the north end of the terrace stands a statue of Samuel de Champlain, watching over the city he founded in 1608. 1 Av. des Carrières (phone: 692-3861).

Jardin des Gouverneurs – Originally the private garden of Château St-Louis, it was opened to the public in 1838. Here stands the Wolfe-Montcalm Monument, erected in 1828. It is one of the few monuments in the world commemorating both the triumphant and the defeated: "Their courage gave them the same lot; history, the same fame; posterity, the same monument." Open daily. No admission charge. Next to *Château Frontenac* at Av. des Carrières and Rue Mont Carmel.

Cavalier du Moulin (Windmill Outpost) – This restful little park once formed an important link in the Old City's defense works. Named for the windmill that once occupied the site, the military outpost was first activated in 1693; its men had orders to destroy the Cape Diamond redoubt and the St-Louis bastion if they were to fall to the enemy. Open daily May through November from 7 AM to 9 PM. No admission charge. Located at the western end of Rue Mont-Carmel.

Musée du Fort – This museum is a good place for visitors to get their historical bearings. A 30-minute sound-and-light show presented on a 450-foot-square model of the 18th-century city re-creates the most important battles and sieges of Quebec, including the Battle of the Plains of Abraham and the attack by Arnold and Montgomery during the American Revolution. There's also a wide variety of guides and history books in English. Open daily (call for hours), except December 1 through *Christmas.* Shows alternate in English and French. Admission charge. 10 Rue Ste-Anne (phone: 692-2175).

Notre-Dame de Québec Basilica – First built in 1647, this Roman Catholic church of the Cardinal Archbishop of Quebec once served the diocese of all French North America, and still serves the oldest parish north of Mexico. The façade is unusual for its two unequal towers; the vaulted interior contains an impressive number of religious works of art. Open daily. No admission charge. Rue Buade and Côte de la Fabrique.

Quebec Seminary – Beyond the iron gates lies a group of 17th-century buildings that were part of a training school for Catholic priests founded in 1663 by François de Montmorency Laval, the first Bishop of Quebec. The main chapel is worth a visit for a look at its marble altars, valuable relics, and sarcophagus of Bishop Laval; the sundial over the door dates to 1773. The museum here has a collection of religious and secular art from both Quebec and Europe as well as some early scientific instruments. The museum is closed Mondays. Admission charge (9 Rue de l'Université; phone: 692-2843). Visits to other parts of the seminary are possible from June 1 to August 31 but must be arranged in advance (phone: 692-3981 for information).

Holy Trinity Anglican Cathedral – This stately structure was the first Church of England cathedral ever built (1804) outside of the British Isles. The pews, including the Royal Pew — which may be occupied only by the British sovereign or his or her representative — are composed of solid English oak; the large stained glass windows are awe-inspiring. Open daily 10 AM to 5 PM from June 1 to September 1; off-season, open 1 to 3 PM, except Mondays. 31 Desjardins (phone: 692-2193).

Ursuline Convent – Founded in 1639, it runs the oldest school for women in North America. The convent itself was twice damaged by fire, but some original walls still stand. A few of the present buildings date from the 17th century. It is not open to the public, but the chapel, which contains a number of relics and valuable paintings, welcomes visitors. Its votive lamp, first lit in 1717, has never been extinguished, and the defeated Montcalm is buried in a tomb in the chapel. His skull is preserved under glass in the *Musée des Ursulines,* adjoining the chapel. Other exhibits in the museum include reproductions of the tiny, rustic cells the Ursuline pioneers occupied in their first years at the waterfront. The chapel is open May through October, Tuesdays through Saturdays; call for hours. No admission charge. The museum is closed Mondays and in December; call for hours. Admission charge. Both are at 12 Rue Donnacona (phone: 694-0694).

Next door, *Centre Marie-de-l'Incarnation* displays a collection of objects belonging to the order's co-founder, Mother Marie-de-l'Incarnation. It also operates a bookstore and shows films tracing the Ursulines' history under French rule. The center is closed Mondays; call for hours. 10 Rue Donnacona (phone: 692-1596). For more information see *Walk 1: Vieux Québec/Upper Town* in QUEBEC CITY/DIRECTIONS.

Montmorency Park – Named in honor of Bishop Laval — François de Montmorency Laval — this park, straddling the hill between the Old Upper Town and Old Lower Town, affords good views of the Lower Town, the harbor, and the surrounding area. A monument to Sir Georges Etienne Cartier, a French Canadian political leader, and another to Louis Hébert (the first farmer to settle in Quebec City), stand in the center of the park. On the hill, off Côte de la Montagne.

Laval Monument – An impressive statue honoring Bishop Laval, Canada's first bishop, who arrived in 1659 and was one of the most prominent citizens of New France. He founded the Quebec Seminary, the predecessor of Laval University. The work, sculpted by Philippe Hébert, was unveiled in 1908. At Côte de la Montagne across from Montmorency Park.

PARLIAMENT HILL AND THE PLAINS OF ABRAHAM

La Promenade des Gouverneurs – This 2,200-foot-long walkway leads from Dufferin Terrace up Cape Diamond, beside the Citadelle, all the way to the Plains of Abraham. The walk offers excellent views of the river upstream to the Quebec Bridge and downstream to the Ile d'Orléans. Open daily from late May to October (closed the rest of the year). No admission charge. Begins at the end of Dufferin Terrace.

Citadelle – This massive star-shape fortress commands a strategic position at the highest point on Quebec's promontory, 350 feet above the St. Lawrence. The French built previous fortifications on this site, but the present citadel was constructed between 1820 and 1832 by the British government as a defense against American attack following the War of 1812. The fortress was never subjected to enemy fire. It was first occupied by British troops, then by the Royal Canadian Artillery, and since 1920 by the Royal 22nd Regiment. From mid-June to the first Monday in September, the Changing of the Guard is performed daily at 10 AM, and the Ceremonial Retreat is enacted at 7 PM on Tuesdays, Thursdays, Saturdays, and Sundays. Closed December through February except to groups with previous reservations (write *Musée de la Citadelle,* CP 6020, Haute-Ville, Quebec G1R 4V7); open during *Carnaval.* Admission charge. Reached by Côte de la Citadelle (phone: 648-3563).

Fortifications of Quebec – The walls encircling the Old City and its four gates, now the domain of Parks Canada, offer a 3-mile (5-km) walk along the western section, which overlooks Old Quebec and the surrounding area. The federal government has been actively restoring the walls since 1971. The Poudrière de l'Esplanade (Esplanade Powder House) is an 1810 defense site at Porte St-Louis which the parks authority has restored as a reception and interpretation center. The departure point for guided tours of the fortifications is the powder house, open daily mid-May through *Labour Day* from 10 AM to 5 PM; off-season by reservation only, except during *Carnaval,* when it opens from 1 to 5 PM. No admission charge (phone: 648-7016).

Parc de l'Artillerie, also part of the fortifications system, preserves defense works raised during the French regime, including the Dauphine Redoubt (built from 1712 to 1748) and military structures installed by the British in the early 18th century. Visit the reception center (an old iron foundry), the redoubt, which has been converted to a heritage initiation center for children, and the Officers' Quarters. Reception and interpretation center open April to October on Mondays from 1 to 5 PM, Tuesdays through Sundays 10 AM to 5 PM. Off-season, Mondays through Fridays 10 AM to noon and 1 to 5 PM. No admission charge. 2 Rue D'Auteuil (phone: 648-4205). For more information, see *Walk 1: Vieux Québec/Upper Town* in DIRECTIONS/QUEBEC CITY.

The Plains of Abraham – Named for Abraham Martin, the first St. Lawrence River pilot, this is where Canada's French-English struggle was decided in 1759. Now part of the 250-acre Parc des Champs de Bataille, the Plains of Abraham were once the site of the battle between the British forces led by General James Wolfe and the French under the Marquis de Montcalm that sealed the fate of New France. Both leaders lost their lives in the struggle and the British gained control of Canada. Many Quebec residents returned to France; those who remained kept alive the idea of a French identity in North America, from which sprang the motto of the province: "*Je me souviens.*" There is an observation post affording excellent river views and various monuments and statues. The *Quebec Museum* (see below) is also on the grounds. Open daily from June 15 to September 14, closed on Mondays for the rest of the year. Beyond the Citadelle to the west, off Grande Allée.

Quebec Museum – Reopened in 1991 after a $23-million expansion, Quebec's museum of fine arts doubled its exhibition space for a collection of Quebecois paintings, sculptures, and decorative arts dating from the late 17th century to the present. The original neo-classical building (1927) is now joined to the restored Old Quebec prison (1871) by a glass-walled Grand Hall with a skylight roof. An artists' garden and 13 galleries display the works of artists from North America and abroad. The museum also hosts major international exhibitions. Open daily from July 15 to *Labour Day.* Closed Mondays the rest of the year, *Christmas,* and *New Years Day.* No admission charge Wednesdays. 1 Av. Wolfe-Montcalm (phone: 643-2150).

Regimental Museum – This 1750 structure displays ancient weapons, uniforms, and rare documents — some dating back to the time of the French regime. Closed January and February, except to groups reserving ahead. Open during *Carnaval.* Admission included in the entrance charge to the Citadelle. Côte de la Citadelle off Rue St-Louis (phone: 648-3563).

National Assembly – Also known as the Parliament buildings, these imposing French Renaissance structures were built between 1877 and 1886. The 12 bronze statues in niches on the façade, commemorating people prominent in Quebec's and Canada's history, were executed by the Quebec sculptor Hébert. Guided tours, in French and English, are conducted daily in July and August and on weekdays from September to November and from January to May. The Assembly is not in session from June 24 to October or from December 22 to mid-March. Bounded by Rue Dufferin, Bd. St-Cyrille E., St-Augustin, and Grande Allée (phone: 643-7239).

Complexe G – This is an example of new Quebec, right down to its straightforward, no-nonsense name. At 31 stories, it is the city's highest building. It houses various ministries and provincial government services. An observation gallery on top is open weekdays from 10 AM to 4 PM and weekends from 1 to 5 PM. Closed December 15 to January 15. No admission charge. Bounded by Bd. St-Cyrille E., de la Chevrotière, St-Amable, and Conroy (phone: 644-9841).

Chapelle Historique Bon-Pasteur – A designated historic monument, the chapel of the mother house of Les Soeurs du Bon-Pasteur de Québec opened in 1868. The high altar of delicately carved wood and gold leaf dates from 1730. Many paintings were done by members of the order more than a century ago. Concerts are held regularly and a special Sunday mass for artists is celebrated at 11 AM, following a 15-minute musical prelude. Open daily except Mondays May through September from noon to 5 PM; open by request the rest of the year. No admission charge. 1080 Rue De La Chevrotière (phone: 648-9720). For more information, see *Walk 4: "New" Quebec* in DIRECTIONS/QUEBEC CITY.

Grand Théâtre de Québec – Another work of modern architecture, this sleek structure built in 1970 comprises a music conservatory and two entertainment halls. 269 Bd. St-Cyrille at the corner of Rue Claire-Fontaine (phone: 643-8131).

SUBURBS

Ste-Foy – This town has grown quickly since the 1960s to become Quebec City's bedroom community of choice, a sprawling, American-style suburb of modern condominiums and apartments. In addition to its Route 175 motel strip, the town supports two large shopping malls, *Place Laurier* and *Place Ste-Foy,* and a growing number of restaurants, bars, and discos. Follow Grande Allée about 2 miles (3 km) west from the National Assembly. Or take bus No. 11 or 25 from downtown.

Sillery – Once the preserve of Quebec City's English-speaking community, today this charming residential neighborhood is more French than English. Only a 10-minute drive from the city center en route to Ste-Foy, it's a tranquil retreat of quiet, tree-shaded streets and expensive homes, surrounded by manicured lawns and well-tended gardens. Avenue Magurie is Sillery's chic commerical zone, with several stylish restaurants.

Villa Bagatelle – An interpretation center devoted to Sillery's past, this gray frame, gingerbread-trimmed Victorian villa recalls the Belle Epoque of Quebec's English and Scots lumber barons and shipbuilders. Today's garden suburb was estate country in the early 19th century, when wealthy lumbermen and shipping magnates built their mansions here close to the St. Lawrence River and the shipyards at the base of the cliffs. In summer, the villa is the departure point for walking tours of what remains of the old baronial domain. The popular Bagatelle Gardens bloom with more than 350 varieties of plants and the adjoining studio exhibits works of promising young artists. Nearby Bois-de-Coulonge is one of the prettiest parks in the Quebec City area. Open Tuesdays through Sundays 11 AM to 5 PM. Admission charge. 1563 Chemin St-Louis, Sillery (phone: 688-8074). Take buses Nos. 11 or 25 from downtown.

Laval University – An outgrowth of the Quebec Seminary founded by Bishop Laval, it is the oldest French-language university on the continent. The construction of a sprawling 465-acre campus was begun in 1948 to accommodate the growing numbers of students. One of the school's 25 modern buildings is the physical education and sports complex. Its excellent facilities, including an Olympic-size pool, are open to the public at certain hours, mainly weekends. Off Bd. Laurier (Rte. 175) and bounded by du Vallon, Myrand, and Chemin Ste-Foy (phone: 656-2131).

Ile d'Orléans – This island in the St. Lawrence River below Quebec was relatively isolated until a suspension bridge connecting it with the mainland was built in 1935. Because of this, the island retains a great deal of its 18th-century French Canadian influence. Most of the islanders are of Norman or Breton stock, and, like their ancestors, most are farmers. (Island apples and strawberries are especially good.) The island is only 21 miles long and about 5 miles wide. Visitors can easily make a complete driving tour in a grand circle, stopping in village after village of 17th- and 18th-century houses and churches. (Route 368 forms a 42-mile/68-km ring around the island.) Ste-Famille has the most interesting church on the island — a triple-spired structure built in 1742. On the east side of the island are some summer cottages and Ste-Pétronille, a summer resort village, 10 miles (16 km) northeast of Quebec.

If you visit during March or April, keep an eye out for smoke coming from some of the buildings off the main road. These are "sugar shacks," stark, wooden structures where Quebec's famous maple syrup is made. More like a scene from a Breton landscape than a village in North America, ruddy-faced men stand around steaming metal bins, waiting and watching for just the right moment when the liquid is ready. Follow the mist: The grounds — maple trees bearing metal spigots and buckets — lead to a shack where, more often than not, the proprietor will invite you in and even give you a sample of his oh-so-sweet wares. Two of the best on Ile d'Orléans are *Sucrerie Jean-Pierre Verret* (Chemin Royal, St-Jean; phone: 522-8217 and 829-3189) and *Cabane L'En-Tailleur* (1447 Chemin Royal, St-Pierre; phone: 828-2344 or 828-1269). Even when the sap is not running these shacks are open for business, selling maple sugar products; both are open from March to November. Those heading west to Montreal (about 20 miles/32 km west on Rte. 40) during March or April can stop at the traditional sugar shack of Ernest Martel (23 Rue Grand-Capsa, Point-Rouge; phone: 875-2842 or 875-2164).

To get to Ile d'Orléans take Autoroute Dufferin down the hill near the National Assembly, then Route 138. *Beautemps Mauvaistemps* organizes personalized tours of the island, year-round (phone: 828-2275).

■ **EXTRA SPECIAL:** Ste-Anne-de-Beaupré is a small village near Mont Ste-Anne dominated by a massive cathedral, which is an internationally renowned Catholic shrine. Millions of people have made pilgrimages here, and the piles of crutches, canes, and folding wheelchairs in the cathedral attest to healings that the faithful believe have taken place. The present basilica (1923) can accommodate 3,000 people. The fountain of Ste-Anne in front is said to have healing powers. The sanctuary has a marble statue of Ste-Anne, as well as other venerable religious items. An information bureau has been set up, and guides are available to lead tours (phone: 827-3781).

Mont Ste-Anne is the most popular winter sports center in the area. Its downhill runs, night skiing, cross-country ski tracks, and lift facilities attract a different breed of pilgrim — in search of miraculous skiing. (See "Sports" in *Sources and Resources,* below.) To reach the ski area, head 5 miles (8 km) beyond the village on Route 138 and turn north onto Route 360 (phone: 827-4561).

Just east of Mont Ste-Anne is the Réserve Nationale de la Faune du Cap Tourmente, developed by naturalists to protect the greater snow goose, along with 250 other bird species, which stop here during their seasonal migrations. The noisy October gatherings can easily attract 100,000 screeching birds. In May, ducks, herons, swallows, and red-winged blackbirds build their nests in the many pounds of the region. The reserve also offers a nature-interpretation center. To visit, head east on Route 138 after leaving Ste-Anne-de-Beaupré and watch for signs for Cap Tourmente (phone: 827-4591, April to October; 653-8186 other times).

En route to Ste-Anne-de-Beaupré or on the return to Quebec City, stop off at the 274-foot-high Montmorency Falls. In 1759, the English General Wolfe established his headquarters near the top. These old buildings have been made into a beautiful, old hotel, the *Manoir Montmorency,* with a dining room offering a fantastic view over Ile d'Orléans. 2490 Av. Royale, Beauport (phone: 663-2877).

SOURCES AND RESOURCES

TOURIST INFORMATION: For tourist information, maps, and brochures, contact the Greater Quebec City Region Tourism and Convention Bureau (60 Rue D'Auteuil; phone: 692-2471) or the reception office of the Quebec Department of Tourism (12 Rue Ste-Anne; phone: 873-2015; 800-363-7777 in the US, except Alaska). The Place Royale restoration has its own information center in *Entrepôt Thibodeau,* open during summer only (Pl. Marché Finlay; phone: 643-6631). Another government tourist information center is in Ste-Foy, off the Pierre-Laporte Bridge. It's open daily, year-round (3005 Bd. Laurier; phone: 651-2882).

English-language city guidebooks are hard to find; most are written in French. *Librairie Garneau* (a bookstore at 47 Buade; phone: 682-3212) and *Musée du Fort* (10 Rue Ste-Anne; phone: 692-2175) have a fair selection. One useful (and free) publication is the *Quebec City Region* tourist guide published by the Quebec government. For information on its availability, call the Quebec City Region Tourism and Convention Bureau (phone: 692-2471 or 651-2882).

Local Coverage – *Le Soleil* and *Le Journal de Québec* are French morning dailies; *Québec Chronicle-Telegraph* is an English weekly that hits the newsstands on Wednesdays. *Voilà Québec* is a bilingual quarterly entertainment, sightseeing, and dining guide distributed free in hotels, at the various tourist information centers, or by calling 692-2471. For English-language television programs, tune to CKMI, Channel 5; the English radio station is CBVE at 104.7 FM.

Food – *Les Restaurants, Le Guide des Restaurants de la Région de Québec,* published by the Quebec Urban Community, lists restaurants in both the city and suburbs and is available (free) at most tourist information offices. Also check *Voilà Québec.*

TELEPHONE: The area code for Quebec City is 418.

CURRENCY: All prices are quoted in US dollars unless otherwise indicated.
  Sales Tax – Quebec has a provincial sales tax of 7% to 9%, depending on what is being purchased. In addition, a 7% federal tax, called the Goods and Services Tax (GST), is levied on most purchases. In many cases, visitors can receive refunds of both the provincial and federal taxes. For details on Quebec tax rebates, call 800-567-4692. For GST rebate information see *Calculating Costs* in GETTING READY TO GO.

GETTING AROUND: Bus – The *Quebec Urban Community Transit Commission (CTCUQ)* operates buses that serve the metropolitan area from approximately 5:30 AM to 1 AM. Exact change, CN$1.75, is required; tickets also can be purchased at tobacconists and convenience stores for CN$1.40. For route information, call 627-2511. During the winter, *CTCUQ* also runs *Skibus*, which serves several ski areas around Quebec from 7 AM to 9:30 PM. Look for the red-and-white snowflake symbol at bus stops throughout the city.

Calèche – Horse-drawn carriages tour Old Quebec, the Parliament area, and the Plains of Abraham year-round. The fare for the 35-minute tour is about $45 for up to five people. A tip is customary for the driver. The *calèches* line up at four locations: near the main information office of the Greater Quebec Area Tourism and Convention Bureau at 60 Rue D'Auteuil; at St-Louis Gate; at Parc Esplanade (on the west side of Rue St-Louis inside the walls); and at Place d'Armes near the *Château Frontenac* (phone: 687-9797 or 648-1888).

Car Rentals – Most major firms serve the city. *Avis* has four locations: *Quebec Hilton International* (3 Pl. Québec; phone: 523-1075); 2785 Bd. Laurier (phone: 651-5087); the *Quebec Inn* near the airport (7174 Bd. Hamel; phone: 872-2861); and *Les Halles de Charlesbourg* (8850 Bd. Cloutier; phone: 626-2847). *Budget* has a number of locations (29 Côte du Palais; phone: 692-3660 or 658-6795; and 5 Pl. Québec; phone: 529-0966). *Hertz* also has several sites (1200 Germain-des-Prés; phone: 658-6785; 44 Côte du Palais; phone: 694-1224 or 694-1226; the airport; phone: 871-1571; and 1176 de la Chevrotière; phone: 647-4949 or 647-4923). *Tilden* has two locations (295 Rue St-Paul; phone: 694-1727; and at the airport; phone: 871-1224). See also "Car Rental" in *On Arrival,* GETTING READY TO GO.

Cruises – St. Lawrence cruises are available aboard the M/V *Louis Jolliet* from Chouinard Pier (10 Dalhousie), in the Place Royale section of the city, from June through September and by request only from May to mid-June and early September to October. Prices range from $13 to $18 (children under 5 free; 5–12, $6.50 to $9.50) depending on the time and day of the cruise (phone: 692-1159). Also available for sailboat lovers are a variety of trips organized by *Vieux Port Yachting,* with cruises of up to 14 days to as far as the Saguenay River, 200 miles north of Quebec City and one of the greatest fjords in the world. Information: *Vieux Port Yachting Inc.* (Quai Renaud, 80 St-André C.P. 1543, Terminus Quebec G1K 7H6; phone: 692-0017).

Ferry – Year-round service links Quebec and Lévis, operating every half hour from 6 AM to midnight, then less frequently. The ferry ride affords panoramic views of both cities (phone: 644-3704).

Taxi – Generally cabs cannot be hailed in the streets but some cabbies are unilingual French so have your phrasebook ready. There are cabstands at the major hotels and in Old Quebec at Place d'Armes and at d'Youville Square. The principal cab companies are *Taxi Co-op* (phone: 525-5191); *Taxi Quebec* (phone: 525-8123); and *Taxi Co-op* in Ste-Foy (phone: 653-7777).

Walking Tours – Quebec City is best seen on foot. To enrich your stroll, rent a tape-recorded tour tracing the city's history from *Sonore Tours* (summers only; Pl. d'Armes; phone: 694-0665). Or pick up a free copy of *Quebec City Region* — which includes walking tours — at the tourist office. The Quebec Ministry of Cultural Affairs publishes a folder about Place Royale, which can be obtained at the Place Royale information center in Entrepôt Thibodeau (Pl. Marché Finlay). *Baillairgé Cultural Tours Inc.* (phone: 658-4799) offers 2¼-hour walking tours of the Old Town, with emphasis on history and architecture, departing from *Musée du Fort,* across the street from the *Château Frontenac,* at 9:30 AM and 2 PM daily. The tour guides are especially interesting and knowledgeable. Tours are available from late June to mid-October. Cost is about $10.50. For those interested in the impressive religious history of the city, the booklet "Living Stones of Old Quebec" outlines three walking tours. The publication, which includes illustrations and brief descriptions of points of interest, is free and can be obtained through any tourist office or by contacting the *Religion Tourism Corporation* (16 Buade St., Quebec City, Quebec G1R 4A1, Canada; phone: 694-0665). Guided tours geared toward the city's religious background also are available. Two tours with different itineraries depart daily from the entrance of the Notre-Dame Basilica. The cost is about $3 per person. Also see Quebec City walking tours in DIRECTIONS.

Note: You can walk down several flights of wooden steps from Dufferin Terrace, the 80-foot-wide boardwalk flanking the *Château Frontenac* in the Old Upper Town, to Place Royale in Old Lower Town. On the return trip take the funicular, an enclosed elevator–cable car that whisks you back and commands a splendid river view — for about 85¢.

   LOCAL SERVICES: For additional information about local services, call the Greater Quebec Area Tourism and Convention Bureau (phone: 692-2471 or 651-2882).

Audiovisual Equipment – *Telav Audio Visual Services,* 352 St-Sacrement (phone: 687-9055).

Baby-sitting – *Service de Gardiennes d'Enfants et d'Aide Familiale de Québec* (phone: 659-3776).

Business Services – *Immeubles Gérard Bouchard* (10-20 Rue St-Jean; phone: 648-8343); *Office Plus,* time-sharing office space and telephone answering services (215 Rue Caron; phone: 648-1431).

Computer Rental – *Hamilton Computer Sales and Rentals,* 3107 Rue Sasseville, Ste-Foy (phone: 651-2328).

Dry Cleaner/Tailor – *Nettoyeurs de la Capitale,* 2 Pl. Québec (phone: 525-6303) and other locations.

Limousine – *Les Limousines de la Capitale* (140-1400 Av. St-Jean-Baptiste; phone: 872-2664), 24-hour bilingual service.

Mechanic – *Garage L.H. Poitras* for emergency service, 1401 Third Ave., corner of Rue Limoilou (phone: 523-5657).

Medical Emergency – *Hôpital l'Hôtel-Dieu de Québec* (11 Côte du Palais; phone: 691-5042); *Dental Emergency* (phone: 653-5412 weekdays; 656-6060 weekends); *Quebec Poison Control Center* (phone: 656-8090).

Messenger Service – *Loomis Courier* (3200 Rue Watt, Ste-Foy; phone: 659-6644); *Purolator Courier* (2225 Av. Chauveau; phone: 843-3236).

National/International Courier – *Federal Express* (phone: 800-463-3339); *Purolator Courier* (phone: 843-3236).

Pharmacy – *Jean Coutu,* 999 Cartier (phone: 522-1235) and many other locations.

Photocopies – *Jet Copie,* 905 Bd. Charest E. (phone 527-2563).

Post Office – Main Post Office (300 Rue St-Paul; phone: 648-3340); Haute-Ville Postal Station (3 Rue Buade; phone: 648-4686).

Professional Photographer – *Photographes Kedl Ltée.,* 336 Rue du Roi (phone: 529-0621).

Secretary-Stenographer – *Drake Office Overload,* 203-320 Rue St-Joseph E. (phone: 529-9371).

Teleconference Facilities – *Le Château Frontenac* (1 Av. des Carrières; phone: 692-3861 or 800-268-9411 in Canada; 800-282-7447 in the US; fax: 692-1751); *Loews Le Concorde* (1125 Pl. Montcalm; phone: 647-2222 or 800-463-5256 in Canada; 800-223-LOEWS in the US; fax: 647-4710); *Quebec Hilton International* (3 Pl. Québec; phone: 647-2411 or 800-268-9275; fax: 647-6488); *Auberge de Gouverneurs* (690 St-Cyrille E.; phone: 647-1717 or 800-463-2820; fax: 647-2146); *Le Germain-des-Prés*

(1200 Germain-des-Près, Ste-Foy; phone: 658-1224 or 800-463-5253; fax: 658-8846); and *Château Bonne Entente* in Ste-Foy (3400 Chemin Ste-Foy; phone: 653-3030 or 800-463-4390; fax: 653-3098).

Telex – *Unitel Communications* (phone: 694-9211).

Translator – *Berlitz Translation and Interpretation Services,* 5 Pl. Québec (phone 529-6161).

Traveler's Checks – *Bank of America Canada, Foreign Currency Service* (24 Côte de la Fabrique; phone: 694-1937); *American Express* in *La Baie* department store in *Les Galeries de la Capitale* (phone: 627-2580) and Pl. Laurier (phone: 658-8820).

Typewriter Rental – *Equipement de Bureau ADA Inc.,* 2094 First Ave. (phone: 529-0829).

 SPECIAL EVENTS: After New Orleans's *Mardi Gras, Le Carnaval de Québec,* a 10-day affair starting on the first Saturday in February, is the biggest blowout in North America. Over half a million people from all over Canada and the US flood the city to celebrate winter. A 7-foot snowman — *Le Bonhomme Carnaval* — presides over the festivities, which include two parades (one in Upper Town, one in Lower Town), international snow sculpture contests, fireworks, a queen's coronation and ball, a variety of theme parties, and lots of winter sports and events — hockey, skiing, and a canoe race on the frozen St. Lawrence River. The biggest events are scheduled over two weekends. Hotels are generally booked solid during *Carnaval,* so make arrangements several months in advance. The best bet for last-minute reservations is through the *Carnaval's* lodging committee, which can sometimes book rooms in motels or guesthouses, from December 15 to *Carnaval* time. (Note: The phone number changes every year.) For general information, contact the *Québec Carnaval,* 290 Joly, Quebec City G1L 1N8 (phone: 626-3716).

For 2 weeks in July, between 600 and 800 artists from all parts of the world and all musical backgrounds gather in the city for the *International Quebec Summer Festival,* one of the largest cultural events in the French-speaking world. Rock, classical repertory, or jazz all can be heard in over 15 public squares and on stages around the city. Most presentations are free of charge. For information, contact the festival office: PO Box 24, Station B, Quebec City G1K 7A1 (phone: 692-4540 or 800-361-5405).

Another critically acclaimed — though more sedate — event, *Quinzaine Internationale du Théâtre de Québec* (Quebec International Fortnight of Theater) features plays performed in their original languages in theaters around the city. Held in even-numbered years during the last 2 weeks in May (phone: 694-0206).

 MUSEUMS: In addition to those mentioned in *Special Places* and *For the Mind,* DIVERSIONS, other noteworthy museums include the following:

Musée des Augustines de l'Hôtel-Dieu-de-Quebec – Dedicated to the founders of Canada's first hospital, the small museum displays antique surgical instruments, furniture, and 17th-century memorabilia related to the order of nursing sisters. Guided tours of cellar vaults. Closed Mondays; call for hours. No admission charge. 32 Rue Charlevoix (phone: 648-4038).

Musée de Cire – Wax museum. Open daily year-round. Admission charge. 22 Rue Ste-Anne (phone: 692-2289).

Parc Cartier-Brébeuf – A replica of Jacques Cartier's ship is moored on the St. Charles River. Open daily. No admission charge. 175 Rue De L'Espinay (phone: 648-4038).

Parks Canada Exhibition Room – Housed on the ground floor of the Louis St-Laurent Building, with a post office that dates from 1871, the Parks Canada salon presents changing exhibitions relating to Canada's national heritage. Open daily; call for hours. No admission charge. 3 Rue Buade (phone: 648-4177).

Urban Life Interpretation Centre – This small museum located in the basement of City Hall concentrates on contemporary life in the provincial capital. Open June 24 to *Labour Day*. Closed Mondays; call for hours. No admission charge. 43 Côte de la Fabrique (phone: 691-4606).

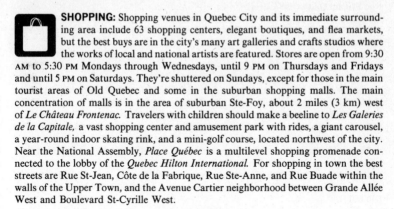 **SHOPPING:** Shopping venues in Quebec City and its immediate surrounding area include 63 shopping centers, elegant boutiques, and flea markets, but the best buys are in the city's many art galleries and crafts studios where the works of local and national artists are featured. Stores are open from 9:30 AM to 5:30 PM Mondays through Wednesdays, until 9 PM on Thursdays and Fridays and until 5 PM on Saturdays. They're shuttered on Sundays, except for those in the main tourist areas of Old Quebec and some in the suburban shopping malls. The main concentration of malls is in the area of suburban Ste-Foy, about 2 miles (3 km) west of *Le Château Frontenac.* Travelers with children should make a beeline to *Les Galeries de la Capitale,* a vast shopping center and amusement park with rides, a giant carousel, a year-round indoor skating rink, and a mini-golf course, located northwest of the city. Near the National Assembly, *Place Québec* is a multilevel shopping promenade connected to the lobby of the *Quebec Hilton International.* For shopping in town the best streets are Rue St-Jean, Côte de la Fabrique, Rue Ste-Anne, and Rue Buade within the walls of the Upper Town, and the Avenue Cartier neighborhood between Grande Allée West and Boulevard St-Cyrille West.

ANTIQUES

Antiquité Brocante – A treasure trove for collectors of old silver and china, heirloom lace, antique furniture, clocks, and estate jewelry. 65 Rue St-Jean (phone: 522-2500).

Antiquités Zaor – A serious collectors' rendezvous for 30 years, it specializes in objets d'art, fine porcelain pieces, silver, and bronze. 112 Rue St-Paul (phone: 692-0581).

La Galerie 141 – An eclectic gathering of furniture, ornaments, and "objets." 97 Rue St-Paul (phone: 694-0896).

Gérard Bourguet Antiquaire – Specialists in 18th-century Quebec furniture and vintage ceramics. 97 Rue St-Paul (phone: 694-0896).

Heritage Antiquité – A favorite of clock collectors, it also carries a selection of furniture, oil lamps, ceramics, and pottery. 109 Rue St-Paul (phone: 692-1681).

Aux Multiples Collections – The best place in town for authentically antique Quebecois furniture, quilts, hand-hooked rugs, and handicrafts. There are signed collectors' pieces. 69 Rue St-Anne (phone: 692-1230); 43 Rue Buade (phone: 692-4298).

Rendez-Vous du Collectionneur – Check out a uniquely Canadian obsession: hockey-card collecting. Antique dolls and old games share the premises. 143 Rue St-Paul (phone: 692-3099).

ART

Brousseau & Brousseau – An exclusive showcase of Inuit artists. Signed prints and carvings are shipped to most destinations around the world. 1 Rue des Carrières (phone: 694-1828).

Galerie Le Chien d'Or – "The Golden Dog" is devoted exclusively to the works of Quebec artists. François Faucher has regular exhibitions here. 8 Rue du Fort (phone: 694-9949).

Galerie Christian Bergeron – This small gallery in the *quartier* features works by artists from Quebec and other parts of Canada. 83 Rue du Petit Champlain (phone: 694-0413).

Galerie Christin – One of a dozen or more galleries along Rue St-Paul, it features works by such well-known national artists as Lemieux, Suzor-Côté, Riopelle, Cosgrove, Roberts, and Picher. 113 Rue St-Paul (phone: 692-4471).

Galerie Eliette Dufour – This salon specializes in the works of such Canadian sculptors as Jordi Bonet, Donald Liardi, and Claude Dufour. Open 7 days a week. 169 Rue St-Paul (phone: 692-2041).

Galerie Estampe Plus – Monthly exhibitions are mounted here. Contemporary artists include Danielle April, Guy Langevin, and Paul Béliveau. 49 Rue St-Paul (phone: 694-1303).

Galerie Georgette Pihay – An award-winning Belgian sculptor, Pihay exhibits works in aluminum and bronze in her own studio-salesroom in the *quartier.* 53 Rue du Petit Champlain (phone: 692-0297).

Galerie Linda Verge – Avant-garde painters Michel Rivest, Guy Labbé, and Joseph Veilleux are featured. 190 Grande Allée W. (phone: 525-8393).

Aux Multiples Collections – The Brousseau family stocks the city's best collection of Inuit carvings, drawings, and prints, each piece signed by the artist. 69 Rue Ste-Anne (phone: 692-1230) and 43 Rue Buade (phone: 692-4298).

Tirage Limité – Works by Calder, Miró, and Riopelle, as well as tapestry art and original prints. 334 Bd. St-Cyrille E. (phone: 522-1234).

Verrerie d'Art Réjean Burns – This innovative Quebec artist exhibits unusual works in stained glass in his own studio/salesroom. 88 Rue du Petit Champlain (phone: 694-0013).

CHOCOLATE

Chocolaterie Erico – Hand-dipped confections in an Upper Town candy boutique. 583 Rue St-Jean (phone: 524-2122).

Confiserie d'Époque Madame Gigi – Homemade chocolate of every conceivable variety. A crowd-stopper in the Lower Town. 84 Rue du Petit Champlain (phone: 692-5325).

Delicatesse Nourcy – Creamy chocolate creations are featured at its Sillery and chic *quartier* Cartier outlets. 1576 Chemin St-Louis, Sillery (phone: 527-2739); 1035 Av. Cartier (phone: 523-4772).

Au Palet d'Or – Hand-dipped chocolates and other custom-made bonbons share the celebrated pastry salon of Roger Geslin in the restaurant complex of chef Serge Bruyère. 60 Rue Garneau (phone: 692-2488).

CRAFTS

Boutique La Corriveau – Two Upper Town outlets specialize in Quebecois arts and crafts, all from the looms, studios, and kitchens of local artists. From homemade jams to hand-carved waterfowl decoys to sheepskin slippers. Two locations: 49 Rue St-Louis (phone: 692-3781) and 42 Rue Garneau (phone: 692-3781).

Créaly – Decorative leather masks, costume jewelry in leather, and other works in semi-precious stones by local artists. 16 Rue du Petit Champlain (phone: 692-4753).

Galerie Le Fil du Temps – Handmade dolls are the stock in trade at this Vieux Québec boutique. Strictly collectibles, these one-of-a-kind creations aren't for kids. 88 Rue du Petit Champlain (phone: 692-5867).

L'Iroquois – An Amerindian souvenir outlet whose best buys are moccasins, toys, baskets, jewelry, and woodcarvings. Also, deerskin jackets and coats, furs, and ceremonial masks. 39 Rue Sous-le-Fort (phone: 692-3366).

Le Jardin de L'Argile – Canada's exclusive outlet for the popular "Lorteau" figurines, the sleepy-faced little people hand-casted by the Quebec ceramist of the same name in clay and glazes in pastel shades of pink and turquoise. Exclusive woodcarvings and ornamental duck decoys range from $300 to $6,000. 51 Rue du Petit Champlain (phone: 692-4870).

O Kwa Ri – Elegant and authentic native Canadian regalia — fringed deerskin dresses and tunics, ceremonial headdresses and jewelry — at "The Sign of The Bear." 59 Rue du Petit Champlain (phone: 692-0009).

Petit Galerie de Pauline Pelletier – Exotica from India, China, Thailand, and Bali complement works of this Quebec ceramist and other Quebec craftspeople. Look for the samurai warrior ceramics in paper robes with mini-swords. 30 Rue du Petit Champlain (phone: 692-4871).

Pot-en-Ceil – Features the work of more than a dozen top potters, ceramists, and wood sculptors from all over Quebec. 27 Rue du Petit Champlain (phone: 692-1743).

Les Trois Colombes – Crafts from Quebec, Atlantic Canada, Ontario, and the Canadian north in a 3-story building. Fashion items include designer sweaters in hand-woven mohair, decorated with leather, silk, and lace, and custom-designed coats, each an original by Quebec designer Lise Dupuis. 46 Rue St-Louis (phone: 694-1114).

For those looking for the best in Native American crafts, there are outlets in Wendake, the Huron Village near suburban Loretteville, about 20 minutes west of the walled city on Route 358. These include *A & Artisanat OKI*, which specializes in snowshoes, moccasins, baskets, dolls, jewelry, fringed jackets, and other hand-crafted items (152 Bd. Bastien; phone: 847-0574); *Artisanat Gros-Louis* (125 Bd. Bastien; phone: 843-2503); *Le Huron* (25 Huron Village; phone: 842-4308); and *Artisans Indiens du Québec* (540 Rue Max Gros-Louis; phone: 845-2150).

FASHION

Atelier Ibiza – This small Lower Town salon specializes in high-fashion leatherwear, handbags, and other accessories. 47 Rue du Petit Champlain (phone: 692-2103).

Atelier La Pomme – House designers work with the finest Argentine leather, suede, and pigskin to produce a *prêt-a-porter* collection of clothing and accessories for men and women. 47 Rue Sous-le-Fort (phone: 692-2875).

Le Capitain D'A Bord – Everything for the well-dressed sailor. 63 Rue du Petit Champlain (phone: 694-0624).

Frederik et Cie. – This well-established boutique in the heart of the Upper Town's old business core features imported woolens from Britain. 49 Rue Buade (phone: 692-5244).

La Maison Darlington – A senior member of Rue Buade's little fashion enclave, it is known for its British tweeds, Scottish cashmeres, and fine mohair shawls. There's also a good selection of Austrian sportswear and a beguiling collection of hand-smocked dresses for infants and little girls. Small sizes in Liberty-print fabrics with matching panties sell for about CN$70. 7 Rue Buade (phone: 692-2268).

La Maison Simons – Established in 1840, the doyenne of Old Quebec department stores stocks its fashion floor with designs by Anne Klein, Ralph Lauren, Marithé and François Girbaud, plus an affordable private-label collection. 20 Côte de la Fabrique (phone: 692-3630).

Peau sur Peau – This high-fashion house of leather features clothing, shoes, and accessories for men and women. Fine leather luggage a specialty. Two locations: 85 Rue du Petit Champlain (phone: 694-1921) and 70 Bd. Champlain (phone: 692-5132).

Promenade du Vieux Québec – The latest arrival on Upper Town's fashion scene has converted *Holt Renfrew*'s stately old store into a stylish complex of boutiques for young fashionables of both sexes. 43 Rue Buade (phone: 647-5964).

Les Vêteries-Blanc Mouton – Distinctive made-in-Quebec fashions in silk and cotton. Best buys are from an exclusive collection of high fashion and après-ski sweaters. 31½ Rue du Petit Champlain (phone: 694-1215).

FURS

J.B. Laliberté – A leading retailer in high-fashion furs. 595 Rue St-Joseph E. (phone: 525-4841).

Joseph Lachance – The long-established furrier in a city famous for top-quality pelts; a large selection of ready-to-wear, too. 634 Rue St-Jean (phone: 523-0530).

Joseph Robitaille – For 100 years this place has been the acknowledged leader of the city's huge fur-trade community. Top-quality skins at realistic prices. 700 Rue Richelieu (phone: 522-3288).

LACE

La Dentellière – Lace curtains to fit all shapes and sizes of windows are a house specialty. It also carries the best in handmade tablecloths and lace accessories for boudoir and bathroom, clothing, and lace trimmings. 56 Bd. Champlain (phone: 692-2807).

MARKETS

Marché de la Place – Fruit and vegetable farmers and flower sellers converge here daily from May through November, and one of the best flea markets in the area, *Marché aux Puces de Ste-Foy,* is nearby. From downtown take buses Nos. 14 and 15. 930 Pl. de Ville, Ste-Foy (phone: 654-4394 and 654-4070).

Marché du Vieux Port – This farmer's market in the restored Old Port area is renowned for its flowers. March through October. Take buses Nos. 1 and 25 from downtown. 160 Rue St-André (phone: 692-2517).

TOYS

L'Echelle – Hand-crafted playthings and other diversions. 1041 Rue St-Jean (phone: 694-9133).

Le Fou du Roi – Wee royals will test their minds (and bodies) in this boutique of educational toys, both domestic and imported. 57 Rue du Petit Champlain (phone: 692-4439).

Le Jardine de l'Argile – Hand-crafted toys, games, rocking horses, child-size chairs, and traditional *gigueurs* — wooden marionettes that dance on a string. 51 Rue du Petit Champlain (phone: 692-4870).

SPORTS: Quebec City has an active sports scene for both spectators and participants.

Golf – Ten 18-hole and an equal number of 9-hole courses are within a 19-mile (30-km) radius of the city. Among the best are *Club de Golf Royal Québec* (Bedard St. in Boischatel, near Montmorency Falls; phone: 822-0331); *Lorette Golf Club* (Cook St. in Loretteville; phone: 842-8441); *Club de Golf Mont Tourbillon* (in Lac Beauport, 12 miles/19 km north of the city; phone: 849-4418); and the two courses at Mont Ste-Anne (25 miles/40 km northeast of the city; phone: 827-3778).

Harness Racing – They're off and running at the *Quebec Hippodrome* on the Exhibition Grounds. Follow Dorchester Boulevard until you see signs for Parc de l'Exposition (phone: 524-5283). Call ahead for schedule.

Hockey – The National Hockey League *Nordiques* face challengers at the *Colisée* on the Exposition Grounds (phone: 523-3333 or 800-463-3333 for tickets; 529-8441 for schedule information).

Skating – Join the locals in Parc d'Esplanade, off Rue d'Auteuil. Other popular spots are the 3-kilometer circuit on the St. Charles River, between the Samson and Marie de l'Incarnation bridges, and Place d'Youville, just outside the St-Jean Gate in Old Quebec. *Village des Sports* in Valcartier (take Autoroute de la Capitale, then Rte. 371) offers skating paths through the woods, and *L'Anneau de Glace de Ste-Foy* is an outdoor Olympic-size skating track. Skating begins mid-October and usually lasts until the end of March (phone: 654-4462).

Skiing – Downhill skiing is best at Mont Ste-Anne, a *World Cup* complex 25 miles (40 km) northeast of the city. The most direct route follows Route 138, but for a more scenic tour leave 138 at Beaupré and continue along Route 360; Route 440 is another alternative. Le Relais (phone: 849-1851) and Mont St-Castin (phone: 849-4277) in Lac Beauport and the Stoneham ski area (phone: 484-2411) also have good slopes only a short drive from the city. All of them offer good night skiing. (See *Skiing* in DIVER-SIONS. For information on buses to the ski areas, see *Getting Around*, above.) For cross-country skiing and snowshoeing, try the Plains of Abraham or the nearby provincial parks with marked trails, and Réserve Faunique des Laurentides, northwest via Route 175. Mont Ste-Anne, Lac Delage, and Duchesnay also have miles of groomed cross-country trails.

Swimming – Some of the hotels have pools; the *Physical Education and Sports Pavilion* at Laval University in Ste-Foy (off Rte. 175; phone: 656-2807) has an Olympic-size pool that is open to the public; the *YMCA* (835 Bd. St-Cyrille W.; phone: 527-2518) and the *YWCA* (855 Rue Holland; phone: 683-2155) also have pools the public can use for a fee at certain hours; call ahead.

Tennis – Indoor and outdoor tennis courts as well as squash courts are available from 7 AM to 11 PM daily at the *Montcalm Tennis Club* (901 Bd. Champlain; phone: 687-1250). Courts are also available for rent at *Club de Tennis Avantage, Inc.* (1080 Bouvier, Charlesbourg W.; phone: 627-3343) and at *Nautilus Plus* (4230 Bd. Hamel; phone: 872-0111).

Tobogganing – There are toboggan runs at the *Village des Sports,* a vast outdoor amusement park near Valcartier, north of the city (phone: 844-3725).

THEATER: A variety of plays is offered in French, rarely in English. Major theaters include the *Grand Théâtre de Québec* (269 Bd. St-Cyrille E.; phone: 643-8131); *Palais Montcalm* (995 Pl. d'Youville; phone: 670-9011); *Bibliothèque Gabrielle Roy* (350 Rue St-Joseph E.; phone: 529-0924); and *Salle Albert-Rousseau* (CEGEP Ste-Foy, 2410 Chemin Ste-Foy; phone: 659-6628). *Théâtre du Trident* (phone: 643-5873) performs French-language works at the *Grand Théâtre*. Student productions are presented at the *Conservatoire d'Art Dramatique* (13 St-Stanislas; phone: 643-9833), and at the *Théâtre de la Cité Universitaire* (on the Laval campus in Ste-Foy; phone: 656-2765). Summer theaters are *Théâtre de l'Ile* (Ile d'Orléans; phone: 828-9530); *Théâtre Beaumont–St-Michel* (on Rte. 2 between Beaumont and St-Michel; phone: 884-3344); and *Théâtre du Bois de Coulonge* (Bd. Laurier; phone: 681-0088). Among the small theaters are *Théâtre Petit Champlain* (68 Petit Champlain; phone: 692-2631), which often hosts folk-singing *chansonniers; Théâtre Périscope* (2 Rue Crémazie E.; phone: 529-2183); *Théâtre de la Fenière* (1500 de la Fenière, Ancienne Lorette; phone: 872-1424); and *Théâtre Paul Hébert* (1451 Av. Royale, St-Jean, Ile d'Orléans; phone: 829-2202).

CINEMA: With two exceptions, Quebec City theaters screen all films in French. English-language versions of current movies are shown at *Cinema Place Québec* (5 Pl. Québec; phone: 656-0592) and at *Cinema Ste-Foy* (Pl. Ste-Foy, 2450 Bd. Laurier, Ste-Foy; phone: 656-0592).

MUSIC: The *Quebec Symphony Orchestra* performs at Louis-Fréchette Hall in the *Grand Théâtre de Québec* (269 Bd. St-Cyrille E.; phone: 643-6976). Touring musical groups usually play at *Palais Montcalm* (995 Pl. d'Youville; phone: 670-9011) or at *Albert-Rousseau Hall* (2410 Chemin Ste-Foy; phone: 659-6629). The small pubs along Rue St-Jean between Rue D'Auteuil and Côte de la Fabrique, on Grande Allée, and in the Old Port area (see *Nightclubs and Nightlife,* below) have live music, ranging from Quebecois folk to rock and blues.

NIGHTCLUBS AND NIGHTLIFE: The city's brightest lights shine along the Grande Allée, on the other side of the walls. In summer, locals and visitors alike gather here from about 5 PM on to plan their evening strategy over a pre-dinner *apéritif* or two. The liveliest corner on this sophisticated strip is at the intersection of the Rue D'Artigny and Grande Allée. Here the triple-threat entertainment complex *Vogue* is hopping until 3 AM, the hour most *boîtes* (*patois* for taverns) in town call it a night. *Vogue*'s café-bar is on the main floor, its disco upstairs. *Sherlock Holmes,* one of the thoroughly British pubs on the francophone scene, shares the premises (1170 Rue D'Artigny; phone: 647-2100 for *Vogue;* 529-9973 for *Sherlock Holmes*). Around the corner, *Brandy* (690 Grande Allée E.; phone: 648-8739), a singles' haunt and terrace café, is a popular summer rendezvous. *Chez Dagobert* (600 Grande Allée E.; phone: 522-0393) is the place where the capital's young and wannabes congregate. There's live music for dancing downstairs, a disco for the under-30 crowd upstairs.

Bar du Grand Hall, the piano bar in the lobby of *Le Château Frontenac,* always attracts an interesting mix of hotel guests and after-dark explorers (1 Rue des Carrières; phone: 692-3861). Many revelers choose to top off the evening romantically under the stars at the *L'Astral* bar in *Loews Le Concorde*'s revolving tower restaurant.

Disco fans — especially the younger set — favor *L'Express Minuit* disco (680 Grande Allée E.; phone: 529-7713). *Le Dancing* at *Loews Le Concorde* attracts first-time customers with its up-market glitter. Often referred to as the "executive's disco," it's open Wednesdays to Sundays (1225 Pl. Montcalm; phone: 647-2222). There's plenty of action in the heart of the old Laval University *quartier,* which still attracts students and their camp followers. However, caution is advised when casing some of the raunchier fun emporia in the walled city's busiest entertainment zone. On the whole it's safe and laid-back but not as geared to the tourist trade as Grande Allée. Try *Bistro Plus* (1063 Rue St-Jean; phone: 694-9252), a singles bar, and *Danse-Bar L'Arlequin* (1070 Rue St-Jean; phone: 694-1422) is for hard-rock addicts. *Bar Chez Son Père* (24 Rue St-Stanislas; phone: 692-5308) is another *boîte à chanson* where a house minstrel serenades night owls with sweet Quebecois ballads. Another Latin Quarter *boîte, Le Petit Paris* (48 Côte de la Fabrique; phone: 694-0383), features *chansonnier* entertainment. *Le Central,* the urbane little piano bar in *A la Table de Serge Bruyère*'s restaurant complex, attracts a more sophisticated clientele (1200 Rue St-Jean; phone: 694-0618). *Zanzibar* (215 Rue St-Jean; phone: 524-3321) is a nostalgic jazz bar where patrons think hippy is hip. Quebec City's only source of authentic contemporary jazz is *L'Emprise,* the art nouveau café-bar in the *Clarendon* hotel (57 Rue Ste-Anne; phone: 692-2480). Four-hour sessions start at 11 PM 7 nights a week.

Confirmed discomaniacs looking for action on a grand scale converge on *Le Palladium Bar* (2327 Bd. Versant N., Ste-Foy; phone: 682-8783), near the University of Laval campus. When 2,000 dancers shake it up in this vast, youth-oriented disco, pandemonium shakes the *Palladium*. *Raspoutine* (2960 Bd. Laurier, Ste-Foy; phone: 659-4318) attracts a more mature disco crowd. So does *Beaugarte* (2590 Bd. Laurier, Ste-Foy; phone: 659-2442), an expense-account singles bar and disco for senior citizens of 35 or so.

BEST IN TOWN

 CHECKING IN: Quebec City has a wide range of hostelries, from the magnificent *Château Frontenac* — a landmark since it was built in the 1890s — to small family-run guesthouses. Four modern high-rise hotels dramatically altered the city's skyline during the 1973–1974 period, when the Municipal Convention Centre was being completed. The city and its immediate surrounding area have close to 10,200 rooms in major convention hotels, motels, inns, and guesthouses. The best bet for motoring visitors is to check into one of the motels in Ste-Foy. Those planning to visit Quebec City during *Carnaval* in early February or during the summer should make reservations as far in advance as possible. During the winter, rooms generally are available, and most places even offer discount rates. Expect to pay $100 to $170 and up per night for a double room in hotels listed as expensive; $70 to $100 for those designated as moderate; and about $65 for those labeled inexpensive. All telephone numbers are in the 418 area code unless otherwise indicated.

Auberge des Gouverneurs – Adjacent to the *Quebec Hilton International,* this modern high-rise has 377 nicely appointed rooms, an elaborate dining room, a health club, and a heated outdoor swimming pool that is open year-round. 690 St-Cyrille E. (phone: 647-1717; 800-463-2820; fax: 647-2146). Expensive.

Le Château Frontenac – The grande dame of Quebec City hotels, this stunning 1892 French Renaissance structure is beautifully situated above the St. Lawrence River. What the Champs-Elysées is to Paris and Red Square is to Moscow, this venerable property is to Quebec City — the point to which tourist tracks are inevitably drawn. The 500-room *Canadian Pacific* property continues to be refurbished, so modern comforts have been added without compromising its Old World appeal. Rooms are air conditioned and many have river views. *Le Champlain* is an excellent dining room (see *Eating Out*); there's also an attractive circular cocktail lounge overlooking the St. Lawrence; café-style restaurants (see *Café de la Terrasse* in *Eating Out);* and a small gallery of shops. (For more information on its history, see *Special Places.*) 1 Av. des Carrières (phone: 692-3861 or 800-268-9411; 800-282-7447 in the US; fax: 692-1751). Expensive.

Hotel des Gouverneurs Ste-Foy – A suburban hostelry, it has 318 attractive rooms, a sophisticated restaurant, a piano bar, and a heated outdoor pool that's open only in summer. 3030 Bd. Laurier (phone: 651-6797; 800-463-2820 in the eastern US; fax: 651-6797). Expensive.

Loews Le Concorde – A dramatic pyramidal structure distinguishes this 424-room hotel. *L'Astral,* the city's only revolving restaurant and bar, sits atop the 29-story pyramid (see *Eating Out*). Other restaurants are available, too, and there is an outdoor pool. During the winter, guests may use the indoor pool at an adjacent club. 1225 Pl. Montcalm (phone: 647-2222 or 800-463-5256; 800-223-LOEWS in the US; fax: 647-4710). Expensive.

Plaza Universel – The straightforward, massive exterior of this building, completed in 1991, contrasts with the refinement of its interior, which is all marble, dark paneling, and cozy stylish furniture. The large interior swimming pool and the dining room are both glass-enclosed. There are 220 rooms and 11 suites. 3031 Bd. Laurier, Ste-Foy (phone: 657-2725; fax: 657-2772). Expensive.

Quebec Hilton International – With one of the best addresses in the city, this striking, modern high-rise has 565 rooms, including 38 suites and 2 executive floors that cater to businesspeople. Service is attentive and friendly. Facilities include a wide variety of restaurants (see *Le Croquembroche* in *Eating Out*); a heated outdoor pool (closed in winter); a health club; and small liquor-vending machines. In addition, the hotel is connected by underground passages with an extensive shopping arcade and the convention center. 3 Pl. Québec (phone: 647-2411 or 800-268-9275; 800-HILTONS in the US; fax: 647-6488). Expensive.

Auberge Ramada Inn – This 99-room establishment, formerly known as *La Nouvelle-Orléans,* is a rustic-looking lodge done up in Canadiana. Rooms have all amenities and there are 28 split-level suites. It offers a choice of restaurants: *Le Leonardo* for continental and Italian specialties, *Le Vivier* for seafood. It has an outdoor pool. Near the Quebec Bridge in Ste-Foy. 1200 Av. Lavigerie (phone: 651-2440 or 800-268-8998; fax: 651-2111). Expensive to moderate.

Clarendon – Within the Old City walls, just opposite City Hall — very convenient for sightseeing — this hotel, built in 1870, is constantly undergoing renovations. The 89 rooms have private baths, color TV sets, and phones, but no air conditioning. The *Charles Baillargé* restaurant serves dinner accompanied by performances of classical music; *L'Emprise* bar, also on the premises, has the best jazz in town. 57 Rue Ste-Anne, near Desjardins (phone: 692-2480 or 800-361-6162; fax: 692-4652). Expensive to moderate.

Holiday Inn Ste-Foy – Formerly the *Châteaubriand,* this property has 235 spacious rooms, including VIP suites with Jacuzzis, an indoor swimming pool, a sauna, a health club, an elaborate dining room, and a cocktail lounge. Free limousine service to and from the airport is available. 3225 Hochelaga Blvd., Ste-Foy (phone: 653-4901 or 800-463-5241; fax: 653-1836). Expensive to moderate.

Manoir Victoria – The most striking aspect of this establishment in a lovely historical setting is its vast and richly decorated entry hall. It has 150 rooms, boutiques, an indoor pool, fitness center, and valet parking. Its 2 restaurants offer continental and French cuisine. Ski packages also are offered. 44 Côte-du-Palais (phone: 692-1030 or 800-463-4093; fax: 692-3822). Expensive to moderate.

Château Bonne Entente – The 11-acre resort setting of this motel-hotel in suburban Ste-Foy draws family travelers and small conventions. The rambling New England–style property is outfitted for business and pleasure with business and conference facilities, an outdoor pool, tennis courts, trout pond, jogging trails, and a children's playground. The *Château* has 170 rooms and suites and 2 dining rooms. 3400 Chemin Ste-Foy (phone: 653-3030 or 800-463-4390; fax: 653-3098). Moderate.

Le Château de Pierre – This 15-room English-style mansion (1853) was converted from a private residence to a guesthouse in 1960 and has much repeat business. The guestrooms are decorated with contemporary furniture; all have color TV sets, and air conditioning; most are large enough for two double beds. 17 Av. Ste-Geneviève, a few steps from the Dufferin Terrace (phone: 694-0429). Moderate.

Fleur de Lys – In the heart of Old Upper Town, 11 of the 33 units here are equipped with kitchenettes. All have color TV sets, air conditioning, and direct-dial phone. Continental breakfast is served in the rooms; other facilities include a laundromat and parking garage. 115 Rue Ste-Anne, near Desjardins (phone: 694-0106). Moderate.

Le Germain-des-Prés – Decorated in European Art Deco, this 127-room hostelry offers personalized service. Rooms include TV sets, AM-FM cassette radios, bathrobes, and fresh fruit. The hotel has a continental breakfast room and is near shopping centers. Transportation to and from the airport is complimentary. 1200 Germain-des-Prés, Ste-Foy (phone: 658-1224 or 800-463-5253; fax: 658-8846). Moderate.

Manoir Ste-Geneviève – One of the best things about this 9-room guesthouse is

Marguerite Corriveau, the friendly proprietress. The house was built in the early 1800s and was one of the first in the Jardin des Gouverneurs. All rooms are furnished with old English furniture but have modern baths, and three have kitchenettes. 13 Av. Ste-Geneviève at Rue Laporte (phone and fax: 694-1666). Moderate.

Auberge du Tresor – Formerly the *Hôtel Le Homestead,* this 300-year-old building has 21 rooms — many overlooking Place d'Armes — each equipped with a private bath, a TV set, and air conditioning. Conveniently situated for those whose main objective is sightseeing, the hotel also has a cocktail lounge, a fine dining room with a multi-ethnic menu, and a café in summer. 20 Rue Ste-Anne at Rue du Tresor (phone: 694-1876). Moderate to inexpensive.

Château Laurier – Near the National Assembly, this 55-room hostelry is quiet and convenient, with a dining room and a coffee shop that's open until 5 AM — a rarity in Quebec City. 695 Grande Allée (phone: 522-8108 or 800-463-4453; fax: 524-8768). Moderate to inexpensive.

Belley – Situated in the Old Port area facing the harbor and marketplace, this small place has 8 rooms and 2 small apartments decorated with stylish, black-lacquered Oriental furniture and Quebecois artwork. Telephones, TV sets, and showers (but no baths) in every room. No restaurant on the premises, but continental breakfast is available at the *Tavern Belley* next door. 249 Rue St-Paul (phone: 692-1694). Inexpensive.

 EATING OUT: Even visitors who don't know the difference between flambé and soufflé will soon become well acquainted with Gallic fare, thanks to the myriad French restaurants in Old Quebec. Although French nouvelle cuisine is on most menus, a few restaurants still serve typical Quebecois meals of pea soup, meat pie, and maple sugar–based desserts. The best of the Quebecois chefs have combined the wild game and succulent lamb of the countryside and farm with the sauces of their French ancestry to create an exciting and ever-changing cuisine. And the city's gastronomic landscape has grown to include a variety of ethnic establishments, including Chinese and Indian. The city also boasts tearooms (*salons de thé*) where one can enjoy the traditional ritual of tea or wonderful chocolate desserts. Expect to pay $85 and up for a very expensive dinner for two; between $70 and $85 in the expensive range; $40 to $60 in the moderate range; and under $40 in the inexpensive range. Prices given do not include drinks, wine, or tip. All telephone numbers are in the 418 area code unless otherwise indicated.

L'Atre – This 1680 farmhouse-turned-fashionable-restaurant is the pride of Ile d'Orléans. The menu is Quebecois. Open daily from mid-June to early September only. Reservations necessary. Major credit cards accepted. 4403 Royal (Rte. 368) near Ste-Famille, east of the island bridge (phone: 829-2474). Very expensive.

Le Croquembroche – An elegant, provincial-style place, it has emerged as one of the top dining rooms in town. It features beautifully prepared French nouvelle cuisine and Quebec City specialties. For starters, try the snails baked in grape leaves and puff pastry or the creamed Arctic char soup with orange zest. Grilled meat and fish, roasted on a spit in the dining area and served with suave sauces, are commendable entrées. Open weekdays for lunch; daily for dinner. Reservations advised. Major credit cards accepted. Lobby level of the *Quebec Hilton,* 3 Pl. Quebec (phone: 674-2411). Very expensive.

Er Michelangelo – For over 20 years patrons have enjoyed the restaurant's homemade pasta and seafood, as well as its other Italian specialties. A favorite of the area's businesspeople. Closed Sundays. Reservations advised. Major credit cards accepted. 3121 Bd. Laurier, Ste-Foy (phone: 651-6262). Very expensive.

Le Paris-Brest – Art Deco decor combined with stained glass windows and brass fittings creates an engaging environment in which to dine on French food, the specialty here. Open daily. Reservations necessary on weekends. Major credit cards accepted. 590 Grande Allée E. (phone: 529-2243). Very expensive.

A la Table de Serge Bruyère – Possibly the best in town. Monsieur Bruyère constantly experiments with nouvelle cuisine and has come up with such dishes as *feuilletée de langoustine à la tomate fraîche* (prawns in puff pastry with tomato) and scallops with leek purée. Only one seating each evening, so reservations are essential. Very expensive. In the same mid-19th-century house, Serge Bruyère Entreprises also operates a small tearoom (inexpensive), *La Petite Table de Serge Bruyère* for light lunches (inexpensive), and the more relaxed but excellent *Le Central* (moderate). Reservations advised for all three. Closed Sundays and Mondays. Major credit cards accepted. 1200 Rue St-Jean (phone: 694-0618).

Le Champlain – The *Château Frontenac's* dining room has changed over to nouvelle cuisine. Try the Brome Lake duckling with cassis vinegar, or the Dover sole soufflé with lobster sauce. Quiet harp and flute music adds to the serenity. Open daily. Reservations advised. Major credit cards accepted. 1 Av. des Carrières (phone: 692-3861). Very expensive to expensive.

La Closerie – One of several restaurants in the region that offer French fare that is more refined than most. The menu changes every season. Chef-owner Jacques Le Pluart has been known to go so far as to import the expensive ($400 per lb.!) black truffles from the Périgord region of France for a special dish on the *menu dégustation.* A business menu is available at lunchtime. Closed Sundays and Mondays. Reservations advised. Major credit cards accepted. 966 Bd. St-Cyrille W. (phone: 687-9975). Very expensive to expensive.

L'Elysée Mandarin – The best place in town for authentic Szechuan and other regional Chinese food. The dining room is spacious in a minimalist environment. The service is very courteous and discreet. Open daily. Reservations advised. Major credit cards accepted. 65 d'Auteuil (phone: 692-0909). Very expensive to expensive.

Le Marie Clarisse – A very good seafood spot near the bottom of the *funiculaire.* Closed Sundays and Mondays. Reservations necessary on weekends. Most major credit cards accepted. 12 Petit Champlain (phone: 692-0857). Very expensive to expensive.

Aux Anciens Canadiens – This house was built in 1675, and was at one time the home of writer Philippe Aubert de Gaspé. It's a wonderful place for a large lunch or brunch (dinner is served, too). Specialties include thick Canadian pea soup, *tourtière* (meat pie), meatball ragout, and, for dessert, sinfully delicious maple syrup pie served with heavy cream. Open daily. Reservations advised. Major credit cards accepted. 34 Rue St-Louis (phone: 692-1627). Expensive.

L'Astral – The only revolving rooftop restaurant in Quebec City. Popular with buffet enthusiasts, it also offers an à la carte menu at lunch and dinner. You're sure to meet Quebecois at Sunday brunch. Open daily. Reservations advised. Major credit cards accepted. Penthouse floor of *Loews Le Concorde.* 1225 Pl. Montcalm (phone: 647-2222). Expensive.

Le Continental – The cuisine could hardly be a surprise — an extensive menu of European specialties ranging from sweetbreads *madère* to steaks *flambé au poivre.* The oak-paneled dining room is attractive and spacious and the service usually very good. For starters, try the *Gaspé en crêpe* (seafood crêpe). Open daily. Reservations advised. Major credit cards accepted. 26 Rue St-Louis (phone: 694-9995). Expensive.

Le Melrose – This exclusive little haven of haute cuisine in the suburb of Sillery can accommodate no more than 60 diners in its charming, rose-trimmed cottage.

Owner-chef Mario Martel takes an innovative approach to French cooking with house specialties based on game and fresh regional products. Closed Mondays. Reservations essential. Major credit cards accepted. 1649 Chemin St-Louis, Sillery (phone: 681-7752). Expensive.

Apsara – A good place for adventurous dining in Quebec, it serves Thai, Cambodian, and Vietnamese fare. The plate of assorted appetizers is a wise and flavorful selection for the uninitiated. Open daily. Reservations advised. Major credit cards accepted. 71 d'Auteuil (phone: 694-0232). Expensive to moderate.

Auberge Louis Hébert – Offers friendly service and an attractive setting, with calico lampshades dangling above the tables. Specialties include fresh Quebec lamb and *confit d'oie,* a goose pâté. The outdoor terrace is open for summer dining. Open daily. Reservations advised. Major credit cards accepted. 668 Grande Allée E. (phone: 525-7812). Expensive to moderate.

Le Bonaparte – This senior member of the Grande Allée restaurant colony evokes nostalgic memories for longtime visitors who don't seem to mind that the food is only so-so. A traditional French menu is served in the formal dining room and on the popular outdoor terrace in summer. Open daily. Reservations advised. Major credit cards accepted. 680 Grande Allée E. (phone: 647-4747). Expensive to moderate.

Café d'Europe – French and Italian dishes are served in cheery and cozy surroundings in Old Quebec. The café also has great little one-person pizza pies and a good dessert cart. Open daily. Reservations advised. Major credit cards accepted. 27 Rue Ste-Angèle (phone: 692-3835). Expensive to moderate.

Café de la Paix – A small, friendly place with French food. The seafood plate, rack of lamb, and, in the fall, various kinds of game such as bison and wild boar are all good bets. Open daily. Reservations advised. Major credit cards accepted. 44 Desjardins (phone: 692-1430). Expensive to moderate.

Café de Paris – French cuisine of the robust variety complements this place's romantic continental atmosphere. Specialities include chateaubriand, leg of lamb, and seafood dishes. A *chansonnier* serenades diners 6 nights a week. Open daily. Reservations advised. Major credit cards accepted. 66 Rue St-Louis (phone: 694-9626). Expensive to moderate.

Café de la Terrasse – Window table diners at *Le Château Frontenac*'s bistro restaurant linger here watching the non-stop promenade on Dufferin Terrace over breakfast, lunch, and dinner. The informal terrace features a bountiful prix fixe buffet and à la carte specials from the grill. Open daily. Reservations advised. Major credit cards accepted. 1 Av. des Carrières (phone: 629-3861). Expensive to moderate.

La Caravelle – Traditional French and Spanish dishes — including a first-rate paella — are featured in this well-respected dining establishment. A *chansonnier* enhances the 18th-century atmosphere in two rustic rooms with wood-burning fireplaces. Open daily. Reservations advised. Major credit cards accepted. 68½ Rue St-Louis (phone: 694-9022). Expensive to moderate.

L'Echaudé – In the Old Lower Town, this spot's Art Deco interior is cool and relaxing, its nouvelle cuisine menu intriguing, and its desserts sumptuous. Try the *bavaroise aux framboises,* a raspberry custard with a tangy sauce. Open daily. Reservations advised. Major credit cards accepted. 73 Sault-au-Matelot (phone: 692-1299). Expensive to moderate.

Gambrinus – Just half a block from the *Château Frontenac,* this place serves fine Italian fare. The pasta dishes with seafood sauces are especially noteworthy, as is the cheesecake for dessert. Open daily. Reservations advised. Major credit cards accepted. 15 Rue du Fort (phone: 692-5144). Expensive to moderate.

Le Graffiti – Connoisseurs relish the creative *cuisine légère* menu here that features such artistically presented dishes as a *millefeuille* of three fish with fresh cucumbers and tomatoes, salmon tartare, and rabbit in a light mustard sauce. A reasonably priced business menu is served at lunch. Open daily. Reservations advised. Major credit cards accepted. 1191 Av. Cartier (phone: 529-4949). Expensive to moderate.

Kyoto – The place to go if you've got a yen for Japanese food. It's decorated in bamboo, with Japanese prints on the wall, and has long tables that seat eight. On a gas burner right on your table, the chef — who loves to show off and make people laugh — prepares authentic Japanese chicken, steaks, shrimp, or lobster dishes, with all the traditional accompaniments. Open daily; no lunch on weekends. Reservations advised. Major credit cards accepted. 560 Grande Allée E. (phone: 529-6141). Expensive to moderate.

Le Paris Gourmet – This small corner of Paris in Old Quebec prides itself on its European atmosphere and service. Nouvelle cuisine specialties include salmon with strawberry vinegar, Brome Lake duckling, and quail Richelieu. A cold buffet is served in the courtyard terrace in summer. Open daily. Reservations advised. Major credit cards accepted. 73 Rue St-Louis (phone: 694-0030). Expensive to moderate.

Restaurant au Parmesan – For those with a taste for Italy, this is the place. Irrepressible host Luigi Leoni presides over traditional Italian meals in a room decorated with his personal collection of wine bottles. Live accordian music from Italy, too. Open daily. Reservations advised. Major credit cards accepted. 38 Rue St-Louis (phone: 692-0341). Expensive to moderate.

La Ripaille – Long-established and well-run, this small eatery specializes in French and Italian food; try the crab dishes and veal escallopes. It's a good place for lunch. Open daily. Reservations advised. Major credit cards accepted. 9 Rue Buade (phone: 692-2450). Expensive to moderate.

Le Saint-Amour – An easy 5-minute walk from all the major hotels, this fine French dining spot specializes in nouvelle cuisine. Try the *lotte,* a white fish, in vinegar and honey sauce. There's also a better-than-average wine list. Open daily. Reservations advised. Major credit cards accepted. 48 Ste-Ursule (phone: 694-0667). Expensive to moderate.

Balico – Off the usual tourist trail, this intimate little place specializes in the food of the Provence region of France. The fish soups are quite delicious, and the *aïoli* (garlic mayonnaise) unforgettable. Closed Mondays. Reservations advised. Major credit cards accepted. 935 Rue Bourlamaque (phone: 648-1880). Moderate.

Le Chalet Suisse – For a change of pace, try the fondues at this festive, multi-storied place. Some suggestions: the Chinese fondue, thinly sliced beef served in a heated beef bouillon; raclette, a grilled cheese dish; or a traditional Swiss cheese fondue. One of the few restaurants in town open past 11 PM, hence its regulars include provincial politicians when the National Assembly is in session. Open daily. Reservations advised. Major credit cards accepted. 26 Rue Ste-Anne (phone: 694-1320). Moderate.

Chez Patrick le Bordelais – This popular Grande Allée rendezvous gets higher marks for its lively bar than its menu, but the traditional fare featuring specialties from Bordeaux is varied and moderately priced. Meals are served in the bar or around the fireplace in the main dining room; there's summer dining on the terrace. A special late-night menu is available after 11 PM. Open daily. Reservations advised. Major credit cards accepted. 570 Grande Allée (phone: 649-0338). Moderate.

Le Fiacre – For a congenial atmosphere, good service, and down-to-earth food — charcoal-broiled steaks or seafood — this large eatery in Ste-Foy fits the bill and the budget. Open daily. Reservations advised Wednesdays through Saturdays. Major credit cards accepted. 1200 Germain-des-Prés, Ste-Foy (phone: 651-4055). Moderate.

Fleur de Lotus – Near City Hall, this Cambodian restaurant also serves Vietnamese and Thai food. Bring your own wine. Open daily. Reservations advised. Visa and MasterCard accepted. 50 Rue de la Fabrique (phone: 692-4286). Moderate.

Mykonos – The total Greek population of Quebec City numbers 150, so it's surprising that there's a Greek restaurant here at all, let alone such a fine one. The menu features a wide variety of Greek dishes, but *agneau* (lamb) is the specialty. Accompanying the lamb is *briam* — fresh string beans, onions, potatoes, zucchini, and eggplant baked in layers. *Galactobouriko,* custard served in phyllo, a thin pastry crust, tops off the meal. Open daily. Reservations advised. Major credit cards accepted. 1066 Rue St-Jean (phone: 692-2048). Moderate.

Nupur – It's off the usual tourist trail, but this Indian spot is well worth the 15-minute drive. Although the decor is modest, the atmosphere is warm and the service exceptional. Try any of the tandoori or curried dishes. Open daily. Reservations advised. Major credit cards accepted. 850 Rue Myrand, Ste-Foy (phone: 683-4770). Moderate.

Optimum – A luxurious, 2-story Victorian house with a Mediterranean deli on the first floor and a café on the second floor, where nouvelle cuisine is served and the desserts are sinful. Open daily. Reservations advised. Major credit cards accepted. 64 St-Cyrille W. (phone: 648-0768). Moderate.

Le d'Orsay – A restaurant-pub with a good location and an excellent selection of European beers. Open daily. Reservations advised. Major credit cards accepted. 65 Rue Buade, just across from City Hall (phone: 694-1582). Moderate.

Le Biarritz – It's an intimate place that can accommodate groups or twosomes for cozy dining. The escargots are a good choice for starters, and any of the many veal dishes will make a satisfying entrée. Open daily. Reservations advised. Major credit cards accepted. 136 Ste-Anne (phone: 692-2433). Moderate to inexpensive.

Café du Monde – Across from the *Museum of Civilization,* this funky diner-style eatery offers everything from an emperor-size Caesar salad to a five-course dinner. The decor — from crystal chandeliers to hot-pink neon — is a whimsical setting at which to enjoy some first-rate fare. Open daily. Reservations advised for groups of eight or more. Major credit cards accepted. 57 Rue Dalhousie (phone: 692-4455). Moderate to inexpensive.

Pub La Faculté – Good pub grub, reasonably priced, attracts patrons at this British-style spot with a summer terrace and a gameroom for darts and billiards enthusiasts. Imported beers and sausages are house specialties. Open daily. Reservations advised. Major credit cards accepted. 595 Grande Allée E. (phone: 529-0592). Moderate to inexpensive.

Café Latin – A lovely place to dawdle over an espresso, sandwich, quiche, or salad to the accompaniment of taped classical music. It also has the best maple sugar pie in town. Outdoor dining on the terrace in summer. Open daily. Reservations unnecessary. No credit cards accepted. 8½ Ste-Ursule (phone: 692-2022). Inexpensive.

Les Délices du Maghreb – Good and inexpensive Mediterranean and Provençal food in unpretentious surroundings. It's in a less than fashionable, but still interesting part of downtown, surrounded by shops and cafés that seem left over from the 1960s. Bring your own wine. Open daily. Reservations unneccessary. Major credit cards accepted. 798 Rue St-Jean (phone: 529-9578). Inexpensive.

La Garonelle – A tearoom and confectionary where only a strong will can keep you away from the chocolate desserts. Pâtés, salads, and fine cheeses also are offered.

Closed Mondays. Reservations advised. Major credit cards accepted. 207 Rue St-Jean (phone: 524-8154). Inexpensive.

Marie Antoinette – For fast food, Quebec-style. Breakfast is especially recommended. Open 24 hours daily. Reservations unnecessary. Major credit cards accepted. There are 10 of these restaurants in the area, including those at 2813 Bd. Laurier (phone: 653-5993) and 44 Kennedy St., Lévis (phone: 837-5809). Inexpensive.

Le Mille-Feuille – This was the first establishment in the region to specialize in vegetarian fare. No clichés about health food hold here, however — the menu features such innovative dishes as fresh pasta with artichoke sauce, and tofu Stroganoff. Open daily. Reservations advised for lunch and weekend brunch. Visa and MasterCard accepted. Two locations: 32 Rue Ste-Angèle, inside the walls (phone: 692-2147), and 1405 Chemin Ste-Foy (phone: 681-4520). Inexpensive.

Au Petit Coin Breton – The Grande Allée branch of this small crêperie chain is best in summer when the terrace café looks out on the passing parade. Crêpes, salads, onion soup, and other light fare are reasonably priced à la carte specials. Open daily. Reservations unnecessary. Major credit cards accepted. 665 Grande Allée E. (phone: 525-6904). Inexpensive.

Le St-Alexandre – One of a dozen English-style pubs that have opened in different fashionable parts of town. The object of the limited but excellent menu (sausages, sandwiches, steaks) is to complement the 175 brands of beer that are served here. Open daily. Reservations unnecessary. Major credit cards accepted. 1087 Rue St-Jean (phone: 694-0015). Inexpensive.

■**Quebec Quaffs:** Pubs, particularly those inspired by the traditional London variety, are increasingly popular in Quebec City. But unlike their British counterparts, most keep late-night hours to compete with the bar trade. *Le D'Orsay* (65 Rue Buade; phone: 694-1582) opposite City Hall is a *soigné* version of the real British thing with rich cashew-wood paneling and all the requisite polished brass appointments (there's a good restaurant upstairs for those tired of pub grub). Across from the Gare du Palais railway station, *Thomas Dunn* (1988 Rue St-Paul; phone: 692-4693) serves imported beer to match its imported atmosphere. *L'Inox* (in the restored Old Port district; 37 Rue St-André; phone: 692-2877) cold-shoulders the trendy import image in favor of the home-brewed product. It's the only independent brewery in Quebec City and pub customers can watch three exclusive brands of suds in the making before deciding on their preference. As notable for its king-size hot dogs as for its house potables. *Le Pub St-Alexandre* (1087 Rue St-Jean; phone: 694-0015) doesn't brew its own brand but it does stock 175 varieties of beer, enough to slake a night-long thirst.

DIVERSIONS

DIVERSIONS

For the Experience

Quintessential Montreal and Quebec City

 Whether it's the roaring St. Lawrence River or the craggy peak of Cape Diamond or Mount Royal — named by a French explorer more than 450 years ago — the past plays a major part in the life of both Montreal and Quebec City. Yet these vibrant cities are filled with new ideas, too. Once the place where the Quiet Revolution began, where the Quebecois learned to stand on their feet in politics and business, there is nothing quiet about French Canada today. Much is shared in spirit, but visitors will delight in the differences.

VIEUX MONTRÉAL/VIEUX QUÉBEC: In few places in North America does the past live so much in the present as in Montreal and Quebec City, and nowhere do you get a better sense of the part played by the French. In Montreal it's a little harder to find those precious pockets of history, while in Quebec City a landscape brimming with the old and revered forms a veritable compact living museum. Although Montreal demolished its city walls, many of its most important early institutions still stand. Surrounding the memorial statue of the founder, Paul Chomedey, "le Sieur de Maisonneuve," in the Place d'Armes are some of the oldest buildings on the continent, including the Sulpician Seminary (1685), which still clings to its original site next door to the Gothic revival towers of Notre Dame Basilica (1829). Wander about Montreal and immerse yourself in a hodgepodge of architectural eras, but in Place Jacques-Cartier take yourself back to the days when it was one of the busiest farmers' markets in the New World. Lined on both sides with sidewalk cafés, bright with flower beds and poster-plastered pillars, with its old-fashioned lamp standards and rough brick paving, the rectangle of history between Rues Notre Dame and St-Paul East could pass for the public square of a small harbor town somewhere in France, the river at its foot, the fussy, Second Empire Hôtel de Ville (City Hall) at its head.

In many ways the past is what Quebec City is all about. Entering the brick-paved market square in Lower Town, you'll suddenly feel at home in the 17th century, surrounded by a gray-stone townscape built in the late 1600s. Although it seems to have aged naturally over more than 300 centuries of careful maintenance, Place Royale, with its small parish Church of Notre-Dame-des-Victoires (1688) and the bust of King Louis XIV at its center, has cost the provincial government millions of dollars and more than 25 years of painstaking restoration. Cobblestones are replaced if they no longer look the part, and huge sums are spent on each building, ensuring the preservation of the halcyon days of French Canada. Like no other place in North America, the story of Vieux Québec unfolds in chronological sequence from its precarious 17th-century beginnings on the waterfront to its full 19th-century flowering in the walled capital on the heights.

QUÉBEC A LA CARTE: With so many restaurants in Montreal and Quebec City devoted to French cuisine you would think that there would be little culinary difference between the French and Canadian cultures. But *vive la différence!* Like their forebears from France, Quebeckers in the sister cities regard their chefs with a reverence usually reserved for poets and philosophers. The best of food here — wild berries, maple syrup, fresh pork, and game birds — has been combined with nouvelle cuisine on menus throughout Montreal and Quebec City. Yet these Canadian comestibles should be enjoyed in their most traditional way, too. For almost 4 centuries French Canada's menu has developed on the edge of a vast hinterland, but some establishments cling to the delicious days of yore. In Vieux Montréal, the *Auberge le Vieux Saint-Gabriel* and, in Québec City, *Aux Anciens Canadiens* have remained true to the old ways. For starters, try a little pot of *ragoût de pattes* (pigs' feet simmered slowly with garlic, cinnamon, cloves, nutmeg, and onions), then a serving of *soupe aux pois* (pea soup) in readiness for a slice or two of *tourtière* (a spicy meat pie — Mom's apple pie to Quebeckers). For the main course order *ragoût de boulettes* (a meatball stew made with lean ground pork). Be sure to save room for dessert: *tarte au sucre* (maple sugar pie) with a dollop of rich cream. That ought to do it. This is no place for calorie counters. Order *tarte au suif* (suet pie), a pastry collection of beef suet, maple sugar, and chopped, tart apples — and start your diet when you get home.

A ONE-HORSE OPEN CALÈCHE: New York has its hansom cab, Charleston, its surrey with the fringe on top. French Canada has its *calèche* and, at times, its one-horse open sleigh. There was a time not that long ago in both Montreal and Quebec City that when the snow flew *calèche* drivers would exchange the wheels of their buggies for gleaming runners that slid over the snow and ice. Sadly, that time has almost past, as modern snow-moving equipment and milder winters have conspired to keep roads clear and keep wheels on *calèches* throughout the year. But it's still possible to catch the feeling of a jingle-bell sleigh: For special occasions, the old-time sleighs pull passengers through Mount Royal Park in Montreal or Battlefields Park in Quebec City (phone: 514-653-0751 in Montreal; 418-687-9797 or 418-648-1888 in Quebec City).

To get a feeling for the difference between the two cities, take a *calèche* ride in both. For your driver in downtown Montreal you'll choose from among frail-looking girls with Rapunzel-length hair and wrists of steel, portly old-timers in *Expos* baseball caps and lumberjack checks, and reedy young gallants in tank tops and tattoos. Like the best of Manhattan cabbies, they take a philosopher's view of big-city life, but they take off from a downtown launching pad, where Montreal motorists give no quarter. Once into the narrow streets of Vieux Montréal, where the horse has the advantage, or up on Mount Royal's peaceful *calèche* road, they relax, listen, and generally are on their best behavior. By comparison, a *calèche* ride in Quebec City is Old World, genteel. Summer drivers for *Danny Doyle, Ltd.* (phone: 418-648-1888) favor jaunty straw boaters with green hatbands to match their green vests and green and white vehicles. Coachmen for *La Belle Epoque* (phone: 418-687-9797) stand out in red-and-white ensembles, harmonizing with their red-trimmed *calèches.* Less fashion-conscious in winter, drivers still look perky in parkas, while their steeds sport equally chic horse blankets. The horse is king of the road in Vieux Québec, setting its own speed limits on streets that become precipitous downhill turns at unexpected corners. Beyond the gates "the old reliables" let themselves go, jogging briskly along the Grande Allée to the carriageways of National Battlefields Park. In either city, it's like journeying back in time.

ICI NOUS PARLONS FRANÇAIS: Listen closely to the voices of Quebec and you're well on your way to learning something even some Canadians don't realize. Bilingual people in the province of Quebec speak two languages in the same conversation. More so in Montreal, but in Quebec City, too, listen to the lunchtime chitchat among locals. A man will speak French, a woman English, each appearing to understand perfectly what the other has said, but both expressing themselves comfortably in their own mother tongue. It happens in intimate conversations between friends and lovers, parents and children, and in convivial groups, where bilingual talk ricochets around the table. The effect is charming, and at the end of the shortest of stays even the most unilingual of English speakers will come away at least knowing when and how to say *salut, très bien, et mais oui.* Relax as you decipher restaurant menus and shop where all public signs are *seulement français* in the comfort that in most places you can fall back on English when the going gets too tough. In the tourist areas of Quebec City, particularly, this is what people have come to expect: Old World charm with built-in communication insurance. And once outside, you'll find that *s'il vous plaît* and *merci beaucoup* will overcome a lot of linguistic barriers — especially in this predominantly French world.

English is more likely to be understood in Montreal, but then so might Turkish, Greek, Russian, or Lithuanian. Although unmistakably French, Montreal has been an international crossroads for a couple of centuries now. Multilingual skills often are taken for granted in a society where "Jean-Marc Brophy" may have an Italian grandmother and "Fiona Laberge" a Scottish grandfather. Though Quebec has always felt the need to safeguard its language and culture from within, its defiance to remain *chez eux* (at home) does not pose much of a handicap for those visitors who want to do their business or have fun in English only.

MOUNT ROYAL PARK, Montreal: From the crush of downtown Montreal, you'll find the mountain beckons through narrow concrete canyons of high-rise towers and office complexes. In getting here, most motorists pass by the best lookout spot over the city on their first drive up "The Mountain" along Camillien Houde Parkway — but if you stay in the eastbound traffic lane you can't miss it. From here you'll get the widest view of the landscape below, and best appreciate what Jacques Cartier must have seen the day he made his way to the top of the mountain along the St. Lawrence more than 450 years ago. Take in the vista from the observatory in front of the Grand Chalet — landmarks are indicated in bronze along the parapet — and think back to the time when this high spot became the center of the French civilization in the New World. Spread out your picnic blanket and basket alongside Montrealers on summer weekends or, if you come in winter, converge on the pine-scented trails with snowshoe enthusiasts and cross-country skiers. You'll be carried along by the spirit and speed of the skaters on Beaver Lake, which is especially pretty and romantic at night under the lights. On sunny days kids are out on the gentle toboggan slide above the natural ice rink; in fact, generations of young Montrealers have learned the rudiments of downhill skiing here on the little rope tow run. Take a whirl around the rink — it's easy to forget you're on a mountain, but don't miss a trip to the main lookout. On a clear day, you'll see the faint outline of the Green Mountains in Vermont — and realize how close the two different worlds of French Canada and the United States can be. For information about Mount Royal Park facilities phone the offices of the City of Montreal at 514-872-1415 (park) or 514-872-2644 (sports and recreation).

SHOOTING THE RAPIDS, Montreal: When it comes to thrill rides, the St. Lawrence River rapids are in a class by themselves. Though you can't prove it by any of the long-gone adventurers who were beaten by the turbulent waters as they set out in search of the riches of China (the rapids themselves were called "La Chine"), you can make up your own mind by riding the waves of the enterprise offered by *Lachine Rapids Tours,* the only company that conducts trips through these rough waters. What amounted to danger and heartache for early explorers has been transformed into excitement and derring-do for latter-day adventurers. The fleet of *saute-mouton* (leap-frogging) craft are durable aluminum vessels, propelled by tow jet-pump engines, strong enough to fight the currents during a river romp, or bob through the chop when the motors idle. Before leaving port, passengers are decked out like Gloucester fisherfolk in bright yellow slickers with matching sou'westers and rubber boots — regulation life jackets complete the ensemble. Soon you're on whirlpool level, in the tradition of the Iroquois, the *coureurs de bois* (gritty fur traders who traveled by canoe into the wilderness), and the woodsmen who went through the stormy passage on log rafts. Out where the river narrows and then descends around the green islands off Lachine's suburban shore, hundreds of standing waves crest above the flood. You bolt headlong into more than a dozen whirlpools and two hydraulics (depressions, or valleys, surrounded by walls of water) caused by the backlash of currents racing through a natural chute. Rearing up like a playful porpoise, the *saute-mouton* dives into the waves, surf crashing over the bow. Imagine yourself as one of those early travelers who, if he was lucky, emerged from an encounter with "La Chine" only soaked to the skin and exhilarated, not battered and defeated. But leave some room for practical details: Despite the rain gear, you'll likely get wet — so wear old clothes and leave something dry to change into at the ticket office. *Saute-mouton* adventures depart Victoria Pier in Old Montreal's Vieux Port restoration every 2 hours daily from mid-May through *Labour Day*. For more information contact *Lachine Rapids Tours,* 105 de la Commune St. W., Montreal (phone: 514-284-9607).

SMOKED MEAT AT SCHWARTZ'S, Montreal: In a city renowned for its fine restaurants you'd think that Montreal might lay claim to the world's best seafood, or the world's finest maple syrup. But move over, Manhattan: Montrealers say they have the best pastrami sandwiches (smoked meat, in Canadian parlance) this side of heaven. Expatriate citizens dream of the *Montreal Hebrew Delicatessen* (a.k.a. *Schwartz's*) the way displaced Viennese dream about *Demel's* café or *tafelspitz* at the *Sacher* hotel. And after years of spreading the word around the international deli circuit, they've established *Schwartz's* as Canada's — if not the world's — most satisfying source of the ultimate smoked meat on rye.

It's been more than 60 years since Ruban Schwartz introduced his home-cured "special" sandwiches and no-frills manner of service — and as the old-timers here will tell you, little has changed. You'll either share a long counter, where the daily specials are printed large and clear on the wall, or crowd together with regulars around arborite tables that clutter the narrow room from entrance to kitchen door. But ignore the clatter and confusion: That's how it's supposed to be, how it's *always* been. Just get your order, a *Schwartz* special, barely containing itself between slices of crusty rye, spread on the extra mustard, and add a dill pickle. Then sprinkle a liberal dose of salt and white vinegar over the best French fries in a province renowned for its *frites* and enjoy. After the first bite, you'll know why the many worlds of this cosmopolitan Canadian city beat a path to this unassuming door. *Montreal Hebrew Delicatessen* is open daily (closed *Yom Kippur*) at 3895 Blvd. St-Laurent, Montreal (phone: 514-842-4813).

UNDERGROUND MONTREAL: Montreal's contribution to travel trade folklore records the fate of one feckless winter visitor who came to town without an overcoat. Unprepared for zero-belt temperatures, the newcomer checked into a deluxe downtown hotel, wined, dined, kept business appointments, saw a movie, attended a symphony concert, went to church — even bought a new overcoat — without venturing out into the snow-banked, traffic-jammed streets. You needn't test this tall tale, but it contains more than a grain of truth. Thanks to the amenities of Montreal's climate-controlled Underground City (there are many separate subterranean complexes but they are referred to collectively in this way) it *is* possible to spend days in coatless comfort. And while Montrealers really don't live like trolls, they do appreciate the weatherproof network of public transport and pedestrian corridors that links the shopping malls, office buildings, hotels, and other major centers in downtown Montreal. You too can escape January blizzards, July heat waves, and rush-hour gridlocks as you hustle around the bright, air conditioned "city below."

Although shopping is the prime attraction, you can travel underground to such diverse destinations as the Université du Québec à Montréal (UQAM), Olympic Park, *Place des Arts* (the city's major center for performing arts), Christ Church Cathedral, and the Montreal Stock Exchange. For *the* French Canadian underground experience try *Complexe Desjardins.* Hardly a day goes by here without some kind of free entertainment on the lower-level concourse. Local rock musicians, school choirs, television crews doing live news spots, and puppet theaters draw big crowds during the lunch hour, when office workers from the towers enclosing the multi-tiered atrium join in on the fun. Life is especially exciting here for children at *Christmas* and *Easter.* But throughout the year the light-filled central plaza, with its jungle of green plants and splashing fountains, is a favorite spot for a subterranean picnic of tasty snacks from the specialty food shops on site — and when blizzards blow it's a great place to wait for the spring thaw.

BATTLES ON ICE, Montreal: Hockey is *the* Canadian game and *Les Canadiens* provide the best of it on their home ice at the *Montreal Forum.* Since the National Hockey League was established in 1924, the *Canadiens* have won more *Stanley Cup* trophies than any other team and practically owned the championship title for years. This is the arena where Maurice and Henri Richard, Jean Béliveau, Ken Dryden, Jacques Plante, and Guy Lafleur, among others, have become legends. Accordingly, Montreal fans follow the action in noisy fervor as plays are announced, first in French, then in English. The game is fast, fierce, yet surprisingly graceful, and the excitement of the fans — Gallic and non — is infectious. You'll soon find yourself cheering along in both tongues, even if you find hockey incomprehensible in any language. During intermission, follow the rambunctious crowd as it spills out to the concession stands. For something different in between-periods snacking, try the tough-skinned Montreal hot dogs ("steamies"), served with small, spicy pickles called *cornichons.* As the venerable old house of hockey nears its 70th birthday, *Les Habs* (*Les Canadiens' nickname, short for Les Habitants*) are about to move next door to a bigger arena in time for the 1995–96 season. Fans are bound to take the loss very hard. (Imagine the chagrin of *Red Sox* fans if their beloved team was to abandon *Fenway.*) Meanwhile, come root for the *Canadiens* at *Montreal Forum,* 2313 Ste-Catherine St. W. (phone: 514-932-2582). They're really good skates.

CANADA'S CASTLE: LE CHÂTEAU FRONTENAC, Quebec City: Though it seems to have been transported from another place and time, there is nothing inaccesible or intimidating about *Le Château,* Quebec City's century-old, fairy-tale castle. Turning off Rue St-Louis through the hotel's great stone archway, you'll half expect a portcullis to come crashing down behind you, or see an armed sentry at the main Rue des Carrières entrance instead of a seasoned doorman. Pause to take in the scene — the multi-towered battlements, the *Château*'s trademark verdigris roofline of ornamental spires and turrets — but don't stop there: The T-shape lobby, a big, richly paneled, seigneurial hall, sets the mood. The floors themselves are vertigious yet beguiling mazes of room-width, richly carpeted corridors. The grand ballroom is a lavishly revived vision of Versailles. At *Le Champlain* (phone: 418-693-3861), decorated in the formal manner of the French colonial regime, waiters in period costume strive to anticipate diners' every whim and a harpist provides soothing sounds. At the *Navigators Bar* next door, you can look out over the river and, 1 floor below, at the *Café de la Terrasse* (phone: 418-629-3861), you're as close as you can be to the site of the Château St-Louis, an old vice-regal palace, onetime home of the Governors of New France. In days past the "castle" has played host to royalty and world leaders, boasting a guest list that has included such luminaries as Franklin D. Roosevelt and Winston Churchill. In the early (and happy) blush of marriage, Britain's Duke and Duchess of York (Prince Andrew and Sarah Ferguson) became the first occupants of a freshly decorated Royal Suite, and although the rates (CN$850 a day) may be a little regal, other suites can be had at about a quarter of that price. *Le Château Frontenac,* 1 Rue des Carrières (phone: 418-692-1751).

DINNER AT SERGE'S TABLE, Quebec City: Long after memories of historic landmarks and colorful street scenes have faded, chances are one name will stay on the tip of your tongue: Serge Bruyère. In a city that claims to support more haute cuisine establishments per capita than anywhere else in the country, gourmets here say *A la Table de Serge Bruyère* is the best restaurant in town. Bruyère stands as one of the new breed of French-schooled chefs who've adapted the basics of nouvelle cuisine to bring out the best in fresh Quebec produce — salmon from the Gaspé, Iles de la Madeleine scallops, tender young lamb from South Shore pastures, and game from the northern forests of Tadoussac. The restaurateur depends on the wild berry fields of Quebec to add a zest to his repertoire of classic sauces for game and fowl, on the local markets for seasonal supplies of vegetables and fruits, and on the good regional cheeses of Quebec farmers. Here your party of two will be joined by only 48 other diners in two intimate upstairs dining rooms in the old walled *quartier.*

Consider, for starters, a bouquet of tiny, smoked salmon roses, or a salmon "sausage" in a creamy sauce of leeks and white wine, followed by Quebec lamb, scented with sweet garlic, or duckling dressed in wild raspberry vinegar. Then an abundant cheese tray, or perhaps a sugar pie. Take your time — you have all night. Pastel linen, fresh flowers, and candlelight provide a delicate contrast to the rough stone and brick walls and the heavy ceiling beams of the restored 19th-century building. In winter, the two upper rooms are warmed by hospitable log fires, burnishing the chef's collection of antique copperware. Don't dwell on the size of the bill, especially if you're an oenophile inclined to get carried away over the best *carte des vins* in the city. But for those who've got a mortgage payment due, try the eight-course "Discovery" menu. It's good value for the money. *A La Table de Serge Bruyère,* 1200 Rue St-Jean (phone: 418-694-0618).

CARNAVAL DE QUÉBEC: For a week and a half in early February, Quebec City breaks out of its winter doldrums and erupts in a northern version of *Mardi Gras* in New Orleans or *Carnaval* in Rio. Merrymakers don 18th-century costume (or at least put toques on their heads and tie *ceintures flechets,* a traditional sash, around their waists); menus feature such Quebec delicacies as maple sugar pie, *tourtière* (a spicy meat pie), and caribou (a potent mixture of wine and pure alcohol); and there is a dizzying array of activities everywhere you turn. The fun begins with an opening ceremony in which the mascot Bonhomme Carnaval (a 7-foot-tall snowman with red cap and *ceinture flechet*) crowns the Carnival Queen at his ice palace before cheering thousands. During the next 10 days there's much to do and see: spectacular ice sculptures and an international ice sculpture competition on Place Carnaval; tobogganing, and — for the brave — luge rides on the nearby hills; dogsled races; auto races on ice; the *International Canoe Race* across the treacherous St. Lawrence; skiing; skating; hockey; and (for the more courageous still) an annual roll in the snow that attracts a surprising number of bathing-suit-clad participants. At night there are fireworks displays, lavish theme parties, a *Queen's Ball,* a night parade with brightly lit floats, and a torch-lit ski run. It's an exciting, invigorating experience in a dazzling wonderland of ice and snow. A half million people flock to Quebec for *Carnaval,* but the mood of the city is more festive than riotous, so in between the parties and parades, it's possible to steal away for a romantic ride in a *calèche* for a more private celebration of the season. Quebec City is at its best in winter. Take a leisurely ride within the walls of the town, where narrow streets and lanes are lined with cafés that serve coffee with steaming milk in large bowls. Listen as the words of the popular song "Mon Pays" by Gilles Vigneault stir the Quebecois heart: *"Mon pays ce n'est pas un pays c'est l'hiver"* ("My country is not a country, it is winter"). After more than 300 seasons of bone-chilling weather, Quebeckers get emotional in the cold; it is *their* time. If you notice that events have a different edge here, that cafés are more jubilant, and that even in the midst of a freezing cold snap the streets are bustling with life, don't forget that Quebeckers are proud to say they have more than a little ice flowing in their veins.

Best Hotels in Montreal and Quebec City

At first glance the story of fine hotels in Quebec's sister cities seems remarkably similar. In Montreal the *Ritz-Carlton* long dominated the scene, and was the unparalleled choice of the discriminating traveler; in Quebec City, *Le Château Frontenac* was No. 1, one of the best-known hostelries on the North American continent. But now there's more — much more. In recent years the *Ritz* has become more of a first among equals, with world class competitors offering the best in accommodations and services for the corporate traveler in Montreal, the more business-oriented of the two cities. Quebec City has its share of hotels devoted to businesspeople, too, but it also boasts numerous high-quality, smaller, *auberge*-type accommodations behind the walls to which tourists flock every year — attracted by their intimate spirit and friendly atmosphere. In Quebec City, more so than Montreal, cozy and traditional flourishes. In the list below you'll find the best: large and modern alongside small and charming.

BONAVENTURE HILTON, Montreal: Located at the top of the *Place Bonaventure* in the heart of the city's business district are 2 stories that provide an oasis of comfort. Guests enter the elevator at the underground level of the most commercial part of Montreal and are whisked up to the lobby to check in, 17 stories above. Here are a Japanese garden and a heated outdoor pool, which in winter is surrounded by evergreens covered in snow (swimmers enter the pool through a narrow covered passageway). Guests with a garden-view room often wake up to the sight of a pheasant strutting across the Japanese courtyard, a landscaped Zen garden, complete with babbling brooks, cascades, and tree-shaded ponds. In a flash you can get back in the fray — only an elevator ride away are the mall and exhibition hall, the Métro, *Place Ville Marie,* and Central Station, all major gateways to Montreal's underground city. There are 400 contemporary rooms in this penthouse location, including 7 executive suites and 13 junior suites. Convention and business facilities are located an escalator ride away on the floor below the hotel's lobby, where the main ballroom can accommodate 2,000, and meeting rooms and secretarial services are available on request. The main dining room, *Le Castillon,* harkens back to the 17th century, right down to its seigneurial decor, baronial fireplace, and the waiters' period garb. Information: *Bonaventure Hilton,* 1 Pl. Bonaventure, Montreal, Quebec H5A 1E4 (phone: 514-878-2332 or 800-268-9275 in Canada; 800-445-8667 in the US; fax: 514-878-3881).

FOUR SEASONS (LE QUATRE SAISONS), Montreal: A leader among the prime properties on Sherbrooke Street, this 27-year-old link in the prestigious Canadian-owned hotel chain has rapidly become a favorite for those who choose contemporary luxury plus traditional comforts. The 31-story, 300-room tower appeals to business travelers, young fashionables, and show-biz bigwigs; its 2 split-level suites are especially popular among Hollywood types. On a visit here, Michael Jackson stayed in La Montagne suite; complete with a spiral staircase, its master bedroom is adjoined by the city's most entrancing bathroom — the only place in town where a guest can float in a sunken tub while enjoying a panoramic view of Mount Royal. Those here on business can plug in a computer, have business calls routed to one of two phones, and work at a larger-than-average, well-lit work desk. Fitness fanatics can stay in shape at the health club, where there is a sauna, a whirlpool bath, a steamroom, and an outdoor pool for all seasons (in winter, the pool is heated to a steamy 90F). There's a minimal charge for computerized Kaiser and Nautilus equipment, aerobics classes, and shiatsu massage. Joggers will find a map in their rooms with directions to the best trails in nearby Mount Royal Park, just a sprint away up Peel Street. In keeping with the lobby's exotic Oriental decor, dinner is served Szechuan-style at *Zen,* the best Chinese restaurant in town. Information: *Four Seasons* (Le Quatre Saisons), 1050 Sherbrooke St. W., Montreal, Quebec H3A 2R6 (phone: 514-284-1110 or 800-268-6282 in Canada; 800-332-3442 in the US; fax: 514-845-3025).

INTER-CONTINENTAL, Montreal: One of the newest members of the famous luxury group, this is a favorite choice in Vieux Montréal. Linked by an interior bridge to the Nordheimer Building (once home of the *Nordheimer Music Hall*), this complex is a stunning blend of old and new. The reception area and 359 rooms are located in a new, 25-story, turret-topped tower, a 20th-century echo of its 19th-century counterpart. Since its opening in 1991, only a privileged (and well-heeled) few have seen the inside of the hotel's $2,000-a-day royal suite. The onetime Victorian music hall, where such stars as Sarah Bernhardt and P.T. Barnum's celebrated Tom Thumb once entertained, now houses the hotel's public rooms and three restaurants. Both the foyer, with its natural wood wainscoting and stenciled frieze, and the ballroom's vast plaster ceiling are sensational. *La Cave des Voûtes* wine-tasting bar and *Les Voûtes* steak and seafood restaurant are down in the restored Nordheimer vaults, which historians claim were part of Montreal's early fortification system. In *Chez Plume,* a casual lounge-café, upper walls are painted with friezes of stylized peacocks in full plumage. All 22 suites and rooms are decorated in gentle pastel shades, with spacious marble bathrooms. A concierge and room service are available 24 hours a day, and other amenities include signature toiletries and complimentary newspapers. Guests can work out in the 10th-floor health club or do laps in the 50-foot pool and then relax in the sauna, steam, and massage rooms. One of the best business centers in town gives you access to secretarial, translations, telex, and courier services, to name a few. Information: *Inter-Continental,* 360 St-Antoine St., Montreal, Quebec H2Y 1P5 (phone: 514-987-9900 or 800-327-0200; fax: 514-987-9904).

RITZ-CARLTON, Montreal: The details matter at this 240-room European-style hotel in the heart of Montreal. Even the ducks in the flower-fringed pond are forever young — when they reach a certain age they are retired to the country and replaced by more youthful birds. Opened more than 80 years ago by the legendary hotelier César Ritz, the Montreal establishment became an instant institution, catering to the high and mighty of Canada, and a loyal international clientele. The *Ritz* secret: making luxury seem natural. The hotel (now managed by the German Kempinski Group, which has not compromised an iota of comfort) sets the standard for amenities — not just the now-ubiquitous toiletries by the sink, but an umbrella in each room and more. The hotel also offers personalized service (two staff members to each guest) and impeccable decor. From the days of transatlantic cruises (the *Ritz* opened in 1912, the year the *Titanic* sailed and sank), the custom of unpacking and packing guests' steamer trunks (or suitcases) remains. Ask and your traveling trousseau or garment bag will be looked after, wrinkled suits pressed, and shoes shined. This is, after all, the *Ritz.* Information: *Ritz-Carlton,* 1228 Sherbrooke St. W., Montreal, Quebec H3G 1H6 (phone: 514-842-4212 or 800-363-0366 in Canada; 800-223-6800 in the US; fax: 514-842-3386).

VOGUE, Montreal: One of the new approaches to up-market innkeeping, this midtown establishment opposite *Ogilvy's* department store has transformed an ordinary office building into a classy little *hôtel particulier.* Although inspired by the discreet and very private hotels favored by well-heeled European travelers, with comforting Old World touches — goosedown duvets and pillows and, in some cases, canopy beds —

there's nothing turn-of-the-century about the amenities. The 126 rooms are equipped with all a business traveler could need, including fax machines and multi-functional phones, and the bathrooms are built for luxury, with whirlpool baths and glassed-in showers. But what really sets this gem apart is the penthouse floor, the work of New York interior designer Stanley J. Friedman. Devotees of the avant-garde admire the classical modernist style: Gray-walled rooms are furnished in black or gray leather and black-and-white marble bathrooms have gold-leaf ceilings. Corporate amenities include three boardrooms equipped with audiovisual and computer projection systems, as well as secretarial, translation, and courier services. Information: *Vogue,* 1425 de la Montagne St., Montreal, Quebec H3G 2Z3 (phone: 514-285-5555 or 800-363-0363 in Canada; 800-243-1166 in the US; fax: 514-849-8903).

CHÂTEAU BONNE ENTENTE, Quebec City: When Col. Charles Hugh Le Pailleur Jones, a retired army officer, invested his savings in estate country around Ste-Foy 70 years ago, the last thing on his mind was a resort hotel: To him, the spacious frame manor house set on 120 acres was home. But 30 years later, the colonel's son, Mowbray, launched the *Bonne Entente* and Quebec's "Other Château" was born. At first a small, 8-bedroom inn, the hospitable country home was an immediate hit with Quebecois and outsiders alike, and before long was sprouting additional wings and services. Today, this château retains the *bonne entente* (good vibes) of the colonel's country retreat in a 170-room mini-resort at the edge of Chemin Ste-Foy's traffic stream. Only 15 minutes by car or No. 11 bus from the walls of Vieux Québec, its many features and attractions make it ideal for family vacationers. In fact, kids are VIP guests at *Le Village de Nathalie,* a complimentary child-care center with an outdoor playground. Guests have the run of what remains of the original estate — 11 landscaped acres with tennis courts, a jogging trail, swimming pool, and trout pond. New owners have refurnished the multi-gabled clapboard hotel-motel complex in the tradition of a rambling New England inn; modern touches include whirlpool baths in the executive suites. The in-house business center provides secretarial and multilingual translation services, as well as audiovisual, photocopy, fax, and telex facilities. Enjoy some of the best-prepared wild game at *Le R.V.,* the *Château*'s gastronomic restaurant, or at any one of the three other less formal settings. Complimentary afternoon tea is a daily ritual at *Le Salon de Thé.* Information: *Château Bonne Entente,* 3400 Chemin Ste-Foy, Quebec City, Quebec G1X 1S6 (phone: 418-653-3030 or 800-463-4390; fax: 418-653-3098).

CHÂTEAU FRONTENAC, Quebec City: Atop the walled city, this 620-room railroad-built hotel designed to resemble a 16th-century French château is a definite landmark — what the Eiffel Tower is to Paris and Red Square is to Moscow, the *Château Frontenac* is to Quebec City. The site of the hotel has had an eventful history (explained in an exhibit in the lobby). Originally, it held a fort built by Champlain in 1620, which became a fortress in 1636, and eventually became known as Château St-Louis, a regal residence of the Governors of New France. In 1834, that structure was razed by fire. The present structure was built in the 1890s. During World War II, Allied officers accompanying Roosevelt and Churchill stayed here and planned the invasion of France. Constantly renovated, the grande dame remains Quebec City's most visible landmark, with its imposing brick walls, turrets and towers, and its copper roof, green with age, visible for miles. Within, modern comforts have been added recently without compromising the hotel's Old World appeal. Rooms are air conditioned, many have river views. There are split-level "spa" units in the central tower attic, where turn-of-the-century travelers had put up their personal maids and valets. Today the former servants' quarters are mini-suites with individual hot tubs. The fare at *Le Champlain,* where waiters wear 16th-century costume, is superb. There's also an attractive circular cocktail lounge overlooking the St. Lawrence, an inviting inner courtyard, a café-style restaurant, and a small gallery of shops. The Dufferin Terrace, built in 1834, has a spectacular view of the historic Old Lower Town and the Ile d'Orléans, and is a lovely place to relax on a summer night. At the *Frontenac,* one can feel the life of official Quebec, while the vibrant life of the city lies just beyond the lobby doors. Information: *Le Château Frontenac,* 1 Rue des Carrières, Quebec City, Quebec G1R 4P5 (phone: 418-692-3861 or 800-268-9411 in Canada; 800-828-7447 in the US; fax: 418-692-1751).

HILTON, Quebec City: Only a 5-minute walk from the walled city, the 563-room terraced tower near Parliament Hill is conveniently close to the capital's legislative and corporate office blocks and all the shopping temptations of Grande Allée. And no other spot is as close to the chic boutiques and fine restaurants of *Place Québec,* the only underground shopping mall of its type in the downtown area — a warm, dry haven when the volatile weather of Quebec City turns mean. Business travelers like its underground link to the Quebec Convention Center, and have 2 floors of executive class accommodations, expansive new meeting rooms, and conference halls. The health club is equipped with the usual gym facilities — pool, sauna, whirlpool bath, massage, and a big Jacuzzi. (Health-conscious guests will also appreciate that 7 floors are reserved for nonsmokers.) *Le Croquembroche* (phone: 418-674-2411), a warm setting conducive to long, relaxed indulgences in nouvelle cuisine, is also *the* place in Quebec City for the best *soupe aux pois* (pea soup) and *tourtière* (meat pie). Information: *Hilton,* 3 Pl. Quebec, Quebec City, Quebec G1K 7M9 (phone: 418-647-2411 or 800-268-9275 in Canada; 800-HILTONS in the US; fax: 418-647-6488).

LOEWS LE CONCORDE, Quebec City: Like the *Frontenac,* its imposing rival at the north end of the Champs de Bataille, this place recently underwent a multimillion-dollar refurbishment. And the investment has paid off. The preferred choice of the business traveler in Quebec City has added a stunner of a lobby, a golden-beige blend of marble, brass, and glass, with a hint of the exotic Orient in its delicate cherrywood paneling and tropical greenery. Set on the verge of Grande Allée's after-dark playground and just a 10-minute walk from Porte St-Louis and Vieux Québec, the geometric pyramid on the Plains of Abraham has a backyard as big as all outdoors in National Battlefields Park. Not surprisingly, the views are the best in town: Every one of the 422 rooms looks out on the St. Lawrence River and the Plains of Abraham. *Club 1225* on the private-access 12th floor has its own exclusive lounge and full American breakfast is included. The 2 top-floor presidential suites feature wood-burning fireplaces in their duplex apartments, as well as saunas and whirlpool baths. Non-presidential guests will more than make do with the hotel's health club, saunas, and whirlpool bath, located next to the heated outdoor pool. Executive amenities include a "Concierge Business Center," with secretarial, photocopy, fax, and telex communication services. The hotel's crowning glory, *L'Astral,* the revolving rooftop restaurant-bar, offers a 360° view of Old Town, picturesque Ile d'Orléans, and a chain of mountains dominated by Mont Ste-Anne. Information: *Loews Le Concorde,* 1225 Pl. Montcalm, Quebec City, Quebec G1R 4W6 (phone: 418-647-2222 or 800-463-5256 in Canada; 800-223-LOEWS in the US; fax: 418-647-4710).

Best Restaurants in Montreal and Quebec City

Montreal and Quebec City boast some of the best French restaurants on the continent, with perhaps the edge going to the gems to be found in Quebec City's Upper Town. Montreal restaurateurs prepare some of the best nouvelle cuisine to be found anywhere and, at the same time, offer more ethnic entrées than any other big city in Canada. Like New Yorkers, Montrealers can be fickle about their favorite spots, more likely to flit from one newborn "find" to another, so that last year's highly touted "in" spot is sometimes out. Diners in Quebec City are more likely to find that their favorite restaurants change little from year to year; but if measured by the hundreds of thousands of people who return season after season to the ancient *quartiers,* it's a tradition that promises to die hard.

BEAVER CLUB, Montreal: Founded in 1785 by the 19 fur-trading partners of the North West Company, which 36 years later united with the Hudson's Bay Company, it was at first a private club that restricted membership to those hardy souls who had spent a winter in the Northwest. Following amalgamation with the Hudson's Bay Company, the club disbanded and was not revived until the 1950s as a dinner club and restaurant in the *Queen Elizabeth* hotel. Though the spirit of the traders is preserved in the restaurant's decor of buffalo hides and other furry trophies, the food is light years beyond the banquet fare of the old Nor' Westers. Chef Edward Merard, one of Montreal's early disciples of nouvelle cuisine, has devised an à la carte menu of great sophistication and variety, featuring such specialties as medallions of deer in a *grand veneur* (master huntsman) sauce with fresh blueberry garnish, *noisettes* of veal with gorgonzola cheese, and pink Atlantic salmon poached in endive-scented cider. Adventuring in food is in the spirit of things, but you might want to take a cue from club regulars; for 4 decades they have been tucking into the best roast beef, either sliced thin, English-style, or in juicy, steak-thick slabs. Although the club no longer has regular meetings, longtime members receive a copper serving plate engraved with their name and the guarantee of a table in a choice location. Information: *Beaver Club,* 900 René-Lévesque Blvd. (phone: 514-861-3511).

CAFÉ DE PARIS, Montreal: Its name is a misnomer for Montreal's most beautiful restaurant, the *Ritz-Carlton*'s main dining room. Better described as an elegant salon, an island of blue-and-gold civility off the mainstream of the Sherbrooke Street shopping strip, its walls are covered in gold watered silk; there are gilt-framed mirrors reflecting intimate groupings of velvet banquettes and French doors that open onto the *Ritz Garden,* a warm weather dining terrace. The cuisine is every bit as fine as the ambience. But be prepared: The golden accents in the decor are reflected in the menu's Midas-like prices: "Gourmet Impérial," a selection of Beluga, Ossetra, and Sevruga caviar, adds up to a $150 appetizer! "Chicken 21" with wild rice is a longtime favorite, as are Dover sole, Gaspé salmon, venison, and other game dishes. The traditional baron of beef — served aboard the *couvercle* (a sparkling egg-shape silver serving dish) atop the *chariot découper* (trolley) — is a carnivore's delight. Former Governor-General Jeanne Sauvé is a longtime patron. Information: *Café de Paris,* 1228 Sherbrooke St. W. (phone: 514-842-4212).

LES HALLES, Montreal: The great charm of this townhouse on the Crescent Street strip is Jacques Landurie, its proprietor, whose hearty welcome sets the tone for a delightful dining experience. A nostalgic version of the bistros that surrounded the historic Paris marketplace of the same name, it's decorated with murals of the long-gone market scene, café signs salvaged from the old *quartier,* and other memorabilia of a sadly missed Parisian landmark. New chef Dominique Crevoisier's robust pot-au-feu (tender boiled beef and fresh garden vegetables) draws the lunchtime crowd; for dinner try the appetizer (served warm) of grapefruit, lobster, and scallops dressed with mayonnaise and French mustard, or the king-size ravioli, with four varieties of imported mushrooms. Marinated venison is a favorite wintertime entrée that gives way to rack of Quebec lamb in summer. Among the wicked temptations from the dessert trolley are strawberries Florentine (strawberry mousse sandwiched between two thin slices of chocolate topped with marinated strawberries and *sauce anglaise*). The *carte des vins* is an encyclopedia of fine but pricey wines. Information: *Les Halles,* 1450 Crescent St. (phone: 514-844-2328).

LA MARÉE, Montreal: Formerly a private residence, this restored property is now home to one of the best seafood restaurants in town. Though meals are served by formally dressed waiters in a velvet-draped dining room, the menu is shaped more by the quality and freshness of the food than by fancy culinary flourishes. Much of the fish and seafood is imported daily from France, and the kitchen turns out such satisfying, yet simply prepared house specials as bouillabaisse, sole *meunière*, halibut in creamy lobster sauce, and poached or grilled salmon. The chef is not adverse to adding hearty old-fashioned favorites such as *soupe à l'oignon gratinée*. Information: *La Marée*, 404 Pl. Jacques-Cartier (phone: 514-861-8126).

LES MIGNARDISES, Montreal: This new entry to the Montreal dining scene is where fashionable diners-about-town like to be seen and devotees of *cuisine légère* like to eat. Host Jean-Pierre Monnet, a former executive chef at *Les Halles*, has transformed a fussy 19th-century townhouse into a complex of three intimate dining rooms (total capacity is 55). Serenity is the key word *chez* Monnet. The small entryway is simply furnished with a few choice antique pine pieces that complement the exposed gray-stone walls and small oak bar. Beyond the bar are two petite dining parlors in an unassuming provincial setting of flower-sprigged wallpaper and oak-framed plaster. Quail sautéed in armagnac or lobster salad with raspberries and limes will sharpen the appetite for a main course of Atlantic salmon cutlets sweetened with pink grapefruit, or guinea fowl in orange sauce. Other popular Monnet entrée suggestions include a robust saddle of rabbit with a rhubarb compote and slices of venison in a delicate sauce of herbs and shallots. The wine list features heady choices (mostly expensive), with a few manageable offerings for customers who prefer to keep *l'addition* in the neighborhood of CN$150 for two. Information: *Les Mignardises*, 3035-07 St-Denis St. (phone: 514-842-1151).

LE SAINT-AMABLE, Montreal: Next door to *La Marée* and under the same ownership, this dining landmark in Vieux Montréal makes its home in the Benjamin Viger House, a heritage property built more than 220 years ago. Opening off lane-width Rue St-Amable, the historic building is just big enough to accommodate a kitchen and a small street-level dining room, cozily encased in the original gray-stone and brick walls and a warm red decor. House specials include roast breast of duckling spiced with red peppercorns and tart apples served in a creamy sauce; sherry-laced filet of veal; filet mignon with truffles; and a classic chateaubriand. The dessert table is a groaning board of chocolate *gâteaux*, pastries, and the *Saint Amable* brand of custard-filled *mille-feuilles*. There's also a memorable cherries Jubilee. Feeling romantic? Ask for a table in the candlelit bar down in the vaulted cellar of the old Viger homestead. If it hasn't been reserved for group dining, this little hideaway is often deserted — just right for dinner *à deux*. Information: *Le Saint-Amable*, 188 Rue St-Amable (phone: 514-866-3471).

ZEN, Montreal: Not your run-of-the-mill Chinese restaurant, this futuristically designed temple of haute cuisine, Szechuan-style, is rated the best of its kind in town. The curved, back-lit glass walls set the stage for a Far East feast that's served seasoned hot-hot or mild, according to taste. (But don't take "mild" too literally.) The long à la carte menu includes such popular choices as aromatic crispy duck, the chef's forte; lobster, prepared in six imaginative ways; salmon garnished with tangerine peel; sesame shrimp; whole abalone; and shark's fin soup for two. The caramelized banana dessert is to die for. It is the only North American branch of the restaurant chain of the same name (with headquarters in London, the group has restaurants in London and Hong Kong). Information: *Zen, Four Seasons*, 1050 Sherbrooke St. W. (phone: 514-284-1110).

AUX ANCIENS CANADIENS, Quebec City: For travelers looking for a complete French Canadian experience this dining spot has no equal. Even if the bill of fare were less than fine, tables here would be filled for the simple reason that the charming, white-walled Maison Jacquet, built about 1675, is the only example of original 17th-century architecture in Old Quebec. It is also one of the more significant: Author Philippe-Joseph Aubert de Gaspé, one of the first French Canadian novelists, wrote his classic of the same name here, dramatizing an incident in the Seven Years' War with the British. And architect Gaspard-Joseph Chaussegos de Lévy, the chief engineer of early 18th-century Quebec who built the early fortifications of Vieux Montréal, lived here. Its 4-feet-thick white plaster walls are crowded with corner cupboards, and bolstered with hand-hewn joists. Furnished in the style of a colonial kitchen with rustic tables covered with blue checkered cloths, it serves customers in four rooms, each decorated differently in an Old Quebec style of antique plates, kitchen utensils, firearms, and other necessities of colonial life. Today's table d'hôte selections go beyond the salt pork and *soupe aux pois* (pea soup) that nourished generations of Quebecois families to include braised goose leg with sour cream and herbs, duckling with maple syrup, and breast of pheasant in puff pastry. Traditional dishes — *fèves au lard* (pork and beans), *les cretons maison* (pork pâté), *tourtière* (meat pie), and *ragoût de pattes de cochon et de boulettes* (pigs' knuckles and meatball stew) — are always available. Information: *Aux Anciens Canadiens,* 34 Rue St-Louis (phone: 418-692-1627).

CAFÉ DE LA PAIX, Quebec City: This Rue des Jardins landmark owes its popularity to the law. It started life quietly back in the 1960s when lawyers from the old courthouse across the street discovered a new lunchtime spot, offering fine food at fair prices. Good news traveled fast. Before long food critics from New York to Los Angeles were singing the praises of chef Jean-Marc Bass and the clubby little café where most customers are on a first-name basis. Now genial host Benito Terzini's convivial establishment is a Vieux Québec tourist tradition but, happily, old patrons turn up regularly to keep the chef *sur le qui-vive.* From the outside, the café is a photographer's dream: a French *auberge* of white-plastered stone, flush with the hillside street, an old-fashioned lantern lighting a narrow doorway, and window boxes brimming with flowers. Inside, it's pure back-street Paris, the kind of *mère-et-père* operation where locals come for lunch and linger through a lazy afternoon, thinking about dinner. Reliable classics include beef *bourguignon,* Dover sole, frogs' legs, rack of lamb, and beef Wellington, and in season, pheasant, partridge, venison, wild boar, and moose. The dessert trolley is loaded with sherry-laced trifle, chocolate cake, custard-filled pastry, and bowls of whipped cream. (Chef Bass isn't into calorie counting). Quebecois émigrés and loyal guests from out of town return to their old haunt hoping the proprietor hasn't changed his cluttered decor of lamp-lit tables, sideboards, hutches, wine racks and bar, and Desrosiers landscapes on the paneled walls. Happily, he hasn't. Information: *Café de la Paix,* 44 Rue des Jardins (phone: 418-692-1430).

LE CHAMPLAIN, Quebec City: A step across the threshold here is like entering a time warp. Attentive waiters in formal colonial dress glide around the richly paneled room; majestic oak pillars and exposed beams support the lofty, stenciled ceiling; there's a massive, hooded fireplace; and high-backed tapestry chairs around damask-covered tables — even a harpist plucks out delicate air. Chef Jean-François Mots oversees the preparation of Old World favorites such as rack of lamb with fresh herbs, peppery buffalo filets, quail in port wine and grape sauce, and beef tenderloin with a truffle and madeira sauce. But Mots pays homage to nouvelle cuisine as well. Try fresh scallops coddled in sea urchin butter and an outstanding, or, more to the point, upstanding crayfish soufflé à l'Américaine. Awesome. The *carte des vins* is long, lavish, and priced accordingly, but wine may be ordered by the glass. This, the best restaurant in the *Château Frontenac,* is open for dinner and Sunday brunch. Information: *Le Champlain,* 1 Av. des Carrières (phone: 418-692-3861).

GAMBRINUS, Quebec City: *Quel outré!* Imagine a modern-looking restaurant in Upper Town — under the *Musée du Fort,* no less — serving nouvelle cuisine in a nouvelle setting. No exposed stone walls or colonial fireplaces here. Despite its ancient surroundings, this place has the contemporary atmosphere of a classy private club, with ceiling beams and wall panels aglow with a satiny mahogany finish; polished brass fixtures; and sheer café curtains. Chefs over the years here are best described as food designers, innovators who confidently bring Italian and French classics together with vivacious Quebecois flair. Try the seafood and veal dishes, usually combined with pasta, or rack of lamb, duckling in madeira sauce, and several variations of beef filet. The chocolate mousse *gâteau* is one of Vieux Québec's best. The menu changes daily for lunch and weekly for dinner. Information: *Gambrinus,* 15 Rue du Fort (phone: 418-692-5144).

LE MELROSE, Quebec City: At first glance it looks like grandmother's cottage, a prim Victorian villa of rose-trimmed gray brick, with rose-colored awnings, and roses growing in rose-colored window boxes. But *Le Melrose* is full of surprises. Since they opened for business in 1990, chef Mario Martel and his partners have built a loyal following, luring gourmets from traditional haunts of Vieux Québec to the charming residential enclave of nearby Sillery. Only a 10-minute cab ride from the walled city, it's as cozy inside as out: There are three small rooms downstairs, three up, curtained in old-fashioned lace, with the original dark wood trim framing plain, pastel-painted walls. No more than 60 guests can be seated at intimate, candlelit tables, arranged around the fireplace in the front parlor, in the dining room, and on the second floor, in what once were the bedrooms (if you cleared the rooms of restaurant furniture, this *could* be grandmother's cottage). Yet no gingerbread cookies bake in chef Martel's ovens. Behind the country-cottage ambience, he's busy inventing house specials: filet of caribou in a sauce of gingery peaches; pink, juicy tenderloin of lamb, seasoned with mustard and green peppercorns; and a mousse of duckling foie gras in chestnut cream. Information: *Le Melrose,* 1649 Chemin St-Louis, Sillery (phone: 418-681-7752).

LE SAINT-AMOUR, Quebec City: Young gourmands-about-town swear by this romantic hideaway in a refurbished Victorian house within the walls of Vieux Québec. They're all fans of chef Jean-Luc Boulay, the master chef from Normandy who first combined rare filets of beef with a white sauce of Roquefort cheese, almonds, and hazelnuts — the rest, as they say, is dining history. Within a few weeks of its modest opening in 1980, when Jean-Luc and his partner Jacques Fortier were still adding sentimental touches to their rose-tinted, lace-curtained salon on Rue Ste-Ursule, local food fanatics were beating a path to his door. The main dining room lives up to its romantic name in a roseate blush of candlelight, pink table linen, and reproductions of Renoir's rose-lipped maidens. From May to November, ask for a table in the glass-enclosed terrace of greenery with a retractable roof. House specials include tiny quail stuffed with roasted scampi, sliced into succulent rounds and served with fresh asparagus; *cornets* of escargot in a creamy herb sauce; and sautéed scallops with snow peas in lobster sauce. Calorie counters can take comfort in the chef's light sauces, which he concocts without butter or flour — but the desserts are bound to undo you. Information: *Le Saint-Amour,* 48 Rue Ste-Ursule (phone: 418-694-0067).

A LA TABLE DE SERGE BRUYÈRE, Quebec City: Like a stay in *Le Château Frontenac,* dinner here is an essential part of the Vieux Québec experience. There's only one sitting per evening in the two small (only 50 diners) rooms of this second-floor dining room in a historic building in the heart of the old walled city. Happily, things haven't changed much since Bruyère, a Lyon-born disciple of Paul Bocuse, opened his establishment 12 years ago: The ambience is pure Old World, with exposed walls of brick and stone, log fires crackling on the hearths, burnished antique copper reflecting the candlelight, and tables set with pastel linen, fresh flowers, and fine china. "Just a perfume" is Bruyère's definitive word on the subject of garlic and other seasonings which enhance the delicate flavor of tender young Quebec lamb, or the way his blueberry sauce complements thin slices of rare pheasant, or the raspberry vinegar that brings out the best in roast duckling. Diners who can't bring themselves to choose between fresh scallops from the Iles de la Madeleine and filet of pork spiced with green peppercorns can solve their dilemma with the nightly eight-course table d'hôte *"Menu Découverte"* (a tasting menu). Bruyère also boasts the best-stocked wine cellar in town, with some selections in the heady price range of $1,200. Information: *A la Table de Serge Bruyère,* 1200 Rue St-Jean (phone: 418-694-0618).

Best Shopping

Even if the snow is 20 feet deep, you can shop till you drop in Montreal — in climate-controlled comfort. A network of fine department stores, shopping malls, and underground city plazas makes up a vast urban marketplace, linked by a subterranean complex and one of the best subway systems in the world. Although the city supports some 150 retail districts and more than 5,000 stores, visitors staying at a midtown hotel are within easy strolling distance of one of the best shopping zones in the country. But do venture above ground. The shopping areas you'll want to visit in Quebec City are concentrated within the walls of historic Upper Town, or down around Place Royale, where Vieux Québec was born more than 3 centuries ago. Stores here are generally small, low-key, and a world apart from the city's suburban malls and its two centrally located plazas, where neither the ambience nor merchandise differs much from similar places across the continent. What sets Quebec City apart is its dozens of *quartier historique* outlets for distinctive Quebecois crafts, and small, designer-wear studios specializing in custom-cut leather, handwoven wools, and accessories.

BIRKS, Montreal: What *Tiffany's* is to New York, *Birks* is to Montreal. Although the Canadian jewelry chain has branches all over the country (and in the US), Montreal is the place where it all began. For generations the familiar blue *Birks* box has been a hallmark of quality in fine china, crystal, silver, home accessories, watches, and jewelry (natch). A regal old treasure house, still clinging to its 19th-century decor of marble columns and crystal chandeliers, *Birks'* headquarters has been a choice of travelers since its first store opened for business in 1879. Information: *Birks,* 1240 Phillips Sq. (phone 514-397-2511).

LES COURS MONT-ROYAL, Montreal: In a city that prides itself on being able to blend the old and new to create something innovative, *Les Cours Mont-Royal* lives up to its namesake: it's the majestic peak. What was once the *Sheraton Mount Royal* hotel has been lovingly turned into the city's most distinguished shopping experience. Heirlooms from the hotel's era include the magnificient coffered ceiling, the giant chandelier that once illuminated the lobby, and the grand staircase. Everything else — white marble salons, reflecting pools and waterfalls, and a cinema complex that could pass for some ancient palace on the Nile (it's called the *Egyptien*) — is part of an exciting approach to mall shopping. Four galleries of boutiques selling designer clothes, fine jewelry, and Italian shoes encircle a central court that once accommodated the lobby and lower level of the former hotel, all tastefully finished in mellow wood paneling and polished brass. Canadian designers Alfred Sung and Simon Chang have boutiques here. The best of Montreal society wends its way through the light, open spaces just as it did 50 years ago down the corridors of the *Sheraton.* Information: *Les Cours Mont-Royal,* 1455 Peel St. (phone: 514-842-7777).

HOLT RENFREW, Montreal: The doyenne of Canadian fashion houses has been catering to the well-dressed crowd since 1837, when the Henderson, Holt and Renfrew fur company first opened its doors in what is now Vieux Montréal. But there is nothing pre-Confederation about its operation today. *Holt's* is still *the* place to shop for furs, ball gowns, and designer fur labels. Birger Christensen, the definitive Danish furrier, has its salon here. Browsers are welcome, and the friendly sales staff is not above telling you a little history about the sleek Art Deco interior of this building in Montreal's vaunted Square Mile district. The city's only *Gucci* boutique is here, too, as are the salons of *Yves Saint-Laurent* and *Georgio Armani.* Information: *Holt Renfrew,* 1300 Sherbrooke St. W. (phone: 514-842-5111).

OGILVY, Montreal: Once a clubby emporium of not-so-distinguished dry goods, the Scottish retail firm has brushed up its image. *Ogilvy* has become the place of choice for high fashion for men, women, and children, as well as for home furnishings. Though older customers still mourn the loss of the *Tartan Room* restaurant, they take comfort in the cranberry glass chandeliers that still sparkle over the main-floor counters. Make a point of being here at noon for the skirl of bagpipes. A kilted bagpiper marches from floor to floor, summoning the thirsty to the basement-level coffee shop. A *Christmas-time* tradition, *Ogilvy*'s windows have been dressed up in festive fashion since 1947. Information: *Ogilvy,* 1307 Ste-Catherine St. W. (phone: 514-842-7711).

ATELIER LA POMME, Quebec City: Even those who don't fancy leather in their wardrobes enjoy browsing through this Quartier du Petit-Champlain boutique, with its multicolored inventory of clothing and accessories of the finest Argentine hides. House designers — who know enough English to consult with their English-speaking customers — create high-fashion leatherwear for men, women, and children in the color of your choice, in smooth leather, suede, or pigskin. Information: *Atelier La Pomme,* 47 Rue Sous-le-Fort (phone: 418-692-2875).

BROUSSEAU & BROUSSEAU, Quebec City: The place to go for Inuit art, this third outpost of the Brousseau family's antiques and crafts empire is one of the best of its kind in Canada. You can spend the day here in what has become a veritable museum of carvings and prints. Some of the large sculptures are museum pieces in themselves, costing thousands of dollars, but the gallery also stocks soapstone carvings in every size and price category. Information: *Brousseau & Brousseau,* 1 Rue des Carrières (phone: 418-694-1828).

LES TROIS COLOMBES, Quebec City: From the outside, this Rue St-Paul emporium looks like the ultimate tourist trap, but the 3-story crafts bazaar is one of Quebec City's best-kept secrets. Anything that's been carved, loomed, knit, stitched, kilned, and painted in eastern Canada and the far north seems to find its way to the shelves of this cluttered storehouse of collectibles. Look for value in the handwoven jackets and reversible coats in mohair and wool by Lise Dupuis, and hand-knit or woven sweaters trimmed with leather, silk, or lace by Marilise Couture. Savvy shoppers will uncover treasures from the Indian settlements of northern Quebec, including hand-sewn deer-skin shirts, jackets, ponchos, and sealskin boots. Information: *Les Trois Colombes,* 46 Rue St-Paul (phone: 418-694-1114).

ANTIQUES

The fur trade may not be what it once was in the heyday of the trappers, but trade in French Canadian pine continues to flourish. Indeed the high quality of antique pine from the Quebec wilderness that is available for sale in antiques houses in and around Montreal and Quebec City draws the most serious of collectors. In Montreal, some canny collectors still strike it rich on Notre Dame Street West, a 10-block stretch of antiques stores and secondhand shops Montrealers refer to as Attic Row. But except for the occasional find in Lower Town's antique row — where lucky discoveries of hand-carved duck decoys, country kitchen utensils, marble-topped washstands, and the occasional piece of good pine are still possible — the best bet for pine pickers in Quebec

City is to head out of town to nearby rural Quebec to discover treasures of your own.

ANTIQUITÉS PHYLLIS FRIEDMAN, Montreal: Those looking for precious pine pieces usually make their first stop here, where blanket boxes, spinning wheels, chests, and armoires are all at least 150 years old. Information: *Antiquités Phyllis Friedman,* 5012 Sherbrooke St. W., Montreal (phone: 514-483-6185).

CIRCA-CIRCA, Montreal: Beyond the western reaches of the city in the town of Montreal West, this long-established New England–like community boasts one main street, on which Fran Porteous keeps a tidy little collectors' rendezvous stocked with Quebecois furniture of pine, ash, oak, and butternut. While some of her wares sell in the $1,000-plus range, most of her offerings are more moderately priced. She carries a selection of sturdy, old, oak country kitchen furniture, stripped down to the grain and its original, natural finish. Information: *Circa-Circa,* 68 Westminster Ave. N., Montreal West (phone: 514-481-3410).

HENRIETTA ANTONY, Montreal: Patient buyers will find beautiful early Quebec furniture among other treasures in this 4-story antiques gallery in Westmount. The collection includes a few rare pieces from the late 1700s, some with traces of the original finish. Period pieces range from traditional farmhouse relics to naïve versions of Versailles elegance that Quebec cabinetmakers made to order for the local seigneurs 200 years ago. Information: *Henrietta Antony,* 4192 Ste-Catherine St. W., Montreal (phone: 514-935-9116).

PIERRE ST-JACQUES, Montreal: One of the first stops for those looking for traditional Quebecois pieces in pine and maple is this spot on Notre-Dame Street. Though many antiques shops in Montreal feature more factory-made Victoriana than hand-crafted *meubles Canadiens,* this shop is not one of them. Information: *Pierre St-Jacques,* 2507 Notre-Dame St. W., Montreal (phone: 514-931-0914).

PETIT MUSÉE, Montreal: Antiques seekers looking for the best of what Montreal has to offer will not want to miss this spot, which is more in the style of a fine-arts gallery than an antiques shop. It has an eclectic collection of fine furniture, china, and objets d'art from Europe, the Middle East, and the Orient, all for sale. Information: *Petit Musée,* 1494 Sherbrooke St. W., Montreal (phone: 514-937-6161).

RON HENRY ANTIQUES, Montreal: It's worth the drive a few miles west of Montreal to the village of Pointe Claire and Ron Henry's house of antiques. Good bargains can be struck here on authentic *Canadien* pieces, as well as reproductions of rustic armoires. Follow Route 20 to the Pointe Claire exit, a few miles west of the Dorval Airport traffic circle. Information: *Ron Henry Antiques,* 17B Cartier Ave., Pointe Claire (phone: 514-694-2597).

ANTIQUE CHEZ TI-PÈRE, Quebec City: Avid collectors who head out to Laurier Station on the South Shore will find good reproductions of country pine. Follow Route 20 from Pierre Laporte Bridge toward Montreal and Exit 278 (about 33 miles/54 km). Information: *Antique Chez Ti-Père,* 128 Rue Olivier, Laurier Station, Quebec City (phone: 418-728-4031).

AUX MULTIPLES COLLECTIONS, Quebec City: This antiques shop in the heart of Upper Town behind the walls of Old Quebec stands as the capital's best and most reputable source of the real Quebecois thing where every item comes with a guaranteed pedigree. Better known for its Inuit carvings, the Brosseau family has been dealing in traditional Quebec furniture and handicrafts for years — and what it doesn't have in stock, it generally can find. Information: *Aux Multiples Collections,* 69 Rue Ste-Anne, Quebec City (phone: 418-692-1230).

For the Body

Downhill Skiing

Canadians can probably be classified in two major groups: Those who ski and those who intend to learn. That's not surprising, considering the usually abundant quantities of snow north of the international border, the mountainous terrain up there, and the number of mountains developed for skiing. Natural snowfall can be expected from late November to late March, but sometimes — particularly in eastern Canada — the "Great White North" is not quite white enough, so many of the major ski areas have installed supplementary snowmaking machinery to ensure good ski conditions even during periods of light snowfall.

In any case, a skier in Canada is seldom very far from a good run. Quebec is undoubtedly the queen of eastern Canada skiing with Parc du Mont Ste-Anne, a giant area outside Quebec City; the Eastern Townships, a quartet of mountains with first class runs for all levels of ability and with a less hectic pace than at some of the older, more popular resorts; and the grand Laurentians, mountains that offer a vacation experience notable as much for the elegant cuisine and the regional specialties served in the restaurants of the quaint villages at the lift base, as for the excitement quotient of the nearly 1,000 slopes and runs of its 125-odd ski areas. That the Laurentians region is one of the few ski areas in the Western Hemisphere where the chef is held in as much regard as the head ski instructor is more important to many skiers than the fact that the runs are shorter and conditions frequently icier and rockier than those in Canada's other great ski region, the ineffably beautiful Rocky Mountains.

LAURENTIANS (LES LAURENTIDES), Montreal: Beginning about 35 miles (56 km) from the city, along the high-speed Laurentian autoroute leading into the hills to the northwest, there is a succession of ski communities — more than 20 major ones in all, each the center of a cluster of ski areas situated just minutes apart. If only for the sheer number of runs in the area — some 300 (80 lit for night skiing) in the space of 40 square miles, a concentration greater than that of any other area of comparable size in the world — the Laurentians would be unique. But the frills of a skiing vacation here also stand out. The region's charming French villages are full of lovely inns, pleasant resorts, and small hotels so close to the skiing that it's easy to schuss right to your doorstep — or, more to the point, to your dining room, where good food is the order of the day.

Every one of the ski areas here has its special charm. At the northern end of this string of resorts is Mont Tremblant, the dowager queen of Canada's winter resorts, which, with a vertical drop of 2,100 feet and runs that extend up to 2 miles in length, offers plenty of good skiing for experts and intermediates. Mont Tremblant has a detachable quad chair lift and jet T-bar, restaurants at the top and the base of the mountain, a nursery, and snowmaking facilities to the very top of the mountain's southern side. Its first-rate hotels include the big *Station Mont Tremblant Lodge* (phone: 819-425-8711 or 800-567-6761) and the smaller *Tremblant Club* (phone: 819-

425-2731 or 800-567-8341 in Canada; 800-363-2413 in the US). Some 3 miles (5 km) away in St-Jovite is the *Auberge Gray Rocks* (phone: 514-861-0187, 819-425-2771, or 800-567-6767), a friendly sprawl of a 252-room Victorian hostelry on 2,600 acres with its own ski hill, Sugar Peak, 100 yards from the inn. The vertical here is a mere 620 feet, but it is a giant in the annals of ski history. In 1938, with war threatening, Austria's famed Snow Eagle Ski School was transplanted here, and since has developed into one of the best anywhere; it's so thorough that there are even a couple of instructors whose sole job is keeping the other teachers on their toes. Graduates number among the best skiers in the world. Among the many aspects that make the lodge outstanding are its new sports complex, indoor swimming pool, whirlpool bath, saunas, nightlife (which is vigorous enough to make the place a good bet for the solo vacationer), and lunches (served on white-linen-covered tables in a dining room practically at the lift base). Other ski areas offer similar delights. Belle Neige (phone: 818-322-3311) in Val-Morin, a small hill with a vertical of only about 520 feet, 2 T-bars, and 2 chair lifts, is distinguished by the proximity of the *Hôtel la Sapinière,* a member of the Relais & Châteaux group and the proud possessor of one of Canada's finest kitchens.

If you only have 1 day to devote to downhill stop at St-Sauveur, only 37 miles (59 km) from Montreal. This pretty, prosperous village, tucked into its namesake valley, serves as the dining, shopping, and entertainment hub for patrons of four neighboring mountains: Mont St-Saveur, Mont Habitant, Mont Christie, and Mont Avila. These four gems form one of the brightest night-skiing conglomerates in Canada, and their popularity is reflected on photogenic Rue Principale, St-Sauveur's main street, lined with fashionable restaurants, bars, and stores. King of the mountain quartet is Mont St-Sauveur, with a vertical drop of 698 feet and 26 runs, the longest of them 4,900 feet. Night skiers can choose from 23 day-bright runs.

For general information and lists of small hostelries contact *Association Touristique des Laurentides,* 14142 Rue de Lachapelle, RR1, St-Jérôme, Quebec J7Z 5T4 (phone: 818-436-8532).

EASTERN TOWNSHIPS (ESTRIE), Montreal: Unlike the Laurentians, which were initially built up to serve as summer resorts and were then strung with lifts to help the communities make it through the winter, the mountains in this northern extension of the Appalachians, 44 miles (71 km) southeast of Montreal and just north of the Vermont border, were developed primarily for skiing, because of the suitability of the terrain. Each one is the peer of Mont Tremblant or any comparable Vermont resort. Mont Sutton, near Sutton, has 54 trails, 9 chair lifts, a 1,509-foot vertical, and unique glade skiing. Owl's Head, near Mansonville, has a 1,770-foot vertical and 25 trails. Mont Orford, near Magog, has a 1,772-foot vertical and 32 trails. Bromont, with a 1,328-foot vertical and 26 trails, is the fourth member of the quartet of major mountains in the area. Headquarter at any one of the four mountains, ski there, and then use your interchangeable lift ticket to sample the other three. All four areas have runs to suit everyone in the family, varied terrain, and good lift service; each has its own unique character.

The area offers accommodations to satisfy almost every taste. Owl's Head has a small lodge right at the base, plus apartment-hotels and condominiums with ski-in/ski-out access to lifts and trails. There is snowmaking equipment and a detachable quad chair lift, plus 6 double chair lifts. Owl's Head attracts an almost fanatically loyal crowd that returns year after year after year. The *Auberge Bromont* (phone: 819-534-2200) at Bromont is a cozy place with views of the illuminated runs. The areas around Mont Sutton and Mont Orford are livelier; they're both close to a couple of other small towns that boast restaurants and other nighttime activities. Among the more interesting hostelries in this area are *Village Archimèd* (phone: 819-538-3440) at Sutton, *Hovey Manor* (phone: 819-842-2421) at North Hatley, and Magog's *Cheribourg* resort (phone:

819-843-3308). Although the Eastern Townships don't bustle with as much activity as the Laurentians, and although this is still very much the farming area that it was before the lifts went in more than 20 years ago, these mountains offer an abundance of amenities for those who've come first and foremost to ski. What's more, the quality of the skiing is among the best this side of the Rockies.

Information: *Quebec Ski East,* 2883 W. King St., Sherbrooke, Quebec J1L 1C6 (phone: 819-564-8989). For reservations and local information: *Mont Orford Resort Centre,* Box 248, Magog, Quebec J1X 3W8 (phone: 819-843-6548); *Owl's Head,* Mansonville, Quebec J0E 1X0 (phone: 819-292-5592); *Sutton Tourist Association,* for lodging, CP 418, Sutton, Quebec J0E 2K0 (phone: 819-538-2646 or 819-538-2537); for skiing, CP 280, Sutton, Quebec J0E 2K0 (phone: 819-538-2339); and *Bromont Ski Area,* CP29, Bromont, Quebec J0E 1L0 (phone: 819-534-2200 or 800-363-8920).

MONT STE-ANNE, QUEBEC CITY: Quebec City skiers can't help feeling a bit smug about Mont Ste-Anne. Unlike their neighbors in Montreal who can spend a traffic-lodged hour creeping *to* a Laurentian Autoroute access, *piste*-bashers from the provincial capital land at the base village of their local mountain within 30 minutes of a midtown takeoff.

Mountain enough to have hosted the first *Canadian Winter Games* in 1967 and now a regular stop on the *World Cup* circuit, Mont Ste-Anne is the biggest of the local areas and so close to the old capital that many of the city's major hotels offer ski packages. Located at Beaupré, a rather nondescript one-street town about half an hour's drive east of the city, it boasted terrain that was already considerable before development of its north and west sides a few years ago doubled the skiable area; today 50 slopes and 12 lifts of varying types allow for an uphill capacity of more than 17,761 an hour. Consequently, there's now the option of enjoying the sunny conditions on the southern slopes (the top three-quarters of them as challenging as any of Vermont's steepest and hairiest), or the intermediate and novice north-facing runs, or even the intermediate and expert trails of the mountain's western exposure. Every year more runs are being backed up by an elaborate snowmaking system; well over 85% of the skiable terrain is currently covered. With the addition of 13 lighted trails, Mont Ste-Anne now claims to have the highest vertical night skiing in Canada. It also offers the cross-country skier over 110 miles of double-track, groomed, and patrolled trails equal to the very best in North America. The base village provides 140 condo units in two 5-story buildings, plus an assortment of boutiques and restaurants, a children's center, and one of the most popular features, a 3-story day lodge adjacent to the existing base chalet with a 550-seat cafeteria and a bar with multilevel sun decks. Over the last several years the park has developed into a year-round resort, with two 18-hole golf courses, camping facilities, and 157 miles of cycling and mountain bike trails. On clear days, year-round, a gondola climbs 2,640 feet to the summit, providing a breathtaking view of the St. Lawrence River, Quebec City, and Ile d'Orléans. There also is Le Massif, the most unusual ski center east of the Rockies. A 2,614-foot-high escarpment that plunges toward the St. Lawrence River, it has 11 2½-mile intermediate and expert trails that boast some of the best powder snow in eastern Canada. Instead of the usual ski lift, it has 8 or 9 buses that transport skiers from the base of the mountain to the top of the slopes. Because the center can accommodate only 350 skiers a day, reservations are a must.

STONEHAM, Quebec City: The region's next most extensive skiing is even closer to the city than Mont Ste-Anne (20 miles/32 km north), and has a respectable 1,380-foot vertical drop. The area, nestled in a valley, is protected from strong winds. About 92% of Stoneham's 25 runs are covered by snowmaking equipment and 15 of the runs are lighted. The lift capacity is now more than 14,000 skiers an hour and skiers who want to be on the slopes when they open can choose from among 50 condos and 2 hotels at the base of the mountain. In addition, it's possible to ski Le Relais and Mont

St-Castin — two areas whose verticals measure 750 and 550 feet respectively — at longtime favorite vacation center Lac Beauport. These areas are so close to the city that each is busy during the week and busier still on weekends. But the attractions of Montreal are such that it's probably best to stay in accommodations in the city and commute to the ski area, rather than the other way around. Ski bus service is available from six Quebec City hotels (phone: 418-627-2511). By car take Autoroute Laurentienne (Rte. 73) to Route 175.

Information: *Greater Quebec City Region Tourism and Convention Bureau,* 60 Rue d'Auteuil, Quebec City, Quebec G1R 4C4 (phone: 418-692-2471); *Parc du Mont Ste-Anne,* PO Box 400, Beaupré, Quebec G0A 1E0 (phone: 418-827-4561); *Le Relais,* 1084 Blvd. du Lac Beauport, Quebec GOA 2CO (phone: 418-849-1851); *Mont St-Castin,* 82 Chemin le Tour-du-Lac, Lac Beauport, Quebec GOA 2CO (phone: 418-849-4277); *Stoneham,* 1420 du Hibou, Stoneham, Quebec GOA 4P8 (phone: 418-848-2411); *Le Massif,* Rte. 138, CP 68, Petite-Rivière-St-François, Quebec G0A 2L0 (phone: 418-435-3593); *RESERVOTEL,* a central reservation service for Quebec City and the Charlevoix region (phone: 800-463-1568).

Cross-Country Skiing

It's not necessary to be an *Olympic*-caliber athlete to enjoy ski touring — cross-country skiing. Nor is it necessary to go anywhere special in parts of Quebec to enjoy the sport. You can ski in city ravines, suburban vest-pocket parks, farmers' fields, and on frozen lakes. But with a long weekend or a week to spare, you'll want to head for the more attractive trails within easy driving distance of Montreal and Quebec City. There, given some wisdom in the ways of the winter wilderness, it's a great adventure to break your own trails through the powder. Or tackle one of the many areas where special cross-country ski trails are marked, groomed, and patrolled. Most provincial and municipal parks have developed at least one trail and try to keep campgrounds open for die-hard winter lovers. Others can be found at a variety of hostelries: downhill ski resorts; luxury resorts (where après-ski means swimming in a big pool and relaxing in a sauna; simple housekeeping cottages in the woods; cozy country inns; and rustic mountain lodges heated by wood stoves and lit by kerosene lanterns. Or you might want to try a lodge-to-lodge or hut-to-hut (tents, actually) tour with accommodations located a day of skiing apart, on an interconnecting trail (luggage is transported separately by road).

LAURENTIANS, Montreal: Twenty-five years ago, cross-country skiing here had the reputation of being for kamikaze-types only. Trails were severe, with frequent cliff-like descents. Today, most of the trails have been redesigned, upgraded, and mechanically tracked. This vast sweep of mountains may well be the ultimate cross-country ski resort area, the Aspen of cross-country skiing. The main attraction, besides the skiing, is the abundance of wonderful restaurants and lodging places. But when you consider their diversity and the variety of the skiing terrain, putting together a Laurentians ski vacation can become terribly confusing. A few basic facts about the area may be helpful. To wit: The northern Laurentians' trails are not quite so well marked as those in the south; and the farther east or west you travel from the Laurentians Autoroute, which bisects the region from north to south, the wilder and less well marked are the ski routes. The trails at the better-known hostelries of the more northerly St-Jovite–Mont Tremblant area — the *Tremblant Club* (phone: 819-425-2731 in Canada or 800-363-2418 in the US), the *Station Mont Tremblant Lodge* (phone: 819-425-8711 or 800-567-6761), and the *Auberge Gray Rocks* (phone: 819-425-2771 or

800-567-6767) — are enjoyable. Most people make their headquarters at one establishment, then spend their vacations exploring its trails and those of its neighbors, accessible via interregional trails. But the very concentration of inns and the proliferation of long-distance trails also suggest the possibility of inn-to-inn touring, and in the south, where the hostelries are situated practically on top of each other, innkeepers are generally quite obliging about transporting your luggage via hotel bus or taxi to your next overnight stop.

Regional trail maps are available from local hotels and ski shops, as is the interregional trail map published by the Laurentian Ski Zone. Information: *Association Touristique des Laurentides,* 14142 Rue de Lachapelle, RR1, St-Jérôme, Quebec J7Z 5T4 (phone: 819-436-8532). Also see *Downhill Skiing,* above.

MONT STE-ANNE AND "LES AUTRES," Quebec City: One of the great charms of being in Quebec City in the winter is its proximity to the great outdoors. Visitors can spend days outdoors pursuing their favorite cold-weather sports (Quebec City is markedly more wintry than Montreal) — and nights in the comfort of the city's splendid hotels, sleeping off the effects of a bountiful French Canadian repast eaten in one of its cozy restaurants. Cross-country skiers will find some of the province's best skiing within an hour's drive of the city. Quebecois themselves take to the Plains of Abraham to keep in shape; and though the skiing isn't the best, the views are outstanding. Quebec's best ski terrain — more than what's possible to explore in a 2-week vacation (let alone a 2-week vacation that leaves time to enjoy the delights of the metropolis) — is at Mont Ste-Anne, 25 miles (40 km) to the east; at Duchesnay Forestry Station, 25 miles (40 km) northwest; and at Camp Mercier, just inside Laurentides Park, 36 miles (58 km) from downtown. Located in the picturesque village of St-Férreol-les-Neiges, 5 miles east of the alpine ski center, Mont Ste-Anne's cross-country ski center has 134 miles of trails in the heart of the Laurentian Forest. The trails have been specifically designed to meet the needs of beginner and intermediate skiers. Expert trails are found at the competition center of Parc Mont Ste-Anne. Duchesnay's more varied woods trails, through mixed hardwood and fir, are better suited to beginners, while the trails at Camp Mercier, far less windy than at either of the other areas, are flatter still; the snow is also better there. Inexpensive group overnight trips are also available.

For those looking to escape the crowds at the three popular locations listed above, the following five centers are devoted exclusively to cross-country skiing and often leave the skier free to wander in the wide open spaces. Within easy driving distance of Quebec City are the following: *Camping Municipal de Beaufort,* with 5 trails of up to 9 miles of touring; waxing room open weekends only; heated relay station; restaurant facilities; and night skiing. Open daily to 10 PM; no admission charge (95 Av. Sérénité, Beauport; access via Rte. 369; phone: 418-666-2228 or 418-666-2155). *Centre de Ski de Fond de Cap-Rouge,* 8 trails of more than 23 miles; waxing room and heated relay station. Open daily to 6 PM; no admission charge (4600 Rue St-Félix, Cap-Rouge; access via Rte. 440; phone: 418-849-9054). *Centre de Ski de Fond Charlesbourg,* 22 trails covering 120 miles; waxing and restaurant facilities; equipment rental; heated relay station. Open daily to 4 PM; admission charge (Rue Dublin, Charlesbourg; access via Rte. 175; phone: 418-849-9054). *Club de Golf de Lorette,* 3 trails of 28 miles; waxing and restaurant facilities; heated relay station. Open daily to 4 PM; no admission charge (12986 Rue Monseigneur Cooke, Loretteville; access via Rtes. 573 or 369; phone: 418-842-8441). *Base de Plein Air de Val-Bélair,* 10 trails of 37 miles; waxing and equipment rental; restaurant. Open daily to 4 PM; admission charge (1560 Av. de la Montagne W.; access via Rte. 369; phone: 418-842-7184; weekends: 418-842-7769). Information: *Greater Quebec City Area Tourism and Convention Bureau,* 60 Rue d'Auteuil, Quebec City, Quebec G1R 4C4 (phone: 418-692-2471).

Note: The *Canadian Ski Marathon,* a mammoth, anyone-can-enter, 2-day cross-country ski event, takes place in the Outaouais region, in the southern section of Quebec. Usually held in mid-February, the marathon ranks among the biggest events of its kind in the world. The starting point is in Montebello, about 40 miles (64 km) east of Ottawa, and the finish line is 160 km (93 miles) west in Gatineau. Entrance fees range from about $38 to $55, depending on the skier's age. For details, contact the *Canadian Ski Marathon,* PO Box 98, Montebello, Quebec J0V 1L0 (phone: 819-423-5157). Information: *Association Touristique de l'Outaouais,* 25 Rue Laurier CP 2000, Hull, Quebec J8Z 322 (phone: 819-778-2222).

Ice Skating and Hockey

Quebec winters and ice go together. From December until May, ponds, lakes, rivers, and streams turn into natural rinks. The tradition of bundled-up businessmen skating to their offices originated with the French traders who skated over the frozen waterways from one trading post to another with their goods. Then, inspired by the ingenuity of the French, the Iroquois strapped bones to their feet and joined the sport, and English soldiers in turn began holding competitions for the most creative and intricate patterns cut into ice. Indoor rinks first appeared in Quebec City and Montreal in the 1880s, and in Montreal today there are 150 outdoor rinks and 21 indoor arenas for hockey and public skating.

Hockey tends to dominate the skating scene, and aspiring professionals begin early in leagues that launch "Henri Richard" and "Patrick Roy" wannabes as young as 7 years old. Drop into any community center/arena across Quebec to see the small fry in action, with parents, family members, and friends cheering them on. If a small town in Quebec or neighborhood in Quebec City or Montreal looks deserted ask directions to the nearest "rink" and take part in one of Canada's favorite winter pastimes.

Figure skating is also booming. The *Canadian Figure Skating Association* (phone: 613-748-5635) has 157,000 members, and some 1,400 clubs based in municipalities nationwide stage seminars for skaters and interclub competitions, sending the winners on to sectional, divisional, national, and international contests. (In 1991, Canadian Kurt Browning captured the *Men's World Figure Skating Championship* title for the third time.) A top Canadian skater in training usually winters in Toronto and summers in the Rockies or England, buying private ice time (usually to the tune of $15,000 annually).

There's fine recreational skating everywhere, but one of the joys of skating in Quebec is the preponderance of lakes and rivers that freeze over and the fact that, because of the sport's popularity, warming huts and hot sandwich stands pop up here and there along the shores.

MOUNT ROYAL PARK AND LAFONTAINE PARK, Montreal: Throughout the week, day and night, Montrealers flock to the city's open-air municipal rinks. Two of the most popular are at Lafontaine Park and Mount Royal Park (both lighted at night and near downtown). Mount Royal Park, whose about 530 acres wrap around the sides of a still-active volcano, is as terrific in winter as it is for summer strolls and *calèche* rides. The skating all takes place on Beaver Lake (Lac des Castors), where there are fine views of the city. After you've unlaced your skates, you can go cross-country skiing, slide down one of a couple of slopes in a toboggan, ride a horse-drawn sleigh, or warm up over an interesting meal. Information: *Mount Royal Park,* Remembrance Rd. (phone: 514-872-1415 or 514-872-2644) and *Lafontaine Park,* Sherbrooke St. E. between Papineau Ave. and Parc Lafontaine St. (phone: 514-872-2644).

ANGRIGNON PARK, Montreal: The large skating rink at this park in the southwest corner of the city is enough to draw the irrepressible Hans (or Heidi) Brinker. Visit the fairy-tale ice palace and labyrinth and plummet down the giant toboggan slide. The children's domain is particularly enchanting in the evening when the fancifully decorated park becomes a place where everyone glides around the skating rink. Cross-country skiers, snowshoers, and brisk strollers are welcome to try out the 260 acres of what Montrealers have come to call their winter wonderland. Open, if winter conditions prevail, from December 21 to the end of February. No admission charge. Information: *Angrignon Park,* 3400 des Trinitaires Blvd. (phone: 514-872-6211).

ILE NOTRE DAME, Montreal: Site of the city's 10-day *Fête des Neiges* festivities from mid-January to early February, the island's summer beach area is transformed into a winter playground once the snow falls. In addition to cross-country skiing, snowshoeing, snowboarding, and the thrills of an ice slide nearly 3 miles long, there's skating on the lake and the mile-long Olympic Basin. Most skaters aim for a mild, sunny day when they plan an island outing: It can be bitterly cold on the open river, and the wind cuts like a knife when the temperature drops. Be careful: Even the most bundled-up skater is not immune to a touch of frostbite. Information: *Ile Notre Dame* (phone: 514-872-6093).

LAURENTIANS, Montreal: The trick here is to arrive after a spell of weather long enough and cold enough to ice over the myriad ponds, lakes, and streams of this lovely area — but before the snow. Then you can skate for miles, play hockey to your heart's content, or trace figures so large that giants might have made them. The great outdoors is one vast skating rink. But even after the snowfall, there's no dearth of places to skate in this skate-happy region. Almost every village has its rink — if not a manmade oval set up in the schoolyard, then a section of a nearby lake kept plowed for the season. Sections of the lakes at several of the area's best resorts (among them *Auberge Gray Rocks* at St-Jovite and the *Hôtel la Sapinière* at Val David) are usually kept clear, as are the lakes at Ste-Adèle and Ste-Agathe. The former has a half-mile oval to speed around as well as the regular rink-size area. And there are indoor rinks as well. The delight of skating here also derives from what goes *après.* The unique European flavor of après-ski in the Laurentians applies to "après-skate" as well, with long sessions at the hearthsides of cozy inns; the satiation of galloping appetites in one of the many fine restaurants in the quaint villages, and the gayer-than-Paris-in-springtime nightlife — some of the happiest to be found at any winter resort on earth. Information: *Association Touristique des Laurentides,* 14142 Rue de Lachapelle, RR1, St-Jérôme, Quebec J7Z 5T4 (phone: 819-436-8532).

ST. CHARLES RIVER, Quebec City: Beautiful as it can be under a hot summer sun, Quebec City seems to have been built to look its best swathed in snow. Quebecois put on skates almost as soon as they learn to walk, and there are hundreds of admission-free skating rinks throughout the region on which to practice. To see for yourself, you've only to lace up your skates and head for the St. Charles River between Samson and Marie de l'Incarnation bridges, where you'll glide along beside one of the city's many parks, serene under its mantle of white. The season generally lasts from mid-December through February and skaters are welcome Mondays through Fridays from noon to 10 PM; Saturdays and Sundays from 10 AM to 10 PM. No admission charge. There's parking by the service hut near Lavigueur Bridge. Information: *Reception area, Marina St-Roch,* 230 Rue du Pont (phone: 418-691-7188).

PLACE D'YOUVILLE, Quebec City: Just beyond the walls of Vieux Québec, opposite Porte St-Jean, this Upper Town square — conveniently located for hotel guests staying within and outside the fortifications — is transformed into a big outdoor rink with the first November freeze. Skaters glide around in an artistic atmosphere here, where sculptor Alfred Laliberté's *Muses* group presides over the ice. The season runs from November through mid-March. Open daily from noon to 10 PM. No admission charge for rink or changing rooms. Information: *Place d'Youville* (phone: 418-628-4685).

VILLAGE DES SPORTS, Quebec City: Famous for its summertime surf pool and water slides, the *Village* goes all out for winter sports when the snow falls. The family complex offers toboggan slides, cross-country ski and snowshoe trails, and racing car rinks from December until the beginning of March. But the most beguiling feature of this commercial playground is its lane-width skating trail, winding 1½ miles through the woods where skaters can skate — or jive — along with the music (speakers are concealed in bird houses); the trail is especially charming under the lights at night. About 20 miles (32 km) north of the city, the winter *Village* is open daily Mondays through Thursdays from 10 AM to 5 PM and 7 to 10 PM; Fridays, Saturdays, and Sundays to 11 PM. Admission charges vary with choice of activities. Information: *Village Des Sports,* 1860 Blvd. Valcartier, St-Gabriel-de-Valcartier (phone: 418-844-3725).

GAÉTAN BOUCHER SPEED-SKATING RINK, Quebec City: Serious skaters enjoy cutting corners around this 437-yard oval of artificial ice, named for Quebec's beloved speed-skating champ. The outdoor facility in neighboring Ste-Foy is groomed for top performance and often hosts international competitions. But that doesn't intimidate some speed-skating wannabes and beginners alike who are out in force all winter whirling and twirling to the music of the day in the park-like setting of the City Hall square. Open mid-October through the end of March Mondays through Fridays from noon to 3:30 and 7:30 to 10 PM; Saturdays and Sundays 1 to 4:30 PM and 7:30 to 10 PM. Admission charge. 930 Rue Place de Ville, Ste-Foy (phone: 418-654-4462). Information: *Greater Quebec City Region Tourism & Convention Bureau,* 60 Rue d'Auteuil, Quebec City, Quebec G1R 4C4 (phone: 418-692-2471).

Good Golf

In summer, Quebeckers trade in the primary colors of their skiwear for the pastels of golf clothes, but they don't switch their destinations. The playgrounds of the Laurentians and Mont Ste-Anne provide some public golf courses and low handicappers and duffers alike will want to spend at least a day on the links during their visit. Golfers teeing off in the foothills of Quebec City will find the weather cool and breezy, rarely humid, and the courses challenging, pristinely kept, and with less expensive greens fees than found at layouts surrounding large US cities. Golfers need not go very far afield either.

In Montreal 50 courses are within a 30-mile (54-km) radius of the city and half of those are public; Quebec City boasts about a dozen 18-hole spreads and 9 sporty little 9-hole courses within 20 miles (32 km) of *Le Château Frontenac.* Avid tee-timers should check with their home country club if they want to take a shot at playing the *Royal Montreal Golf Club* or the *Royal Quebec* golf course, the two oldest country clubs in North America. Some private clubs in the US have reciprocal agreements with the *Royal Montreal,* where members first drove the green in 1873, just 6 months before the *Royal Quebec* opened for business. It may be hard in peak season to fit into a tee-off schedule at the more popular courses without advance reservations; some links restrict weekend play to members. But if you reserve a couple of days in advance, you usually can find a weekday time slot at any of the following courses. Information: *Royal Montreal Golf Club,* 25 Southridge Rd., Ile Bizard (phone: 516-626-3977); *Royal Quebec Golf Club,* 65 Rue Bedard, St-Jean-de-Boischatel (phone: 418-822-0331).

CARLING LAKE GOLF CLUB, Montreal: Designed by Harold Watson, this challenging course in the foothills of the Laurentians was rated 2 years ago by *Golf Digest* as the No. 1 public course in Quebec and the No. 3 in Canada. Spread over rolling terrain, the lakeside fairways and greens are demanding enough to test the skill of the lowest handicapper. While it's not the longest course in Canada (6,650 yards), the par 72 tantalizer draws a lot of top tournament events. Reserve well in advance for a tee-off time on weekends. Take Laurentian Autoroute north to Rte. 158 West and Brownsburg, then Rte. 327 to Pine Hill. Information: *Carling Lake Golf Club,* Rte. 327 (phone: 514-476-1212).

LE CHANTECLER GOLF CLUB, Ste-Adèle: One of the best of 25 Laurentian layouts that welcome greens-fee players by the day, this course spreads its 6,200-yard, par 70 field around 2 mountain lakes. The mature, 40-year-old course is next door to *Le Chantecler* hotel's resort complex, 28 miles (45 km) north of Montreal, about an hour's drive. To complement the beautiful mountain scenery and the challenge of its well-kept alpine fairways, the course has a newly renovated clubhouse. Weekend golfers first tee up at 7 AM on a shotgun schedule. Take the Laurentian Autoroute to exit 67 at Ste-Adèle, then Route 15. Information: *Club de Golf Chantecler Ste-Adèle,* 2520 Chemin de Golf, Ste-Adèle (phone: 514-229-3742).

GOLF DORVAL, Montreal: This 36-hole complex was laid out in 1982 over hilly, wooded terrain with plenty of water hazards. The par 72 *Oakville* course, at 6,359 yards, is the more challenging of the two, with narrow fairways and rolling greens, while *Gentilly's* broader fairways were designed for tournament action. It's shorter by about 400 yards and carries a par of 70. Like most public courses in the area, the *Dorval* complex extends full clubhouse privileges to day players, including pro shop facilities and club rental. Reservations required for Friday, Saturday, and Sunday morning tee-off. Take Autoroute 20 west to the Sources Boulevard exit north. Information: *Golf Dorval,* 2000 Reverchon St., Dorval (phone: 514-631-6624).

LAC ST-JOSEPH GOLF CLUB, Quebec City: This compact, 18-hole testing ground never seems to play the same from one day to the next and some of the par 5 holes are extremely difficult. The first 9 holes were laid out on hilly, wooded terrain 45 years ago. Another 9 completed the par 72 teaser in the mid-1970s. The club is open to visitors during the week, but weekends are reserved for members and their guests. Take Autoroute Charest (Rte. 440) to exit 295, then Rte. 367 north to Ste-Catherine-de-la-Jacques-Cartier. Information: *Club de Golf Lac St-Joseph,* 5292 Blvd. Fossambault, Ste-Catherine-de-la-Jacques-Cartier (phone: 418-875-2074).

MONT STE-ANNE, Quebec City: The 18-hole *Beaupré* course in Mont Ste-Anne Park ranks among the best in the area. Far less challenging is the park's executive course. Both demand par 72 play and offer greens-fee visitors a full range of club facilities. Make reservations well in advance for weekend starting times. From town, take Autoroute Dufferin-Montmorency to Rte. 138 and Beaupré, then Rte. 360 to the park. Information: *Golf du Parc du Mont Ste-Anne,* Beaupré (phone: 418-872-3778).

SAINT-LAURENT GOLF CLUB, Quebec City: One of the most scenic layouts in the Quebec City region, this breezy, 18-hole, par 72 site on Ile d'Orléans is known locally as the place where "fore!" is first cried out at the end of winter and where birdie putts are first sunk. Because of its location high on the southeast shore of the island, it's the area's first course in condition for early spring play. The closest thing to a traditional windblown links west of the famous resort area of Murray Bay (La Malbaie), you'll shoot uphill for 9 holes, downhill for the rest, always into a stiff wind. Spread out in long, wide-open fairways above the Chenal des Grands Voiliers (Big Ship Channel), the course commands a wonderful view of the St. Lawrence River traffic lanes of ocean-going vessels. Reserve well ahead for weekends and weekdays. Take Autoroute Dufferin-Montmorency to exit 325 and the island bridge, then Route 367 clockwise to the village of St-Laurent. Information: *Club de Golf Saint-Laurent,* 758 Chemin Royal, Ile d'Orléans (phone: 418-829-3896).

Smooth Sailing and Boating

 Montreal and Quebec City have their very beginnings rooted in sailing. The first French sailors to arrive at the base of Cape Diamond in Quebec and near Mont Royal in Montreal weren't in it for kicks (they had a trade route to China to find, after all). They employed the best of their skills to negotiate the rolling waves, tricky winds, and the cold of the St. Lawrence. Today serious sailors can relive that challenge for the thrill of it all. The St. Lawrence River offers some of the best and hardiest river sailing anywhere in the world and both cities have well-serviced ports to accommodate sailors of all kinds and abilities. In Montreal, the river is a little less wild, because the city's islands slow down the current, and sailing is smoother on Lac St-Louis (where the river widens west of the city) and the Lake of Two Mountains. Visiting sailors can crew up for a day if their home club has a reciprocal arrangement with a port of call near Montreal. In the Quebec City region, downstream past Ile d'Orléans, where the surge of fresh water meets the first hint of salt, sailors can sense the pulse of the distant Atlantic. Although it's 650 miles from the Cabot Strait, the island has recorded tides as high as 19 feet in its time. But never fear: If most of your sailing has been done on summer cottage lakes, the following ports of call will test and hone your skills — all on a safe course.

ROYAL ST. LAWRENCE YACHT CLUB, Montreal: One of Canada's oldest private clubs for sailors, this place has occupied a breezy site on the shores of Lac St-Louis since 1888, when the busy suburb of Dorval was still summer cottage territory. A 15-minute drive from midtown Montreal, it's a hospitable harbor for visitors with courtesy privileges. Members of any "Royal" club in the world rate automatic entrée and many other clubs have reciprocal ties with this fine old establishment. Information: *Royal St. Lawrence Yacht Club,* 1350 Lakeshore Dr., Dorval (phone: 514-631-2720).

ECOLE DE VOILE DE LACHINE, Montreal: The best port for serious sailors near the city, the sailing school marina is a gateway to Lac St-Louis, where the St. Lawrence widens into a lake. Private and group lessons have the approval of the Quebec Sailing Federation and you can rent light sailboats and lasers, as well as windsurfing equipment by the hour or the day. Open May 15 to September 30. Take Autoroute 20 west to the Lachine exit. Information: *Ecole de Voile de Lachine,* 2105 St. Joseph's Blvd., Lachine (phone: 514-634-4326).

RECREATIONAL SAILING, Montreal: Those without club connections and content with a low-key sailing experience make tracks for little Regatta Lake on Ile Notre Dame, where *Club Nautique,* a sailing club, rents sailboats and sailboards, or Boucher-ville Islands Recreation Park, a few miles downstream from the Port of Montreal, just east of the Lafontaine Bridge and Tunnel. The water sports center on the island is open from mid-June to September. The park at Boucherville is open all year, from 8 AM until sundown. Call ahead to check out the sailing schedule. Take Rte. 25 south to exit 89, Iles de Boucherville. Information: *Club Nautique,* Ile Notre Dame (phone: 514-872-6039); *Boucherville Islands Recreation Park,* Ile Ste-Marguerite, Boucherville (phone: 514-873-2843).

BOAT TOURS, Montreal: Newcomers to St. Lawrence waters can explore the river the easy way, with cruise boat skippers who know their way around the busy harbor area. *Montreal Harbor Cruises* charts a variety of mini-voyages up and down the river, lasting from 1 to 3 hours, from May 1 to October 15. Tickets are available at major hotels and kiosks on Victoria Pier. Five or more excursions a day depart from the foot of Berri Street. Phone ahead for reservations at peak season. *Les Tours Saint-Louis* schedules several 2-hour cruises daily around Lac St-Louis. M.V. *Saint-Louis IV* boards 180 passengers per voyage (tour season lasts from May 15 to October 15; advance reservations are advised). The adventurous prefer the wild water of Lachine Rapids and boat rides arranged by *Lachine Rapids Tours.* Five voyages a day depart Victoria Pier from April 28 to September 29 at 10 AM, noon, 2, 4, and 6 PM. Information: *Montreal Harbor Cruises,* Victoria Pier, Old Port (phone: 514-842-3871); *Les Tours Saint-Louis,* 300 Chemin du Canal, Lachine (phone: 514-367-2840); *Lachine Rapids Tours,* 105 de la Commune St. (phone: 514-284-9607).

BAIE DE BEAUPORT, Quebec City: A 10-minute drive from the Old Port of Quebec, this sheltered bay opposite the southern tip of Ile d'Orléans is a popular playground for sailors and windsurfers. Beginners can take lessons here and rent catamarans and storm sails. Bay facilities are open daily from the end of April through mid-October. Admission charge. Information: *Baie de Beauport,* access off Blvd. Henri-Bourassa, Port of Quebec (phone: 418-666-8368).

LAC ST-JOSEPH, Quebec City: Sailors who want to work up to the challenge of the Great River are within a half-hour drive of this sizable lake, which has two outdoor recreation centers in the Duchesnay Forest nature preserve, about 30 miles (48 km) northwest of the city. A campsite at Germain Beach offers facilities for sailing, canoeing, and windsurfing; *La Vigie,* a small inn with accommodations for 120, rents sailboats, catamarans, and windsurfing equipment by the hour. Follow Autoroute Charest (Rte. 440) west to the intersection with Route 367 north, which leads directly to the forest reception center. The park is open year-round, but call for information about the summer sailing schedule before heading out. Information: *Camping Plage Germain,* 7001 Blvd. Fossambault N. (phone: 418-875-2242); *La Vigie,* 550 Blvd. Thomas Maher (phone: 418-875-2727).

PARC NAUTIQUE DE CAP-ROUTE, Quebec City: Nautical types can rent sailboats and get professional guidance to the St. Lawrence in this water sports park at the mouth of the Cap-Rouge River. Located upstream from Ste-Foy, the center is near the historic site where explorer Jacques Cartier made an unsuccessful attempt to establish a colony around Cap-Rouge harbor in 1541. In addition to sailing, windsurfing, and other river recreations, the park is the scene of summer concerts and picnics. Facilities include a landing ramp, equipment rental, a bar, and a terrace café. Visiting sailors without their own wheels can make the half-hour voyage from town aboard buses Nos. 14 and 15. Admission charge. Open daily June 1 through *Labour Day;* weekends only May 1 through June 1 and during the month of September. Information: *Parc Nautique du Cap-Rouge,* 4155 Chemin de la Plage Jacques-Cartier (phone: 418-653-0593).

Best Biking

The first thing most people notice about Canadian cities is the quality of open spaces within easy view of the high-rises and downtown malls. Wide green expanses of parkland, with ribbons of bike paths snaking through them, stand out as some of the most picturesque and best planned in the world. Both Montreal and Quebec City proudly reflect this tradition, particularly

Quebec City outside the historic *quartier,* where some of the most rewarding bike paths in eastern Canada can be found. For sheer length and diversity, Montreal takes the lead with almost 150 miles (240 km) of trails, many close to the city center. The Métro leaves the last two doors of its tail car open to cyclists and their wheels (limited to four at a time) Mondays to Fridays after 7 PM and Saturdays and Sundays at all hours for transportation to trails. For biking maps in Montreal call the city department of parks and recreation (7400 St-Michel St.; phone: 514-872-6111) and rent wheels at *La Cordée* (2159 Ste-Catherine St. E.; phone: 514-524-1515); *Cycle Peel* (6665 St-Jacques St. W.; phone: 514-486-1148); and *Cyclo-Touriste* (*Centre Infotouriste,* 1001 Dorchester St.; phone 514-393-1528). For rentals in Quebec City try *Location Petit-Champlain* (94 Rue du Petit-Champlain; phone: 418-692-2817). Following is a list of places where you'll get a rolling, intimate view of the country in the city.

   LACHINE CANAL, Montreal: This 7.8-mile (11-km) path is lit for evening biking along the old canal, once the only way to bypass the Lachine Rapids. But take your first ride along the historic trail by light of day. For more than a century until it was closed to navigation in 1967, this canal routed ships around the rapids, opening up the Canadian interior and the young nation to its trading partners around the world. As the gateway to the Great Lakes, the canal was once lined with shipyards and foundries, rail lines, factories, and mills. The industrial area fell into a decline when the waterway closed, leaving a lot of empty ghosts behind, but the path gets prettier as it nears Lachine and René Lévesque Park. Bikers can see the Lachine Rapids from here as they cycle along the waterfront to St. Louis Park, where most travelers stop for a breather or a picnic snack under the trees before the return trip. If you are driving here and planning to rent a bike, pick up the Lachine Canal route and follow de la Commune Street west from the Old Port to Mill Street under the Bonaventure Autoroute and park in the car park there. Information: *Parks Canada,* 7115 Peel St. (phone: 514-283-6054).

   ST. LAWRENCE SEAWAY, Montreal: After a trip down memory lane alongside the Lachine Canal, bike with the big boys of the St. Lawrence Seaway. Heading west from Lambert Locks, where oceangoing vessels creep through on their way upriver or downriver to the sea, cyclists can ride for miles, keeping up with the slow-moving vessels as they negotiate this narrow part of the seaway. (The seaway opened in 1959 and its series of locks make it possible for full-length oceangoing vessels to trade goods into the very heart of North America.) The seaway bike route is 10 miles (16 km) long and begins at the locks on its south side and ends in the community of Côte Ste-Catherine at the foot of the Lachine Rapids, as far east as Ile Notre Dame. Take the Victoria Bridge from downtown across to St. Lambert on Rte. 15. Open May to mid-October; weekends only September and October. Information: *St. Lawrence Seaway* (St. Lambert Locks), St. Lambert (phone: 514-672-4110).

   THE ISLANDS, Montreal: Both Ile Ste-Hélène and Ile Notre Dame are captivating places to explore on two wheels, although neither maintains trails exclusively for bikers. Choose a sunny warm day because the weather on the islands can be a few degrees colder and windier than downtown. Weekend cyclists can transport their wheels via Métro to the Ile Ste-Hélène station, and spend a full day taking in the sights of Montreal's mid-river playgrounds. The islands are linked by two bridges. In the floral park on Ile Notre Dame, *Quadricycle International* (phone: 514-768-9282) rents only pedal-powered, four-wheeled "vehicles" that seat up to six (no traditional two-wheelers). The rental service operates June 5 through September 1 from 11 AM to 6 PM. Information: *Société de l'Ile Notre Dame,* PO Box 805 Station C (phone: 514-872-6093).

   OLD PORT, Montreal: Vieux Montréal's ever-growing waterfront park maintains a scenic bike path that parallels de la Commune Street from Berri Street west to McGill Street, an easygoing, lazy path of about 1½ miles (2.4 km) with lots to see along the way. The path is well illuminated for night riders. From the port path, cyclists can continue west to join the Lachine Canal route. Visiting bikers can rent wheels of all kinds at the port, including the ubiqutous quadricycles. *Accès Cible* (phone: 514-525-8888) rents bicycles and tandems. Open mid-May through *Labour Day,* Mondays, noon to 8:30 PM; Tuesdays through Sundays, 9 AM to 5 PM. *Quadricycle International* (phone: 514-768-9282), which rents the four-wheeled variety only, is open June 1 to September 1, daily from 10 AM to midnight; September 1 to October 1 and May 1 to June 1, open Saturdays and Sundays only, 10 AM to midnight. Information: *Old Port (Vieux Port),* 333 de la Commune St. W. (phone: 514-283-5256).

MAISONNEUVE PARK, Montreal: This 525-acre parkland has room to spare for bikers in a vast green domain that includes Montreal's Botanical Garden, a 9-hole municipal golf course, and a well-maintained bicycle track. Take the Métro to Viau station. Information: *Maisonneuve Park,* 4601 Sherbrooke St. E. (phone: 514-872-6555).

ANGRIGNON PARK, Montreal: Out in the southwest section of the city, the home of Montreal's so-called winter wonderland (see *Ice Skating and Hockey*), reveals a 4-mile (6.5-km) cycling path when the snow melts. This cool summer retreat of little lakes and picnic groves is the last stop from downtown on the Angrignon-Honoré-Beaugrand Métro line. Bikers wheel out of the station into the north end of the park. Information: *Angrignon Park,* 3400 des Trinitaires Blvd. and the city's department of sports and recreation, 7400 St-Michel St. (phone: 514-872-6211).

NATIONAL BATTLEFIELDS PARK, Quebec City: The most convenient trail for Sunday cyclists interested in some mild exercise in pleasant surroundings is the scenic route along Avenue George VI in the capital's best-known park. Less than 1 mile (1.6 km) long, it stretches along the western reaches of the 18th-century battleground, from the corner of Avenue George VI and Grande Allée, just beyond Porte St-Louis to the intersection with Avenue Wolfe-Montcalm. Bikers are welcome to wheel all over historic park territory, and the return jaunt along the avenue adds up to nearly 2 miles (3 km) of peaceful, parkland touring, with plenty of shady rest stops along the way. Information: *Parks Canada,* 3 Rue Buade (phone: 418-648-4177).

ST. CHARLES RIVER BIKEWAY, Quebec City: Those who take their exercise a little more seriously can follow a path along the south bank of the St. Charles River. Nearly 3 miles (5 km) of riverside trail lead from Samson Bridge, just northwest of the restored Old Port area, to the foot of Rue Marie de l'Incarnation. History buffs can cycle across the bridge that spans the river at the halfway mark to visit Cartier-Brébeuf Park, a national historic site on the north shore, where French explorer Jacques Cartier and his party spent a cruel wilderness winter in 1535–36. The park is also the site of a 17th-century mission that Jesuit Jean de Brébeuf founded in 1626; a replica of Cartier's flagship, *La Grande Hermine;* and a reproduction of an Iroquoian longhouse. There's a reception and interpretation center on site, featuring exhibits related to the park's history.

MONTMORENCY BIKEWAY, Quebec City: A challenging path of just over 6 miles (10 km) leads all the way out to Montmorency Falls, 1½ times higher than the mighty Niagara, as any civic booster around the capital will gladly tell you (also see "Extra Special" in *Quebec City,* THE CITIES). The falls are surrounded by a park, with picnic sites, nature trails, and lookout points, welcome rest stops before the return trip to town. The bike path starts just north of the city, off Boulevard Montmorency at Domain Maizeret, a small park west of Autoroute 440. Unfortunately, the busy highway is always between the cyclist and the river, but there are some fine views of the St. Lawrence and Ile d'Orléans en route. If the thought of pumping out to the falls fazes leisurely bikers, there's a branch trail to Parc des Cascades that meets the Montmorency path at Baie de Beauport near Avenue de la Station. It follows and crosses the Beauport River from its estuary up to a riverbank park, a distance of about a mile.

MONT STE-ANNE PARK, Quebec City: Mountain biking is a favorite summer pastime at *Mont Ste-Anne Park,* Quebec City's all-seasons playground. The big ski domain maintains 157 trails for cyclists and mountain bikers. Explorers can rent wheels in the park at *Bicycles Marius* (phone: 418-827-2420 or 418-827-4561).

For the Mind

Historic Churches

Quebec's churches, more than any other other single institution, tell the tale of the land's foreign settlers. From their earliest days until the last *voyageur* traveled upriver in the 1820s, Montreal and Quebec City were but crude trading posts of fur and lumber barons, distingushed only by the huge churches and basilicas built by a growing Catholic church and the smaller houses of worship erected by the Protestant English. Many of these buildings survive and today serve as symbols and reminders of the spirit, determination, and faith of its early settlers.

CATHEDRAL OF MARY, QUEEN OF THE WORLD, Montreal: A replica (though much smaller) of St. Peter's Basilica in Rome, complete with a row of statues that depict the patron saints of the Archdiocese of Montreal on the roof and a reproduction of Bernini's altar columns, this cathedral was under construction from 1870 to 1894. Its vast interior space (architects of the time believed that the darker the church, the brighter the candles would glow and, thus, the brighter the stained glass would appear) is a symbol of the era when the Catholic church was a powerful influence on the city and the province. The domed mass is now dwarfed by the towers of modern Montreal, but it remains a monument to the Catholic heritage of Quebec. Information: *Cathedral of Mary, Queen of the World,* Rue Dorchester W. (phone: 514-866-1661).

ST. JOSEPH'S ORATORY, Montreal: Founded as a tiny chapel in 1904 by Brother André, a member of the Holy Cross Order of Roman Catholic brothers, by 1922 this oratory had grown into a 5,000-seat basilica. Brother André — almost illiterate and in ill health — purportedly had healing powers, and had a vast following among the faithful of Quebec (he is entombed here). He is said to have cured hundreds of people, invoking the aid of St. Joseph, husband of Jesus's mother, Mary. Today, more than 2 million people visit the site each year, many climbing the 99 steps to the basilica in the hopes of saintly intercession or a divine cure. A museum houses a collection of religious art and a few relics of the founder, including one of his cassocks; during the *Christmas* season exhibitions feature a collection of 200 crèches from more than 60 countries. The church commands the hillside on the northwest slopes of Mount Royal, with flights of steps cut into the steep slope below the main entrance. At one time the most humble of suppliants made the ascent on their knees. Its carillon of bells was designed for the Eiffel Tower but in the end was judged unsuitable for the famous landmark and came to the oratory on loan in 1955; it was later purchased as a permanent fixture. At 860 feet above sea level, the oratory observatory is the highest point on the Montreal skyline, with a view that stretches as far west as Lake St-Louis and over the northwest section of the city. Carillon concerts are held Wednesdays through Saturdays at noon and 5 PM; Sundays at noon and 2:30 PM. Organ recitals are given Wednesday evenings in the summer, and *Les Petits Chanteurs du Mont-Royal* children's choir performs on Sunday mornings. The oratory is open daily 6:30 AM to 9 PM; no admission charge.

The museum is open daily, 10 AM to 5 PM; donations accepted. Information: *St. Joseph's Oratory*, 3800 Queen Mary Rd. (phone: 514-733-8211).

NOTRE DAME BASILICA, Montreal: This twin-towered Gothic-revival church, designed by New York architect James O'Donnell (who is buried in the church vault), was completed in 1829. Today's basilica is notable for its lavishly decorated interior, which includes a monumental altar, exquisite woodcarvings and paintings, exceptional stained glass windows, and a 5,772-pipe organ. There also is a museum in the sacristy with a silver statue presented by Louis XV. Adjacent to the main church is the restored Sacred Heart Chapel, whose stained glass windows depict the history of Montreal. It is a place of calm in the crush of Old Montreal. After leaving the basilica, step into Place d'Armes and glance up at the twin spires for a true perspective on the church's scale. One spire houses Le Gros Bourdon bell, a 6-foot, 12-ton monster that once taxed the muscle power of 12 burly bellringers. Powered by electricity now, Notre Dame's massive *cloche* remains one of the world's largest and is sounded only on rare occasions. The basilica has seating for 5,000, standing room for 2,000, and its chapel is the scene of French Montreal's most fashionable society weddings. Open *Labour Day* to June 24, 7 AM to 6 PM; June 25 to *Labour Day,* 7 AM to 8 PM. Guided tours mid-May to June 24 and *Labour Day* to mid-October, weekdays, 9 AM to 4 PM; June 24 to *Labour Day,* daily 9 AM to 4:30 PM. Museum open weekdays only; no admission charge. Information: *Notre Dame Basilica,* Pl. d'Armes (phone: 514-849-1070).

NOTRE-DAME-DE-BON-SECOURS CHAPEL, Montreal: While it doesn't pretend to the grandeur of the Notre Dame basilica, the modest little chapel at the bottom of Rue Bonsecours is much older than its neighbor on Place d'Armes. It's said that the founder himself, French career soldier Paul de Chomedey, Sieur de Maisonneuve, felled the first timber and laid the cornerstone for the tiny chapel beyond the stockades of Ville-Marie in 1657. And although none of that timber remains (the present structure dates from 1772), the church has never moved from its original site. The chapel owes its beginnings to Marguerite Bourgeoys, the first Catholic saint to live and die in Canada. A pious 30-year-old French schoolteacher who de Maisonneuve recruited and brought to New France in 1653, Bourgeoys had a dream soon after her arrival of building a shrine to the glory of the Virgin Mary in the no-man's land beyond the settlement stockade. Later she would distinguish herself as Canada's first schoolmistress and found Congrégation de Notre-Dame, the first Canadian order of non-cloistered nuns; but her vision of extending the boundaries of Old Montreal was truly ahead of its time. Bourgeoys persisted in her plans and eventually — 2 decades after the first cornerstone was laid — the chapel was completed, ready to enshrine an ancient wooden statue of the Virgin, donated to the cause by a benefactor in France. Reputed to work miracles of salvation for sailors on perilous seas, Our Lady of Good Help was unveiled at the chapel's official opening in 1675.

Although it is the third church to occupy the site and a new façade was added in 1895, the "Sailors' Church" retains the simple, unpretentious character of early Quebecois architecture. Inside, a tile mosaic of de Maisonneuve acknowledges a debt to Montreal's founder, who donated the land for the building site. A little fleet of votive lamps, in the form of model ships, is suspended above the pews; they were gifts from grateful sailors who still believed in miracles. The chapel's rooftop Madonna is a familiar beacon for mariners making port in Montreal. A small chapel museum tells the story of Ste-Marguerite Bourgeoys with a collection of doll-size figurines in historically correct dress. Visitors can climb to the observation deck above the apse for a rooftop view of the port and Vieux Montréal. The chapel is open daily, November through April, 10 AM to 5 PM; May through October, 9 AM to 5 PM. The museum is open daily except Mondays, May through October, 9 AM to 4:30 PM; November through April, 10:30 AM to 4:30 PM. There is an admission charge for the museum.

Information: *Notre-Dame-de-Bon-Secours Chapel,* 400 St-Paul St. E. (phone: 514-845-9991).

ST. PATRICK'S BASILICA, Montreal: It wasn't designed to work out that way, but English-speaking Catholics don't have to use a lot of imagination to find their house of worship in downtown Montreal. A bank of buttresses on the east wall of the largest English-language Catholic church in the city is as green as old Erin. Environmentalists blame a combination of acid rain and the dissolving patina from the copper roof for the verdigris stain, but whatever the cause, the color seems appropriate for a church named for the patron saint of Ireland. Opened on *St. Patrick's Day* in 1847, the church offered spiritual shelter for Irish-born Montrealers following one of the most devastating periods of the community's history. A typhus epidemic was sweeping the city at the time, and residents of "Little Dublin," those living in tenements between today's de la Gauchetière Street and René-Lévesque Boulevard, were struck down with particular severity. Hundreds died, but the living kept the faith. In more prosperous times, parshioners learned to love the vast, brown-and-gold interior and the mighty columns, each hewn from an 80-foot pine tree. Unity was underscored by an interior decor of shamrocks, Celtic crosses, and fleurs de lis, a nod to the Sulpicians who'd helped them acquire the building site. The nave is splendid; its fine oak wainscoting is inset with paintings of 150 saints. The church was also the site of the funeral of Thomas D'Arcy McGee, a Father of Confederation; a silver-tongued orator, he was given one of the grandest send-offs of any Montrealer. Open during the summer from 7:45 AM to 6 PM; in winter from 10 AM to 6 PM. Information: *St. Patrick's Basilica,* 460 René-Lévesque Blvd. (phone: 514-866-7379).

CHRIST CHURCH CATHEDRAL, Montreal: Members of Montreal's Anglican community have grown accustomed to giving their cathedral a second glance these days. For years the Christ Church congregation, and most of downtown Montreal, watched with apprehension as one of the finest examples of Gothic architecture in Canada teetered over a huge canyon shopping mall that developers were burrowing beneath it. Now for all practical purposes the church is firmly grounded again (although the faithful still say little prayers of protection for the landmark), with *Les Promenades de la Cathédale*'s (father of the subsurface *Les Promenades*) underground retail world open for business. Reflected in the pink glass tower of *Maison des Coopérants,* the cathedral's delicate spire casts a frail image. Completed in 1857, the building was designed to reflect the cross-shape form of 14th-century English church architecture; 70 years later the original spire of Canadian stone was removed because of fears of structural damage and was replaced by an aluminum replica. The reredos at the altar is a war memorial, depicting seven scenes from the life of Christ; the monument in what's left of the cathedral grounds honors Francis Fulford, Montreal's first Anglican archbishop. Christ Church maintains an open-door policy 7 days a week, with frequent noon-hour concerts and evening recitals. Open 8 AM to 6 PM. Donations suggested for concerts. Information: *Christ Church Cathedral,* 1444 Union Ave., corner Ste-Catherine St. W. (phone: 514-843-6577).

EGLISE NOTRE-DAME-DES-VICTOIRES, Quebec City: Built over the foundations of the *habitation* (residence or dwelling) settlement that Samuel de Champlain founded in the early 1600s, the small gray-stone church on Place Royale has been clinging to its original Lower Town site for more than 3 centuries. Despite its meek appearance, Notre-Dame owes its name to two French victories over British aggression, one in 1690, just 2 years after celebrating its first mass, and another in 1711. Destroyed in the bombardment that preceded the Battle of the Plains of Abraham and the conquest of 1759, the church has been restored twice. Today it looks much as it did when it was the heart and soul of community life in the French colony's burgeoning port district.

The pretty, pastel-tinted interior is dominated by an unusual castle-shape high altar. A scale model of a ship, suspended above the nave, recalls *Le Brezé,* the vessel that transported troops to New France in 1664. Services are still conducted. Open daily May 1 to October 15, 9 AM to 4:30 PM; Sundays, 7:30 AM to 1 PM. Information: *Eglise Notre-Dame-des-Victoires,* Pl. Royale (phone: 418-692-1650).

NOTRE DAME BASILICA, Quebec City: The Quebec basilica, probably the finest example of baroque architecture in Quebec, stands on the site of Notre-Dame-de-Recouvrance, built in 1633 by Samuel de Champlain, who was buried there. It was destroyed by fire 7 years later and rebuilt as Notre-Dame-de-la-Paix, the place where Monseigneur François Xavier de Montmorency-Laval, first Bishop of Quebec, established the first Roman Catholic diocese in North America outside Mexico in 1674. Like the Eglise Notre-Dame-des-Victoires, it was destroyed during the British bombardment of 1759. Repairs, changes and additions, which took place over the next century, resulted in a building that is reminiscent of the 18th-century structure. Restored several times due to warfare, fire, and weather, the ornate interior (which was largely reconstructed after a fire in 1922) is decorated with works of art and illuminated by stained glass windows. Basilica treasures include an Episcopal throne and a chancel lamp presented by French King Louis XIV. Three governors of New France and most of the Bishops of Quebec are buried in the crypt. Open daily from 6:30 AM to 8 PM; guided tours of basilica and crypt from May 1 through November 1 from 9 AM to 5 PM. No admission charge. Information: *Notre Dame Basilica,* 16 Rue Buade (phone: 418-692-2533).

CATHEDRAL OF THE HOLY TRINITY, Quebec City: One of the city's historic church properties that has no associations with the old French regime, Holy Trinity is a relic of the British colonial era in Quebec. The first Church of England cathedral ever built beyond the British Isles, it has served the capital's Anglican community since 1804. Built by royal decree of King George III — who donated the silver communion set now used on royal occasions — it was inspired by London's St. Martin-in-the-Fields with pews of stalwart English oak. The cathedral still honors the British monarchy with a sacrosanct Royal Pew reserved for the exclusive use of a visiting British sovereign or designated representative. Memorial plaques under the stained glass windows trace the history of Quebec City's English-speaking establishment in war and peace. Open May and June from 9 AM to 5 PM Mondays through Saturdays, noon to 5 PM Sundays; July and August from 9 AM to 9 PM Mondays through Saturdays, noon to 9 PM Sundays. Call for off-season hours. Information: *Cathedral of the Holy Trinity,* 31 Rue des Jardins (phone: 418-692-2193).

BASILIQUE STE-ANNE-DE-BEAUPRÉ, Quebec City: Back in the 1650s, ship-wrecked sailors rescued from the treacherous waters off Cap-Tourmente showed their gratitude to Ste-Anne by founding a chapel in her name in the little village of Beaupré, about 25 miles (40 km) downriver from Quebec City. In part because of the good saint's reputation as a miracle worker with extraordinary healing powers, the faithful flocked here; the little wooden chapel was replaced a decade later by a sturdy fieldstone church. By 1876 Ste-Anne's shrine had grown to basilica size, providing a wellspring of hope for millions of pilgrims seeking a cure for all their bodily ills. Destroyed by fire in 1922, the celebrated shrine was rebuilt the following year in neo-Roman style. A vast edifice, with twin towers, lovely rose windows, and a marble statue of the saint in the sanctuary, the basilica can accommodate a congregation of 3,000. More than 1½ million suppliants a year come here, leaving crutches, wheelchairs, and canes behind them as testaments to their faith in the mother of the Virgin Mary. The Ste-Anne Fountain in front of the basilica is believed to have healing powers. Open daily for masses at varying hours. An on-site information center is open from early May through mid-September, daily from 8:30 AM to 5 PM. Information: *Basilique Ste-Anne-de-Beaupré*, 10018 Av. Royale, Ste-Anne-de-Beaupré (phone: 418-827-3781).

Memorable Museums

The best of Quebec's museums reveal and celebrate the ideas and artifacts of the province's — and Canada's — history and culture. There are museums devoted to its prehistoric past, to the Inuit and Indian peoples who were its first inhabitants, to the Europeans who explored and settled here, to the artists, past and present, whose work bears the distinctive stamp of the land, and to the country's military, anthropological, scientific, and technological history. These collections offer visitors more insight into the province and the country than they'll find anywhere else.

The museums described here are best enjoyed when given a visitor's unhurried attention. Be sure to allot sufficient time for a museum visit — a half day is about right — and remember that return trips are usually worthwhile. Most of these museums also host special exhibits and offer demonstrations, films, lectures, concerts, short courses, and other special programs that are worth investigating. Hours vary and many are closed 1 day a week so be sure to call ahead.

MUSEUM OF FINE ARTS, Montreal: Canada's oldest fine-arts museum (1860), this neo-classical building houses a first-rate permanent collection of Canadian, European, and Oriental paintings and sculptures, and frequently stages important international shows. It has undergone many expansions; in the most recent (in 1991), the complex branched out into a new building across the street, which is linked by an underground passage and 4 tiers of catwalk corridors. The permanent collection, much of which has been under wraps for years for lack of exhibition space, includes Western European art from the medieval period to the contemporary, as well as relics of ancient civilizations in Europe, Egypt, China, Japan, and pre-Columbian America. Works by Canadian, Inuit, and Amerindian artists are noteworthy, as is the collection of period furnishings. The new building also houses touring shows. In recent years, the musuem has mounted exhibitions from the Vatican Collection, and works by Picasso, Miró, and da Vinci. Open Tuesdays through Saturdays from 10 AM to 5 PM. Admission charge. Information: *Montreal Museum of Fine Arts*, 3400 Av. du Museum (phone: 514-285-1600).

McCORD MUSEUM OF CANADIAN HISTORY, Montreal: More than 100 years ago, when Montreal was growing as fast as any city anywhere, industrialist David Ross McCord had a vision. The Irish-born immigrant feared the city he had come to love was disappearing under the weight of change, and although he was powerless to stop it, he set about capturing its landscape on canvas. What resulted was a series of street scenes commissioned by McCord and painted by former British army officer W. H. Burnnett, a legacy Montrealers and visitors can enjoy today at this newly expanded museum. As it happened, other Canadian collectors shared McCord's vision and contributed their works to the museum's collection; today the *McCord* boasts one of the largest bodies of aboriginal art and artifacts in the country, as well as a good selection of the works of such masters as Cornelius Kreighoff and Théophile Hamel. In 1965 the museum was moved to the McGill University Union building, a hybrid of baroque, Gothic, and classical architecture; it reopened last May after a 3-year expansion project, just in time to celebrate Montreal's 350th anniversary. New galleries now provide improved exhibition space for a treasure trove of period costumes, furniture, religious art, toys, and photographs from the Notman Archives, a collection of some 700,000 glass negatives and prints of Montreal scenes, some of which date from the 1850s. Open Tuesdays, Wednesdays, and Fridays, 10 AM to 6 PM; Thursdays, 10 AM to 9 PM; Saturdays and Sundays, 10 AM to 5 PM. Closed Mondays and holidays. Admission charge. Information: *McCord Museum of Canadian History,* 690 Sherbrooke St. W. (phone: 514-398-7100).

CONTEMPORARY ART MUSEUM OF MONTREAL, Montreal: Devoted to contemporary work by Quebecois, Canadian, and international artists, the museum reopened last spring in its new location on the west side of Place des Arts Plaza. (It's the second move in the museum's 29-year history; previously it was located on the grounds of *EXPO '67.*) Only works of art completed after 1939 are displayed here; included are pieces by Quebec-based artists Jean-Paul Riopelle, Paul-Emile Borduas, David Moore, and Alfred Pellan and Canadian artists Barbara Steinman, Jack Bush, and Michael Snow. Open Tuesdays through Sundays, 11 AM to 6 PM; Wednesdays, 11 AM to 9 PM. Admission charge. Information: *Contemporary Art Museum of Montreal,* 185 Ste-Catherine St. W. (phone: 514-873-2878).

CANADIAN CENTRE FOR ARCHITECTURE, Montreal: Conceived primarily as a museum and reference center for students of architecture, this relative newcomer to Montreal's museum community has drawn raves worldwide for its design innovations, spawning pilgrimages of the architecturally inclined from around the globe. What captivates visitors and pilgrims alike is the story of the museum's founder, award-winning architectural innovator Phyllis Lambert. With her own personal resources, the Canadian-born Lambert oversaw the development of the museum — the world's first nonprofit institution devoted solely to the study and celebration of architecture — from its conception to the official opening. People sensitive to Canadian history also watched the development of the museum with great interest. The Canadian architect started her project when she bought the old Shaughnessy House — a formidable gray-stone pile of the Second Empire domestic style — when it was on the brink of destruction. The 1874 "double house" was once the home of Lord Thomas Shaughnessy, American-born third president of the *Canadian Pacific Railway,* the so-called King of Railway Presidents, who occupied one of the semi-detached mansions for years. Another *CPR* executive, Donald Alexander Smith, fur trader, politician, banker, philanthropist, and first Baron of Strathcona and Mount Royal, had once called the other half of the property home.

Both residences form the core of a contemporary complex, co-designed by Lambert and Montreal architect Peter Rose. In contrast to the ornate Victorian façade of Shaughnessy House, two wings of the austere gray limestone extend east and west from the rear of the historic property. The additions accommodate study and research facilities, a library, a lecture hall, and the personal treasures of the founder — an exhaustive collection of manuscripts, folios, books, artwork, photographs, and archives that includes 47,000 prints and drawings, 45,000 photographs, and 35,000 books spanning the history of architecture from the Renaissance to the 20th century. Original works by Leonardo da Vinci and Michelangelo are on display. The center also has a state-of-the-art conservation area in the basement. A sculpture garden across René-Lévesque Boulevard West from the Shaughnessy complex is an enchanting spot to rest during a visit here. Open Wednesdays and Fridays, 11 AM to 6 PM; Thursdays, 10 AM to 8 PM; Saturdays and Sundays, 11 AM to 5 PM. Admission charge. Information: *Canadian Center for Architecture,* 1920 Baile St. (phone: 514-939-7026).

BIODOME OF MONTREAL, Montreal: What was once an oval track of high-speed thrills and spills has given itself over to a pace of a different kind in this most unique of city museums. Housed in the Olympic Park's former *Velodrome,* where cycling champions competed for medals in the 1976 *Summer Olympics,* are four natural ecosystems, growing at their own speed beneath the dome. Each of the environments represents a typical climate zone — in the two zones in South, Central, and North America, more than 4,600 animals, birds, and marine creatures make themselves comfortable in such settings as the foliage of a tropical rain forest, a beaver lake, a salt marsh, and an arctic snowbank. In the St. Lawrence Marine Ecosystem, 23 species of fish and other ocean-dwellers patrol a salty artificial "sea," while scores of starfish, anemones, crabs, sea urchins, and other invertebrates inhabit a tidal pool near the salt marsh home of black ducks and shorebirds. The Polar Ecosystem represents the two icy worlds of the Arctic and Antarctic, which can be viewed from a glass-enclosed observation site. Open daily; call for hours. Admission charge. Information: *Biodome of Montreal,* 4545 Pierre de Coubertine Ave. (phone: 514-252-8687 or 514-252-4737).

CHÂTEAU RAMEZAY, Montreal: Travelers from the 20th century take a giant step back to 1705 with an intimate glimpse of domestic life under the French colonial regime at this small museum in Vieux Montréal. The château was built as the official residence of Claude de Ramezay, 11th Governor of Montreal, who occupied this modest version of a Norman château during his 20 years in office. Even though his 25-room home was palatial by colonial standards, it was barely big enough to contain the de Ramezay brood of 13 children, an office staff of civil servants, and the domestic help Madame de Ramezay needed to meet the governor's social obligations. The museum has been enlarged over the years to accommodate a collection of Amerindian and other artifacts, but some of the rooms still recall the de Ramezay era, furnished with traditional 18th-century pieces and decorated in the period. The big cellar kitchen, with its cavernous fireplace and the latest innovations in 18th-century appliances, is particularly noteworthy. Some of the rooms, such as the richly paneled Grand Salon, represent a later period, but on the whole, the restoration is pure de Ramezay. American visitors will be interested to learn that today's museum originally was the domicile of choice for such visiting countrymen as Generals Benedict Arnold and Richard Montgomery, and Benjamin Franklin. The generals used the building as army headquarters and both slept here. Franklin stayed here, too, with other members of the Continental Congress, who'd come on their vain quest to persuade French Canada to renounce British rule and join the 13 colonies (see *Walk 1: Vieux Montréal* in DIRECTIONS/MONTREAL). Open 10 AM to 4:30 PM; closed Mondays except June through August. Admission charge. Information: *Château Ramezay,* 280 Notre Dame St.W. (phone: 514-861-7182 or 514-861-3708).

MUSÉE DU QUÉBEC, Quebec City: Not many museums of fine arts boast a "criminal" connection, but Quebec City is proud to claim a city jail as part of its landmark museum complex on the Plains of Abraham. An expansion project launched in 1988 linked the *Musée*'s original neo-classical gallery in National Battlefields Park with the somber old "Prison on the Plains," a 19th-century jail that hadn't seen an inmate in nearly 20 years. Former cell blocks have been transformed into airy new exhibition space, with five galleries, a library, a documentation center, and administrative offices adding to more than 4 acres of fine-arts property in the heart of the historic park. Now known as the Baillairgé Pavilion, the restoration opens on a Grand Hall, the hub of the expanded museum complex and the link between the old and new pavilions. With its glass walls and lofty cruciform skylight, the main entrance hall is a work of art in itself. Built partially underground, its connecting corridors are roofed in landscaped lawn to blend harmoniously with the natural park setting. The dramatic entry houses all the museum's public facilities, including a 180-seat auditorium, a gift shop, and a restaurant with a terrace overlooking the Plains and the St. Lawrence River. A sculpture garden occupies an inner court between the Grand Hall and the original Gérard Morisset Pavilion, where six galleries are devoted to a permanent collection that traces Quebec's fine-arts history from the late 1700s to the present. More than 18,000 works by artists from Quebec and other parts of the world make up the collection. Open daily June 15 to *Labour Day* from 10 AM to 5:45 PM, Wednesdays 10 AM to 9:45 PM. Closed Mondays the rest of the year. No admission charge Wednesdays. Information: *Musée du Québec,* 1 Av. Wolfe-Montcalm (phone: 418-643-2150).

MUSÉE DE LA CIVILISATION, Quebec City: If you want some peace and quiet when you visit here, call ahead: Schoolchildren from all parts of the province are more likely to be on a class tour at this place than at any other other museum in the capital. All aspects of the human experience as it relates to Quebec society are explored in this stunning complex in the restored Old Port of Quebec near Place Royale. Architect Moshe Safdie brought old and new together in 1988, joining a contemporary core to three historic properties and crowning the whole with a space-age steeple of glass and steel that covers a city block between Rues Dalhousie and St-Pierre. Summer visitors can stroll from one street to the other via a series of connecting stairways and terraces, taking in the port panorama as they go. Students of architecture consider the Safdie innovation the highlight of the museum experience, which begins in an arena-size entrance hall. The centerpiece here is a reflecting pool where Astri Reusch's *La Débâcle* sculpture symbolizes the drama of the spring thaw on the ice-choked St. Lawrence. The museum takes a hands-on approach, involving children and adults in many of the exhibits through computers and video screens. Open daily June 21 to September 7 from 10 AM to 7 PM; Tuesdays through Sundays the rest of the year, 10 AM to 5 PM; Wednesdays year-round 10 AM to 9 PM. Admission charge every day but Tuesday. Information: *Musée de la Civilisation,* 85 Rue Dalhousie (phone: 418-643-2158).

MUSÉE DES URSULINES, Quebec City: It's easy to pass this modest little museum by as part of the convent complex on Rue Donnacona (the order doesn't go in for heavy promotion), but don't: This is a fascinating repository of early Quebec memorabilia, some of it dating from 1639, when three intrepid members of the French teaching order arrived in the port of "Kebec." With the blessing of King Louis XIII, they set up their first convent in the waterfront settlement: two rooms with a cellar and garret they ironically called "The Louvre." The sisters eventually moved uptown, but they brought everything with them, including the original front-door key and a cauldron in which bubbled a noxious stew called sagamite. This dubious treat for Indian visitors included such ingredients as a bushel of black prunes, a dozen tallow candles, and 3 pounds of lard. The recipe, and other trappings of convent life — furniture, kitchenware, and richly embroidered altar clothes — are exhibited on 3 silent, dimly lighted floors. It's an oddly touching collection. Replicas of the sisters' enclosed "cabin beds" — for warmth (they didn't install stoves in the convent until 1668) — share exhibition space with the elegant furniture of the order's wealthy co-founder, Madame de la Peltrie, and the skull (under glass) of Marquis Louis-Joseph de Montcalm, defeated commander of the French army in the Battle of the Plains of Abraham. The general is buried in the convent chapel next door, and many of his personal effects are on display in the museum. One of the more endearing exhibits is the shirt that Murdoch Stewart, a British soldier and paymaster, the first of the "enemy" to marry a Canadian girl after the conquest of 1759, wore to his wedding to Angelique Cartier. Hand-stitched in sheer linen, with a bonny frilled jabot, the Fraser Highlander's dress shirt is as fresh as the day it was made more than 2 centuries ago. Closed Mondays and December; call for hours. Admission charge. Information: *Musée des Ursulines,* 12 Rue Donnacona (phone: 418-694-0694).

The Performing Arts

 Montreal and Quebec City offer a range of opportunities to enjoy fine concerts, plays, opera, and ballet; Montreal's symphony is considered a major force in the music world. For those nimble enough in Canada's other official language, finding professional-grade and avant-garde theater is no obstacle, but pickings tend to be slim for the English-only crowd. In Montreal, you should be able to find a play or two by Canadian-born playwrights of world class caliber or touring shows at the *Centaur Theatre,* the only professional English-language house in the city. But music and dance, in both centers, particularly in Montreal, are memorable. The following is a sampling of the best venues, those that consistently present fine performances. For more information and the names of local newspapers and magazines that carry arts information see "Sources and Resources" in *Montreal* and *Quebec City,* THE CITIES.

PLACE DES ARTS, Montreal: A product of the building boom that surrounded *EXPO '67,* this lavish complex of stages housed in a pyramid-shape building is the heart of Montreal's cultural life. The complex contains a stunning and acoustically excellent concert hall, the 3,000-seat *Salle Wilfred Pelletier* (the largest in the city), and three smaller theaters that house another 2,000 people. This is the home of the *Montreal Symphony Orchestra, Orchestre Métropolitan de Montréal, Les Grands Ballets Canadiens, L'Opéra de Montréal,* and *Opéra de Québec.* It's also the setting for *Les Ballets Jazz Montréal* performances, and a variety of chamber music concerts, ballet recitals, and plays. The 1,300-seat *Théâtre Maisonneuve* on the upper level reserves its large, adjustable stage for drama, dance, and recitals; the smaller *Théâtre Port-Royal* and pocket-size *Café de la Place* theater complete the complex. (It's linked to Montreal's Underground City through a pedestrian corridor to *Place des Arts* Métro station.) Tapestry murals by Quebec artists of the mythical meeting of Orpheus and Dionysius at the River Styx and the legend of Icarus adorn the main lobby. On Sunday mornings there's "Sons et Brioche" in the center lobby — informal concerts and continental breakfast. Information: *Place des Arts,* 1501 Rue Jeanne-Mance (phone: 514-842-2112).

CENTAUR THEATRE, Montreal: The city's only professional English-language theater has been at home in the former Stock Exchange building since 1965. The 1903 Beaux Arts temple of finance still looks like its imposing old self on the outside, but the interior has been transformed into an award-winning playhouse that includes two small theaters, one primarily a workshop stage for experimental endeavors. Works by Canadian playwrights are given priority here. French-language productions and dance companies share both stages with the English-repertory players. Information: *Centaur Theatre,* 453 St-François-Xavier St. (phone: 514-288-3161).

THÉÂTRE ST-DENIS, Montreal: The second-largest facility after *Salle Wilfred Pelletier,* the grand old theater of Montreal (1916) can accommodate audiences of 2,500. The theater, with its rebuilt Art Deco façade that traditionalists have never been able to forgive, plays host to the best French-language theater, to many of the events of the *Just for Laughs Festival* each July, as well as music and dance programs. (Also see "Special Events" in *Montreal,* THE CITIES.) Information: *Théâtre St-Denis,* 1594 St-Denis St. (phone: 514-849-4211).

POLLOCK CONCERT HALL, SALLE CLAUDE CHAMPAGNE, Montreal: For the best in classical music outside *Place des Arts,* the music halls at McGill University and the University of Montreal are the best in town. Designed by New York architect Bruce Price, the *Pollock* has been the recital hall for students from McGill University's faculty of music since 1899 and is now the home of the *McGill Chamber Orchestra.* Its concert schedule runs from September through May. Performances start at 8 PM; call for program dates. Most performances have no admission charge. Students from the University of Montreal's music faculty perform in concert and recital at *Salle Claude Champagne* from September to July. The 1,000-seat auditorium also features folk music groups. Performances start at 8 PM; no admission charge, with some exceptions. Information: *Pollock Concert Hall,* 555 Sherbrooke St. W. (phone: 514-398-4547); *Salle Claude Champagne,* 220 Vincent d'Indy Ave. (phone: 514-343-6000).

LE GRAND THÉÂTRE DE QÚEBEC, Quebec City: The preeminent stage of French culture since it opened more than 20 years ago, this is the home of the *Quebec Symphony Orchestra,* the oldest symphony orchestra in Canada, *Opéra Québec, Théâtre du Trident* repertory company, and the *Danse-Partout* dance company. The symphony schedules a full concert season in *Salle Louis Fréchette,* one of *Le Grand's* two splendid auditoriums. From September through May, the theater company mounts productions that range from the classics to new works by Canadian, European, and American playwrights, and the opera takes over the big stage twice a year for a series of spring and fall productions. Designed by Victor Prus, the huge building is a stunning piece of contemporary architecture. The interior is decorated with three massive murals in concrete by Spanish artist Jordi Bonet titled *Death, Space,* and *Liberty.* Both the building and the murals are controversial — not everyone likes Prus's bold design or Bonet's aggressive style — but they're worth seeing even if you're not staying for the concert. Information: *Le Grand Théâtre de Québec,* 269 Blvd. St-Cyrille E. (phone: 418-643-6967).

A Shutterbug's View

Photographers have just about everything going for them in photogenic Montreal and Quebec City. Both cities abound in exciting photo opportunities, with 20th-century skylines towering over well-preserved 17th-century birthplaces, river ports alive with dockyard activity, colorful Latin Quarters, and acres of public greenspace and landscaped gardens. For something completely different, Montreal has its extinct volcano (Mount Royal) and Quebec City its rugged cliff (Cape Diamond). The contrast of old and new charms visiting shutterbugs when they happen on some unexpected relic of the past, reflected in the glittering shaft of a newborn corporate tower, or the sight of a horse-drawn *calèche,* wheeling nonchalantly through high-rise condo territory in Montreal or riding merrily along near the expanse of the Plains of Abraham in Quebec City.

With opportunities around every corner, even neophyte enthusiasts can't go far wrong with good basic equipment and a limited set of filters and lenses. (For detailed information on equipment, see *Cameras and Equipment* in GETTING READY TO GO.)

Don't be afraid to experiment. Use what knowledge you have to explore new possibilities. At the same time, don't limit yourself by preconceived ideas of what's hackneyed or corny. Because Notre Dame Basilica or *Château Frontenac* have been photographed thousands of times before doesn't make them any less worthy of your attention.

In Montreal and Quebec City, as elsewhere, spontaneity is one of the keys to good photography. Whether it's a sudden shaft of light bursting through the clouds and hitting the St. Lawrence River just so, or farmers setting up their wares at an outdoor market as dawn creeps over the horizon, don't hesitate to shoot if the moment is right. If photography is indeed capturing a moment and making it timeless, success lies in judging just when a moment worth capturing occurs.

A good picture reveals an eye for detail, whether it's a matter of lighting, of positioning your subject, or taking time to frame a picture carefully. The better your grasp of the importance of details, the better your results will be photographically.

Patience is often necessary. Don't shoot a view of the memorial monument of Maisonneuve if a cloud suddenly dims its glow. A rusted old Volkswagen in the center of Rue St-Louis in Quebec City? Reframe your image to eliminate the obvious distraction. Watch for other intrusions, like overhead wires, which can ruin an otherwise stunning composition. Try recomposing the shot from a different angle to cut out the wiring. People walking toward a scene that would benefit from their presence? Wait until they're in position before you shoot. After the fact, many of the flaws will be self-evident. The trick is to be aware of the ideal and have the patience to allow it to happen. If you are part of a group, you may well have to trail behind a bit in order to shoot properly. Not only is group activity distracting, but bunches of people hovering nearby tend to stifle spontaneity and overwhelm potential subjects.

The camera provides an opportunity, not only to capture Montreal's and Quebec City's varied and subtle beauty, but to interpret it. What it takes is a sensitivity to the surroundings, a knowledge of the capabilities of your equipment, and a willingness to see things in new ways.

LANDSCAPES, RIVERSCAPES, AND CITYSCAPES: Vieux Montréal and Vieux Québec are most often visiting photographers' favorite subjects. But the cities' green spaces and waterways provide numerous photo possibilities as well. In addition to *Le Château Frontenac* and Place Royale in Quebec City and Place Jacques-Cartier and Notre Dame Basilica in Montreal, be sure to look for natural beauty: seabirds while on a boat tour, the flowers and vegetables of the farmers' markets, the towering stands of trees on Mount Royal, and the squirrels and chipmunks of National Battlefields Park, for example.

Color and form are the obvious ingredients here, and how you frame your pictures can be as important as getting the proper exposure. Study the shapes, angles, and colors that make up the scene and create a composition that uses them to best advantage.

Lighting is a vital component in landscape and seascapes. Take advantage of the richer colors of early morning and late afternoon whenever possible. The overhead light of midday is often harsh and without the shadowing that can add to the drama of a scene. This is when a polarizer is used to best effect. Most polarizers come with a mark on the rotating ring. If you can aim at your subject and point that marker at the sun, the sun's rays are likely to be right for the polarizer to work for you. If not, stick to your skylight filter, underexposing slightly if the scene is particularly bright. Most light meters respond to an overall light balance, with the result that bright areas may appear burned out. In both cities the best views of the skylines are shot across water; a harbor cruise in Montreal or the Quebec City–Lévis ferry can be the best way to see the urban profile from a different perspective. But you'll be on the move without much time to linger over artful compositions and, by early afternoon, you'll be shooting into the sun. Try angles that leave out at least half the sun when framing the picture, use a polarizer, and bracket your shots. Better still, board the first available morning cruise or an early morning ferry (although on a bright day, you'll still be coping with reflected light). Near shore, you'll get good results with a wide-angle lens, and even better results on terra firma. In Montreal, board the Métro or drive over to Montreal's satellite islands where you'll have time to frame the city properly in your zoom lens from the north shores of Iles Ste-Hélène and Notre Dame. At the right time of the day you'll focus on some spectacular sunset views.

Although a standard 50mm to 55mm lens may work well in some landscape situations, most will benefit from a 20mm to 28mm wide-angle. Place Royale, with Cape Diamond and *Le Château* looming in the background in Quebec City, for example, is the type of panorama that fits beautifully into a wide-angle format, allowing not only the overview, but the opportunity to include people or other points of interest in the foreground. A pedestrian, for instance, may be used to set off a view of Christ Church Cathedral; overhanging branches can provide a sense of perspective in a shot of Mount Royal Park. Wide-angle shots of the old market square in Montreal and the 18th-century buildings that flank its colorful length will take in the Nelson Column and the Hero of Trafalgar, with the flower market at his feet and the bright poster pillars and flowerbeds stretching down the slope of the central mall to the river. Pay strict attention to the light meter when focusing on the old financial district in Montreal. The ghosts of once-powerful financial houses still cast long shadows. Time your shooting schedule to coincide with office hours when most employees will be off the street and busy at their desks. Or better still, poke around on a weekend when the street is almost deserted and there's elbow room for shooting architectural details from different angles.

Summer and winter, photographers with an eye for composition will achieve dramatic results with Mount Royal as their subject. Catch it in an autumn mood, shooting up from the south end of McGill College Avenue into the slope of fiery foliage backlighting McGill University campus. Early morning and late afternoon shoots in Mount Royal will result in the purest color reproduction of natural settings. Use a zoom lens for best results here, or when taking the long view from the corner of Atwater Avenue and Sherbrooke Street West. Up on top of Mount Royal Park you'll be shooting under ski slope conditions on a bright winter day; 80% or 90% of the light will be reflected off the snow. A polarizing filter will reduce the reflection, but watch the light meter, which tends to go crazy under these conditions, and consider your exposure carefully. A polarizer will increase the contrast between sky and snow, especially if you underexpose to compensate for the glare. You could end up with a dark sky in the background. Always bracket your shots when using a polarizer.

To isolate specific elements of any scene, use your telephoto lens. Perhaps there's a particular carving in a historic church that would make a lovely shot, or it might be the interplay of light and shadow on a cobblestone street. The successful use of a telephoto means developing your eye for detail.

PEOPLE: As with taking pictures of people anywhere, there are going to be times in Montreal and Quebec City when a camera is an intrusion. Your approach is the key: Consider your own reaction under similar cicumstances, and you have an idea as to what would make others comfortable enough to be willing subjects. People are often sensitive to having a camera suddenly pointed at them, and a polite request, while getting you a share of refusals, will also provide a chance to shoot some wonderful portraits that capture the spirit of the city as surely as the scenery does. For candids, an excellent lens is a zoom telephoto in the 70mm to 210mm range; it allows you to remain unobtrusive while the telephoto lens draws the subject closer. And for portraits, a telephoto can be used effectively as close as 2 or 3 feet.

For authenticity and variety, select a place likely to produce interesting subjects. Place Jacques-Cartier is an obvious spot for visitors in Montreal, as is La Citadelle in Quebec City, but if it's local color you're after, try the *Complexe Desjardins* in Montreal or the St. Charles River in snowy Quebec City, sit at a café on St-Denis Street or Grande Allée and watch the fashion parade, or walk around the central *places,* where everyone from elderly Quebecois to college students to street people flock to enjoy a sunny day. Aim for shots that tell what's different about Quebec City and Montreal. In portraiture, there are several factors to keep in mind. Morning or afternoon light will add richness to skin tones, emphasizing tans. To avoid the harsh facial shadows cast by direct sunlight, shoot in the shade or in an area where the light is diffused. In summer, the sidewalk cafés on Place Jacques-Cartier are busy long before the sun's over the yardarm and the harsh midday glare burns out any subtlety of color and shadow. Exchange your regular skylight filter for a polarizer when you move down to the Old Port waterfront at the foot of the *place.* If the day is particularly bright, underexpose slightly to offset the reflected water light.

Escape the crowds in Old Montreal on at least one Sunday so that you can capture Montreal's skyscraper zone on film. Enough strollers and window shoppers will be on hand to add to the big-city atmosphere, but you won't be knocked off your pins by the crush of weekday crowds when you pause to click off a few frames. Use a polarizing filter when the sun is glancing off the glass of the city's new steel-and-concrete canyons, and your zoom lens for long shots of the skyline. Don't miss the statue groups: the *Illuminated Crowd* reflected in the gleaming façade of the bank tower complex (1981 McGill College Ave.), or Rodin's *Jean D'Aire, Burgher of Calais* in from the *Dominion*

Gallery (1438 Sherbrooke St. W.). Montreal is filled with statue subjects and you can frame them at close quarters with a standard 50mm lens or move in from a distance with a zoom. No single day is better than any other to shoot Quebec City beyond the walls; the time of year means everything. The Grande Allée seems busy 24 hours a day, 365 days a year, but during off-season, photos of the sidewalk cafés can be taken with some success as breaches appear in the sea of endless pedestrians. When Parliament is in session, pictures taken outside the National Assembly are more enlivened and colorful. Have your zoom lens handy for photos of the statues high up the façade of the National Assembly or better yet get your tripod and set up for a night shot when the building, a modified version of the Louvre, is lit to perfection.

SUNSETS: Montreal is the better city of the two for sunsets. Take a trip to Ste-Hélène Island as the shadows lengthen and then shoot from the island back toward the skyline, which is crowned with magical clouds of pink and lavender, purple and red. In Quebec City get the best view of its monumental skyline at sunset from Lévis, a short ferry ride across the St. Lawrence.

When shooting sunsets, keep in mind that the brightness will distort meter readings. When composing a shot directly into the sun, frame the picture in the viewfinder so that only half of the sun is included. Read the meter, set, and shoot. Whenever there is this kind of unusual lighting, shoot a few frames in half-step increments, both over and under the meter reading. Bracketing, as this is called, can provide a range of images, the best of which may well be other than the one shot at the meter's recommended setting.

Use any lens for sunsets. A wide-angle is good when the sky is filled with color-streaked clouds, when the sun is partially hidden, or when you're close to an object that silhouettes dramatically against the sky.

Telephotos also produce wonderful silhouettes, either with the sun as a backdrop or against the palette of a brilliant sunset sky. Bracket again here. For the best silhouettes, wait 10 to 15 minutes after sunset. Unless using a very fast film, a tripod is recommended.

Red and orange filters are often used to accentuate a sunset's picture potential. Orange will help turn even a gray sky into something approaching a photogenic finale to the day, and can provide particularly beautiful shots linking the sky with the sun reflected on the ocean. If the sunset is already bold in hue, the orange will overwhelm the natural colors. A red filter will produce dramatic, highly unrealistic results.

NIGHT: If you think that picture possibilities end at sunset, you're presuming that night photography is the exclusive domain of the professional. If you've got a tripod, all you'll need is a cable release to attach to your camera to assure a steady exposure (which is often timed in minutes rather than fractions of a second).

For situations such as evening concerts or nighttime harbor cruises, a strobe does the trick, but beware: Flash units are often used improperly. You can't take a view of the skyline with a flash. It may reach out as far as 30 feet, but that's it. On the other hand, a flash used too close to a subject may result in overexposure, resulting in a "blown out" effect. With most cameras, strobes will work with a maximum shutter speed of 1/125 or 1/150 of a second. If you set the exposure properly and shoot within range, you should come up with pretty sharp results.

CLOSE-UPS: Whether of people or of objects such as antique door knockers, close-ups can add another dimension to your photography. There are a number of shooting options, one of which is to use a 70mm or a 210mm lens at its closest focusable distance. Unless you're working in bright sunlight, a tripod will be worthwhile. If you are very near your subject and there is a good deal of reflective light, it may pay to underexpose a bit in relation to the meter reading.

If you do not have a telephoto lens, you can still shoot close-ups using a set of magnification filters. Filter packs of one-, two-, and three-time magnification are available, converting your lens into a close-up lens. Even better is a special macro lens designed for close-up photography.

The following are some of Montreal and Quebec City's truly great pictorial perspectives.

A SHORT PHOTOGRAPHIC TOUR OF MONTREAL

MONTREAL BOTANICAL GARDEN: With 30 gardens to choose from, it's hard to miss a flowery photo opportunity within this 180-acre Maisonneuve Park preserve. For exotic scenes, focus on the Japanese Garden, a beguiling transplant from the Orient, with iris-banked reflecting pool, a tea house, graceful little bridges and whimsical rock formations. Move to the Chinese Garden and shoot across the Dream Lake and pagoda rooftops to the space-ship roof of the *Olympic Stadium* and its inclining tower. This reproduction of a Ming dynasty garden is in itself a joy to capture on film, with its flowering trees, brooks, cascades, and such poetically named pagodas as the "Where Purple Clouds Hang in the Sky" pavilion. Schedule your shooting session on a weekday morning or late afternoon when there won't be too many people around to disturb the serenity.

PLACE D'ARMES: No self-respecting photographer leaves Montreal without capturing its founder on film. A dramatic statue of Paul de Chomedey, Sieur de Maisonneuve, stands with drawn sword and flaring banner atop his fountain monument with historic figures from the early days of the Ville Marie settlement at his feet. Approached from almost any angle on Place d'Armes the statue photographs well; there's also a stirring view of Notre Dame Basilica from the north side of the square with the monument in the foreground. From another angle you'll register the full effect of the basilica's neo-Gothic towers.

CITY CENTER: Set Sunday morning aside to patrol the midtown blocks between René-Lévesque Boulevard West and Sherbrooke Street West and from University Avenue to Peel Street, where the city's towers of power glitter in the sun. One of the most memorable contrasts between Old and New Montreal is the sight of Christ Church Cathedral's 19th-century steeple reflected in the pink glass shimmer of La Maison des Coopérants' skyscraper. On a quiet Sunday morning you'll be able to focus on the reflection from the best positions on University Avenue without getting crowded off the sidewalk. A good spot for a wide-angle shot is the corner of University and Ste-Catherine Street West.

La Tour CIBC, with its 45 stories of tympanum walls covered in gleaming green slate at the corner of René-Lévesque Boulevard and Peel Street, is Montreal's most sensational vertical shot, and for a close-up few parallel Henry Moore's *Reclining Figure in Three Pieces* nearby.

PRINCE ARTHUR STREET MALL: On fair-weather weekends this is *the* people place. Find a vacant table on a café terrace and focus in on the world strolling by. The mall is lined on both sides with small cafés, so feel free to snap away, capturing clowns, magicians, street magicians, and fellow tourists on Montreal's most colorful pedestrian strip.

ST-DENIS STREET: The home address of the city's largest concentration of bars, restaurants, antiques shops, art galleries, and handicraft studios, this street is a fertile field for capturing the spirit of young French Canada at play. If your visit coincides with the *International Jazz Festival* in June, when part of the street is closed off for open-air performances, you won't have enough film to record the action.

A SHORT PHOTOGRAPHIC TOUR OF QUEBEC CITY

THE SKYLINE: The famous urban landscape of the old capital presents photographers with a classic dilemma: How do you get a picture of one of the best-known views in Canada and *not* make it look like just another postcard? It is not an easy matter, but try working from the bottom up. Most people head straight for the waterfront or the deck of the Quebec-Lévis ferry, but the most unusual shooting site, and one newcomers often miss, is from Rue St-Paul's antiques row. Here the turrets and towers of the omnipresent *Château Frontenac* present themselves in a unique and captivating angle across the colorful rooftops of a row of centuries-old buildings huddled under the cliff.

LOWER TOWN: The crowds and the narrow streets where old buildings lean close together in the Place Royal *quartier* just don't cooperate. (Try early morning if you are determined to bring home a relatively people-free shot.) Close-ups of architectural details and people are easy, however, and there's a fine view up Rue du Petit-Champlain at its junction with Boulevard Champlain. But you'll snap some of your best shots en route between the Upper and Lower Towns. The landings on Escalier Casse-Cou (Break-Neck Staircase) overlook some good views of the town at the foot of the stairs and, on top, in Parc Montmorency, there are some great spots to take overviews.

UPPER TOWN: A favorite postcard composition takes in the Champlain Monument, with the city's founder on top and street performers attracting a crowd at the bottom. The horse-drawn *calèche* queue, waiting at the top of Rue St-Louis, near *Le Château,* is always a distinctive summer subject. Try different angles of the old square area itself, with the graceful Gothic fountain of the Recollet Memorial in the foreground. For café-society studies, move down to the colorful sidewalk terraces on Rue Ste-Anne. Be quick about framing a mood piece of the artists and browsers on little Rue du Trésor before moving on. Here is where a zoom lens will come in handy because crowds can converge at any time to spoil a shot. Walking the walls of Upper Town will open new perspectives, too, as shutterbugs look down on the spires and domes of Vieux Québec's upper level from the footpath on top of the wall's western section, between Porte St-Louis and Parc d'Artillerie, as well as of the "new" city beyond the walls.

"NEW" QUEBEC: Just beyond the gates, but still the vital core of the city's old defense network, the Citadelle sets the stage for some exciting film footage. Time your visit to catch the daily changing of the guard ceremony, when the Royal 22nd Regiment — complete with furry busbies and regal red coats — puts on a show at 10 AM, mid-June to *Labour Day.* The National Assembly building is photogenic from any angle, an imposing Second Empire presence on Parliament Hill since 1886. And don't miss the constant, colorful parade of pedestrians on Grande Allée, where the action goes on from noon to midnight.

DIRECTIONS

Montreal Directions

Don't let Montreal's size as the number two city in Canada (behind Toronto) fool you; this city is made for walking. Caught between river and mountain, old Ville Marie (the city's original name, said to have been bestowed by missionaries in honor of the Virgin Mary) has many modern and historic attractions that are within easy strolling distance of the midtown hotel area. So it's easy to walk from one century to another in less than half an hour — about the time it takes to wander downhill from the contemporary crossroad at Ste-Catherine Street West and McGill College Avenue to the threshold of the 17th century on Place d'Armes.

"Down" is the operative word. You'll climb plenty of hillside streets between the historic *quartier* of Old Montreal and the heights of Mount Royal Park — unless you follow resident pedestrians to the underground escalator and elevator services that link the old financial district to the new. The so-called Underground City, separate commercial areas underground that Montrealers refer to as if they were all interconnected, and its speedy, efficient Métro afford convenient connections to more widely separated walking zones. It's a long hike between the Sherbrooke Street hotel strip, the Montreal Botanical Garden, a 180-acre complex of exhibition greenhouses and outdoor gardens, and Olympic Park, the site of the 1976 *Summer Olympic Games* — about 70 city blocks — but the subway ride takes less than 20 minutes.

But when you're not following parkland paths or wandering the narrow streets of Vieux Montréal, be sure to keep your wits about you and your eyes on the intersections. Montreal drivers have a propensity for entering the traffic fray in a combative mood, girded for the daily battle of wills with fellow motorists, buses, cruising patrol cars, cyclists, *calèche* drivers, and pedestrians. Jumping traffic lights is a point of honor. And the native habit of cutting corners around slower senior citizens adds a certain zest to the conflict.

Montrealers are also accomplished jaywalkers. Some inner voice urges them into the path of oncoming traffic, against the light, against all reason. Don't even think about plunging into the stream after them. Keep an eye out for cyclists even when navigating an intersection *with* the light; rules of the road don't mean much to them, either. But *pas de problème.* Once you understand the system, walking in downtown Montreal can be safe and satisfying. Just keep your head up — and *bonne chance!*

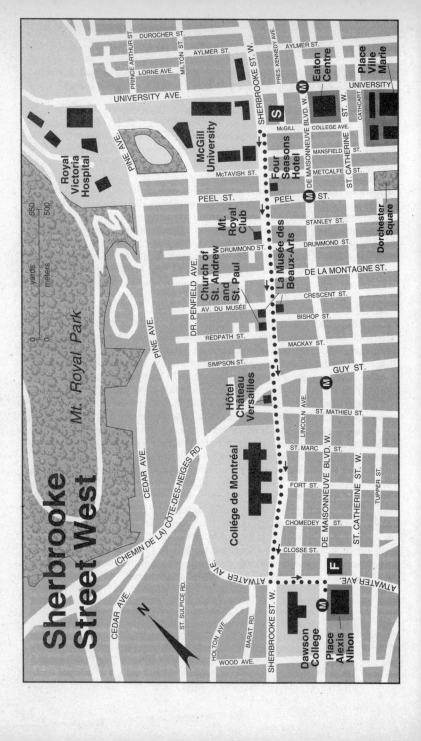

Sherbrooke
Street West

Mt. Royal Park

N

DUROCHER ST.
PRINCE ARTHUR ST.
MILTON ST.
LORNE AVE.
AYLMER ST.
PRES. KENNEDY AVE.
AYLMER ST.

Place
Ville
Marie

Eaton
Centre

UNIVERSITY

UNIVERSITY AVE.

SHERBROOKE ST. W.

McGill

CATHCART

ST. CATHERINE ST. W.

COLLEGE AVE.

Royal
Victoria
Hospital

PINE AVE.

McGill
University

Four
Seasons
Hotel

DE MAISONNEUVE BLVD. W.

Mansfield ST.

Metcalfe ST.

McTAVISH ST.

PEEL ST.

PEEL

ST.

Mt.
Royal
Club

STANLEY ST.

Dorchester
Square

DRUMMOND ST.

DRUMMOND ST.

Church of
St. Andrew
and
St. Paul

La Musée des
Beaux-Arts

DE LA MONTAGNE ST.

DR. PENFIELD AVE.

AV. DU MUSÉE

CRESCENT ST.

BISHOP ST.

REDPATH ST.

MACKAY ST.

SIMPSON ST.

GUY ST.

Hôtel
Château
Versailles

LINCOLN AVE.

ST. MATHIEU ST.

PINE AVE.

CEDAR AVE.

(CHEMIN DE LA) CÔTE-DES-NEIGES RD.

ST. MARC ST.

DE MAISONNEUVE BLVD. W.

Collège de Montréal

FORT ST.

ST. CATHERINE ST. W.

TUPPER ST.

CHOMEDEY ST.

CLOSSE ST.

ATWATER AVE.

F

ATWATER AVE.

CEDAR AVE.

ST. SULPICE RD.

SHERBROOKE ST. W.

HOLTON AVE.

BARAT RD.

WOOD AVE.

Dawson
College

Place
Alexis
Nihon

yards 0 550
meters 0 500

Walk 1: Sherbrooke Street West

Back in the glory days when Montreal's merchant princes and financial power brokers controlled two-thirds of Canada's wealth, midtown Sherbrooke Street ranked as the city's most prestigious residential neighborhood.

Lined with baronial Victorian and Edwardian mansions, it was the elm-shaded main drag of the Square Mile, a precinct of privilege and influence on the southwest slopes of Mount Royal that stretched north from René-Lévesque Boulevard (then Dorchester Boulevard) to Pine Avenue, with Guy Street and Chemin de la Côte-des-Neiges marking its western border, and the campus of McGill University to the east.

Within this tightly controlled enclave, descendants of the North West Company's Scottish and English fur traders and the frontier entrepreneurs who flocked into Montreal after the British conquest of 1759–1760 reigned supreme over the city's — indeed Canada's — social, economic, and political scene. Their forebears, primarily canny Scots from the threadbare Highlands, had pretty well cornered the market in British North America by the early 19th century, founding banks, industrial empires, and shipping lines, amassing personal fortunes in an age when land was cheap and income taxes an unconscionable affront.

Early Square Milers, like Nor' Wester Simon McTavish and his fur-trading contemporaries, James McGill and William McGillivray, staked out lordly estates on the mountainside and along the western stretches of a country road that became Dorchester Boulevard. But their woodland domains shrank as the old walled city by the river burst its bounds and "uptown" real estate values soared. Wealthy newcomers from town soon enhanced the fast-growing suburb with Victorian versions of Renaissance châteaux and medieval castles, surrounded by acres of lawns, orchards, and landscaped gardens. Despite the influx of French gentry stock who began to move up the western slope of the mountain and join in business and marriage with the self-made Scots, English, and Irish, the Square Mile flourished as a proud outpost of Britain's empire.

At the height of their exuberant heyday, from the 1840s until the 1880s, Square Milers (a term that wasn't coined for another generation; it was later upgraded to the Golden Square Mile by over-enthusiastic travel writers) enjoyed a winter social season that reminded international visitors of czarist St. Petersburg. Montreal's close-knit aristocracy claimed knighthoods and baronies, hosted royalty, and imported their butlers and hunting pinks from London, their governesses and gowns from Paris. Their ballrooms, bloodstock stables, and vintage wine cellars lived up to the highest British standards. The mile-long stretch of Montreal's longest street, patriotically named for Governor-General Sir John Sherbrooke, was the ultimate carriage trade route to social and financial standing in Canada.

As the 1920s roared in, a new generation of first families abandoned the cumbersome Gothic fortresses their grandfathers had built to last forever in favor of a more contemporary lifestyle, unhampered by the armies of servants required to maintain a 50-room family seat. In 1925, the razing of Rokeby, the intimidating limestone stronghold of Andrew Frederick Gault, Canada's "Cotton King," to make way for an apartment block, marked the beginning of the end of Sherbrooke Street as an avenue of stately homes. But it was the stock market collapse of 1929 that hastened the decline of the Square Mile. One by one the Tuscan villas, Tudor manors, and Second Empire châteaux crumbled under the wrecker's ball. In time they would give way to hotels, apartment complexes, and office towers that changed the street's residential character forever. Tall terrace houses turned into high-fashion boutiques and art galleries. Finally, the last of the great family-occupied mansions, the 52-room, century-old bailiwick of *Canadian Pacific Railway* czar Sir William Van Horne, was demolished in 1973 — gold-leaf wallpaper, Art Nouveau fireplaces, and all.

Today, only a few ghosts of the Square Mile's Belle Epoque cling to their Sherbrooke Street roots. But while the empire builders and the merchant princes have departed along with the triumphal arch of elms, Sir John's namesake avenue is still gentry row, its period-piece lamp standards reminiscent of Europe's gaslight era, its sidewalk planters blooming with summer flowers. This is still Montreal's most elegant strolling strip.

A long walk through yesterday and today takes about 90 minutes, not counting stops for browsing and snacking. It begins at the Roddick Gates to McGill University campus (see *Walk 5: McGill University–Prince Arthur Street*), where McGill College Avenue meets Sherbrooke Street West. (Métro passengers should disembark at the McGill station and take the McGill College exit).

Today's campus was the home of the original Montrealers, residents of the pallisaded Iroquois village of Hochelaga, who encountered their first foreign visitors in 1535 when Jacques Cartier and his crew dropped anchor. Before turning west to see the Hochelaga Stone, a small plaque commemorating that meeting, through the fence on the north side of Sherbrooke, look back down the length of city blocks that links Place Ville-Marie to the campus — this is a vista of downtown Montreal at its most dramatic. This mini–Champs-Elysées, with its flowery boulevard and ranks of soaring glass towers, still stops Montrealers in their tracks — especially when they recall what McGill College Avenue was only a few years before: a common strip of retail shops, undistinguished restaurants, and lackluster bookshops.

Now cross Sherbrooke at McGill College to the south side and proceed west to *Henri Vezina's* up-market boutique for fashionable men (920 Sherbrooke St. W.; phone: 514-844-1971). Continue on to the International Civil Aviation Organization (ICAO), established in 1976 at No. 1000, the site of

Sir George Drummond's turreted brownstone mansion. The only United Nations organization with headquarters in Montreal, ICAO promotes the orderly development of civil aviation and sets international standards for air safety. McGill University's McLennan-Redpath Library faces International Aviation Square from the north side of Sherbrooke (enter the library at 3495 McTavish; phone: 514-398-4698).

The flamboyant rose granite heights of Tour Scotia, the Bank of Nova Scotia's controversial contribution to Montreal's carriage trade route, is located at the southeast corner of Sherbrooke and Metcalf Streets. Pause for a moment here and look up to the mountain. To the north, McTavish Street (Metcalf changes names on the north side of Sherbrooke) opens onto the much-photographed view of Mount Royal and its Eiffelesque cross, and the Allan Memorial Institute, the psychiatric center of the Royal Victoria Hospital. The Allan, once the stateliest of stately Square Mile homes, started life as Ravenscrag, a lofty limestone perch carved into the mountainside above Pine Avenue in the 1860s by transatlantic shipping magnate Sir Hugh Allan. Newspaper accounts of the day claimed Sir Hugh's castle excelled "in size and cost any dwelling house in Canada."

Back on space-age Sherbrooke Street, the *Four Seasons* hotel (*Le Quatre Saisons;* at No. 1050; phone: 514-284-1110) dominates the block between Metcalf and Peel Streets. The *Four Seasons* is popular with visiting stars of stage, film, and video: Michael Jackson stayed in one of its posh VIP suites during his last visit to the city. *Le Circle* restaurant is a pleasant lunchtime retreat for strollers who start their walk around midday (see "Checking In" in *Montreal,* THE CITIES).

Across the traffic stream at the northeast corner of this busy intersection is *Le Shangrila Best Western* on Peel Street (phone: 514-288-41410), a tranquil Oriental spot (also see "Checking In" in *Montreal,* THE CITIES).

Across Peel at 1115 Sherbrooke, *Le Cartier,* with its posh apartments, offices, and boutiques-filled mall, towers over the northwest corner. Some of Montreal's most fashionable heads are groomed here by the trend-settting hair stylists at *La Coupe* (phone: 514-288-6131). *Le Cantlie,* an upscale apartment-hotel (1110 Sherbrooke) shares the south side of the block between Peel and Stanley with Tour Central Guaranty's corporate space and *Paradis Maternité* (also at No. 1110), a chic specialty store for shoppers with great expectations (phone: 514-845-4350). Across the street the head office of Air Liquide (No. 1155) now occupies the site of the former Van Horne mansion at the corner of Stanley.

Continue along Sherbrooke to its southwest juncture with Stanley to discover one of the city's most imaginative urban renewal projects at Maison Alcan (1188 Sherbrooke St. W.). What other developers knocked down on millionaires' mile, Alcan Aluminum conserved in its world headquarters, opened in 1983. The Maison's conservation includes the century-old cut-stone townhouse of the late Lord Atholstan, founder of the *Montreal Star,* the city's largest English-language daily newspaper until its demise in 1979. Alcan incorporated the press lord's corner property and some of its Sherbrooke Street neighbors into a stunning complex that features a skylit atrium, hung with brilliant banners and decorated with modern tapestries, sculptures, and works of art. The main entrance (No. 1188) leads through the triple archway of the abandoned *Berkeley* hotel's Art Deco façade into a light-filled interior plaza where free noontime concerts are staged twice a month from March to December (check for notices in the window for details). From concert-stage level, music lovers can see how the shell of the *Berkeley*'s gracious old lobby and the rear walls of Lord Atholstan's neighbors were used to enclose the lower levels of the 8-story atrium.

Le Pavillon de l'Atlantique restaurant (phone: 514-285-1637) opens off the atrium, across the passage from *Dixversions Mobilier,* one of a chain of home furnishing and accessory shops for the young at heart (phone: 514-284-1013). Alcan's Stanley Street entrance (No. 2100) leads to *La Tulipe Noire,* a Parisian-style café and pastry shop (phone: 514-285-1225), and to *Moby Dick's* (phone: 514-285-1637; also see "Eating Out" in *Montreal,* THE CITIES). An affiliate of *Le Pavillon de l'Atlantique,* this hip wood-paneled bar with its glass-walled seafood café is a popular after-five watering hole for uptown singles and a restful spot to enjoy lunch with a garden view. Rear entrances to *Giorgeo of Montreal*'s haberdashery (phone: 514-287-1928) and *Giorgeo Donna Boutique* (phone: 514-287-1570) at 1176 Sherbrooke open off the atrium. So does a door to the *Walter Klinkhoff Gallery,* a long-established showcase for Canadian artists (1200 Sherbrooke; phone: 514-288-7806; also see "Shopping" in *Montreal,* THE CITIES). Alcan offers guided tours of its headquarters on request (phone: 514-848-8487). Lunchtime concerts are scheduled every other week, March to December.

Opposite Maison Alcan a trio of Square Mile monuments takes up the north side of the block between Stanley and Drummond Streets. The Mount Royal Club (1175 Sherbrooke) was founded in 1899 by refugees from the St. James's Club, who decided their old refuge on Dorchester Boulevard (now René-Lévesque Boulevard) was getting too crowded. They moved into the home of former Prime Minister Sir John Abbot (1891–1892) and flourished there until the mansion went up in smoke in 1904. The present structure was raised on the same site. The work of American architect Stanford White, it's a cool, uncluttered contrast to the overwrought Second Empire home of the United Services Club next door at No. 1195. The USC has occupied the imposing gray-stone building since 1927. Its previous occupant was the former Senator Louis-Joseph Forget, the onetime President of the Montreal Stock Exchange and founder of the most powerful brokerage house in Canada.

Corby House on the club's western flank (No. 1201) is an 1882 Square Mile relic that fell on hard times. Degraded to rooming-house depths during the Second World War, it regained its stately status in 1952 when Corby's Distilleries reclaimed the red sandstone centenarian and its coach house for executive office space.

If you're here during the summer, rally round the *Ritz-Carlton* (No. 1228; phone: 514-842-4212) about now for tea in the hotel's duck pond garden, one of Montreal's most enchanting fair-weather interludes. In winter, visit the *Ritz Bar,* where you're apt to run into Canadian political leaders, visiting potentates, and other public personalities. Founded in 1916 with the personal blessing of César Ritz himself, the *Ritz* doesn't admit to rivals and the faithful always have considered the Square Mile landmark the *only* place to stay (see *Montreal's Best Hotels* in DIVERSIONS).

Once beyond the *Ritz,* you're in high-fashion territory, with *Holt Renfrew,* the prestige emporium for designer furs and imported couture collections (1300 Sherbrooke St. on the southwest corner of de la Montagne St.; phone: 514-842-5111), and *Ralph Lauren Polo* (next door at No. 1316; phone: 514-288-3988).

Across Sherbrooke the Château Apartments (No. 1321), with their towers and turrets, gargoyles and courtyard arches, maintain a high feudal profile next door to the stolid stone presence of the 100-year-old Erskine and American United Church. But the apartment house is not nearly as old as its 19th-century neighbor on the corner of Sherbrooke and Avenue du Musée. The 3-section luxury compound didn't make the Sherbrooke scene until 1925 when its battlements rose over the site of vanquished Rokeby. The row of tall, gray townhouses on the opposite side of the block, between de la Montagne and Crescent Streets, are older, too, but their upstairs/downstairs boutiques are stocked with the styles of the 1990s. Shoppers find Sonia Rykiel and Thierry Mugler designs at *Clubissimo* (1320 Sherbrooke St.; phone: 514-844-5555). *Lippel Gallery* (No. 1324; phone: 514-842-6369), 1 floor above *Clubissimo,* is Montreal's foremost showcase for pre-Columbian art.

West of Crescent, *Le Musée des Beaux-Arts de Montréal* (Montreal Museum of Fine Arts) dominates both sides of Sherbrooke. The classic Vermont marble home of the "old" fine-arts museum (1379 Sherbrooke on the west corner of Av. du Musée; phone: 514-285-1600) dates from 1912, when the oldest established museum in Canada moved west from Phillips Square. Across the street and linked to the older building by underground tunnel, Moshe Safdie's striking addition opened in 1991. The gleaming white companion piece to the Greek temple across the street adjoins a neo-Renaissance apartment block that the museum restored to accommodate its archives, library, and offices. The *Beaux-Arts* boasts several important collections of Canadian and international paintings and sculpture (see "Special Places" in *Montreal,* THE CITIES).

While in the neighborhood, visit the historic Church of Saint Andrew and Saint Paul (3415 Redpath St.; enter on Sherbrooke), the Presbyterian regimental Church of the Black Watch (Royal Highland Regiment) of Canada. Tapestries by Sir Edward Burne-Jones decorate the chapel and Louis Comfort Tiffany created the stained glass windows.

But don't look for any traces of Calvinism on Sherbrooke's worldly little rialto across the street. The stretch of big spenders' shopping blocks between Crescent and Guy Streets is a sophisticated, exclusive enclave of designer boutiques, art galleries, and antiques shops, great for browsing, if not for buying. On the strip's eastern approaches, *Ungaro* (No. 1430; phone: 514-844-8970) caters to label-conscious shoppers who rely on a top designer to keep them one jump ahead of the fashion pack.

Nearby (No. 1438), a Rodin casting of *Jean d'Aire, Bourgeois de Calais* stares grimly past the window shoppers from his pavement stand outside the

Dominion Gallery, an unlikely medieval figure in the company of Henry Moore's *Upright Motive. Dominion Gallery* (phone: 514-845-7474) takes credit for introducing Moore to Canadian collectors. *Les Créateurs* (No. 1440; phone: 514-284-2101) is a salon outlet for such high-profile prêt-à-porter designers as Claude Montana.

Shopped-out strollers can take a break here and turn into *Passage du Musée,* a mini-mall of shops and services, for a pick-me-up at *Café Il Cortile* (1442 Sherbrooke; phone 514-843-8230) before moving on toward Guy Street. En route, stop by *Pratesi* (No. 1448; phone: 514-285-8909), if only to admire the window display in this boudoir of pricey designer linen and bath accessories. *Davidoff* (No. 1452; phone: 514-289-9118) is the haunt of smokers in search of imported tobacco products, pipes, lighters, and other expensive necessities. *Les Gamineries* (1458 Sherbrooke, corner MacKay St.; phone: 514-843-4614) caters to style-conscious children with well-heeled parents, while *Brisson et Brisson* (No. 1472; phone: 514-937-7456) caters to style-conscious men.

On the north side of Sherbrooke two rewarding art galleries — *Galerie du Cygne* (phone: 514-935-6971) and *Galerie de l'Isle* (phone: 514-935-9885) — share an address (No. 1451) with the handsome white Port Royal complex of offices and apartments. Back on the south side the *Galerie Claude Lafitte* showcases Canadian, especially Quebecois, art (No. 1480; phone: 514-939-9898). *Le Petit Musée* (No. 1494; phone: 514-937-6161) is an Aladdin's cave of rare collectibles that has served generations of local antiques browsers. *Cartier* (No. 1498, corner Sherbrooke and Simpson Sts.; phone: 514-939-0000) is a sumptuous little green marble *bijouterie* of costly gems and signature handbags.

Facing shoppers' row across Sherbrooke is the Linton (No. 1509), the grande dame of Square Mile apartment houses. Mountain View House, a separate building constructed by James Linton — the Victorian-era owner of the property — still stands behind the Beaux Arts apartment landmark on the west corner of hillside Simpson Street. For a view of Mountain View (which alas, hasn't much of a view of anything now), detour around the corner of Simpson, where the forlorn ghost of this 1862 edifice waits for some form of restoration. Used over the years as casual apartment and office space, it once ranked among the loveliest properties on Sherbrooke.

Continuing west on the north side to the traffic-clogged intersection where Guy Street becomes Chemin de la Côte-des-Neiges, you'll see at the northwest corner of Sherbrooke the last of the Square Mile's Romanesque houses raised on the neighborhood's western limits. Built in 1891 for the son of one of Montreal's biggest property owners, it came down in the world to trade and commerce after Robert Stanley Bagg died in 1911.

The Guy Street–Côte-des-Neiges intersection marks the official western boundary of the Square Mile, but Sherbrooke follows a graceful course west under its distinctive, Parisian-style lampposts. *Hôtel Château Versailles* (1659 Sherbrooke W.; phone: 514-933-3611), the city's best-publicized "European" hotel, occupies four ample gray-stone townhouses built by venturesome developers between 1911 and 1913 outside the Square Mile on the north side of the street.

The charming hotel puts up its overflow clientele in the *Hôtel Tour Versailles* (No. 1808; phone: 514-933-3611; see "Checking In" in *Montreal,* THE CITIES), its more contemporary property across the street. Both are close neighbors to one of the city's oldest historic landmarks: Grand Séminaire de Montréal. Five years after moving into their newly built Ville Marie seminary in 1685 (see *Walk 2: Vieux Montréal*), the missionaries of St-Sulpice opened an Indian mission about 2 miles northwest of the walled town. By 1694 the outpost was securely enclosed within fortified walls, with four stone martello towers defending a community of Indian villagers, a farm, a school, and the Château des Messieurs, a large limestone structure on the north side of today's Sherbrooke Street. Two of the towers were razed in the 1850s to make room for an imposing entrance to the Grand Séminaire de Montréal, a college for the sons of Montreal's French-speaking élite. But two towers remain on their original site, facing Fort Street, still guarding the walled seminary (now the faculty of theology of the University of Montreal), the Collège de Montréal at 1931 Sherbrooke, and what's left of the Sulpicians' vast seigneurial estates. Ste-Marguerite Bourgeoys, Montreal's first schoolmistress, held classes in both towers. There's a sad little urban myth connected with one of the dank stone classrooms where she taught Indian girls hymns, prayers, and useful needlework: According to local legend, in the first tower on the west is the tomb of a young Indian convert who lived within the Sulpician fortress from early childhood. She died shortly after taking the veil and, as the story goes, the little nun was buried in the tower, far from the forest freedom she craved all her short life.

On the northeast corner of Atwater Avenue, one of the "Priests' Farm" properties, as the vast Sulpician domain is called, has been adapted to the condominium era, its stern granite walls merged with an airy hillside high-rise on the slopes of Atwater. Cross Atwater here to its southwest corner and stroll past the elm-shaded campus of Dawson College (3040 Sherbrooke St. W.), where Quebec's largest junior college for English-speaking students got its start in the former Maison Mère des Soeurs de la Congrégation de Notre-Dame. Classified now as a historic site, the Mother House was the order's headquarters, retirement home, and hospital, as well as a private school for girls, until the collegian contingent took over the huge Beaux Arts building and its beautiful grounds in 1988.

The eastern boundary of Dawson campus follows Atwater south to de Maisonneuve Boulevard and, if weary strollers take the same route, they'll arrive at *Place Alexis Nihon,* the Atwater Métro station — and a speedy trip back to midtown Montreal on Métro line No. 1.

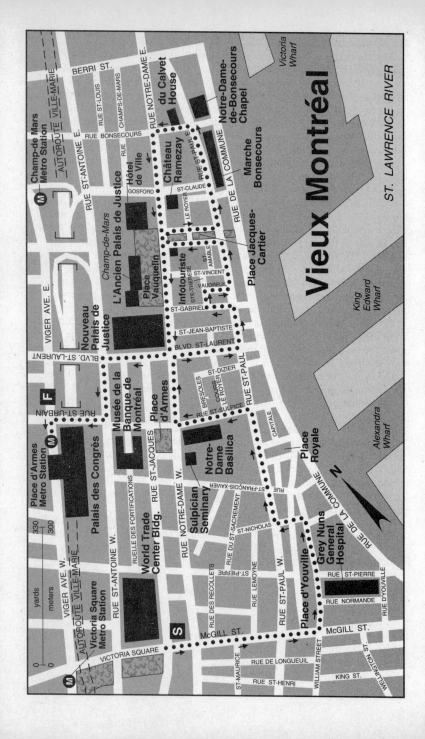

Walk 2: Vieux Montréal

Exploring the birthplace of Canada's second-largest city can add up to an hour or a lifetime. In fact, resident historians often do make Vieux Montréal a lifelong career, charting the latest restoration projects in the once-neglected waterfront neighborhood. Self-appointed watchdogs of their hometown's deepest roots, they distrust a 20th-century approach to 17th-century territory. A missing wall plaque, an archaeological dig, a builder's crane, still inspire a spate of concerned letters to the editor from the undeclared sidewalk superintendents of Old Montreal.

History buffs will want to devote more time, but visitors should set aside at least 3 hours to visit the dominant landmarks and museums and relax over lunch or dinner in one of the fine restaurants or terrace cafés of the protected historic preserve.

Take the *Henri-Bourassa* (No.2) Métro line to Victoria Square station and exit via the square's southern outlet at the corner of McGill Street and St-Jacques Street West. Following McGill south toward the waterfront, you'll be tracing the course of the stone wall that once guarded the city's western approaches from, at various times, the Iroquois, the English, and the American colonists.

Look back now to the World Trade Center Building on the east side of McGill between Rue St-Jacques and Rue St-Antoine. The center straddles Ruelle des Fortifications (Fortifications Lane), where, in 1716, urban planners began construction of the town's northern ramparts. Within 20 years they'd enclosed some 95 acres of the continent's fur-trading capital with an 18-foot-high fortification that commanded the waterfront from McGill to a point just east of present-day Berri Street. The walls and their gates were leveled less than a century later when the port city outgrew its obsolete defense system.

Where the southwest corner of the wall once stood, the former Grand Trunk Building (at 360 McGill) faces Place d'Youville. Turn east here; 1 block farther is a broad, brick-paved pedestrian island, surrounded by historic buildings. Pass them by for the moment and proceed to the granite obelisk at the eastern point of the wedge-shape plaza. Bronze plaques at its base commemorate the arrival of Montreal's first settlers; on May 18, 1642, some 3 dozen pioneers and their leader, Paul de Chomedy, Sieur de Maisonneuve, took their first hopeful steps into a primeval wilderness. Caught up in the religious revival that blazed through 17th-century France, the landing party's leading lights had come to found a mission and spread the gospel among Canada's first citizens. Protégés of wealthy sponsors of the *Société de Notre-Dame* in Paris, they'd spent a sheltered winter in the Quebec settlement before sailing upstream with de Maisonneuve, a career soldier the society had hired to direct them in what was to be a "glorious enterprise." Few had any conception of the sacrifice that lay ahead.

Try to imagine that springtime landing at a riverbank site Samuel de Champlain had explored and approved 3 decades earlier. At Point-à-Callière, the grassy meadow where the devout little mission band knelt over the firelight to celebrate its first mass of thanksgiving, stands the new *Archaeological History Center of Montreal;* a work in progress, upon its completion (scheduled for the end of this year) visitors will be able to look down into the archaeological digs that recount the centuries. Historians believe they've discovered the foundations of the stockade the founders erected around their vulnerable mission outpost before the first ghastly winter set in. The museum covers the location of the small Fort Maisonneuve, garrisoned near the meeting of the Little St-Pierre and the St. Lawrence rivers centuries before landfill and harbor construction pushed the waterfront far beyond the lush, green common where the colonists' cattle once grazed. The paved stretches of Rue de la Commune were once a 17th-century village green, and parklands of the Vieux Port restoration cover the riverbank with bike paths and decorative planting.

Before leaving the cradle of Vieux Montréal, stroll around one of the city's early market squares, opened in the 19th century over the dried-up riverbed of the Little St-Pierre. At 335 Place d'Youville the *Montreal History Center* (phone: 514-872-3207) is at home in a 90-year-old fire station (see "Special Places" in *Montreal,* THE CITIES). On the square's south side, the weathered stone walls of the Grey Nuns' General Hospital (138 Rue St-Pierre) still dominate the block between Rue St-Pierre and Rue Normand. One of the original wings of the 1694 refuge for the ailing, elderly, and orphaned has been restored (phone: 514-842-9411 for guided tours) in the place where a Montreal saint, Mother Marie-Marguerite d'Youville, founder of the Congrégation des Soeurs de la Charité (Grey Nuns) and North America's first home for abandoned children, died in 1771. Still on the south side of the square (at 296-316 Place d'Youville), the old warehouses of the *Youville Stables* have been brought back to useful life around a tranquil garden courtyard. Parts of the complex date from the 1700s, but the reborn storage depot for 19th-century grain merchants and soap manufacturers is one of the historic quarter's most attractive restorations, with office space and artisans' studios sharing a picturesque location with *Gibby's,* a popular steakhouse (phone: 514-282-1873).

From Place d'Youville follow Rue St-Nicolas uphill to Rue St-Paul and turn east. Before it had a name or a street sign, St-Paul was a narrow path through the woods, linking the fort to Montreal's first hospital. It was a dangerous route to follow once Iroquois scouts discovered the new settlement. Mortal enemies of the Algonquian and Huron — whom the French had befriended — the Iroquois were ill-disposed to the settlers expanding their river colony, and for the next 50 years villagers and their forest-dwelling allies lived in a virtual state of war with the Iroquois intruders. Happily, this first thoroughfare is a safer path today.

After 5 PM some walkers interrupt their rovings for a while at *L'Air du Temps* (191 Rue St-Paul; phone: 514-842-2003), a small, smoky jazz *boîte* on the northeast corner of Rue St-François-Xavier. Or you could take time out for coffee at *Le Pot aux Roses Café* next door (No. 184; phone: 514-282-1509). But if you manage to resist these temptations and continue east along the settlers' Main Street, you'll come upon Place Royale. This was the mission's first public square, where, within 3 years of their arrival in 1642, headstrong first families were settling into new housing. Maisonneuve drilled his defense forces and punished the colony's lawbreakers here. Appropriately, the parade ground was called Place d'Armes; later it served as a public market and fur-trading center, with the requisite gallows and pillory, a town crier's corner, a fountain — and plenty of dueling space for the hot-headed. Built in 1837, the neo-classic Customs House in the center of the square marks about the midpoint of Montreal's long history.

Nearly 2 centuries earlier, Maisonneuve's home faced the square from the north side of his namesake street. Nothing remains of the founder's household today, but if you turn into the open courtyard at 147 St-Paul you'll see a wall plaque marking the spot.

A few yards to the east, another wall plaque marks the birthplace of Charles Le Moyne, eldest of a remarkable brood of 11 brothers sired by a Dieppe innkeeper who immigrated to Ville Marie during the early Maisonneuve regime. A linguist who soon learned the Iroquois dialect, Le Moyne served as the colony's interpreter in its rare cease-fire encounters with the enemy; eventually, he found his place among the frontier town's leading citizens, first as Baron of Longueuil and later, Governor of Montreal. The Le Moyne household covered an area in the northeast corner of St-Paul and Rue St-Sulpice. A family compound for 14 children, Père Le Moyne's property extended north on St-Sulpice, where a wall plaque honors Montreal's first Canadian-born hero. Charles's brother, Pierre Le Moyne d'Iberville (1661–1706), was a leading figure in the Anglo-French power struggle for New World supremacy. Admiral of the Sun King's fleet, he won the decisive naval confrontation with the British in the Battle at Hudson Bay. He then went on to found Biloxi, Mississippi, and Mobile, Alabama, and add all Louisiana to the North American empire of French King Louis XIV. His younger brother, Jean-Baptiste Le Moyne de Bienville, founded New Orleans and was three times Governor of Louisiana.

Jeanne Mance was a hero who marched to a different drummer. One of the original founding group, she opened Ville Marie's first hospital at the northeast corner of St-Paul and St-Sulpice 2 years after the Pointe-à-Callière landing. North America's first secular nurse kept a small farm here to support her fortified compound of hospital wards and chapel, commuting daily from the fort when the Iroquois threat was at its worst. Her Hôtel Dieu stockade once enclosed part of what is now the stylish Cours Le Royer condo development, which strollers can admire today as they climb up St-Sulpice to Place d'Armes. Double rows of massive stone warehouses that once belonged to Hôtel Dieu's Soeurs Hospitalières de Saint-Joseph now house offices, shops, and condominiums. They line both sides of a long pedestrian courtyard where fountains play in geranium garden plots and old-fashioned lamp standards light a brick-paved promenade.

St-Sulpice follows the east walls of Sacré-Coeur Chapel and Notre-Dame

Basilica (see "Special Places" in *Montreal,* THE CITIES) to Place d'Armes and the oldest building in Montreal. Next door to the basilica (a relative newcomer to the *place*), the venerable Sulpician Seminary still stands on the plot the gentlemen of St-Sulpice staked out for it in 1685. The Sulpicians were the first parish priests; but by the time they built their administrative center they'd acquired full seigneurial rights over the entire island of Montreal, giving them the power to administer the courts and appoint governors.

The west section of the seminary (at 130 Rue Notre-Dame W.) has been standing, unchanged, behind its rough fieldstone walls for 308 years. The clock over the façade is the oldest public timepiece in North America. Rue Notre Dame, the first street the Sulpicians laid out, forms the south side of Place d'Armes, the flower-banked stage for Montreal's famous memorial to Maisonneuve and his fellow colonists. The founder's bold soldierly figure tops the fountain monument, drawn sword in one hand, the banner of France in the other, marking a near-fatal encounter with the Iroquois when Place d'Armes was still a forest clearing. Forewarned of an Indian attack, Maisonneuve led his outnumbered garrison out beyond the palisades to confront a force of 200 foes. Legend has it Maisonneuve covered a successful retreat with pistols blazing in both hands. He suffered a serious wound before the Iroquois chief fell under fire and the warriors fled.

Statues at the base of the monument represent nurse Jeanne Mance tending an Indian child, citizen Charles Le Moyne, Major Lambert Closse, commanding officer of Ville Marie's militia, a subdued Iroquois brave, and Pilote, the mission's one-dog early-warning system. As resident historians will tell you, Pilote and her uncanny canine knack of sensing approaching danger saved the day for embattled Ville Marie on more than one occasion.

Leaving Place d'Armes, follow Rue Notre-Dame eastward to the corner of Boulevard St-Laurent, the division between old west end Ville Marie and "new" 18th- and 19th-century Montreal. Walk down St-Laurent toward the river and the boulevard entrance to Cours Le Royer. Just inside the court on the north wall, a window display shows the plan of the original Hôtel Dieu. Continue now down St-Laurent to its intersection with St-Paul and a shopping spree along the north side of Montreal's first commercial street.

Near the corner of Rue St-Jean-Baptiste, *Sonja Rémy's* little boutique (1-A St-Paul E.; phone: 514-393-9023) vibrates with the latest colorful fashion trends. On the east corner, *Chez Brandy* (25 St-Paul; phone: 514-871-9178), moves to a different beat after dark when its regular bar-hopping clientele shows up. At midday it's a reasonably priced lunch stop. Next door, at the same address, *The Keg* caters to steak and seafood enthusiasts after 5 PM and to party animals late into the night (phone: 514-871-9093).

At the corner of Rue St-Gabriel, *Restaurant du Vieux Port* (39 Rue St-Paul E.; phone: 514-866-3175) features a lunch and dinner *brochetterie* menu at modest table d'hôte prices. If you have something more festive in mind, turn north on St-Gabriel to the *Auberge le Vieux St-Gabriel* (426 Rue St-Gabriel; phone: 514-878-3561). The *auberge* has been a going concern on this spot since 1754, keeping fresh its claim as the oldest continuously operated inn in North America. A sprawling conglomerate of cavernous, stone-walled dining rooms in the old Quebecois style, it also boasts intimate café corners and a historic beer-and-sausage snack bar, all combined under one oak-beamed roof (see "Eating Out" in *Montreal,* THE CITIES).

You're in the heart of 18th-century fur-trading territory now. The inn's cellar bar and its access tunnel were storage vaults for beaver pelts and other products of the trap. Across St-Gabriel on the east side, Rue Ste-Thérèse leads to a rakish-looking condo dwelling at the corner of Rue Vaudreuil. Built in 1759, this was the warehouse trader John Jacob Astor operated when he was building the power base for one of America's wealthiest families.

Rue Vaudreuil leads back to St-Paul and the birthplace of Canadian banking. The Bank of Montreal was founded at 32 St-Paul at the corner of Vaudreuil in 1817. A wall plaque marks the site of the bank's first office, where Canada's first currency was issued. Continue east now to the corner of Rue St-Vincent, and then north to see one of Vieux Montréal's oldest examples of domestic architecture in Maison Beaudoin. The historic monument (at 427 St-Vincent) was built in 1690 while Louis XIV still ruled New France, reconstructed in 1750, and restored in 1972. Today it's the home of *Le Père St-Vincent* restaurant (431 Rue St-Vincent; phone: 514-397-9610).

Genial hosts at the *Hôtel Richelieu* used to refresh their guests with noggins of punch and ale in the ornamental gallery of their 1861 hostelry. It's now home to *Restaurant Claude Postel* (443 Rue St-Vincent; phone: 514-875-5067) where genial host Claude Postel serves his distinctive brand of Canadian cuisine.

Backtracking to the north side of Rue St-Paul you'll be on the western frontier of Place Jacques-Cartier, the thoroughly quaint Old World town square travelers expect to see when they visit Vieux Montréal (see *Quintessential Montreal/Quebec City* in DIVERSIONS).

Coming upon this broad hillside plaza from the crowded confines of Rue St-Paul is like walking into a stage setting for a historic film. Only the cast of characters, in their unsuitable 20th-century costumes, seems out of place on Montreal's 19th-century market square. Still, the *place* itself lives up to every expectation, suitably bricked with ankle-testing paving stones, its center mall bright with flowers, its terrace cafés shaded with colorful awnings and umbrellas.

Turn to the river and you'll find the *calèche* queue waiting for weary explorers who decide to finish their tour under horsepower. Beyond the horse-and-carriage line at the south end of the long, rectangular *place,* Vieux Port's promenades and parklets open on breezy views of the St. Lawrence, the *Expo '67* islands, and the south shore skyline. Turn to the plaza's northern limit to see Admiral Horatio Nelson in an uncharacteristic pose. Back turned to the waterfront, he gazes inland across Rue Notre-Dame from the top of his 1809 column. In summer a flower market blooms around the base of this oldest remaining monument in Montreal.

There's a wide choice of restaurant options on either side of the *place.* Walk north from St-Paul up the west side to the house Pierre del Vecchio built in 1807 at 404 Place Jacques-Cartier. In family hands until 1946, the handsome old home now houses *La Marée,* an expensive seafood restaurant that many local connoisseurs consider the best in Montreal (phone: 514-861-8126). Next door is the Benjamin Viger House, built in 1772. A radical lawyer and publisher, Viger was jailed for 18 months for his part in the rebellion of 1837, under Louis Joseph Papineau (see below). The home of the former rebel now harbors *Le St-Amable,* another French dining establishment, with plenty of stone-wall-and-candlelight atmosphere and prices to match (188 St-Amable; phone: 514-866-3471; also see *Montreal's Best Restaurants* in DIVERSIONS). Wander down quaint lane-width Rue St-Amable to find the front door of its namesake restaurant and you'll pass a street gallery of artists and craftspeople displaying their wares.

At the corner of Rue Notre-Dame, INFOTOURISTE, Montreal's tourist information center (174 Rue Notre-Dame E.) now occupies the house built in 1811 by master mason Nicolas Morin. At its most notorious, the Morin Building became the home of the *Silver Dollar Saloon,* where patrons could boast they "walked on a fortune" when they bellied up to the bar. The floor was paved with 350 US silver dollars.

Cross to the east side of Place Jacques-Cartier now for a corner view of the Hôtel de Ville (City Hall), a majestic Second Empire fixture at 275 Notre-Dame E. since 1878. Only the exterior walls of the original building were salvaged from the ashes of a 1922 fire and much of its early elegance has been diminished by additions and alterations.

Meander down the east side of the *place* to No. 421 and the old (1866) *Nelson* hotel, once the folksy rendezvous for farmers who set up their wagons and stalls when the area was a working marketplace. The last stalls disappeared in the 1960s and, after many attempts to revive the hotel, its facilities have disappeared, too. Now the building is a branch of the city's cultural affairs deparment and in one of Vieux Montréal's secret gardens is tucked away a delightful restaurant, *Maison Cartier* (ca. 1812; 407 Pl. Jacques-Cartier; phone: 514-861-5731). A wrought-iron archway opens off the street and, in summer, the *Maison* becomes a cool oasis under the trees where reasonably priced alfresco meals are served to the sounds of live chamber music. Crêpes, salads, and sandwiches are *spécialités de la maison.*

On a lazy summer afternoon it's a temptation to linger in the shade of Terrasse Nelson, but those caught in the spirit of Old Montreal will find treaures await: Most of the best restorations in Montreal line both sides of Rue St-Paul's last few blocks. Turn toward the river again and head for St-Paul, past the corner house (No. 401) that Amable Amyot added to the Place Jacques-Cartier scene in 1812. On the north side of the block (281 St-Paul E.) facing little Rue du Marché Bonsecours, a sturdy survivor of Victorian Montreal's tourist boom recalls an era when *Rasco's* hotel was one of North America's finest. Celebrities of the day throughout Montreal's long history stayed here, including Charles Dickens, who stayed in splendid style at the *Rasco* in 1842 when he made his debut as an actor, winning a rave review for his role in a farce called *High Life Below Stairs. Rasco's* was almost brand-new at the time, a classic-revival extravagance of salons, concert hall, and ballroom that Italian hotelier Franco Rasco introduced to Montreal's beau monde in 1836. Neglected for years at the end of its golden era, it was restored 10 years ago by the city as municipal office space.

Look for the silvery white dome of Marché Bonsecours (330 St-Paul E.), another landmark now housing civil servants. The neo-classical building has dominated the waterfront skyline since 1864, when it was erected over a capacious public building that stretched over 3 city blocks. Built in 1845 to accommodate Montreal's City Hall, the multipurpose complex also housed reception rooms, council chambers, and the police headquarters. A city market was once installed in the basement and around the exterior walls, on the site of the 17th-century *Marché Neuf*, which replaced Ville Marie's first shopping mall on Place Royale. The mayor and his councilors moved up to their new Rue Notre-Dame palace in 1878, but the market prospered under its graceful Renaissance dome for more than a century. The city renovated the interior 30 years ago; current plans call for the building to one day be open to the public as a museum.

East of the market at the corner of Rue Bonsecours, Notre-Dame-de-Bon-Secours Chapel (400 St-Paul E.; phone: 514-845-9991) stands out as Montreal's most appealing historic property. Still the spiritual sanctuary Ste-Marguerite Bourgeoys dreamed it would be in 1675 when she chose the site for a tiny chapel beyond the safety of Ville Marie's stockades, today's edifice is the third incarnation of the original. But while the building has changed, the spirit within remains. Enter here and sense the aura of Old Montreal. Enshrined within is an ancient wooden image of the Virgin, reputed to work miracles for sailors on dangerous seas. Still referred to as the Sailors' Church, its rooftop Madonna, arms outstretched to the harbor, presents a welcoming, nostalgic sight to Montreal mariners returning home after a week or a lifetime. Take time to visit the chapel's upstairs museum, dedicated to the life of one of Canada's truly great women — the first schoolmistress, first saint, and founder of the first Canadian order of non-cloistered nuns, Congrégation Notre-Dame. For a spire-high view of Vieux Montréal and the port, climb up to the observation deck above the apse; then go up Rue Bonsecours to admire a block of impeccably restored 18th- and 19th-century houses (see "Special Places" in *Montreal,* THE CITIES).

US history buffs should not miss a visit to du Calvet House (on the east corner at 401 St-Paul E.), where the enthusiastic supporter of the War for Independence once lived. In 1775, American soldiers invaded and held Montreal for 7 months in the hopes of convincing French Canada to renounce the British crown and join the fledgling republic. They did not have to convince Pierre du Calvet, a Huguenot merchant who during the occupation supported the revolutionary cause with goods and services. But when the effort failed and the Americans withdrew, du Calvet was tried for his "treason," served a long prison term, and was eventually banished. Ponder the tragic fate of the patriot of American causes over a ham and cheese on rye or a smoked meat sandwich at the deli counter in the current building. The house has been restored and the ground floor is a neighborhood lunchroom, with a few snack tables for deli customers, plus take-out sandwiches, house specials, and wine.

Encounter history of a more commerical type at *Les Filles du Roy* restaurant, halfway up the block (415 Rue Bonsecours; phone: 514-849-3535), where a 17th-century past is preserved in an authentically restored 18th-century building (see "Eating Out" in *Montreal,* THE CITIES). Today's waitresses dress according to the frontier fashions of 1662–1672, a decade when "The King's Girls," royally dowered by Louis XIV, were shipped off to find husbands among the lonely bachelor settlers and the Carignan-Salières Regiment, 400 men who chose to stay in Canada after quelling an Iroquois uprising, and to keep the cradles rocking.

A century after the first brides-to-be disembarked at Ville Marie, local architect Jean-Baptiste Cérat built a fine 4-story house (440 Rue Bonsecours) with walls 4-feet thick and a noble carriage entrance to an inner courtyard and garden. Louis-Joseph Papineau, a member of the legislative assembly and leader of the 1837 rebellion in Lower Canada, bought the house 10 years after the ill-fated uprising; 440 Rue Bonsecours was then a fashionable address. The property remained in Papineau family hands for 6 generations, but it declined with the neighborhood, neglected and defaced with ugly additions until it was salvaged by a dedicated Montreal conservationist. Music critic Eric McLean, an urban pioneer, bought the deteriorating property in the early 1960s and restored it at his own expense, marking the beginning of the revitalization of Old Montreal.

Turn west onto Rue Notre-Dame at the corner and walk back toward Place Jacques-Cartier. Opposite City Hall you'll discover one of the best-preserved relics of the French colonial regime in *Château Ramezay,* built in 1705 as the oficial residence of Claude de Ramezay, 11th Governor of Montreal (see "Special Places" in *Montreal,* THE CITIES). The château museum (280 Notre-Dame E.; phone: 514-861-3708) has been restored to reflect its original role as combined colonial office and family home of 13 children and furnished in the period — from governor's office to basement kitchen.

Cross Notre-Dame to Place Vauquelin on the north side where the statue of a French naval hero stares across the traffic stream — and the centuries — at the victor of Trafalgar. Lieutenant Jean Vauquelin, who defended New France to the last in the 1759 battle for Quebec, faces Admiral Nelson from a statue base above the *place* fountain.

Pause here for a moment for a sweeping view of Champ-de-Mars, once a spiffy military parade ground where crack regiments from the British garrison put on a daily show of regulation drill and promenading Montrealers gathered to listen to the bands. A city works project is returning the raised terrace to its original use as a public promenade. Back on the north side of the street, just west of Place Vauquelin, L'Ancien Palais de Justice is one of three courthouses you'll pass on Notre-Dame, each built at a different period in the city's history. The old Palais at No. 155 was raised in 1856 on the site of an older courthouse, designed in the popular classic-revival style. The dome was added later, at a cost that generated the kind of public outcry that besieged the controversial retractable roof on today's *Olympic Stadium.*

Across Allée des Huissiers is the Nouveau Palais de Justice; built in 1926, its magnificent copper doors and Art Deco lamp standards were designed by Montreal architects Amos, Saxe, and Cormier. Today the Ernest Cormier Building (100 Notre-Dame E.) is devoted more to culture than criminal cases; Quebec's Ministry of Cultural Affairs maintains a conservatory of music and dramatic arts here.

Across St-Laurent on the northwest corner of Notre-Dame, a link in *Mc-Donald's* golden-arched chain serves Big Macs on a site the founder of Detroit once called home. Antoine Laumet, also known as de Lamothe Cadillac, Seigneur of Port-Royal and Governor of Louisiana, built a corner house here in 1694. Walk down the slope of St-Laurent past Ruelle des Fortifications to Rue St-Antoine, where a stream of the same name once ran below the north wall of Vieux Montréal. Two blocks to the west is Rue St-Urbain, the nearest entrance to Place d'Armes Métro station, a convenient underground route back to home base from the birthplace of Montreal.

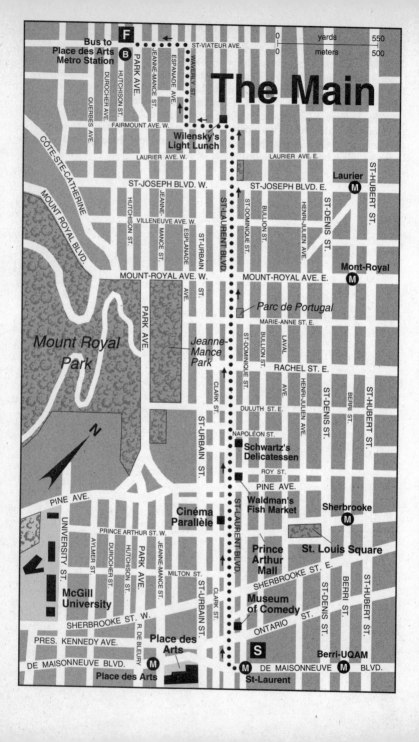

Walk 3: The Main

It may be a concrete jungle now, but The Main was not always this way. Try to imagine bustling St-Laurent Boulevard as a pleasant country road through apple orchard farms and hillside meadows. It was along this road that Montreal pushed beyond its walls and linked the picturesque Rivière-des-Prairies on the island's north shore and became the road to divide east and west Montreal.

By the 1830s it was the road to suburbia and the country retreats well-heeled townsmen staked out among the habitant farms below the eastern slopes of Mount Royal. But, St-Laurent (or St. Lawrence) Boulevard is better known among locals as Main Street or The Main, the Great Divide between east and west — from its ox-cart beginnings to its traffic-jammed present.

Once the shopping preserve of the horse-and-carriage trade, The Main stream and its east-west tributaries opened up to the average-income citizen when the first horse-drawn trams struggled up the hill to Plateau Mont-Royal in the gaslight era. In the 1880s, a new surge of settlers, refugees from the Russian and Polish pogroms, began building new lives on or around St-Laurent Boulevard. As the Jewish community moved north, successive waves of newcomers from Greece, Eastern Europe, Portugal, Spain, Latin America, and the Middle East, settled into the neighborhood's old cold-water flats and cramped Victorian cottages.

Wave after wave of immigrants have changed the face of Old St-Laurent, in modern times transforming a once-dingy, abandoned industrial strip into a crucible of ethnic vitality — from its Ukrainian bakeries and Polish sausage shops to its Hungarian restaurants and Mexican coffee bars. The latest migratory trend, led by a young pioneer force of artists, designers, and architects, spruced up upper Main not that long ago when they established studios and apartments in the abandoned factory lofts. Entrepreneurs joined the trend, opening bars, boutiques, restaurants, and other public places, reshaping nondescript buildings with glass tubing, suspended sheet metal, and halogen spot runners. The urban revival has not extended to lower Main, however. After dark, the Ste-Catherine Street intersection is a place that strollers can afford to miss.

By day avid explorers along lower Main will find two disparate civic monuments. Built in 1894, 2 years after tracks for electric streetcars were laid along The Main, the old Union National Building at 1182 St-Laurent displays little of its old glory; at one time its theater provided the stage for first-rate drama and rousing political meetings. The *National Theater School* moved in in the 1970s and still mounts student productions on the original stage. And connoisseurs of local food history will appreciate the *Montreal Pool Room* (200 St-Laurent; phone: 514-861-1397). For longer than anyone can remember the *Pool Room* has been serving "steamies," Montreal's exclusive version of the hot dog. Even the city's most finicky food fanatics find no conflict in enjoying the taste of the city's most notable junk food. When former Mayor Jean Drapeau was in office, he made the *Pool Room* a regular port of call. It was the source of his favorite nosh, a steaming-hot, juicy frankfurter on a doughy roll, garnished with onions, *cornichons* (small, sweet pickles), mustard, coleslaw — the works — with a side order of *frites*. Steamies still sell for $1.05, "all-dressed or plain — same price," says the current cook.

The St-Laurent station on the No. 1 Métro line is the best place to start a sunny-day Saturday stroll up The Main. Allow about 4 hours for the tour if you're into serious window shopping, snacking, and detours along some of the more intriguing side streets.

If you'd like a drink, cross Sherbrooke and indulge yourself while you see how an imaginative new design approach has upgraded a working man's tavern into a chic restaurant. *Boulevards* (3435 St-Laurent; phone: 514-499-9944) has replaced a utilitarian pub decor with a black-and-russet marble theme, sectioned off space into a convivial bar and three small dining areas, and stretched a cloud-covered "sky" over the whole. For a bite, a few storefronts north at No. 3479 is *Csarda,* which hasn't joined the nouvelle *"vague"* of interior decoration. Old-fashioned lace curtains and a window of red geraniums create a cozy, Old World atmosphere on the second floor of this Hungarian restaurant complex, which features dinner-theater productions Saturday and Sunday nights (phone: 514-843-7519). If you catch the shopping bug or want to watch the young and flashy Montrealers picking out their new ensembles, try *Parachute* (No. 3526; phone: 514-845-7865), the flagship of the Parnass-Pelly fashion fleet of four boutiques where the firm's original couture creations are available. The St-Laurent outlet is a stark cement-and-steel warehouse of tomorrow-designed fashion that caters to local and transient trendies. Back on the east side of the street is *Shed Café* (No. 3515; phone: 514-842-0220), the current "in" spot where bright young French-speaking party people gather to see and be seen, hopefully in the vicinity of French network television stars.

Pause at the Prince Arthur Street intersection now, where the pedestrian mall of the same name begins. Take a moment to look down this colorful restaurant row to St. Louis Square, but don't venture in if you've reserved the day for The Main. *Prince Arthur Mall,* with its strolling minstrels, moderately priced ethnic restaurants, and terrace cafés, is a walk for another day (see *Walk 5: McGill University–Prince Arthur Street*).

Opposite the mall entrance note the trees among the lampposts and, proceeding north, the benches and sidewalk planters — all part of a beautification project for "Village St-Laurent." North of Prince Arthur on The Main's west side *Cinéma Parallèle* (No. 3682; phone: 514-845-6001) is the driving force behind the annual October *Festival International du Nouveau Cinéma de Montréal,* Canada's oldest international cinema and video event. Between festivals, the theater screens intellectual and experimental films and operates *Café Meliès* next door (phone: 514-281-0525). *Librairie Gallimard* (No. 3700; phone: 514-499-2012), Montreal's most prestigious multilingual bookstore, translates the spirit of a staid academic reading room into an ultra-contemporary setting designed by architect Shulim Rubin.

From food for thought to something more substantial move on to Pine Avenue and a European-style sausage fix at the *Zagreb Charcuterie* (3766 St-Laurent; phone: 514-844-3265). Or cross over to 3711 St-Laurent for a quick sushi fix at *Sushibar* (phone: 514-845-2881). Almost next door, *Le Sam* (No. 3715; phone: 514-842-0653) is one of the new, scrupulously austere restaurants the young lions of Montreal's design community have added to the folksy east side section of The Main.

At Roy Street turn east off St-Laurent for a salty shopping experience in one of North America's largest wholesale-retail fish markets. On Saturday mornings all of Montreal's multicultural world seem to meet at *Waldman's Fish Market* (74 Roy St. E.; phone: 514-842-4483). Even if your shopping list doesn't include fresh Dover sole, pompano, and abalone, it's fun to go fishing in Waldman's pond and observe a buyers' feeding frenzy over the freshest catch of the day.

Back on The Main track, stop at *La Vieille Europe* (No. 3855) to sample the cheese selection before calling in at *Warshaw's Supermaket,* a St-Laurent landmark since 1935, when the Warshaw family left Poland to open a small green-grocery at the rear of a butcher shop. Another landmark that's a legend among Montrealers is *Montreal Hebrew Delicatessen and Steak House* (3895 St-Laurent; phone: 514-842-4813), commonly known as *Schwartz's* (see *Quintessential Montreal/Quebec* in DIVERSIONS). Old St-Laurent is the nosh-belt of Montreal, so loosen a notch or two on your belt and try one of the sandwich favorites here. A fixture on The Main since 1927, this crowded, steamy shrine to the smoked meat (a.k.a. an almost pastrami/corned beef) sandwich claims it's the last of the perfectionists in Montreal to smoke its own house special.

Cross Napoléon Street now for a look-see at *Moishe's Steak House* (3961 St-Laurent; phone: 514-845-1696), where the tenderly aged western Canadian beef comes in Texas-size portions and the tab comes to match. Moishe Lighter founded this granddaddy of Montreal steakhouses 55 years ago when hungry customers knew big was better and cholesterol hadn't entered the diner's vocabulary (see "Eating Out" in *Montreal,* THE CITIES).

Before continuing north into Montreal's Little Soho district (so named for its similarity of character to New York City's Soho), turn east at Rachel Street into Place des Amériques, which reflects the Latin American influence on this section of The Main. Another small park farther up the block north of Marie-Anne Street is a nostalgic reminder of the boulevard's Portuguese connection. Parc de Portugal lives up to its name with a quaint little bandstand with colorful tiles lining its plaza, recapturing travel-poster memories of a village square back on the Iberian Peninsula.

Across the street, *Oslo Furs* (4316 St-Laurent; phone: 514-499-1777) is one of The Main's main outlets for quality fur and leatherwear. *Bagel-Etc* (No. 4320; phone: 514-845-9462), just south of Marie-Anne, is a late-night, diner-style restaurant for chic insomniacs, featuring an eclectic menu and taped jazz. Open weekdays from 11 AM to 4 AM (9 PM to 6 AM Fridays and Saturdays), it's also a popular rendezvous for Sunday brunchers.

Four blocks north, one of Montreal's great halls of fire dominates the corner of Laurier Avenue and The Main. The baronial No. 30 fire station started life pretentiously in early French Renaissance style as the City Hall for suburban St-Louis du Mile End in 1905. Only 10 years ago, the blocks between Laurier and St-Viateur Avenues were gray areas of small businesses and factories, corner variety stores, and quick lunch counters; today, the neighborhood gets busier by the year with new fashion outlets, design studios, and restaurants. *Prego* (5142 St-Laurent; phone: 514-271-3234; see "Eating Out" in *Montreal*, THE CITIES) was the first to introduce nouvelle cuisine to the upper Main in 1984. The following year *Eclectic* (No. 5133; phone: 514-270-9144) opened in an aesthetic black-and-white temple of unisex beauty that designers Jacques Bilodeau and Jean-Pierre Viau created for compulsive trendsetters. A hair styling here includes a 10-minute scalp massage, wine, coffee, and a predictably high tab.

Just north of Fairmount Avenue *LUX* (No. 5520; phone: 514-271-9272) set the tone for the old business area's new ambience when it pioneered the northern frontiers of Little Soho. Luc Laporte designed this quirky core of late-late nightlife on The Main to accommodate an inexpensive restaurant, bar, snack counter, magazine store, pastry shop, and T-shirt boutique under one leaded-glass roof. Open 24 hours a day, *LUX* is at its multicultural best after midnight, when the upstairs piano bar draws the young and the restless from all corners of the city. The magazine racks on the mezzanine gallery are stocked with publications from around the world and the second-floor T-shirt collection features exclusive *LUX* creations you can't buy anywhere else in town. A local TV show is taped on the premises every Friday afternoon about 5 PM.

Turn west off The Main at Fairmount and you'll be in the heart of Mordecai Richler country. The world-renowned author and one of Montreal's most prominent citizens, Richler grew up on St-Urbain Street in the 1930s, when the Fairmount–St-Urbain crossroads was the hub of Jewish community life. But the neighborhood he described so vividly in his best-selling novel, *The Apprenticeship of Duddy Kravitz*, has changed since Richler brought the irrepressible Duddy to life 34 years ago. Only a few memories of the Kravitz era linger in cosmopolitan Fairmount today, among them a scrap of film history regular customers know as *Wilensky's Light Lunch* (34 Fairmount, corner of Clark St.; phone: 514-271-1247). Scenes from the 1974 movie version of Richler's novel were shot at Moe Wilensky's pokey little fast-food establishment. Step inside for a chapter of urban history in this pint-size luncheonette, where the daily specials are marked up over a foggy mirror behind the counter and an all-male clientele perches on tipsy stools. The Main and its west-side arteries used to support one of these salami-and-seltzer parlors on every other corner, but they're a dying breed in the age of chi-chi cafés and sophisticated restaurants.

Another old-timer on Fairmount is the *Bagel Factory*, founded a few blocks to the south by Itzac Shalfman in 1929 and relocated at 74 Fairmount West 20 years later. Shalfman's son and grandson still run the family business, which has served at least 4 generations of bagel mavens, all firmly convinced the Shalfman product is Canada's — if not the world's — most delectable (phone: 514-272-0667).

Take time to pause at the corners of Fairmount's north-south intersections between Clark Street and Park Avenue to admire the gentrification of a time-worn neighborhood. The prim little 2-story houses, with their pointed dormers and Victorian trim, are flushed with the colors Greek and Portuguese newcomers splashed over weathered brick, stone, and wood when they moved up The Main. Waverly Street is still lined with Montreal's famous balcony flats with their steep outside staircases, and St-Urbain is now one of the district's most attractive streets. Walk up from the Fairmount intersection toward St-Viateur Avenue past modest homes where Portuguese residents mark their presence with religious pictures at the front door and an Orthodox synagogue shares the block with a Buddhist house of worship and a Roman Catholic church. Byzantine Saint Michael the Archangel (5580 St-Urbain) accommodated a predominantly Irish congregation when it was built in 1915 and until the end of the Second World War it served the second-largest English-speaking parish in Quebec. Now affiliated with a Polish mission, Saint Michael celebrates mass bilingually — in English and Polish.

Walk west on St-Viateur past a kosher butcher, an Italian meat shop, and a Greek grocery to the *Bagel Shop* (No. 263; phone: 514-276-8044), also known as *Maison du Bagel*. Patrons of the aforementioned *Bagel Factory* and this St-Viateur shop have been engaged in an often touchy rivalry since the latter opened in 1956: Each side claims to bake the world's best bagel. *Bagel Shop* customers can watch the bakers at work any day of the week when they come to pick up their orders.

Walk west to Park Avenue now; here you can hop a No. 80 bus to *Place des Arts* Métro station and return to the midtown hotel strip on Sherbrooke Street East or West. But before boarding, stop by Montreal's newest venue for French-fried potato freaks. *Frite Alors* (5235A Park Ave.; phone: 514-948-2219) keeps busy on the lower floor of a renovated house across the street from *Club Soda*. While the daily bill of fare includes sausages, hot dogs, brochettes, and burgers, the house special is *frites*. Local connoisseurs claim this latest arrival on Park Avenue is the best thing that's happened to the spud in years. A small order (about $2) may be all you'll have room for after your gastronomy-oriented tour of The Main.

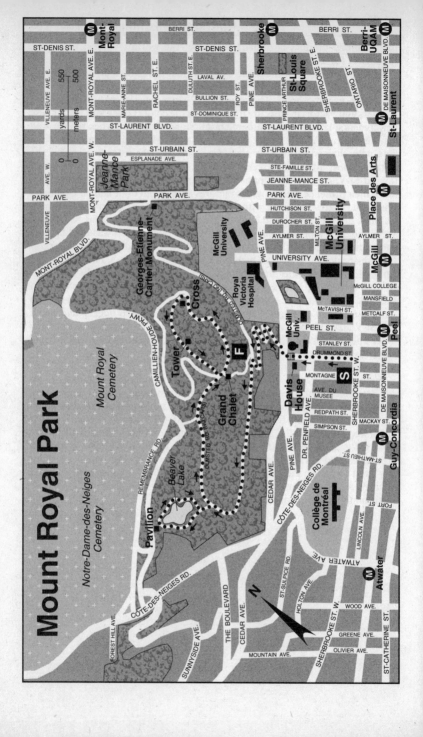

Walk 4: Mount Royal Park

When Montrealers crave a breath of fresh air, they don't necessarily join the autoroute trek to the Laurentians. After all, they have a perfectly adequate mountain right on their doorstep. Mount Royal Park's 496 airy acres of natural woodlands, grassy dells, and sylvan paths are all within a 10-minute cab ride of the city center.

No one makes better use of a resident mountain than the citizens of Quebec's high-rise metropolis. They ski it, toboggan it, and skate it; bird-watch its woods, jog and cycle its paths, sail toy boats on its willow-banked lake, picnic in its maple-treed shade, and admire the view from the heights of its observation terrace. But mostly they simply walk on it, happy to escape the noise and tensions of urban life for an hour or so, feed the fat, sassy squirrels, and listen to the sing-song of the birds.

Visitors who've overdosed on the wealth of dining, shopping, and other Montreal temptations learn to love the mountain, too — once they find their way around. Fanciers of New York City's Central Park may notice some similarities in the design of the landscape when they get here. And small wonder. Central Park's designer, American landscape architect Frederick Law Olmsted, planned Mount Royal Park in 1874 on the enduring premise that "the possession of charming natural scenery is a form of wealth."

There are many approaches to the mountain-crest oasis. The easy way to the top is by car, cab, or public transportation. If you have your own wheels, approach the western flank of the mountain via Côte-des-Neiges Road, driving north to Remembrance Road; turn right into the park, just beyond the Côte-des-Neiges Drill Hall. Remembrance Road leads to two meter-equipped public parking lots, one near Beaver Lake and a second, larger facility farther to the east where the road merges with Camillien-Houde Parkway. West-end bus passengers should board the No. 165 bus at the Guy-Concordia Métro station and transfer to No. 11 at the Forest Hill Avenue stop. No. 11 is the park's only public transport service. It follows Remembrance Road and the parkway along Mount Royal's northern crest from Côte-des-Neiges to Mont-Royal Avenue, with stops at Beaver Lake and other points along the route.

The eastern approach for motorists is via the same parkway, named for Camillien Houde, one of the city's more colorful and controversial mayors in the 1930s and 1940s. The scenic mayoral route merges with Mont-Royal Boulevard, Mont-Royal Avenue, and Park Avenue just west of Jeanne-Mance Park. The No. 11 bus embarks on its east-west parkway journey from Mont-Royal Métro station.

The parkway and Remembrance Road skirt the southern fringes of two city cemeteries, one Protestant and one Catholic, which spread over the north side of the mountain where hillside farms flourished until the 1850s. These were the first planned greenspaces in Montreal, the results of a 19th-century bylaw prohibiting burials within the city limits (no one at the time could have forseen that the city would spread up to and even beyond this area). Opened 20 years before Olmsted designed the mountain park, Protestant Mount Royal Cemetery is a park in itself, with roadways and paths winding through a peaceful retreat of towering old trees and flowering shrubs.

Among the monuments to the soldiers, politicians, fur traders, explorers, and financiers who shaped 19th-century Canada, the modest grave of Mrs. Anna Leonowens is easy to pass by. But don't if you've ever caught yourself humming "Shall We Dance" or "Getting to Know You." Anna Leonowens was the spunky Anna, governess to the children of the King of Siam, whose story formed the basis of *The King and I,* one of Broadway's most successful and best-loved musicals. How she ended up in Montreal is a story in itself: After finishing her grueling stint with the king she went home to England, where she wrote two books, the *English Governess at the Siamese Court* in 1870 and the *Romance of the Harem* in 1872. She then journeyed to New York with her two daughters to seek her fortune by trying to get the work adapted to the stage. But after repeated failures (*The King and I* did not become popular until long after her death — the play that was first staged in 1951 was based on a popular book about Anna's life, *Anna and the King of Siam,* written 8 years earlier by Margaret Landon.) In 1876, Anna followed to Halifax her daughter who was marrying a Canadian banker, and there became secretary of the Halifax Council of Women, a suffragette association, and helped form the Victorian School of Art and Design. She later moved to Montreal, where her daughter and son-in-law had moved, and died there in 1915. She would never know how well known her story would become.

Next door is the Catholic Cimetière de Notre-Dame-des-Neiges, opened in 1854. Larger than its Protestant neighbor, Mount Royal Cemetery, this vast space is the final resting place of more than a million Montrealers, among them Calixta Lavallée, composer of Canada's national anthem ("O Canada"), two Fathers of Confederation, and, the parkway's namesake, Camillien Houde.

The Camillien Houde–Remembrance Road route is the park's only concession to motor traffic. Olmsted Road, the old bridle path that loops around Mount Royal from the Sir Georges-Etienne Cartier Monument on Park Avenue to the meadows above Beaver Lake and the Grand Chalet at center park, is reserved for *calèche* traffic, bikers, and strollers. Olmsted Road meets a footpath that follows the park's eastern threshold to the massive monument to French Canada's great statesman and Father of Confederation. The monument site marks the most convenient eastern access to Mount Royal for walkers who'd rather putter along than pant up a series of steep pathways. A more challenging trek snakes up Drummond Street to the southwest slopes above Pine Avenue, one of the most accessible park gateways for midtown hotel guests in the Sherbrooke Street West area. Following this route, explorers will spend a good 3 hours on the mountain and its network of paths and trails.

Puffing uphill from the corner of Sherbrooke and Drummond, it's hard to believe the posh *Ritz-Carlton* hotel and its neighbors mark a half-way plateau on Mount Royal's long southwest slope. Now that it's paved and built over, most Montrealers forget their mountain's past, when the foothills' forest climbed upward from St-Antoine Street not far from the riverfront. Jacques Cartier knew it well, however, in 1535, when he pushed up from the river through a majestic forest of red oak and maple to the Indians' mountainside village of Hochelaga. "As beautiful as any forest in France," he gushed after his hosts led him on to the top of their world and the summit site of today's park.

The explorer who christened the "Royal Mountain" probably followed a trail a few blocks east of Drummond. Conjure up thoughts of that lost forest as you climb up through today's apartment-tower canyon to Dr. Penfield Avenue. Cross at the light to the northeast corner of this traffic speedway and take a breather by the landscaped terrace in front of the Phytotron, the greenhouse laboratory McGill University's biology department maintains for the advanced studies of plant development. The rotund tower overlooking the lab is the McIntyre Medical Building, another university property. Directly opposite (3654 Drummond) is Davis House, a red-brick replica of an English manor house, built in 1909 for a prominent Montreal family; it now accommodates McGill's department of physical and occupational therapy. The department also occupies the somewhat shabby sandstone mansion at 3630 Drummond. But the once-opulent relic of the Beaux Arts building boom was the talk of the town in 1907 when it was built for Charles Rudolph Hosmer, who made his fortune developing a telegraph system for the *Canadian Pacific Railway.*

Drummond dead-ends at a steep flight of steps to Pine Avenue. At the top, cross Pine at the stoplight and bear right to the serpentine access to Olmsted Road. There's a shortcut path on the left that cuts down the distance between the bridle path's elongated loops and a set of staircases halfway up the switchback road. But it's easier to gradually zigzag up the slope and leave the bypaths to conditioned climbers. The loopy roadway coils up into the woods and the junction with Olmsted's namesake carriageway, where you'll meet lots of fellow travelers on bikes, *calèches,* and, in winter, horse-drawn "sleighs" jingling along on fat rubber wheels instead of traditional runners. For reserving an honest-to-goodness sleigh (available from time to time during special occasions) try calling 514-653-0751.

Turn left at the junction and stroll on past the old horse trough, following the road to Beaver Lake. En route you'll pass through what's left of Jacques Cartier's forest. Some of the stands of red oak and maple, offspring of the Cartier-era groves, still attract the bluejays, cardinals, chickadees, and other representatives of the more than 150 feathered species that flutter through the park in their season. But most of today's coniferous and deciduous wood-lands — mountain ash, chestnut, and birch, wild cherry, spruce, and pine — are less than a century old. Replanting of the mountain forest began on a wide scale in the 1870s. Before that, hillside residents cut into the forest for firewood; but after one particularly severe winter public outcry against the practice was so intense that city fathers invited Olmsted to create a mountaintop preserve in keeping with his conviction that unspoiled nature was the great healer of body and soul.

Since the 1950s, when the instigators of a prissy public morality campaign tried to discourage amorous rendezvous by thinning out the maple groves and and slashing away the thickets, more than 100,000 trees have been planted over the mountain's bald spots, including the stands of pine and spruce the City Parks Department introduced to Mount Royal. Now, along with 600 species of herbaceous plants, the forest is home to not only chipmunks, squirrels, and rabbits, but groundhogs, skunks, and the occasional red fox.

A series of footpaths leads off the carriage road into the woods and a network of cross-country ski trails. If you climb the public staircase to the right, clamber up past the pumping station and turn right again at the first path — you'll be on the fast track to the Grand Chalet and its observation terrace, Mount Royal Lookout. Continuing west along the Olmsted route, less adventurous mountaineers come upon the gentle slopes of the park's toboggan slide and rope-tow ski run. Follow the first path to the left beyond the drinking fountain; Beaver Lake will take its free-form shape below the hill. Skaters cut a fine figure here in winter, warming up over hot chocolate at the lakeside pavilion, where there's a fast-food restaurant, washroom facilities, and pay telephones. In summer, the circuit around the large, manmade pond is a popular promenade and the shady groves above the water one of the city's coolest retreats. On weekends, taped music echoes through the trees to the open lawns where sun worshipers congregate and toy boat armadas bob along in the breeze. The stage by the pavilion is the scene of free summer concerts and folk-dancing sessions in which all comers are invited to take a whirl.

After rounding the lake, return to Olmsted Road the way you came and strike out on a quarter-hour walk to the Grand Chalet. Olmsted, whose mission was to keep the mountain park as close to its natural state as possible, probably would not be amused by the intrusion of this vast, echoing hall, a $200,000 work project constructed by the city in 1931–1932. Beaver Lake, on the site of a natural beaver pond, was another Depression-era product.

The chalet is used primarily for civic functions and exhibitions, but between galas it's well used as a rest stop for park regulars. Washroom, phone, and snack-bar facilities are tucked tactfully into the rear of the hall behind a seigneurial fireplace bearing the city crest. Here you can admire an impressive interior decor of heraldic crests and murals depicting highlights of the city's early history.

Out on the brink of the observation terrace, Mount Royal Lookout (see *Quintessential Montreal/Quebec City* in DIVERSIONS) is usually lined with horizon-scanners. US-born enthusiasts with a pang of homesickness swear they can see the Green Mountains of Vermont on a clear day. Centre de la Montagne, a nature interpretation and education center, conducts guided walks from its mountain headquarters next to the chalet. It also publishes a colorful walkers' map of Mount Royal and other informative literature (phone: 514-844-4928).

From the terrace, turn east and follow the inner circle of Olmsted Road toward one of Montreal's best-known beacons, the illuminated cross on the eastern summit of Mount Royal. And if you're a bird watcher, take time for a detour along any of the small paths laced through the wooded slopes on the left. Depending on the season, your binoculars will focus on cedar waxwings and yellow-bellied sapsuckers, rock doves and red-breasted nuthatches, even a visiting pheasant or two on an excursion from their Mount Royal Cemetery nesting grounds. The main track leads around the base of the Cross on Mount Royal, erected by the St-Jean-Baptiste Society in memory of the long-vanished wooden original that Paul de Chomedy, Sieur de Maisonneuve, planted on the mountaintop more than 3 centuries ago. The city's founder carried a rough-hewn oak cross 3 miles up into the mountain wilderness on a bitter January day in 1643, just weeks after a flood had threatened to destroy his frail riverside settlement. Maisonneuve had vowed to raise the cross in thanksgiving for Ville Marie's miraculous escape and, for years, the symbol of the colonists' gratitude drew worshipful pilgrims up the mountain. Such history easily comes to mind as you gaze at this meaningful Montreal landmark. Installed on *Christmas Eve* 1924, the 100-foot steel structure shines in different colors on special occasions, in purple for the death of a pope, for example.

A footpath on the right side of Olmsted's way circles the cross and leads directly to Mount Royal's highest point (763 feet) and the City of Montreal's Communications Tower, the "mast" through which vital information about fire, crime, and road conditions is transmitted. Follow the path down through the spruce glades for a close-up view of the Canadian Broadcasting Corporation's Tower. Although it's a CBC property, the candelabrum of antennas at the tower's tip, 1,100 feet above sea level, also transmits programs for other Montreal television and radio stations. (That was part of the deal CBC made with the Canadian government when the tower was built in 1963; it ensures against a forest of antennas sprouting up all over the mountaintop.)

A short-cut path leads down from the tower to a curve in Olmsted Road where the carriageway's inner circle joins the main circuit, just west of the Grand Chalet. A right turn here leads to the large parking complex and the No. 11 bus stop, probably a welcome sight for flagging trailblazers. Turn left and you'll be back at the chalet. Hardier souls can take the pathway down from the east side of the observation terrace to the public staircase and the lower level of Olmsted Road. Turn left to take the long road back to Park Avenue (and add 45 minutes to the tour). A right turn at the foot of the stairs leads back the way you came, down the meandering route to Pine Avenue and the stairs to Drummond Street.

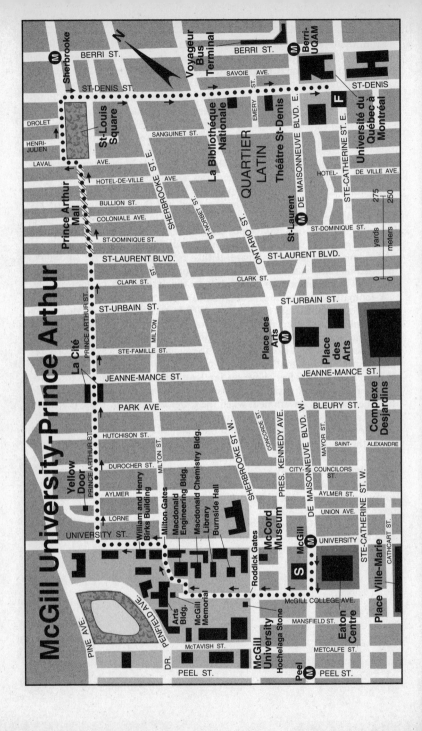

Walk 5: McGill University–Prince Arthur Street

Walking through the groves of academe is a pleasure the University of McGill shares with anyone who cares to pass through its Roddick Gates. They're always open at 805 Sherbrooke Street West, a courtesy downtowners appreciate in a neighborhood of corporate towers, hotels, and apartment blocks, where greenspace is at a premium. Visitors appreciate the open invitation, too, because the campus is the departure point for one of the city's most interesting walking tours, from one seat of higher education to another. This 2-hour stroll begins at McGill and ends at Université du Québec à Montréal (UQAM). It's a journey through changing times and neighborhoods, with a colorful pedestrian mall to bridge the gap between two student cultures.

The tour begins at the McGill College exit from McGill Métro station. Walking up the broad boulevard of McGill College Avenue, you'll see the campus vista opening below a wooded mountain backdrop, the octagonal dome of its first on-site lecture hall crowning the historic Arts Building at the end of a central driveway. The university's oldest building on campus didn't open its doors until 1839, a long 26 years after James McGill left his 46-acre mountainside estate and £10,000 sterling to the Royal Institute for the Advancement of Learning, on the understanding a university would be established in his name.

The founder was an enterprising Scot from Glasgow who made his mark (and his wealth) as a fur trader, merchant, army officer, and legislator. Unlike most of his Scottish contemporaries — who had left school early to seek their fortunes in booming 18th-century Montreal — McGill was a graduate of Glasgow University. Making a case for higher education in Quebec's business and financial capital was one of his priorities, and, dying childless, he bequeathed his beloved Burnside Hall ("burn" is a Scottish word for stream) to the cause. After years of litigation with other claimants, the Institute finally received its Royal Charter from King George IV in 1821 and the university's first college was founded. The first student body of 20 attended lectures in Burnside Hall, the unpretentious country home McGill built on the south side of today's Sherbrooke Street.

The squire's garden grew opposite the site of the Roddick Gates, but the grand entrance and its carillon clock was a later bequest. The imposing Greek-revival gateway opened in 1924 as a memorial to Sir Thomas George

Roddick, a benefactor and distinguished member of the university's medical faculty. Walk through them, past the security guard's post, and turn left off the drive to the Hochelaga Stone. The small granite boulder just inside the formal black iron fencing along Sherbrooke Street commemorates the Indian village of Hochelaga, which was still thriving behind its wooden stockade when Jacques Cartier visited more than 450 years ago.

The Iroquois villagers had moved on when Montreal's first European settlers arrived less than a century later. But McGill makes a point of remembering. It also remembers the Founder's Elm with a plaque on the tree stump on the right-hand side of the main drive in front of the Macdonald Physics Building (ca. 1890). Campus historians are convinced James McGill planted the tree himself in 1790 (before anyone knew about Dutch Elm disease). The afflicted tree was cut down 17 years ago, but still is revered as part of the philanthropic Glaswegian's legacy.

Turn back to the central drive and walk up toward the Arts Building. On the right is Burnside Hall, the modern computer center on the south border of the campus, just inside the fence; then the vintage physics building, home to the science and engineering library, followed by the Macdonald Chemistry Building (1896) and the Macdonald Engineering Building (1908). On the left, the university's old playing fields sweep up to Gertrude Vanderbilt Whitney's charming statue group of the Three Graces, irreverently known around campus as "The Three Bares."

Continue up the drive to the McGill Memorial in front of the Arts Building, where the founder's tomb rests under a quadrangular column topped by a funereal urn. (The monument, with McGill's remains, was moved from the Protestant cemetery on Dorchester Square when the old burial ground was closed in 1878.) The Arts Building behind the monument is the city's oldest academic structure still extant — although only the central façade and its dome date to 1839.

Return to the east branch of the drive, where neighborhood mothers bring their tots to play in the small children's park under the willow trees. Bear right past the McConnell Engineering Building and pass through the Milton Gates onto University Street. (For a more extensive tour, take advantage of the guided excursions around the campus, which McGill offers on 24 hours' notice; phone: 514-398-6555.)

You're on the threshold of the old student ghetto now, the never-never land of the 1960s and early 1970s when flower children roamed their romantic realm between the campus and Park Avenue, Sherbrooke Street, and Pine Avenue. Those were the Little Bohemia days when students could rent affordable rooms in rundown houses and apartment buildings along Milton and Prince Arthur Streets and the byways in between. But the flower children have faded away and the neighborhood has come an interesting full-circle to its genteel 19th-century beginnings.

Back in the 1850s when McGill was developing according to the founder's plan, the area east of University Street was still rural, sweet with apple orchards and hayfields. But at about this time upwardly mobile citizens made their escape from the crowded city below and moved into the fringes of uptown estate country in the shadow of Mount Royal. Here the newly wealthy built the next best thing to stately homes: substantial gray-stone terrace houses with big back gardens and tidy front lawns. Yet this desirable enclave of Victorian- and Edwardian-era households started to disintegrate in the 1920s as the old families sold out and the rooming-house operators moved in. Before long student strays who weren't living in university residences discovered a good thing in inexpensive rented rooms and shared apartments — and a new community of blithe spirits was born. Now Montreal's young families have reclaimed this most convenient of midtown neighborhoods and gentrified it beyond the means of the average student. Along with those who never bothered to leave, they've renovated near slums into cooperative housing, expensive condominiums, and single-family townhouses. Indeed, the old student ghetto is a prime piece of real estate today.

To explore one of its main thoroughfares, turn north from the Milton Gates and follow the west side of University up to Prince Arthur Street. This side of the campus boundary once was lined with mansion class housing, some of which McGill has salvaged or inherited. Other donations — such as the School of Social Work and School of Nursing and the William and Henry Birks Building, on the left as you make your way uphill — were built in the collegiate Gothic style to the specifications of wealthy benefactors. Built around 1864, the gray-stone row houses on the east side of University, most of which operate as rooming houses today, were built on a less imposing scale.

Turn east onto Prince Arthur and you'll be making royal progress. Originally designated Bagg Street (for Stanley Clark Bagg, who developed much of the area's eastern suburbs), the 14-block avenue between University and Laval Avenue was renamed for Prince Arthur, Duke of Connaught, son of Queen Victoria and a popular governor-general, the Crown's representative in Canada. Pause at the first corner to look up Lorne Avenue, another loyal reference to the Crown, named for the Marquess of Lorne, the old queen's son-in-law and former governor-general. Here's an example of suburban planning 1880s-style, with dignified rows of 3-story houses leading to a charming residential crescent of the same name. If you ignore the big apartment building on the west side of the street the block of snug Victorian buildings looks pretty much as it did more than a century ago when a comfortable middle-income community took root here.

For a nostalgic step back into a more recent past, turn north at Aylmer Street, where a landmark of the student-ghetto days is still hanging in at the *Yellow Door,* Canada's oldest coffeehouse (3625 Aylmer St.; phone: 514-398-6243). Opened in 1967, it was a rallying point for disaffected young Americans during the Vietnam War and a stage for the folksongs of protest. Jesse Winchester enthralled some of his earliest audiences here and folksinging is still the highlight of the Friday-night gatherings (8 PM to midnight; $2 cover). The coffeehouse operates under the chaplaincy of McGill University. The handsome red-brick house at 481 Prince Arthur has interesting student connections, as well. In its time, the commodious old (1897) relic has served as a fraternity house, a Hare Krishna temple, and a youth hostel.

But student activism was mild compared to the shock waves an earlier resident sent through the neighborhood around the turn of the century. In Montreal society of the day, feisty Canadian suffragette Madame Benoit made her mark at a time when her peers shied away from any sort of confrontation with men. A leading civil rights advocate of the day, Benoit fought bravely for the feminist cause in a province that denied women a vote in Quebec elections until as late as 1940. Now the house is in private hands again, beautifully restored, from stepped gables to elaborate front gate and fenced lawn.

Another Prince Arthur Street property with a long collegian connection is *Le Marché Campus* (No. 461). The neighborhood convenience store started life as a stable (look for the upper-story hatch that once opened on the hayloft), but it's been a handy stop-and-shop for campus-area residents since the 1940s.

At the Durocher Street intersection, you'll be on the corner of the oldest street in the district; cut through farm fields in 1837 as a private road, it was later expropriated by city developers. The old farmhouse at the corner (3592 Durocher), with a gingerbread trim frilling the central dormer and an unfortunate aluminum awning over the front door, very likely predates the road itself. The Beaux Arts building on the west corner (3612 Durocher) was a luxury hotel that failed even before the first guest registered. Converted to a residential apartment building in 1915, the Halcion Apartments are still an attractive presence on a tree-shaded street of period-piece homes. Most of the unadorned gray-stone veterans of the neighborhood's earliest settlement — prim red-brick row houses with fussy Victorian trimmings, and Edwardian latecomers with turret-topped towers and oriel windows — have been restored as single-family units or condominiums.

Return to Prince Arthur, and you're back in the 20th century with an imposing view of the high-rise, high-rent tenement complex of La Cité. Three apartment towers soar above their older neighbors on either side of Prince Arthur between Jeanne-Mance Street and Park Avenue, linked below the surface by a huge underground village of shops and services that includes a theater, a pool-equipped health club, a restaurant, and a bank. The *Ramada Renaissance du Parc* (3625 Park Ave.; phone: 514-288-6666) shares this underground facility with La Cité tenants (see "Checking In" in *Montreal,* THE CITIES).

Cross Park Avenue to the southwest section of the historic St-Louis district, which up-and-coming suburbanites colonized in the fields west of St-Laurent Boulevard in the 1870s and 1880s. Only a brisk 10-minute jog from McGill campus, the new neighborhood flourished as a solid middle class community of academics, merchants, and professionals, who settled into rows of 3-story Victorian houses, with fashionable wood-trimmed gables and little cubes of enclosed front porches. That image dimmed after the First World War as the population shifted to greener pastures beyond the city center; now, like the reincarnated campus zone, it's been adopted by a new wave of prosperous householders. Rows of neglected buildings destined for demolition have been salvaged and transformed into cooperatives and condominiums, notably the onetime church on the corner of Prince Arthur and Jeanne-Mance, now a condominium.

Continue east to St-Laurent Boulevard, where a welcome feature of a revived neighborhood opens up on the east side of the street. The 5-block pedestrian mall between St-Laurent and Laval Avenue is one of the city's more successful experiments in urban renewal. The mall is really a legacy from the 1960s, when Prince Arthur was known as "hippie alley" and a transient craftsperson could rent a store for $60 a month. Dreamy members of the flower-child generation who opened the original offbeat clothing outlets and bangles-and-beads boutiques drifted away once these casual agora of head shops and low-tab hangouts turned commercial and acceptably trendy. But the carefree tone they set lingered on after the city transformed the blocks west of Laval into a village square for pedestrians in 1981.

Now that it's been dressed up with a fountain and flower beds, old-fashioned lamp standards, and Parisian-style "Morris" columns plastered with posters, the mall is a popular promenade for diners in search of an inexpensive meal in picturesque surroundings. Ethnic restaurants of every variety line both sides of the old residential street, and with the first breath of spring they set up sidewalk cafés along the brick-paved length of the plaza. In summer, clowns, magicians, and street museums add more color to a lively street scene. The restaurants, none of which pretend to make the grade in the haute cuisine league, aren't as cheap as they once were, but the tradition of encouraging patrons to bring their own wine to the table has not been lost. But check the house policy before arriving with your little brown bag: Some of the new places are licensed.

With dozens of options on both sides of the mall, it's hard to make a choice — although half the fun of dining here is casing the territory, picking out a likely-looking spot and then shopping around for an acceptable wine to accompany a meal of Greek, Italian, Polish, Vietnamese, Swiss, Japanese, or Quebecois specialties. Both *Donat Vezina Groceries* (27 Prince Arthur St. E.; phone: 514-842-8044) and *Marché Nascimento & Brito* (67 Prince Arthur St. E.; phone: 514-845-5751) carry a stock of inexpensive wines for brown-baggers.

Walking west to east, you might be tempted by *Minerva* (No. 17; phone: 514-842-5451), a BYOW seafood house with a Greek accent, or *Coimbra* (No. 20; phone: 514-845-7915), a licensed Portuguese dining room featuring grilled specialties. *Xuan* (No. 26; phone: 514-849-4923) has a chef from Vietnam and *Le Prince Arthur* (No. 54; phone: 514-849-2454) is a traditional French *brochetterie*. The *Mazurka* (No. 64; phone: 514-844-3539) is the dean of the mall's restaurant community. The Polish pioneer was the first kid on the block when it opened in 1964. *La Fondue du Prince* (No. 70; phone: 514-845-0183) caters to fondue enthusiasts but offers other appetizing choices. Another well-established Prince Arthur landmark is *La Cabane Grecque* (No. 102; phone: 514-849-0122), a BYOW restaurant with a sidewalk café made for people watching. *Pizza Mella* (No. 107; phone: 514-849-4680) is a good choice on the mall for pizza (what else?). *Vespucci* (No. 124; phone: 514-843-4784) outclasses most of its Italian neighbors in decor with a white-tablecloth dining room and a stained glass wall mural. Tidy little *Akita* (No. 166; phone: 514-499-8412) serves traditional Japanese fare.

In your browsing, don't mistake *Le Chat Botté* (No. 108; phone: 514-844-

1850) for a pet-food store. It's been selling designer boots on Prince Arthur since the pre-mall era. *Vol de Nuit Bar Salon* (No. 14; phone: 514-845-6243) is a popular singles bar.

On the east side of Laval Avenue you'll come to the end of the mall and the beginning of St-Louis Square, which the city transformed from a reservoir into a park in 1867. Once the grass grew, a colony of prosperous French bourgeoisie built their Victorian townhouses and prudent 3-family residences along both sides of an almost-private residential garden. Several generations of artists and poets favored the tranquil little sanctuary with its bower of shade trees and playful fountain — and the square never quite lost its original cachet.

Here are formal, 4-story Victorian buildings, some of which are still private homes with steep front staircases and ornamental balconies. Condo conversion has changed some of these historic structures, but many are house-size duplexes and triplexes, designed for a gracious, drawing-room era, with fine, high ceilings and long, park-view windows. In recent years, householders who've invested in expensive renovations have chafed at the decline in the state of the park, a nighttime haven for drug dealers and their customers and the homeless. But during the day St-Louis Square still evokes memories of a gentler society.

Take a turn around the square before heading south on St-Denis Street (see "Special Places" in *Montreal,* THE CITIES) toward Montreal's legendary Quartier Latin, the francophone scholars' domain that grew up around Université de Montréal in the 1920s. Lately, the street evokes wistful visions of Paris, the Left Bank, and the café culture of Boulevard St-Michel. But the heart of St-Denis's intellectual world throbs around the Ste-Catherine Street intersection where Université du Québec à Montréal (UQAM) boasts a student body of 25,000. The newly fashionable blocks north of Ontario Street East draw more big spenders than thrifty collegians to their up-scale bistros, boutiques, and haute cuisine restaurants.

One of the city's most expensive dining spots is on the east side of the street, just south of Sherbrooke Street. At *Les Mignardises* (2035-37 St-Denis St.; phone: 514-842-1151), master chef Jean-Pierre Monnet has transformed an elegant little 1880s townhouse into a temple of gastronomy (see *Montreal's Best Restaurants* in DIVERSIONS). This stretch of St-Denis was a preferred residential avenue for well-heeled French Canadian suburbanites who moved up the hill into subdivided estate country about the same time the new neighborhoods west of St-Laurent were settled. Walk south and note the gray limestone façades of their mini-châteaux, crowned with elaborate gables and turrets, camouflaged now by storefront additions and restaurant marquees. Crossing Ontario Street, there's a change of urban scene that began as early as 1876, when Laval University opened a branch of the historic Quebec City institution in Montreal.

The Latin Quarter came to life with the university's decision to extend its faculties of law and medicine to sites around St-Denis Street and with the construction of l'Ecole Polytechnique in 1905. In 1920 Laval's outpost of higher learning won its autonomy as Université de Montréal and an expanding student population took over the Victorian-era homes of southern St-Denis. Before the university moved to its new mountainside campus on the north slope of Mount Royal in 1943, the stretch of St-Denis between René-Lévesque Boulevard and Ontario Street was the intellectual and cultural nerve center of French-speaking Montreal. The focus changed when the largest French-language university outside Paris abandoned St-Denis. But not for long. UQAM (Université de Québec à Montréal) opened in 1969 and now a new generation of student activists, poets, and philosophers charts Quebec's future in the smoky bars and affordable *brochetteries* of a new Latin Quarter.

Stroll south from Ontario Street; stop to admire La Bibliothèque Nationale du Québec (1700 St-Denis St.; phone: 514-873-1100). A Parisian-looking Beaux Arts building, it is one of three city centers associated with the National Library of Quebec. The St-Sulpice Building on St-Denis, which the Sulpician Order donated to the province in the 1960s, was built in 1912. Today it's the library's reference center and showcase for the collection of Canadiana the Sulpicians donated with the building. A variety of cultural activities take place in St-Sulpice Hall, a period-piece concert hall with exquisite stained glass skylight panels set into a beamed ceiling.

For a raucous change of pace, drop by *Café de Picasso* (1621 St-Denis St.; phone: 514-843-3533), a student hangout with a high-decible approach to conversations. By mid-evening, this is the spot to hear young Montreal in full voice. Across the street *Faubourg St-Denis* (1660 St-Denis St.; phone: 514-843-4814) is another popular student rendezvous.

Before crossing de Maisonneuve Boulevard stop by *Théâtre St-Denis* (1594 St-Denis St.; phone: 514-849-4211) to inspect the Art Deco façade of Montreal's second-largest concert hall (see "Music" in *Montreal,* THE CITIES). It covers the original 1916 face of the 2,500-seat theater where Sarah Bernhardt won standing ovations; many traditionalists are not pleased with its new look. But it seems to harmonize with thousands of summertime visitors who come here for such events as Montreal's *International Jazz Festival* and *Just for Laughs* comedy festival. *Théâtre St-Denis* can accommodate such mega-productions as *Les Misérables* and French pop extravaganzas.

At the junction of St-Denis and Ste-Catherine Streets is a red-brick university that boldly looks to the future, not the past. UQAM, its St-Denis campus now only 22 years old, was designed more for effficiency than aesthetic appeal.

Still, no Montreal institution would be complete without at least a wink at the past. On the grounds of the university, don't miss visiting Cathédrale St-Jacques, which enlightened Montreal architects managed to save from the wrecking ball when the university acquired the property. Instead of demolishing a Gothic-revival landmark that had stood its ground on Ste-Catherine Street East since 1860, the university integrated the highest church steeple in Montreal and the cathedral's south transept into the UQAM complex at 405 Ste-Catherine Street East (phone: 514-987-3125). Place 350, a new park the city created on Berri Street to celebrate its 350th anniversary last year, adds the requisite laid-back touch to the "all-business" student scene.

The university is linked to Montreal's underground city through the Berri-UQAM Métro station, a boon to students who commute from all quarters of

Montreal Island and beyond. Watch out for the traffic here, though. Students make up only a tiny proportion of the passengers who come through this hub of the Montreal subway system. More than 750,000 weekday travelers use the underground branch of the urban community's mass-transit system.

For a close encounter with Montreal on the move, turn into the Métro station on the west side of St-Denis opposite the university and join the flow. Four subway lines converge here on four different levels and the rush-hour mob scene can be an eye-opener for strangers in town. But case-hardened regulars take it all in stride. Don't be surprised if you're the only one taking any time to admire the outsize stained glass window that covers an entire wall of Berri-UQAM's underground art gallery.

The station is connected to the *Voyageur* bus terminal and *Les Atriums* shopping galleries, a 7-story atrium with its own in-house waterfall cascading into a tropical garden. The multi-tiered mall is worth a visit before hitting the fast track to home base.

Quebec City Directions

Quebec's historic capital is Canada's most walkable city — its many charms are best discovered on foot. If you come to Quebec City by air, on arrival you'll probably be driven behind its walls by taxi, but that could be the last time during your stay that you travel in such a way. It's easy to get caught up in the spirit of the street here.

Indeed, using a car to navigate the maze of one-way thoroughfares in the confines of the ramparts is more nuisance than convenience. Public parking in Upper Town is limited, particularly on weekends and during the summer tourist season when early birds snap up the available spaces, and the local *gendarmerie* keep an eagle-eye on restricted parking zones. Sightseers from beyond the walls can avoid the frustration of traffic tie-ups and parking tickets by leaving the car in the hotel garage.

The historic *quartier* is an easy walk for hotel guests in the Parliament Hill–Grande Allée district, and the No. 11 bus plies a regular course along Grande Allée, Chemin St-Louis, and Boulevard Laurier, linking the motel strip of suburban Ste-Foy to the heart of the walled city. Many of the larger Ste-Foy hotels operate a shuttle service to and from Upper Town. Parking is less of a problem in the Vieux Port area of Lower Town, where the facilities are new and expansive, but still it's best to leave the car behind: Much of Place Royale is restricted to pedestrian traffic in summer.

Uptown or downtown, walking through history is one of the great rewards of this compact, split-level city. It's almost impossible to get lost inside or outside the walls. The turrets and spires of the *Château Frontenac* hotel are a constant point of reference, always visible on the Vieux Québec skyline. Down by the river, or out beyond the fortifications, head toward the *Château*'s high profile to find the way back to Place d'Armes and the heart of Upper Town.

Few cities in Canada make life easier for strolling visitors. From mid-June through *Labour Day,* bilingual tourist-information agents zip around both levels of the Old Town on bright green mopeds, on the lookout for confused wanderers. When in doubt, look for the little white flag with the big black question mark; at the crossroads of key pedestrian routes there's usually a well-informed driver beneath the flying pennant.

Day or night, *la vieille capitale* is a safe city for strolling. Civic boosters take pride in Quebec City's low crime rate, pointing out the only real hazard on Vieux Québec's streets are the streets themselves. Plunging downward at unexpected corners, or newly surfaced with historically correct paving stones, the lane-width roads of the *ancien quartier* call for stout walking shoes with good, thick soles. Oh, and keep an eye peeled for *calèche* traffic. The horse rules in traffic here, forcing rental-car drivers and local motorists alike to give way.

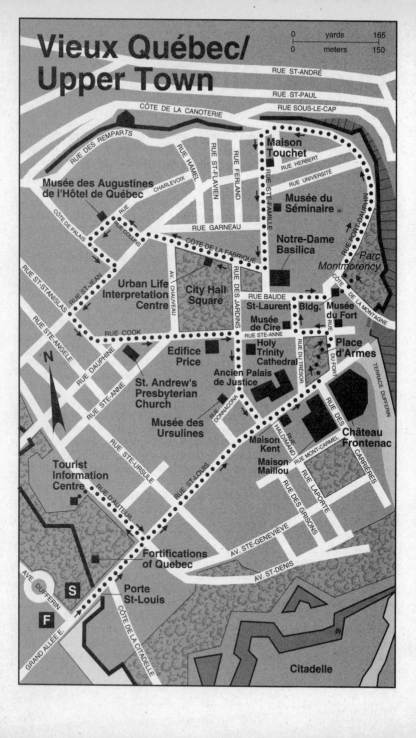

Vieux Québec/ Upper Town

| 0 | yards | 165 |
| 0 | meters | 150 |

RUE ST-ANDRÉ

RUE ST-PAUL

CÔTE DE LA CANOTERIE

RUE SOUS-LE-CAP

RUE DES REMPARTS

RUE HAMEL

RUE ST-FLAVIEN

RUE FERLAND

RUE STE-FAMILLE

Maison Touchet

RUE HERBERT

RUE UNIVERSITÉ

CHARLEVOIX

Musée des Augustines de l'Hôtel de Québec

RUE

CÔTE DE PALAIS

RUE COLLINS

RUE GARNEAU

CÔTE DE LA FABRIQUE

Musée du Séminaire

Notre-Dame Basilica

RUE PORT-DAUPHIN

Parc Montmorency

CÔTE DE LA MONTAGNE

RUE ST-STANISLAS

RUE ST-JEAN

AV. CHAUVEAU

Urban Life Interpretation Centre

City Hall Square

RUE DES JARDINS

RUE BAUDE

St-Laurent

Bldg.

RUE

Musée du Fort

RUE STE-ANGELE

RUE COOK

Musée de Cire

RUE STE-ANNE

Place d'Armes

RUE DAUPHINE

Edifice Price

Holy Trinity Cathedral

RUE DU TRÉSOR

RUE STE-ANNE

St. Andrew's Presbyterian Church

Ancien Palais de Justice

RUE DONNACONA

Musée des Ursulines

RUE HALDIMAND

RUE

TERRASSE DUFFERIN

Maison Kent

RUE MONT-CARMEL

Château Frontenac

RUE DES

RUE STE-URSULE

Maison Maillou

RUE LAPORTE

RUE DES GRISONS

CARRIÈRES

RUE ST-LOUIS

N

Tourist Information Centre

RUE D'AUTEUIL

AV. STE-GENEVIÈVE

Fortifications of Quebec

AV. ST-DENIS

AV. DUFFERIN

S

F

Porte St-Louis

GRAND ALLÉE E.

CÔTE DE LA CITADELLE

Citadelle

Walk 1: Vieux Québec/Upper Town

For visiting history buffs, nothing in Canada surpasses the thrill of walking for the first time through Porte St-Louis into the Upper Town of Vieux Québec. There are other gateways to the only walled city in North America, but they don't lead back to the 17th century as dramatically as this western approach to the historic *quartier* of Quebec's provincial capital.

This is where guests from hotels outside the walls are one up on the insiders, who generally arrive by car or taxi through other breaches in the ramparts to check in to Upper Town accommodations. Caught up in the traffic stream, they miss out on the sensation of walking into history along the oldest tourist route in Canada. Years before modern-day explorers, Indian braves followed this very trail down to what they called "Kebec" (Where the Waters Narrow) to observe the funny foreigners in their vulnerable riverbank settlement and do a little business at the new fur-trading post.

Today's visitors should leave the No. 11 bus at Avenue Dufferin and make the grand entrance to Vieux Québec on foot. Follow a centuries-old path and you'll be surprised to discover the neo-Gothic Porte St-Louis isn't as old as it looks. The original was built in 1693, along with nearby Porte St-Jean, as part of the colonial defense system, but both were located closer to the center of town. Moved several times during the French regime, today's imposing portal wasn't reconstructed until 1878. Still, it's easy to imagine it funneling frontier traffic into Upper Town's main thoroughfare and on to Fort St-Louis at the opposite end of the street where the *Château Frontenac* now stands.

Enter the upper reaches of this old split-level town (known affectionately by those who live here as Le Grand Village) to begin a walking tour of about 2 hours; the Poudrière de l'Esplanade (Esplanade Powder House) is set back in the park on the left. Built in 1810, it's part of the Fortifications of Quebec, a national historic site maintained by Parks Canada. The Poudrière is a reception and interpretation center now, featuring special activities for military-minded children on the green of Esplanade Park. It's also the departure point for tours of the 3-mile wall circuit (see *Walk 3: Vieux Québec Wall Tour*). As you stroll, note that many of the windows in these old buildings have been covered over in brick or stone. In the 19th century, homeowners were taxed by the number of windows in their houses; the sealing of these openings not only saved on taxes, it greatly reduced the need for extra firewood for heating.

Continue along the verge of the park to the intersection of Rue d'Auteuil and St-Louis and look to the right, up the picturesque slope of Avenue St-Denis where rows of fine mid-19th-century homes are tucked under the

wall of La Citadelle (see *Quebec City,* THE CITIES). Turn left on Rue d'Auteuil
at the Boer War Monument and follow the park to the Tourist Information
Centre of the Greater Quebec Area Tourism and Convention Bureau (60 Rue
d'Auteuil; phone: 418-692-2471), a must stop. The bureau distributes free
guidebooks, maps, brochures, and other tourist literature in French and
English, and the bilingual staff has the answer to almost any question flustered
newcomers care to ask.

Armed with information and suggestions, visitors can return to the Rue
St-Louis intersection with confidence and proceed down the most colorful
street within the walls. Spring through fall, the 8-block link between Porte
St-Louis and the *Château Frontenac* seems to be *en fête* (decked out) 7 days
a week. In summer look up at the flashes of color coming from the old-style
window boxes that brighten up historic stone façades and the baskets that
hang from lampposts. Stop to smell the flowers in café window boxes, to
admire the 17th-century buildings. In winter the spirit is different, but no less
festive. In the cold and swirling snow, restaurant windows glow with welcoming light and warmth, and gaily painted doorways mark the friendliness and
comfort that lies within.

But winter or summer, the restaurants always beckon: St-Louis is Quebec
City's restaurant row. Get out a notepad here to write down the ones you like
the looks of because there are many from which to choose. Starting with *Le
Paris Gourmet* on the right-hand side of the street (73 Rue St-Louis; phone:
418-694-0030), you can crisscross from one fine dining room to another. *La
Caravelle* (No. 68; phone: 418-694-9022) serves traditional French and Spanish fare to the tunes of a dinner-hour troubadour (try the mussels with
rosemary — they're superb). Almost next door, at *Café de Paris* (No. 66;
phone: 418-694-9626), diners are beguiled by serenades of a resident *chansonnier,* while *Restaurant au Parmesan,* farther down the street (No. 38; phone:
418-692-0341), serves robust Italian fare to the accompaniment of Italian and
French folksongs.

At the corner of Rue des Jardins, *Aux Anciens Canadiens* (No. 34; phone:
418-692-1627) is Vieux Québec's most famous purveyor of traditional French
Canadian cuisine — good substantial reliables, like *soupe aux pois grand'mère*
(Grandma's pea soup), *fèves au lard* (pork and beans), *tourtière* (pork pie),
and ragoût de pattes de cochon et de boulettes (pigs' knuckles and meatball
stew). François Jacquet, a slate roofer, wasn't thinking in terms of a quaint
restaurant when he built his little peak-roofed stone cottage in 1675, but he'd
probably be pleased to know his handiwork has withstood more than 3
centuries of war, weather, and wear. Though a dining spot nearby, *Le Continental* (No. 26; phone: 418-694-9995), can't claim historic monument status,
it is the dean of restaurant row's dining establishments. The Sgobba family
has been living up to the high standards of haute cuisine in this peaceful
formal dining room since 1956 (see "Eating Out" in *Quebec City,* THE CITIES
for all of the above).

Cross to the opposite side of the street now to the corner of Rue Haldimand,
where Maison Kent (25 Rue St-Louis) has been a main-street landmark since
1650. Quebec's fate was sealed in this stately 17th-century home where the

capital of French Canada was officially surrendered to victorious British forces after the Battle of the Plains of Abraham in 1759. Just 32 years later, the proud relic of the old French regime adopted the name of a royal resident from England. The Duke of Kent, father of Queen Victoria, resided here as governor from 1791 to 1794. A few yards down the street (at No. 17), Maison Maillou houses the Quebec City Board of Trade in a handsome example of early Quebecois architecture, built by Jean Maillou between 1736 and 1753.

This is the historic heart of Upper Town. Take a break here. The green, tree-shaded square of Place d'Armes, with its memorial fountain glorifying the faith of the early Récollet missionaries, is the place to stake out a park bench and consider the lay of the land.

Towering over the south side of the *place,* on Rue St-Louis, *Château Frontenac* has commanded the strategic heights above the St. Lawrence River for 100 years; built in 1883 by the *Canadian Pacific Railway,* it is the ultimate in Canadian grand hotels (see *Quintessential Montreal and Quebec City* in DIVERSIONS). Looking down from his statue column by the hotel's east corner, Samuel de Champlain surveys the site of the fortress he built in 1620 to defend his riverside colony at the base of the cliff. Dufferin Terrace, which flanks the east side of the hotel, has obliterated all traces of Fort St-Louis (the founder died here in 1635), but the memorial statue of the Father of New France remains a focus of Upper Town life. Clowns, acrobats, and other street entertainers draw crowds around the monument base from early spring through the fall foliage season, and the *calèche* fleet of horse-drawn carriages is always lined up on the nearby Place d'Armes to tempt footsore explorers. The 92-year-old Champlain Monument now shares the Dufferin Terrace stage with a much younger historic memorial — the sphere of bronze and glass that proclaims Vieux Québec as a UNESCO World Heritage site.

West of the busy monument area, Place d'Armes came to life during the French regime as Grande Place, a combined speakers' corner and military parade ground. From here, sightseers can follow a path down to the square's northern boundary at Rue Ste-Anne. On the west side of the colonial meeting ground, look for the Ancien Palais de Justice (Old Courthouse), built over the site of a church and convent founded by the Récollet Order of Franciscan missionaries in the early 1600s. Next door, the east façade of Holy Trinity Cathedral (1804) — the first Anglican cathedral built outside the British Isles — faces the *place* from its churchyard in the ancient Récollet Gardens. Follow the chain of lamp-lined paths across the *place* to its eastern border on Rue du Fort and continue north to the Rue Ste-Anne intersection. To the right is the *Musée du Fort* (10 Rue Ste-Anne; phone: 418-692-2175), a museum devoted to the six military sieges of Quebec (see "Museums" in *Quebec City,* THE CITIES). Cross Rue du Fort and continue along Rue Ste-Anne, a lively enclave of sidewalk cafés, bistros, and restaurants made even livelier in summer by wandering minstrels and other curbside performers. Compulsive brochure collectors may wish to visit the Quebec Ministry of Tourism's Maison du Tourisme (12 Rue Ste-Anne), which the province operates in the former *Union* hotel. Back on the pedestrian section of the street you can sort out a booty of brochures for every region in the province around the umbrella-shaded tables of *Auberge du Trésor* (20 Rue Ste-Anne; phone: 418-694-1876), a stalwart, half-timbered veteran of the 17th-century tourist trade that bills itself as "North America's Oldest Inn" (see "Eating Out" in *Quebec City,* THE CITIES).

On the corner of Rue du Trésor is *Le Musée de Cire* (Wax Museum; 22 Rue Ste-Anne; phone: 418-692-2289), another vintage landmark of the French colonial period (1732), where a permanent collection of wax figures in period settings depicts major events in early American and Canadian history.

Now turn down the narrow alley of Rue du Trésor, a casual outdoor gallery for the street artists of Vieux Québec, who cover every inch of wall space with their work and sketch portraits from life on the spot. The cramped passage of cheery bohemia was not always like this. Once upon a time disgruntled settlers tramped down this strip to the colony's tax bureau, where they paid their dues to the Royal Treasury. Hence the name Treasury Street.

At the bottom of the lane, turn right on Rue Buade. This Upper Town shopping street adopted the family name of Louis de Buade, Count Frontenac, the famous soldier-governor of Canada during the French colonial period whose title lives on in the city's most well known landmark. At the intersection of Rue du Fort, take a moment to window shop at *La Maison Darlington* (7 Rue Buade; phone: 418-692-2268), a long-established import outlet for British tweeds and woollies (see "Shopping" in *Quebec City,* THE CITIES). Save selecting from *Darlington*'s stock of Shetland sweaters and mohair rugs for your shopping spree in Quebec City and cross Rue du Fort to the Louis St-Laurent Building (No. 3; phone: 418-648-4177). Crowning the crest of a hill at Côte de la Montagne, the post office building was erected in 1871 on the site of the old *le Chien d'Or* (Golden Dog) hotel, immortalized in a 19th-century romantic novel of the same name set in New France. (The English-born author, William Kirby, who settled in Canada in the 1830s, was a popular writer of his day whose work included *Annals of Niagara* and *The U.E.: A Tale of Upper Canada.*) A relief on the façade shows a dog chewing a bone over a bitter little ditty that reflects the vengeful spirit of the universal underdog:

> *I am a dog that gnaws his bone*
> *I crouch and gnaw it all alone*
> *A time will come, which is not yet*
> *When I'll bite him by whom I'm bit.*

On the main floor of the post office building visit the displays in the Parks Canada Exhibition Room for a quick lesson in Canadian history. The St-Laurent Building was named for Louis St-Laurent, one of Canada's most popular prime ministers (1948–57), affectionately known in Liberal Party circles (and most of Canada) as "Uncle Louis." The statue opposite the post office on Rue Port-Dauphin is a monument to Monseigneur François-Xavier de Montmorency-Laval, the first Bishop of Quebec and founder of the seminary that became Laval University (see "Special Places" in *Quebec City,* THE CITIES).

Cross Côte de la Montagne (with a sharp eye on the traffic taking the precipitous route down to Lower Town) and pause to enjoy the view from Bishop Laval's namesake park, *Parc Montmorency* (see "Special Places" in

Quebec City, THE CITIES). The park ramparts are part of the city fortifications and strollers can look down from this section of the wall to the town below — where the first settlers came ashore in 1608 — and out across the St. Lawrence to the opposite shore. Greening the hill that divides Upper and Lower Town, this shady retreat was a wheat field in 1618; it was tilled by Louis Hébert, the first French Canadian farmer, whose statue stands in the park. The first official residence of the Bishops of Quebec was built on the park site from 1691 to 1696. The statue of Sir Georges-Etienne Cartier, French Canada's great statesman and Father of Confederation, shares the hilltop greenspace with farmer Hébert's monument.

Leave the park at the corner of Côte de la Montagne and Rue Port-Dauphin; the Archeveché (Bishop's Palace) has commanded this crossroads since 1844 when the Palladian-style residence replaced the original palace that was across the road. Rue Port-Dauphin changes its name to Rue des Remparts as it follows the wall around the heights past the cannon that once guarded the city's northern flank.

Now turn left into Rue Ste-Famille to one of Upper Town's best-preserved historic houses. Maison Touchet (No. 15) dates from 1774, reflecting the traditional 18th-century building style in its high chimneys and steeply pitched roofline. Continue up the street to its intersection with Rue Université and examine the eclectic collection of historic treasures at *Le Musée du Séminaire* (Seminary Museum; 9 Rue Université; phone: 418-692-2843), which houses a diverse collection of Canadian and European art, old coins, gold ornaments, and scientific instruments (see "Special Places" in *Quebec City,* THE CITIES).

From the museum return to Ste-Famille and proceed up to the corner of Côte de la Fabrique and the spiritual and intellectual heart of Catholic Quebec. The Basilique Notre-Dame-de-Québec and its historic seminary make up a venerable ecclesiastical complex at the intersection of Côte de la Fabrique and Rue Buade, opposite Place de l'Hôtel de Ville (City Hall Square).

To the left of the basilica at 1 Côte de la Fabrique an ornate wrought-iron gate — crowned with the monogram of the Paris Foreign Missions seminary — leads to the interior courtyard of Séminaire de Québec; the seminary was founded in 1663 by Bishop Laval to administer parishes and bring "The Word" to the first Canadians. At about the same time a minor seminary trained young colonists for the priesthood. In 1852, seminary authorities founded Laval University, the first French-language Catholic university in America; the university relocated to suburban Ste-Foy in 1946, but the minor seminary continues in the spirit of learning, serving today as a private high school for boys and a coed college. In summer, guided tours of the seminary precincts include a visit to the Outer Chapel, a Romanesque relic of 1888 that replaced an 18th-century original, and the 1950 memorial crypt of Bishop Laval. While touring the seminary don't miss the bishop's kitchen and its original baronial fireplace and the former refectory (see "Special Places" in *Quebec City,* THE CITIES).

Next door to the seminary, the Notre-Dame Basilica (main entrance at 16 Rue Buade) ranks among the finest examples of baroque architecture in all of Quebec. Notre-Dame started life as a humble parish church in 1647 and was elevated to cathedral status 27 years later when North America's first Roman Catholic diocese outside Mexico was established here under Bishop Laval. Indeed, the cathedral stands as a worthy symbol for the resilence and determination of the French people. Since it was first built (almost 350 years ago), the cathedral has been enlarged several times, bombarded during the British siege of Quebec in 1759, ravaged by fires (the latest in 1922), and always lovingly reconstructed on the same site. Four Governors of New France, including Count Frontenac, and most of the Bishops of Quebec, are buried in the crypt. Guided tours through the basilica and crypt are conducted daily from May 1 to November 1 (phone: 418-692-2533; see "Special Places" in *Quebec City,* THE CITIES).

Cross over to City Hall Square (at its center is a monument honoring Cardinal Taschereau, Canada's first cardinal) and follow Côte de la Fabrique to the *Urban Life Interpretation Centre* (43 Côte de la Fabrique; phone: 418-691-4606) in the basement of City Hall. The center's host building was built in 1895 on the site of a former Jesuit college (1635). Maintained by the Quebec Historical Society, the basement museum interprets contemporary life in an old city with a large model of the capital as it looked in 1975. Video displays, electronic hands-on presentations, and other exhibitions tell the story of the growth of the modern city and its distinctive cultural life.

Côte de la Fabrique — the area north and west of the seminary which classical scholars from Laval University traversed — was one of the main thoroughfares of Canada's first Latin Quarter. Slip into these scholars' shoes as you follow their original route to the corner of Rue St-Jean. On the right is Rue Collins, which leads to Rue Charlevoix and the *Musée des Augustines de l'Hôtel-Dieu de Québec.* The museum is housed on the first floor of the Monastère des Augustines, which adjoins North America's first hospital. (Members of the Augustine Order founded l'Hôtel-Dieu Hospital in 1639.)

Some of the personal effects and the medical instruments of the first nursing sisters are on display in the small museum, along with paintings, antique furniture, and 17th-century ornaments. Guided tours are conducted on request through the church and into the deep, vaulted cellars where the nuns found safety and shelter during the various bombardments of Quebec. 32 Rue Charlevoix (phone: 418-692-2492).

Continue along Rue Charlevoix to Côte du Palais; turn left to Rue St-Jean. Walk south along St-Jean to its intersection with Rue St-Stanislas, then turn left toward Rue Cook. St. Andrew's Presbyterian Church (1810), on the corner of Rues Cook and Ste-Anne, is one of the major symbols of the introduction of British ways after the conquest in Upper Town. Presbyterian sons and daughters of members of James Wolfe's army first worshiped here, yet many would marry French girls and raise Quebecois families of their own. These roots are recalled today in such names as Jean-François Stewart and Sandy Larocque.

From the church follow Rue Ste-Anne along the south border of City Hall Square toward Rue des Jardins. On the right is the Art Deco Edifice Price, Quebec's first high-rise office building. At the corner, turn right on Rue des Jardins and walk up the hill to Rue Donnacona. Just before the intersection is the main entrance to Holy Trinity Cathedral (31 Rue des Jardins; phone:

418-692-2193). A copy of St. Martin-in-the-Fields in London, the cathedral was built by royal decree of British monarch George III, who personally donated many of the church's treasures, including the silver communion service. During the summer visitors can attend weekly organ concerts and a festival evensong every afternoon at 4:45 PM. Daily guided tours are conducted from May through the first week in October.

Just around the corner (12 Rue Donnacona; phone: 418-694-0694) is the *Musée des Ursulines;* Quebec City's most endearing small museum, it is dedicated to the Ursuline Order's 354 years of service. Adjoining the Chapalle des Ursulines, where the sisters founded the oldest school for girls in North America, the museum sits so modestly behind its plain, gray-stone walls that many sightseers pass it by. But don't: The dimly lit interior, tranquil as a tomb, affords a poignant glimpse of French Canada's history, from the time three unflappable Ursulines set up their primitive 2-room convent on Lower Town's waterfront in 1639 to the last days of the French regime. The nuns moved up to the Donnacona site 3 years later and they've been conducting classes in the convent school ever since. The charming little chapel next door (10 Rue Donnacona; phone: 418-694-0694) contains the tombs of Reverend Mother Marie de l'Incarnation, who founded the order with Madame de la Peltier, and General Montcalm, defeated leader of the French army in the Battle of the Plains of Abraham.

The Marquis Louis-Joseph de Montcalm owes his final resting place to a nosy little schoolgirl with a long memory. In the confusion and sorrow that followed the fateful battle, no one noticed 9-year-old Amable Dubé following the torch-lit funeral cortege through the streets to the Ursuline Chapel. Little Amable watched the burial of the fallen hero as his hastily built coffin was lowered into a grave near the chapel grating. Seventy-four years later Amable, then an Ursuline nun, told this story that she had carried with her all her life to nuns who were contemplating erecting a tomb to honor Montcalm. The only living witness to the burial, she was even able to point to the exact gravesite.

Take a peek into the adjoining *Centre Marie-de-l'Incarnation* (phone: 418-692-2569), which combines a bookstore with films about the order's co-founder and a collection of her personal belongings.

If it's lunchtime, stop just down the street at *Café de la Paix* (44 Rue des Jardins; phone: 418-692-1430), a cozy spot reminiscent of Left Bank Paris that's become a tourist tradition since it opened 30 years ago. You're sure to enjoy your experience here or when you return for dinner (be sure to make reservations for dinner). Frequent visitors make a point of dropping by Benito Terzini's intimate main-floor restaurant just to make sure he hasn't changed the comfortable clutter of lamp-lit tables, pastry carts, wine racks, and Desrosier landscapes.

Continue up the block after lunch to Rue St-Louis and head back toward the starting point at the town gate at the top of the street. Halfway up, on the corner of Rue Corps de Garde, look for the tree with remnants of a cannonball wedged into its lower trunk — a reminder that walls and fortified gates were one of life's necessities when Vieux Québec was a battleground in Europe's struggle for mastery of North America.

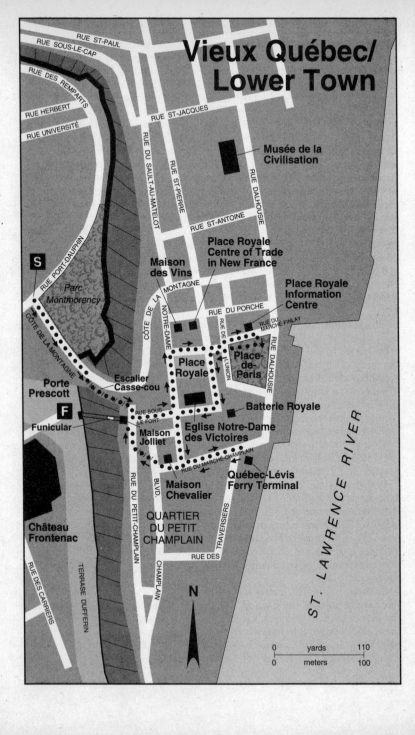

Walk 2: Vieux Québec/Lower Town

There's an easy way down to the birthplace of Quebec City and a 90-minute walking tour of the first permanent settlement in New France. A funicular at the north end of Dufferin Terrace, opposite the memorial statue of Samuel de Champlain, cranks passengers down over the rooftops to a safe landing in the heart of Lower Town in less than 5 minutes.

But that's hardly the historic way to go. The founder himself charted the original "road" between the upper and lower levels of the new colony in 1623, 3 years after he built Fort St-Louis on the heights above the waterfront village. The Côte de la Montagne trail was hacked out of the sheer cliff face of Cape Diamond to link port and fort. So conscientious historians generally leave the funicular for the return ascent, when an easy way up can be much appreciated. Going down you can trace Champlain's route from the corner of Rue Port-Dauphine and still-precipitous Côte de la Montagne, following the grassy southern slope of Parc Montmorency to Porte Prescott, one of four remaining gateways to the walled city.

Porte Prescott suffered the same fate as other historic entries to town in 1871 when it was demolished along with its guardhouse to ease the kind of traffic congestion Champlain never imagined. A replica of the 18th-century original was erected on the site only 8 years ago.

Pass under the gate's arched bridge; to the left is a cross indicating the site of the settlement's first cemetery, opened after the first terrible winter of 1608–09 when at least 20 of the founding party died of scurvy. Halfway down the hill, to the right, l'Escalier Casse-Cou (Break-Neck Staircase) isn't as dangerous as it sounds — and certainly nowhere near as taxing as the flights of 17th-century steps colonial pedestrians climbed during the French regime. The city's first iron staircase replaced them in 1893; now wooden steps follow the iron-railed descent to the cliff in easy stages to Rue du Petit-Champlain.

At the foot of the stairs is one of the best seafood restaurants in Vieux Québec. Tucked into a centuries-old fieldstone building, *Le Marie Clarisse* (12 Rue du Petit-Champlain; phone: 418-692-0857) has a devoted following of regulars from Upper Town. Make advance reservations if your Lower Town walking tour includes a long, relaxed lunch (see "Eating Out" in *Quebec City*, THE CITIES).

Next door, at the corner of Rues Petit-Champlain and Sous-le-Fort (Under the Fort), Maison Louis Jolliet is the funicular's Lower Town station. From the outside, the durable, white-plastered building maintains a traditional 1683 image, much as it was when Jolliet — the explorer who co-discovered the

Mississippi River — came here to retire. Don't bother going inside unless you're in the mood for examining the latest trinkets and T-shirts in an all-too-commonplace 20th-century souvenir shop.

Walk down Rue Sous-le-Fort and turn left at Rue Notre-Dame, which leads into Place Royale. Entering Vieux Québec's earliest market square you're probably walking over the site of Champlain's first *habitation*. Somewhere in the immediate vicinity nearly 4 centuries ago, the founder, who'd arrived from France with two shiploads of recruits on July 3, 1608, paced out a fortress plan on a stretch of level land between river and cliff. He set the shore party to work immediately, clearing the woods, then building a storehouse and living quarters, surrounded by a stout palisade and ditch. But it was not all smooth sailing for the man who was to become known as the Father of New France. Within weeks malcontents were hatching a plot to assassinate him and and escape to sea with the company stores. Undismayed, Champlain promptly put down the mutiny, executed the ringleader, and carried on with preparations for the winter ahead.

Nothing remains of that first fragile outpost of French civilization in North America, but archaeologists have discovered the foundations of a second *habitation* (1624) under Eglise Notre-Dame-des-Victoires (Our Lady of Victories Church; Place Royale; phone: 418-692-1650). Indeed, the quaint little gray-stone church on the south side of the *place* is literally the cradle of New France.

By the time Notre-Dame was built over the earliest settlement ruins in 1688, Champlain had died and left New France to his successors; Place du Marché had become Place Royale, a proper colonial setting for the new bust of King Louis XIV, which was installed at this crossroads of the young frontier town. But today's square, with its authentic, sole-testing paving stones and center-stage replica of the original Sun King effigy, remains an economic crossroads, of sorts. But tourists — not furs, or lumber — are the stock in trade, buzzing in and out of the district's boutiques, galleries, snack shops, and restaurants.

After visiting Notre-Dame to admire the beautifully restored interior and its unusual, castle-shape high altar, wine fanciers won't want to miss the *Maison des Vins* (House of Wines; 1 Pl. Royale; phone: 418-643-1214) on the opposite side of the square. Colonial merchant Eustache-Lambert Dumont had this substantial stone domicile built to order a year after Notre-Dame appeared on the Place Royale scene. Now his deep storage vaults, some of which predate the building, are stocked with a small fortune in rare, vintage wines, which visitors are invited to inspect before getting down to business in the street-level retail outlet. Customers have a choice of 1,000 bottles of wine at their disposal — anything from the ordinary table variety to connoisseur extravagances at $1,000 a cork.

Now look around for the best in historically correct restorations that envelop the square in the spirit of the 17th and 18th centuries. Many of these buildings remain private homes, while others are business offices and crafts studios. Like their ancestors, Quebecois live and work here, adding an infectious zest and vibrancy to the historic *quartier*.

Visitors can see how colonial shoppers did their marketing when they stop by *Place Royale, Centre of Trade in New France,* one of two Place Royale interpretations centers, next door to *Maison des Vins.* At the sign of 17th-century merchant Nicolas Jérémie, three restored properties are devoted to exhibits and a multimedia show that traces the development of a young country during the halcyon days of the fur trade.

From here take Rue de la Place on the east side of the square to Rue St-Pierre. Turn to the right and cross the threshold of another reclaimed townhouse (25 Rue St-Pierre; phone: 418-643-6631). This colonial homestead has been converted to another interpretation center, *Place Royale, 400 Years of History,* where exhibitions tell the story of Lower Town's early beginnings as a trading post to its prosperous heyday as the financial hub of New France to the present day.

Return to the corner of Rue de la Place and head toward the river and Rue du Marché Finlay. Here at the Place Royale Information Centre (215 Rue du Marché Finlay; phone: 418-643-6631) you can join a guided/audio tour of the neighborhood that is steeped in stories of Lower Town's past and get handy information about activities or enterainment on or around the *place.* The center overlooks Place-de-Paris, where Champlain's settlers came ashore (the river was higher then) at the corner of Rues de la Place and de l'Union. A contemporary geometric sculpture, *Dialogue avec l'Histoire,* is believed to mark the exact spot of the first landing.

Also well worth a visit is Batterie Royale, south across Place-de-Paris, at the corner of Rues St-Pierre and Sous-le-Fort. Buried for years under a sprawl of wharf development, the original 1691 defense system was unearthed 16 years ago and rebuilt in the image of its 18th-century self, complete with gun ports and cannon. The battery was part of the city's defense during the siege of Quebec, when Wolfe's army lobbed 40,000 cannonballs and 10,000 fire bombs into the capital.

Three stalwart neighbors of the battery escaped the worst of the enemy fire to eventually become a cultural center, maintained by *Le Musée de la Civilisation.* To visit them, follow Rue Sous-le-Fort west to its intersection with Rue Notre-Dame and turn left toward Rue du Marché Champlain, where Maison Chevalier (60 Rue du Marché Champlain; phone: 418-643-9689) offers a glimpse of Lower Town life in the 17th and 18th centuries. The trio of historic buildings that make up the complex was built by master mason Pierre Renaud for the Chenaye de la Garonne, Frérot, and Chevalier families between 1695 and 1752. All have been restored to their prime as handsome, 5-story dwellings with massive chimneys towering over their steep, red rooflines. Designed for safety and warmth to accommodate the leader's of Lower Town's merchant society, Renaud used stone that was 4-feet thick for the walls.

On the corner opposite Maison Chevalier, *La Vieille Maison du Spaghetti* (Old Spaghetti House; 40 Rue du Marché Champlain; phone: 418-694-9144) has adopted a row of refurbished 18th-century homes to house a reasonably priced pasta parlor. Warm-weather customers can sit out on the flower-banked terrace and think about the next leg of the tour over a fortifying pizza. From the umbrella-shaded tables it's a short stroll back down Rue du Marché

Champlain to the waterfront and the Québec-Lévis ferry terminal at 10 Rue des Traversiers (phone: 418-644-3704). Add half an hour to the excursion for a return trip across the river to the Lévis shore. The commuter service departs every hour on the half hour between 6 AM and 7:30 PM; less frequently in the evenings. At any hour, the 15-minute return crossing costs CN$2.20. Sightseers going along for the ride aren't expected to disembark with the commuters. From the ferry deck, passengers can enjoy a superb view of the city: the little gray port with the multicolored rooftops huddled at the base of the cliff, the turrets and spires of the *Château Frontenac* dominating the heights.

For those wanting to forgo the St. Lawrence and its views, walk west from the *Old Spaghetti House* into Rue Cul-de-Sac, which forms a little shopping corner around the rear walls of Maison Chevalier before it merges with Boulevard Champlain. Take the first staircase to the right, just beyond *Anse aux Barques* restaurant at 28 Boulevard Champlain (phone: 418-692-4674).

At the top of the stairs is Rue du Petit-Champlain, the heart of Vieux Québec's first shopping street and the oldest of such streets in Canada. Once Quebec was established as a lucrative trading post the waterfront settlement flourished into a busy port with plenty of opportunities for canny dealers and fortune seekers. Quartier du Petit-Champlain was the colony's main financial district, its namesake street lined with the homes, shops, and counting houses of newly prosperous tradesmen and ship owners. But the district fell into a decline toward the end of the 19th century as former residents moved onward and upward, abandoning Lower Town to the wharf and the businesses there. Thirty years ago visitors determined enough to see all sides of Quebec rattled down Lower Town's old main drag in horse-drawn *calèches* and gawked at a sad little slum of a street, a narrow plank road where barefoot children scrambled around the tourist traffic begging for coins and candy.

Today the old broken-down tenements and shanties have been restored to make Rue du Petit-Champlain the oldest shopping center in Canada. These days the pedestrian route could pass for the High Street of a seaport village in France, flanked with interesting boutiques, galleries, and crafts studios. Take time to window shop both sides of the street, from the corner of Rue Sous-le-Fort, down to the junction with Boulevard Champlain.

For a short shopping spree on this, the best little shopping strip in Quebec City, stop first on the north side at *Pot-en-Ciel* (No. 27; phone: 418-692-1743), which displays the works of Quebec potters, ceramists, and carvers. Nearby, *Les Vêteries Blanc-Mouton* (No. 31; phone: 418-694-1215) features high fashion in wool, silk, mohair, and cotton. The following is a select list from which to choose, or visit them all — you won't be disappointed: *Atelier Ibiza* (No. 47; phone: 418-692-2103) is a reliable source of fine leatherwear and *Le Jardin de l'Argile* (No. 51; phone: 418-692-4870) is Canada's only outlet for sweet, sleepy-faced "Lorteau" figurines, each an individual work of glazed clay in delicate pastel colors. The Quebec City artist creates just 300 pieces a year, which the store will ship to almost any address in the world. *Studio d'Art Georgette Pihay* (No. 53; phone: 418-692-0297) is the atelier-gallery of the popular Belgian-born sculptor. At *Le Fou du Roi* (No. 57; phone: 418-692-4439) have fun learning with its stock of educational toys, domestic and imported. *Peau sur Peau* (No. 85; phone: 418-694-1921) offers high fashion in leather for men and women, and *O Kwa Ri* (At the Sign of The Bear; No. 59; phone: 418-692-0009) marks the place for Indian crafts in Lower Town.

Cross the street now to the south side for a look at the handmade dolls at *Galerie Le Fil Du Temps* (No. 88; phone: 418-692-5867); here, exquisitely crafted dolls can cost anywhere from $100 to $6,000. Or satisfy yourself with a chocolate fix at *Confiserie d'Epoque Madame Gigi* (No. 84; phone: 418-692-2825) where hand-dipped bonbons are the *spécialité de la maison. Théâtre du Petit-Champlain* (No. 66; phone: 418-692-2631) mounts regular productions in French near *Le Lapin Sauté* (No. 52; phone: 418-692-5325), a modest but agreeable little café, open for breakfast, lunch, dinner, and after-theater supper. Pauline Pelletier's *Petite Galerie* (No. 30; phone: 418-692-4871) is a showcase for the works of this innovative Quebec ceramist and other regional artists who share the gallery's retail space with imported exotica from India, China, Thailand, and other faraway sources. *Créaly* (No. 26; phone: 418-692-4753) is the retail outlet for Quebec artists and artisans and a source of such unusual finds as decorative leather masks and costume jewelry set with semiprecious stones.

This walk has come full-circle back to Maison Jolliet. Hardy souls who want to walk in the shoes of a typical 17th-century Canadian, don't hesitate: The stairs await. But the funicular may seem a better way to go. Just pay your 85¢, crowd into the often-packed glass-walled funicular, enjoy the view, and *voilà,* you're at Dufferin Terrace.

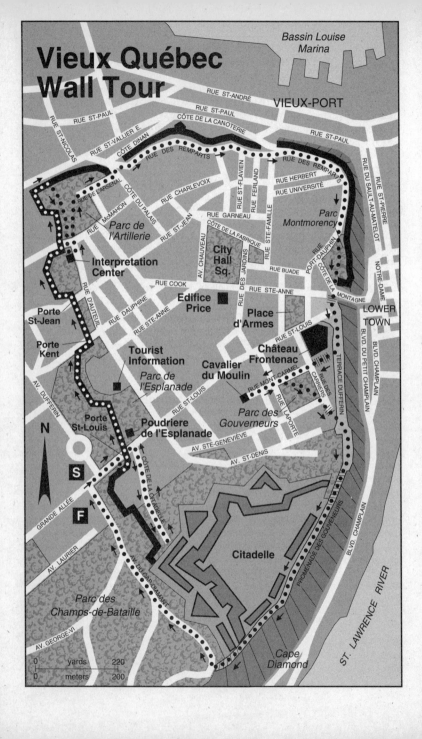

Vieux Québec
Wall Tour

Bassin Louise
Marina

VIEUX-PORT

RUE ST-ANDRÉ

RUE ST-PAUL

CÔTE DE LA CANOTERIE

RUE ST-PAUL

RUE ST-NICOLAS

RUE ST-PAUL

RUE ST-VALLIER E.

CÔTE DINAN

RUE DES REMPARTS

RUE DES REMPARTS

RUE ST-PIERRE

RUE DU SAULT-AU-MATELOT

RUE DE L'ARSENAL

CÔTE DU PALAIS

RUE CHARLEVOIX

RUE ST-FLAVIEN

RUE FERLAND

RUE HERBERT

RUE UNIVERSITE

Parc
Montmorency

Parc de
l'Artillerie

RUE McMAHON

RUE ST-JEAN

RUE GARNEAU

RUE STE-FAMILLE

RUE PORT-DAUPHIN

CÔTE DE LA FABRIQUE

CÔTE DE LA MONTAGNE

NOTRE-DAME

Interpretation
Center

AV. CHAUVEAU

City
Hall
Sq.

RUE DES JARDINS

RUE BUADE

LOWER
TOWN

RUE COOK

RUE D'AUTEUIL

RUE DAUPHINE

RUE STE-ANNE

Edifice
Price

RUE STE-ANNE

Place
d'Armes

BLVD. CHAMPLAIN

BLVD. DU PETIT CHAMPLAIN

Porte
St-Jean

RUE ST-LOUIS

Porte
Kent

Château
Frontenac

Tourist
Information

Cavalier
du Moulin

RUE DES CARRIÈRES

TERRASSE DUFFERIN

Parc de
l'Esplanade

RUE MONT-CARMEL

RUE ST-LOUIS

AV. DUFFERIN

Porte
St-Louis

Poudriere
de l'Esplanade

RUE LAPORTE

Parc des
Gouverneurs

N

AV. STE-GENEVIÈVE

S

AV. ST-DENIS

CÔTE DE LA CITADELLE

F

GRANDE ALLÉE

PROMENADE DES GOUVERNEURS

AV. LAURIER

Citadelle

AV. DU CAP-DIAMANT

BLVD. CHAMPLAIN

Parc des
Champs-de-Bataille

ST. LAWRENCE RIVER

Cape
Diamond

AV. GEORGE-VI

| 0 | yards | 220 |
| 0 | meters | 200 |

Walk 3: Vieux Québec Wall Tour

Doing your own version of sentry duty on the ramparts of Vieux Québec is a unique tourist attraction in Canada; no other Canadian city — no North American one, for that matter — is enclosed by historic walls that you can walk upon. No longer protection against invading armies, Quebec City's walls are open to all who care to trace the course of the city's history — although they're closed from December through February when ice and snow make the route hazardous. At other times, though, visitors are welcome to walk on top of a long, western section of the fortifications when they make the traditional 3-mile circuit of *la vieille capitale's* defense system.

Allow 3 hours for this inspection tour, taking time out to explore the military highlights along the way and to savor the magnificent views from the heights.

The logical departure point for a wall walk is the Citadelle (on Côte de la Citadelle), the star-shaped fortress commanding the city's critical southern flank. The "Gibraltar of North America" wasn't part of the 17th-century defense network French army engineers started in 1690. The French had intended to encircle the entire capital with a protective wall, but when New France fell to the British in 1759 only the western section between Cape Diamond and Côte du Palais was finished.

After the conquest, the British followed the original plan for 63 years, building additional ramparts and fortified gates; from 1820 to 1832 they constructed their own "Gibraltar" 350 feet above the St. Lawrence River.

Today the fortifications, part of a national park administered by Parks Canada, have been designated as a historic monument. The Citadelle, from which a hostile shot has never been fired, is the largest manned fortress in North America, home of the Royal 22nd Regiment, the legendary "Van Doos," and Quebec residence of Canada's governors-general. Although the Van Doos — a phonetic equivalent of the French word for 22 — have not been called upon to defend Canada at home, they have distinguished themselves in battle in both World Wars and are regarded as one of the country's most valiant and loyal regiments.

From the Porte St-Louis entrance to Upper Town, turn right into Côte de la Citadelle and continue up the hill to the fort's visitors' entrance. The military complex includes 25 buildings, the Cape Diamond Redoubt (1693), and five heavily fortified bastions. Tour guides lead visitors around the public areas, through the *Royal 22nd Regiment Museum,* located in a former powder house (1750), and an old military prison. The big treat here is the Changing of the Guard ceremony (mid-June to *Labour Day*) when the Van Doos in their natty red tunics and bearskin busbies put on a daily show at 10 AM, weather permitting (see "Special Events" in *Quebec City,* THE CITIES).

From the citadel retrace your steps down to Rue St-Louis and cross to Poudriere de l'Esplanade (Esplanade Powder House), the reception and inter-pretation center just inside Porte St-Louis (see *Walk 1: Vieux Québec/Upper Town*).

Conducted tours of the fortifications begin here. Or, if you prefer to explore on your own, go back through the gate toward Grande Allée and climb the staircase to the wall on the citadel side of the street. Follow the footpath west over Parc de l'Esplanade, Porte Kent, and Porte St-Jean to Parc de l'Artill-erie, a strategic defense site for more than 250 years. This oldest section of the wall owes its life to Lord Dufferin, a far-sighted Governor-General of Canada who took office just as Quebec was preparing to demolish the entire defense system to further urban sprawl.

With the departure of British troops from the citadel in 1871, a change in the landscape of Old Quebec occurred when federal authorities, bowing to public pressure, had the walls torn down; at the same time, they lowered the eastern ramparts. The decision shocked and angered the governor-general of the day, Lord Frederick Temple Hamilton-Temple-Blackwood, the First Marquess of Dufferin of Ava. Realizing the value of the fortifications, he had the decision overturned and launched a salvage operation to preserve the walls and rebuild some of the gates.

Leave the wall via the stairs at the northwest end of Parc de l'Artillerie at Rue de l'Arsenal and walk back across the green to the Interpretation Centre (2 Rue d'Auteuil; phone: 418-648-4205). Three buildings are open to visitors here — the center itself, where, among other educational exhibits, an intricate scale model of Quebec reproduces Upper and Lower Town as they were in 1808; the Redoute Dauphine (1712–1748); and the 1820 Officers' Quarters.

Return across the park to the intersection of Rue de l'Arsenal and Côte du Palais and turn left to the junction with Rue des Remparts. Follow the north section of the fortifications at sidewalk level, pausing to look across the wall to the Vieux Port restorations, its farmers' market, and Bassin Louise marina.

Turn away from the view and the cannon-mounted walls at 51 Rue des Remparts and look for the plaque on the left side of the house that marks Maison Montcalm, the residence French General Montcalm occupied for only a year until he fell in the Battle of the Plains of Abraham. Once a gracious country home, in recent times the house has been decked out in ways that doubtless would not amuse its first occupant, the Seigneur of Château Candiac, the rightful heir to a family seat near Nîmes in Provence, France. Montcalm's old lodgings seem to change color with the seasons. (The current owner has splashed a rainbow of colors on it — many Quebecois paint the roofs of their homes in bright colors — mostly red — to brighten the often dreary winter landscape.) Currently, the private house is painted an eye-popping purple.

Continue around the northeast curve of the defense works into Parc Mont-morency, a restful spot to find a park bench under the trees at the halfway mark on the tour (see *Walk 1: Vieux Québec/Upper Town*). The wall rings the east side of the clifftop park and continues over the Porte Prescott Bridge across Côte de la Montagne to Escalier Frontenac (Frontenac Staircase), one of 25 stairways that link one level of the old city to another. From the top of the stairs you'll see Dufferin Terrace, the broad boardwalk promenade that follows the ramparts along Upper Town's eastern approach.

The brainchild of colonial Governor Lord John George Lambton Durham, the terrace emerged in 1838, an expansive version of an English seaside "prom," and was extended 40 years later with pavilions for gull's-eye viewing above the chest-high walls by order of Governor-General Lord Dufferin. That work was done by architect Charles Baillairgé, the designer of the current façade of Notre-Dame-de-la-Paix de Québec, the Quebec basilica. Spring through fall (the breezy terrace is a bone-chiller in winter), the boardwalk is the capital's most popular rendezvous, as much a part of Quebec City's tourist image as *Château Frontenac.*

Follow the promenade south, past the Champlain Monument and *Château Frontenac,* toward Cape Diamond and the Citadelle. If hunger strikes, this may be the time to stop by the *Château*'s *Café de la Terrasse* (phone: 418-692-3861), where window-table customers can watch the passing parade in comfort. (Look for an entrance to the *Terrasse* at the hotel's northeast corner by the ice cream counter. The hotel's main entrance is a few yards away, off Rue St-Louis at 1 Rue des Carrières.) For strollers who prefer to snack while walking or while seated on a boardwalk bench, refreshment is also available at a couple of outdoor stands along the way.

Find a spot along the boardwalk for a peek over the wall at Lower Town below and beyond to the ocean-bound river traffic that shares St. Lawrence River sea lanes with fleets of local sailboats. On clear days you can see downriver as far as Côte de Beaupré and Ile d'Orléans, and well beyond the Lévis skyline on the opposite shore.

From the river-view ramparts, turn inland at the south corner of the *Château* and mount the steps to Rue Mont Carmel. At the west end of the street is Cavalier du Moulin (Windmill Outpost), a pretty, tranquil park, located on land that once upon a time was a strategic military site. Named for the windmill that once stood here, it was converted to a military outpost in 1693, with orders to destroy the Cap-Diamant redoubt and the St-Louis bastion if either fell into enemy hands.

Turn back from the park on Rue Mont Carmel and cut across Parc des Gouverneurs toward the boardwalk. When Château St-Louis stood at the north end of the terrace, residents of the colonial governor's palace claimed the park as their private garden. Now it's the peaceful setting for an unusual war monument, dedicated to two opposing generals — James Wolfe and Louis-Joseph, Marquis de Montcalm. In one of the bitter quirks of history, both were personal losers in the battle for Quebec. British commander Wolfe died on his field of victory. The defeated French general was carried off the battleground mortally wounded. He died the following day, thankful to know "I shall not live to see the English masters of Quebec."

At the park's southeast corner — where Av. Ste-Geneviève meets Rue des

Carrières — at the end of a row of fine old 19th-century houses is the United States Consulate (2 Pl. Terrasse Dufferin; phone: 418-692-2095). Once occupied by officers from the citadel garrison, nearly all of the houses have been converted to small private hotels. Take the first set of steps down to the terrace and continue south to the staircase and Promenade des Gouverneurs.

The view from the stairway clinging to the rim of the cliff is well worth the climb. The governors' walk extends along the east flank of the citadel to the tip of Cape Diamond, where hardy souls can press on into Parc des Champs-de-Bataille (Battlefields Park) — or save that excursion for another day.

From the Cape Diamand lookout, follow the park path or Avenue du Cap-Diamant down the grassy hillside, past the citadel's southwest bastions, to the city wall and Porte St-Louis, where the fortifications tour begins and ends.

Walk 4: "New" Quebec

Newcomers to Quebec's famous walled city often get so caught up in the romance of the *quartiers historiques* they overlook life beyond the walls. Many leave thinking they have seen what there is to see here, done what there is to do, like someone who visits central London and the theater district and then "ticks" London off as an experience.

The story of the provincial capital is a tale of two cities. Old Quebec, the 323-acre UNESCO World Heritage preserve, includes the community within the ramparts and the waterfront village below the fortifications where the first settlers arrived in 1608, while "New" Quebec, which took shape in the early 1800s when prosperous townsfolk began moving out toward the country villages of Sillery and Ste-Foy, covers a vast area of residential neighborhoods, industrial zones, government and corporate office towers, and suburban shopping malls. But here too is where the most fateful battle in Canadian history took place, and where the National Assemby, the legislature for the province of Quebec, is charting the province's strategy in its constitutional negotiations with the rest of Canada.

Porte St-Louis is the traditional gateway to New Quebec, the start of this 4-hour walk from the Old World to the new along Grande Allée. This gracious avenue, which Quebeckers proudly compare to the Champs-Elysées, is a charming section of Route 175, the main link between Vieux Québec and Ste-Foy.

Beyond Parc des Champs-de-Bataille (Battlefields Park), Grande Allée becomes Chemin St-Louis and, beyond Sillery, Boulevard Laurier. But its eastern section, just beyond the walls, is one of the capital's most beguiling strolling venues. Once Quebec City's most prestigious residential enclave, the thoroughfare is lined on both tree-shaded sides by stately Victorian and Edwardian mansions, most of which have been converted to restaurants, bars, and discos. In summer, when every restaurant opens bright umbrellas and awnings over its sidewalk cafés, the stretch of conviviality between Place George V and Place Montcalm is transformed into a round-the-clock block party. Compulsive party animals prowl here until the last bar closes, and daytime strollers can always find a lively *terrasse* oasis for people watching.

As you cross Avenue Dufferin onto Grande Allée you'll be following a trail that Indian trappers tramped out of the wilderness in the early 1600s when they brought their furs to the French trading post of "Kebec." During the French regime, this was the colony's longest road, the main link to other frontier outposts. Walking in the same direction, you'll pass an entrance to National Battlefields Park (at Av. George VI); just beyond the park entrance look up to see the modern buildings with Orwellian-sounding names — Complexe H and Complexe J — that house the offices of Quebec's premier, Robert

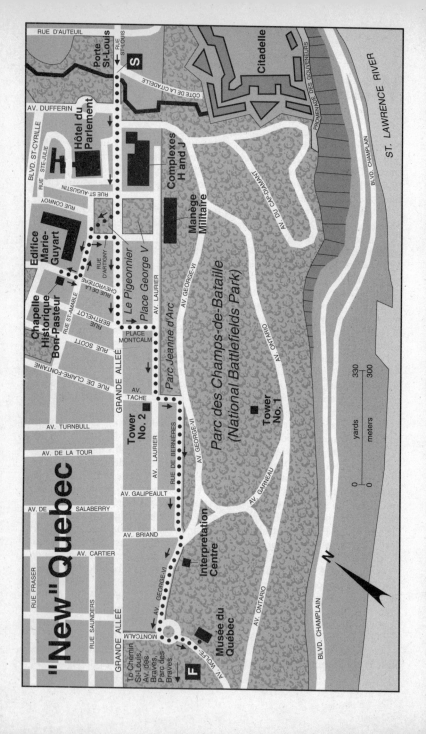

"New" Quebec

RUE D'AUTEUIL

RUE ST-LOUIS

Porte St-Louis

S

Citadelle

ST. LAWRENCE RIVER

COTE DE LA CITADELLE

AV. DUFFERIN

PROMENADE DES GOUVERNEURS

BLVD. ST-CYRILLE

RUE STE-JULIE

Hôtel du Parlement

RUE STE-JULIE

RUE ST-AUGUSTIN

Complexes H and J

BLVD. CHAMPLAIN

RUE CONROY

Edifice Marie-Guyart

RUE D'ARTIGNY

Le Pigeonnier
Place George V

Manège Militaire

AV. DU CAP-DIAMANT

Chapelle Historique Bon-Pasteur

RUE ST-AMABLE

RUE DE LA CHEVROTIERE

RUE BERTHELOT

AV. LAURIER

AV. GEORGE-VI

Parc des Champs-de-Bataille
(National Battlefields Park)

RUE SCOTT

PLACE MONTCALM

Parc Jeanne d'Arc

RUE DE CLAIRE-FONTAINE

GRANDE ALLÉE

AV. TACHE

AV. ONTARIO

Tower No. 1

AV. TURNBULL

Tower No. 2

AV. LAURIER

RUE DE BERNIÈRES

AV. GEORGE-VI

AV. DE LA TOUR

AV. GARNEAU

AV. DE QUEBEC

AV. GALIPEAULT

SALABERRY

AV. BRIAND

AV. CARTIER

Interpretation Centre

AV. GEORGE-VI

AV. ONTARIO

RUE FRASER

Musée du Québec

BLVD. CHAMPLAIN

RUE SAUNDERS

GRANDE ALLÉE

MONTCALM

AV. WOLFE

To Chemin St-Louis,
Av. des Braves,
Parc des Braves

F

N

yards   0   330
meters   0   300

Bourassa. On the opposite side of the Allée, Hôtel du Parlement, home of Quebec's National Assembly, dominates the landscaped greens of Colline Parlementaire (Parliament Hill) at the corner of Avenue Dufferin and Grande Allée.

The first legislative assembly in New France was housed in the bishop's palace on the site of today's Parc Montmorency (see *Walk 1: Vieux Québec/ Upper Town*). In 1869, when the legislators for the then 2-year-old Quebec province decided they had outgrown their *palais épiscopal* accommodations, they chose a place beyond Porte St-Louis where the English once played cricket; the seat of government still exists today. A modified version of the *Louvre* in Paris, the National Assembly was designed and built between 1877 and 1886 under the direction of architect Eugène-Etienne Taché, whose place in Quebec history was assured when he personally carved *"Je me souviens"* ("I remember") into the building's provincial crest, a quotation latter-day Quebec Province has adopted as its motto.

Guided tours are scheduled for visitors who'd like to see the Legislative Council Chamber and the Renaissance-style National Assembly Chamber where Quebec's elected representatives meet. *Le Parlementaire,* the parliamentary restaurant, is open to the public between noon and 9 PM when the Assembly is in session.

The bronze statue facing Grande Allée from the legislature lawn is of Maurice Duplessis; the most dominant man in the history of Quebec politics, he ruled the province between 1936 and 1939 and from 1944 until his death in 1959. Beyond Parliament Hill, Grande Allée bisects two small parks: Place George V and Le Pigeonnier (Pigeon Park). Bird-loving Quebecois maintain a heated birdhouse and feeder in the center of the Le Pigeonnier; local pigeons seem to like the cuisine, but few choose to stay the night. From Place George V you'll see the Manège Militaire (Drill Hall) in National Battlefields Park, another Eugène-Etienne Taché work, dating from 1888. Militia units still perfect their parade-ground technique here.

Detour off Grande Allée now by cutting across Pigeon Park to Rue St-Amable and turn right at the corner of Rue de la Chevrotière. Stop at No. 1037 for the best panoramic view in Quebec City. *Galerie Anima G* is at home on the 31st floor of Edifice Marie-Guyart (Complexe G), the city's highest observation point; visitors can tour an exhibition of works by Quebec artists and enjoy views of the city and the raging river beyond (phone: 418-644-9841).

From Complexe G cross the street to Chapelle Historique Bon-Pasteur (1080 Rue de la Chevrotière; phone: 418-648-9710). Here tour the Romanesque-baroque chapel of Les Soeurs du Bon-Pasteur de Québec (1868), leaving plenty of time to admire the intricately carved and gilded high altar and works of art by members of the order (see "Special Places" in *Quebec City,* THE CITIES). Next return to Rue St-Amable and walk back toward Le Pigeonnier, where on a summer day you're likely to happen upon an outdoor concert.

Follow the west side of the park along Rue D'Artigny to Grande Allée; this is the threshold of the Allée's most sprightly R & R area. At the corner, *Vogue*

(1170 Rue D'Artigny; phone: 418-647-2100) is a split-level rendezvous, with a café-bar on the ground floor and a disco upstairs. *Sherlock Holmes,* one of the new breed of British pubs to make the capital scene, shares the premises (phone: 418-529-9973). Around the corner, *Brandy* (690 Grande Allée; phone: 418-648-8739) is a popular hangout for the thirtysomething crowd. Now follow the lineup of outdoor terraces (they're open on sunny days till the end of September) to *L'Express Minuit* (Midnight Express; No. 680; phone: 418-529-7713), another hot spot for young and young-at-heart discomaniacs.

Le Bonaparte, a veteran member of Grande Allée's top-ranking restaurant colony, shares the street address, if not the spirit, of the *Midnight Express.* Diners can enjoy classic French cuisine on *Le Bonaparte's* terrace or in the formal dining room indoors (phone: 418-647-4747). A few steps along the Allée, *Auberge Louis Hébert* (No. 668; phone: 418-525-7812) combines a small, upper-floor hotel of 10 rooms with a street-level restaurant and summer terrace. Back in the kitchen the chef takes a nouvelle cuisine approach to such traditional game dishes as wild boar, moose, and venison. Across the street, *Au Petit Coin Breton* (No. 655; phone: 418-525-6904) serves reasonably priced crêpe specialties indoors and out, and a few doors west *Pub La Faculté* (No. 595; phone: 418-529-0592) is a Quebecois version of the real British thing, specializing in imported beers and sausages. Back on the opposite side of the Allée, *Le Paris Brest* (No. 590; phone: 418-529-2243) has contrived a winning combination of traditional French fare and Art Deco flair.

Chez Patrick le Bordelais (No. 570; phone: 418-649-0338) offers a realistic prix fixe menu in a picturesque gabled house with an adjoining greenhouse. Depending on the weather, meals are served on a lamp-lit terrace, around the fireplace in the main dining room, or out in the glass-walled bar, a popular watering hole for all seasons (see "Eating Out" in *Quebec City,* THE CITIES).

Patrick's folksy little establishment is directly opposite the terrace of *Loews Le Concorde* (1225 Pl. Montcalm; phone: 418-647-2222), a striking, tomorrow-designed presence on the stately home strip of 19th-century Quebec, topped by *L'Astral,* the city's only revolving tower restaurant (see also *Best Hotels* in DIVERSIONS).

Cross Grande Allée here, where a statue of French General Montcalm stands at the head of Place Montcalm Boulevard. It's a replica of the original monument in Candiac, the Provençal estate near Nîmes, France, where Louis-Joseph, Marquis de Montcalm, was born in 1712. The defeated general died within the walls of Old Quebec, but he suffered his fatal wounds not far from here on the historic battlefield above Cape Diamond.

Walk down Place Montcalm to Avenue Laurier to the verge of the Plains of Abraham, the undulating expanse of wheat fields and pasture land where British General James Wolfe and soldiers under his command clashed with the French defenders of Quebec on a sunny September morning in 1759. The land, first cleared by a Scot, Abraham Martin, more than a century earlier, was still open farmland on that day when the English surprised the French so close to the walls of the city. The skirmish — involving some 9,000 soldiers — was over in 20 minutes, as New France fell to England and both sides lost their military leaders.

Today the battlefield has healed into a National Park protectorate, encompassing 250 acres of green meadows, woodlands, and gardens laced with paths and scenic motorways. Since 1908, when the battlefield was landscaped in its current form, the land has become a haven for cyclists, joggers, picnickers, and park-bench readers in summer, and cross-country skiers in winter. *Calèche* drivers take their passengers through the park in every season. Commemorative plaques, stones, and artillery pieces trace the course of the conflict, but they're scattered throughout the Plains, easily missed in grassy hollows and wooded glades. Strolling historians keen to explore the battleground in detail should follow Avenue Laurier to the Reception and Interpretation Centre (390 Rue de Bernières; phone: 418-648-4071), where they'll find information about the park highlights and background literature related to the battle. The center is open May through early September, but phone for opening hours.

En route to the center you'll pass Jardin Jeanne d'Arc, with its flower-banked equestrian statue of the warrior saint; this is the site where, in 1880, Canada's national anthem "O Canada" was played for the first time. At the corner of Avenue Taché and Avenue Laurier, Tower No. 2, one of four martello towers Britain added to its Quebec defense arsenal between 1801 and 1811, still stands guard over the Plains, in line with Tower No. 1, located closer to the cliffs above the St. Lawrence River. Both are open at certain hours during the summer. Check with the reception center for times.

Now continue along Rue de Bernières to Avenue George VI, a scenic parkway that leads to the *Musée du Québec* (1 Av. Wolfe-Montcalm; phone: 418-643-2150). At the Grande Allée end of the avenue, a monument to General Wolfe marks the spot where the 32-year-old commander died in a sheltered dell behind the lines. Wounded three times as he led the charge, he lived just long enough to hear of the French defeat. "God be praised, I die happy," he sighed, with his last breath.

But the French do not associate the Plains only with defeat. Six months after the Battle of the Plains of Abraham the French fought for — and very nearly won back — their beloved city. Under Gaston-François, Chevalier de Lévis, Montcalm's second in command, a force of 7,000 soldiers, some armed with no more than hunting guns and knives, captured Ste-Foy and whipped the over-confident Brits on the Plains before laying siege to the town. Only the arrival of the British fleet dashed hopes of further victories and Lévis was forced to lift the siege and retreat to Montreal, where he was soon surrounded by superior forces. The final capitulation, signed the following September, officially ended the French regime in Canada.

Leave the Plains now for the *Musée du Québec,* which stands at the opposite end of Avenue Wolfe-Montcalm (phone: 418-648-4071). Two years ago the original 1933 neo-classical building was linked to the Old Quebec jail next door to create a stunning new complex of galleries and administrative offices, with a modern library and auditorium. Art lovers may decide to end the tour here and spend the rest of the day viewing a collection of Quebec art that spans the centuries, from the early French colonial period to the 1990s. International and Canadian artists are well represented in this permanent collection.

A glass-roofed Grand Hall opens on an attractive restaurant and terrace café overlooking the Plains, where weary walkers can map out the next stage of the tour over lunch or tea, while history buffs who haven't yet had their fill will want to stop first at the Battlefields Park Exhibition Room on Level 1 of the Baillairgé Pavilion, where they can locate the important battle sites on a model of the plains. Strollers who've wound up their tour admiring the art in one of the 11 galleries of the *Musée* will want to stop in its well-stocked gift boutique for cards, books, and gift items.

In summer, a free shuttle-bus service departs from the museum area on guided tours of the battlefield. Determined walkers should follow Avenue Montcalm out to Terrasse Earl Grey for one more dramatic view of the river before wandering back to town through the park. Or they can leave the national preserve at the junction of Avenue Montcalm and Chemin St-Louis (the extension of Grande Allée) and walk 2 blocks west to Avenue des Braves. At the end of the avenue, a monument in Parc des Braves (Park of the Brave) recalls Lévis's short-lived victory of 1760. Avenue des Braves intersects with Chemin Ste-Foy, one of the old colonial roads, where strollers who've decided to call it a day can catch the No. 7 bus back to the walled city via Porte St-Jean or, if their arches hold up, they can walk back to town along Grande Allée and on to Rue St-Louis and the heart of Vieux Québec.

INDEX

INDEX

Index

Insurance (*cont.*)
  trip cancellation and
    interruption, 39–40
International Jazz Festival
  (Montreal), 112
International Quebec Summer
  Festivals, 146
Islands, the (Montreal), biking, 191
ITX fares, 16

Jardin des Gouverneurs (Quebec
  City), 138
Jet-boat tours (Montreal), 119
Jogging, 119
Just for Laughs Comedy Festival
  (Montreal), 112

Lachine Canal (Montreal), biking,
  191
Language, 164–65
  See also Words and phrases,
    useful
Last-minute travel clubs, 27–28
Laurentians (Les Laurentides,
  Montreal), 109
  cross-country skiing, 183–84
  downhill skiing, 180–81
  ice skating/hockey in, 186
Laval Monument (Quebec City),
  139
Laval University (Quebec City),
  141–42, 256, 257
Legal aid, 67–68
Les Autres (Quebec City),
  cross-country skiing, 184–85
Les Cours Montréal (Montreal),
  102
Local transportation. *See*
  Transportation
Low-fare airlines, 18

Mackay to de la Montagne
  (Montreal), 108
Magazines, 77
  See also Publications
Mail, 61–62
Main, the (Montreal)

walking tour of, 230–35
  map, 230
Maison Chevalier (Quebec City),
  137, 263
Maison des Vins (Quebec City),
  137
Maison Fornel (Quebec City), 136
Maison Jolliet (Quebec City), 137
Maison Radio-Canada (Montreal),
  108
Maisonneuve Park (Montreal),
  biking, 192
Maisons Bruneau, Drapeau, and
  Rageot (Quebec City), 136
Maps
  Main, the (Montreal), 230
  McGill University/Prince Arthur
    Street, 242
  Montreal, 4–5
  Mount Royal Park, 236
  New Quebec, 272
  Quebec, 6–7
  Sherbrook Street West, 212
  Vieux Montréal, 220
  Vieux Québec/Lower Town, 260
  Vieux Québec/Upper Town, 252
  Vieux Québec Wall Tour, 266
Marc-Aurèle Fortin Museum
  (Montreal), 113
Marguerite d'Youville Centre
  (Montreal), 113
Markets (Quebec City), 150
McCord Museum of Canadian
  History (Montreal), 107,
  198–99
McGill Chamber Orchestra
  (Montreal), 202
McGill University (Montreal), 107,
  242–50
McGill University/Prince Arthur
  Street
  walking tour of, 242–50
  map, 242
Medical assistance, 64–65
  See also Health care
Metric system. *See* Weights and
  measures